新编应用商务英语丛书

Business English

实用商务旅行与会展英语

桑龙扬 杜清萍◎主编

参编（按姓氏笔画排序）

公佳颖 何晓灵 侯泊华 李堉华

沈丽华 魏 华 姚丽娜 周龙英

审校 陈绵水

■ 本书的编写目的是为参加国际会展的企业管理人员、营销人员以及其他各类国际商务人员，金融、旅游、商业等行业服务人员，会展活动的组织者、翻译人士和涉外工作者以及其他涉及会展的各类人士提供必要的专业知识和语言素材，为商务活动、翻译活动和翻译工作的成功创造必要的条件。

■ 本书共分为四个部分：概述、筹备会展、商务旅行和参加会展。另附12个附录，为读者提供与会展相关的各种表格、样板、指南等实务内容。

机械工业出版社
China Machine Press

本书的编写目的是为参加国际会展的企业管理人员、营销人员以及其他各类国际商务人员，金融、旅游、商业等行业服务人员，会展活动的组织者、翻译人士和涉外工作者以及其他涉及会展的各类人士提供必要的专业知识和语言素材，为商务活动、翻译活动和翻译工作的成功创造必要的条件。

本书共分为四个部分：概述、筹备会展、商务旅行和参加会展。另附12个附录，为读者提供与会展相关的各种表格、样板、指南等实务内容。

本书也可作为大中专院校相关专业师生的教科书和参考书。

图书在版编目（CIP）数据

实用商务旅行与会展英语／桑龙扬，杜清萍主编．—北京：机械工业出版社，2010.8

（新编应用商务英语丛书）

ISBN 978-7-111-31481-3

Ⅰ.①实…　Ⅱ.①桑…　②杜…　Ⅲ.①商务-旅游-英语　②展览会-英语　Ⅳ.①H31

中国版本图书馆 CIP 数据核字（2010）第150384号

机械工业出版社（北京市百万庄大街22号　邮政编码100037）

策划编辑：余　红　　责任编辑：安　婧　朱慧芳

版式设计：张文贵　　责任印制：杨　曦

北京中兴印刷有限公司印刷

2010年10月第1版·第1次印刷

132mm×214mm·11.125印张·397千字

标准书号：ISBN 978-7-111-31481-3

ISBN 978-7-89451-712-8（光盘）

定价：26.00元（含1CD）

凡购本书，如有缺页、倒页、脱页，由本社发行部调换

电话服务

社服务中心：（010）88361066

销售一部：（010）68326294

销售二部：（010）88379649

读者服务部：（010）68993821

网络服务

门户网：http://www.cmpbook.com

教材网：http://www.cmpedu.com

封面无防伪标均为盗版

Preface

前言

近年来，我国会展业发展迅速，急需大批既懂专业又懂外语的专门人才。但是，目前既具备会展专业知识，又精通英语的应用型、复合型人才日益紧缺，已成为制约我国会展行业发展的障碍。目前国际会展人才的培养要解决的基本问题有两个：一个是掌握商务旅行与会展的基本知识，另一个就是熟练运用商务旅行与会展英语。本书通过我国企业作为参展商参加广交会同时接待国外采购商，我国企业作为参展商参加国外会展与外国会展组织方和采购商的接触以及外国参展商参加广交会与我国有关方面的接触，完整、真实地展现了商务旅行与会展活动的全过程，有助于帮助读者了解和掌握商务旅行与会展的基本知识和英语词汇与句型。

本书编写的目的就是希望能为那些参加国际会展的企业的管理人员、营销人员以及其他各类国际商务人员，金融、旅游、商业等行业的服务人员，会展活动的组织者、翻译人士和涉外工作者以及其他涉及会展的各类人士提供必要的专业知识和语言素材，为商务活动和翻译工作的成功创造必要的条件。本书也可以作为大中专院校相关专业师生的教科书和参考书。

在安排本书内容和结构的时候，充分考虑了商务工作者的实际需要，选取了商务旅行和会展业务中所经历的各种情景和环节，做到了实用性与知识性相结合。全书共分四部分，其中包含一篇概述，24 章课文；另有 12 个附录。第一部分是概述，第二部分是筹备会展，第三部分是商务旅行，第四部分是参加会展。第一部分和第二部分以书面语言为主，其中第二部分也根据实际需要安排了口语环节；第三和第四两部分都以口语为主。各个章节的结构是：第一部分有两个商务旅行与会展实务，每个实务前都设置了一个背景介绍；第二部分是业务链接，介绍相关业务知识；第三部分是常用句型，包含了商务旅行中和会展过程中所能用到的各类基本句型和表达方式。第二部分里包含了必要的书面材料和口语对话，主要介绍会展主办方筹备会展的过程和英国的参展商参加广交会的过程。第三和第四部分的业务包含两个情景对话。此部分有两条主线，两笔业务：一个是加拿大公司来广州参加广交会，由中方参展企业深圳Ugo运动鞋有限公司接待，双方最终签订了购销合同；另一条线是中方企业澄海玩具贸易有限公司参展团参加纽约玩具展的过程。这两条线贯穿了整本书和完整地参加国内和国外国际会展的全部流程。为便于理解和自学，每组对话和句子后面都附上中文译文。附录部分有各类会展邀请函样板、广交会参展商服务指南、商务旅行与会展词汇表、海关申报表等表格。

本书由江西九江学院外国语学院桑龙扬教授和广东省汕头市鮀滨技术学校杜清萍老师担任主编。参加编写的老师有：九江学院外国语学院公佳颖、侯治华、李堉华、沈丽华、姚丽娜、周龙英，广东省汕头市鮀滨技术学校何晓灵、魏华。留荷经济学博士、九江学院党委书记陈绵水教授对该书进行了审校。本书在编写过程中，得到了北京理工大学珠海学院吴伟雄教授的悉心指点，在此一并表示感谢。本书在编写过程中，征询了多位企业界人士和担任过广交会等大型国际会展的翻译人员的意见，也接受了部分专家和大中专从事商务英语教学的一线教师的建议，参考了大量的国内外相关书籍，经过多次修订调整。本书所选用的材料主要来源于国内外企业的宣传资料、国内外专业商务和会展英语教材、互联网以及编者实际工作中所获得的资料等，也来自于编者在国内担任口译、笔译和在国外留学和工作期间获得的第一手资料。

由于编者水平有限，书中不足之处在所难免，敬请专家和读者不吝赐教。联系邮箱是：Sangly@126.com

编　者

目　录 CONTENTS

Part I 概述 (General Introduction)

一、商务旅行

商务旅行又称公干、出差等，是旅游行业中细分出来的一个概念。主要涉及交通、迁移、住宿、体育赛事、文化、饮食活动或饭店行业的宴会。在世界绝大部分国家的旅游统计中，到异地从事商务活动的人，都是被作为旅游者进行统计的。由此可知，商务活动也是旅游活动，到异地从事商务活动的人也是旅游者。会议、展览和奖励旅游，是商务活动的组成部分，是商务旅游市场中的细分市场。会展活动也应是旅游活动，会展也是旅游的组成部分。商务旅游可以划分为奖励旅游（Incentive Travel）、会议旅游（Meeting Tourism）、个人商务差旅（Business Personal Trip）、展览会旅游（Exhibition Tourism）、特殊活动旅游（Special Events Tourism）和教育培训旅游（Training & Education Tourism）。将上述几种类型的英文第一个字母组合起来，可以简称为"IMBEST"市场。

二、会展

广义上来说，会展是指会议、展览、大型活动等集体性活动的简称。其概念内涵是指在一定地域空间，许多人聚集在一起形成的定期或不定期，制度或非制度的传递和交流信息的群众性社会活动。其概念的外延包括各种类型的博览会、展览展销活动、大型会议、体育竞技运动、文化活动、节庆活动等。

因此，国际上一般把会展定义为（M：Meetings 公司业务会议；I：Incentive Tour 奖励旅游；C：Conventions 协会或社团组织会议；E：Events 节事活动或 Exhibition 展览会）。

会议、展览会、博览会、交易会、展销会、展示会等是会展活动的基本形式，世界博览会为最典型的会展活动。

狭义上来说，会展仅仅指会议和展览会等展会。

三、会议的分类

1. 按照举办单位划分

一般认为，按照举办单位性质划分不同，可将会议分为三大类，分别为公司类会议，协会类会议和其他组织会议。

（1）公司类会议

公司类会议规模大小不一，小到几个人，大到上千人。公司管理者强调的是信息传递，而信息传递的最基本方式便是会议。因此公司类会议的数量极其庞大。有关机构在作会议数量统计时，很难准确统计公司类会议的数量，因为很多公司并不愿意对外宣传内部会议。如果将公司类会议比做冰山，那么它们被纳入统计资料的仅是冰山一角。

（2）协会类会议

协会类会议在会议市场中同样占有相当重要的位置。协会因人数和性质而互不相同，它们的规模从小型地区性组织、省市级协会到全国性协会乃至国际性协会不等。协会大致可以划分为行业协会、专业和科学协会、教育协会和技术协会等类型。

（3）其他组织会议

这类会议的典型代表是政府机构会议，许多人在电视上看到过政治性会议。电视镜头中显现的虽然是主会场，但是不难想象背后对小型会议室、套房和宴会等设施的需求。

2. 按会议规模划分

根据会议的规模即参加会议的人数的多少，可将会议分为小型会议、中型会议、大型会议及特大型会议。

（1）小型会议：出席的人数少则几人，多则几十人，但是不超过100人；

（2）中型会议：出席人数在100～1 000人之间；

（3）大型会议：出席人数在1 000～10 000人之间；

（4）特大型会议：人数在10 000人以上，例如节日聚会、庆祝大会等。

3. 按照会议的性质和内容划分

（1）年会（Convention）

年会是就某一特定主题展开讨论的聚会，议题涉及政治、经济、科学、教育、技术等领域。年会通常包括一次全体会议和几个小组会议。年会可以单独召开，也可以附带展示会，多数年会是周期性的，最常见的周期是一年一次。

（2）专业会议（Conference）

专业会议的议题通常是具体问题并就其展开讨论，可以召开分组小会，也可以召开大会。就与会者人数而言，专业会议的规模可大可小。

(3) 代表会议（Congress）

这个词最常在欧洲和国际活动中使用。它常指在本质上类同专业会议这样会议的事件和活动。只有在美国，这个词用来指立法机构。代表大会的出席人数差别很大。

(4) 论坛（Forum）

论坛的特点是反复深入的讨论，一般由小组组长或演讲者来主持。它可以有许多的听众参与，并可由专门小组成员与听众就问题的各方面发表意见和看法，两个或更多的讲演者可能持相反的立场，对听众发表讲演而不是互相讲给对方听。主持人主持讨论会并总结双方观点，允许听众提问，所以饭店必须对这种论坛会议提供多个话筒。

(5) 座谈会、专题讨论会（Symposium）

这种座谈会和专题讨论会除了更加正式外，与论坛那样的会议是一样的。不管个人还是专门小组参加，方法就是进行一种陈述讲演，有一些预定好的听众参加，但是一般要少一些论坛会议所拥有的那种平等交换意见的气氛和特征。

(6) 讲座（Lecture）

讲座要更正式一些，更有组织一些，常有一位专家进行个别讲演，讲座后观众可以提问。讲座规模大小都有。

(7) 研讨会、专家讨论会、讨论会（Seminar）

这种讨论会形式通常有许多参与的活动，出席者有许多平等交换意见和分享知识和经验的机会，一般由讨论主持人主持。这种形式明显地在相对范围内进行，当这样的会议规模变大时，它就变成了论坛 forum 或 symposium 这样的讨论会或专题讨论会了。

(8) 专题讨论会（Workshop）

专题讨论会（workshop）的形式仅指处理专门问题或特殊分配任务的一般性小组会议，不管 workshop 这个词是否被采用，workshop 这种形式都是经常被培训负责人所采用来进行技术培训的，参加这实际上能互相学习，同时分享新的知识、技能和对问题的看法。很明显它是以面对面商讨和参与性强为其特征的。

(9) 专门小组就某一问题公开进行的讨论会（Panel）

这种就某一问题公开进行的讨论会需要两位或者更多的提供观点或某一领域专门知识的讲演者，并和专门小组成员或听众一起公开进行讨论。这种研讨会总是由主持人掌握，可以是大型会议的一部分。

(10) 培训性会议（Training Sessions）

一般至少要用一天的时间，多则几周。这类培训会议需要特定场所，培训内容高度集中，由某个领域的专业培训人员教授。

(11) 奖励会议 (Incentive Meetings)

公司为了对员工、分销商或客户的出色工作表现进行表彰奖励。

4. 按照会议活动特征划分

(1) 商务型会议 (Business Meeting)

一些公司、企业因其业务和管理工作发展需要在饭店召开的商务会议。出席这类会议的人员素质比较高，一般是企业的管理人员和专业技术人员，他们对饭店设施、环境和服务都有较高的要求，且消费标准高。召开商务会议一般选择与公司形象大体一致或更高层次的饭店，如大型企业或跨国公司一般都选择当地最高星级的饭店。商务型会议在饭店召开常与宴会相结合，会期短，会议效率高。

(2) 度假型会议 (Holiday Meeting)

公司等组织利用周末或假期组织员工边度假休闲，边参加会议。这样既能增强员工之间的了解，以及企业自身的凝聚力，又能解决企业所面临的问题。度假型会议一般选择在风景名胜地区的饭店举行。这类会议通常会安排足够的时间让员工观光、休闲和娱乐。

(3) 展销会议 (Show Meeting)

参加商品交易会、展销会、展览会的各类与会者入住饭店，同时，还会在饭店举办一些招待会、报告会、谈判会和签字仪式等活动，有时晚间还会有娱乐消费。另外，一些大型企业或公司还可能单独在饭店举办展销会，整个展销活动全部在饭店举行。文化交流会议，各种民间和政府组织组成的跨区域性的文化学习交流的活动，常以考察、交流等形式出现。

(4) 专业学术会议 (Academic Meeting)

这类会议是某一领域具有一定专业技术的专家学者参加的会议。如专题研究会、学术报告会、专家评审会等。

(5) 政治性会议 (Political Meeting)

国际政治组织、国家和地方政府为某一政治议题召开的各种会议。会议可根据其内容采用大会和分组讨论等形式。

(6) 培训会议 (Training Meeting)

用一个会期对某类专业人员进行的有关业务知识方面的技能训练或新观念、新知识方面的理论培训。培训会议形式可采用讲座、讨论、演示等形式。

四、展览会类别

在实际应用中，展览会名称相当繁多。英语国家中，有 exhibition，general exhibition，industrial exhibition，agricultural exhibition，consumer exhibition，international exhibition，regional exhibition，local exhibition，private exhibition，major exhibition，minor exhibition，solo exhibition，exposition，show，trade show，moveable show，road show，boat show，plane show，catalogue show，fair，multi-trade fair，display 等。

在中文里，展览会名称有博览会、展览会、展览、展销会、看样订货会、展览交流会、交易会、贸易洽谈会、展示会、展评会、样品陈列、庙会、集市、墟、场等等。另外，还有一些展览会使用非专业名词。比如：日（澳大利亚全国农业日 Australian National Field Days），周（柏林国际绿色周 Berlin International Green Week）、市场（亚特兰大国际地毯市场 International Carpet and Rug Market）、中心（汉诺威办公室、信息、电信世界中心 World Center for Office-Information-Telecommunication）等，加上这些非专业的名称，展览会名称更多。

展览会名称虽然繁多，但其基本词是有限的，比如英文里的 fair，exhibition，exposition（Expo）和 show，即中文里的交易会、展览会、博览会或会展。其他名称都是这些基本词派生出来的。本书所介绍的会展即是展览（Exhibition）、博览会（Expo）或交易会（Fair）。

一般认为，博览会是高档次的，对社会、文化以及经济的发展能产生影响并能起促进作用的展览会。但是在实际生活中，"博览会"有被滥用的现象。不时可以在街上看到由商店举办的"某某博览会"。

五、世界博览会

世界博览会（World Exposition，简称 World Expo，或称为 Universal Expo，International Exposition，Expo 是 Exposition 的缩写；也称 World Fair 或 World's Fair）是一项由主办国政府组织或政府委托有关部门举办的有较大影响和悠久历史的国际性博览活动。就其在经济与文化方面的影响来说，是仅次于奥林匹克运动会（Olympic Games）和世界杯（the World Cup）的世界第三大盛况。它已经历了百余年的历史，最初以美术品和传统工艺品（arts and crafts）的展示为主，后来逐渐变为荟萃科学技术与产业技术的展览会，成为培育产业人才不可多得的场所。世界展览会的会场不单是展示技术和商品，而且伴以异彩纷呈的表演，富有魅力的壮观景色，设置成日常生活中无法体验的、充满节日气氛的空间，成为普通市民娱乐和消费的理想场所。

世界博览会有综合性博览会和专业性博览会两类或注册类世博会和认可类世博会。按国际展览组织的规定，专业性博览会分为 A1，A2，

B1, B2 四个级别。A1 级是专业性博览会的最高级别。上海世博会就是注册类的世博会，它是层次最高的、规模最大的世博会，所以规模是区别之一。注册类的世博会一般要有 100 个以上的国家参与，展出的时间是 6 个月。上海世博会的展出时间是 184 天左右，参展的内容更综合性一点。而认可类的世博会参加的国家和国际组织相对比较少，一般 25 个以上就可以了，而且展出的时间比较短。2008 年的西班牙萨拉戈萨世博会就是一个认可类的世博会，它举办的时间是 3 个月，参与的国家相对较少。参观人次大概是 700 万到 800 万人次之间。

第三类就是世界园艺博览会，主要是由世界园艺组织举办的，当然只是认可里面的 A1 类，A2 类它就不认可。昆明世博会就是世界园艺博览会中间的 A 类，也属于国际展览局认可的展览。2006 年沈阳园艺博览会就是属于 A2 类到 B1 类的博览会，所以不属于国际展览局认可的，但是它是国际园艺组织认可的展览。所以，昆明的世界园艺博览会与上海世博会的区别就在于此，上海世博会是一个综合性的注册类世博会，规模应该大得多。

六、国际及国内重要会展管理组织

1. 国际展览局 BIE

负责协调管理世界博览会的国际组织是国际展览局。它的法文是 the Bureau Interna-tional des Expositions（英文: International Exhibitions Bureau），英文简称为 BIE。国际展览局成立于 1928 年，总部设在法国巴黎，其章程为《国际展览公约》（Convention on International Exhibitions）。该公约由 31 个国家和政府代表于 1928 年在巴黎签署，分别于 1948 年、1966 年及 1972 年作过修正。

国际展览局属政府间国际组织，其作用包括组织考察申办国的申办工作；协调展览会的日期；保证展览会的质量等。它的存在对规范、管理和协调世博会的举办，起到了很好的效果。国际展览局的收入，主要来自申办展览会的注册费和举办期间门票收入的一定比例。目前 BIE 已有 155 个成员国。

国际展览局每年由在职主席主持召开两次全体成员国代表大会，会议由成员国代表和国际组织的观察员参加出席。会议由代表们评审新项目（世博会）的申请，评估那些申办国申办世博会的报告。大会也听取分管各方面工作的四个委员会的工作报告。国际展览局（BIE）的宗旨是通过协调和举办世界博览会，促进世界各国经济、文化和科学技术的交流和发展。国际展览局的常务办事机构为秘书处，秘书长为该处的最高领导。

2. 国际展览联盟 UFI

国际展览联盟（原为法文 Union des Foires Internationales，后改为英文 Union of International Fairs，简称 UFI），于 1925 年在意大利米兰成立，并将总部设在法国巴黎。在 2003 年 10 月 20 日开罗的第 70 届会员大会上，该组织决定更名为全球展览业协会（The Global Association of the Exhibition Industry），仍简称 UFI。国际展览联盟是迄今为止世界展览业最重要的国际性组织。对国际性展会进行权威认证是国际展览联盟的核心任务。经 UFI 认可是高品质贸易展览会的标志。

截止到 2004 年 8 月，国际展览联盟所拥有的 256 个正式会员来自世界 72 个国家的 155 个城市，获得国际展览联盟认可的国际性展览会或贸易博览会共有 629 个。此外，国际展览联盟还拥有 40 个协作会员，以各国的全国性会展行业协会为主。如德国的 AUMA 和 FKM、美国的 IAEM、中国的展览馆协会和深圳市会展业协会等。

3. 国际大会及会议协会 ICCA

国际大会及会议协会（The International Congress and Convention Association）创建于 1963 年，总部位于荷兰首都阿姆斯特丹，是全球国际会议最主要的机构组织之一，是会议业最为全球化的组织。目前在全球 80 多个国家（地区）拥有 700 多个机构和企业成员。目前，我国有 14 家单位加入 ICCA，其首要目标是通过对实际操作方法的评估以促使旅游业大量地融入日益增长的国际会议市场，同时为他们对相关市场的经营管理交流实际的信息。作为会议产业的领导组织，ICCA 为所有会员提供最优质的组织服务，为所有会员间的信息交流提供便利，为所有会员最大限度地发展提供商业机会，并根据客户的期望值提高和促进专业水准。

4. 国际专业会议组织者协会 IAPCO

国际专业会议组织者协会（The International Association of Professional Congress Organisers）成立于 1968 年，其前身是英国专业会议组织者协会（The Association of British Professional Congress Organizers，ABPCO）。这是一个由专业的国际国内会议、特殊活动组织者及管理者组成的非营利性组织，服务于全球的专业会议组织者，其总部设在英国伦敦。目前拥有 29 个国家的 80 名成员。

5. 国际奖励旅游协会组织 SITE

国际奖励旅游协会组织（Society of Incentive and Travel Executives，SITE）成立于 1973 年，是目前国际上奖励旅游行业最知名的一个国际性的非营利性的专业协会，主要向会员提供奖励旅游方面的信息服务和教育性研讨会。目前该组织有2100多个会员，分属35个地区的87个国家，总部设在美国芝加哥。国际奖励旅游协会组织的会员的专业涉及航空、游轮、目的地管理公司（DMC）、顾问、酒店和度假地、奖励旅游公司、旅游局、会议中心、旅游批发商、研究机构、旅游景点、餐馆，供应商等。

6. 国际会议中心协会 AIPC

国际会议中心协会（Association International des Palais de Congress，AIPC）于1958年成立于罗马，为非营利组织，目前有来自世界49个国家和地区的160个国际会议中心会员。中国北京国际会议中心、中国香港会议和展览中心、中国台湾地区台北国际会议中心都是其会员。

AIPC的宗旨是：为结合全世界会议中心资源，通过会员间的交流，交换有关会议管理、会议技术、会议沟通以及会议新需求等信息，向会员提供有关会议管理和顾问服务；通过会员间的交流，提升有关会议硬件管理与营运、财务运作、组织与员工发展、行销与客户管理和环保诉求等相关议题的水准。协会在行业术语的释义方面，统计数据方面以及国际会议等其他方面起着非常重要的作用。AIPC每年都要在世界上不同地方举行年会和委员大会，来自全球各地的人士互相讨论行业议题并交换意见。

7. 中国国际贸易促进委员会 CCPIT

中国国际贸易促进委员会（China Council for the Promotion of International Trade）简称中国贸促会，是由中国经济贸易界有代表性的人士、企业和团体组成的全国民间对外经贸组织，成立于1952年5月。中国贸促会的宗旨是：遵循中华人民共和国的法律和政府的政策，开展促进对外贸易、利用外资、引进外国先进技术及各种形式的中外经济技术合作等活动，促进中国同世界各国、各地区之间的贸易和经济关系的发展，增进中国同世界各国人民以及经贸界之间的了解与友谊。

经中国政府批准，中国贸促会1988年6月组建了中国国际商会（China Chamber of International Commerce，CCOIC）。目前，中国贸促会、中国国际商会已同世界上200多个国家和地区的工商企业界建立了广泛的经贸联系，与300多个对口组织签订了合作协议，并同一些国家的商会建立了联合商会；同时，中国贸促会还在16个国家和地区设有驻外代表处。在国内，中国贸促会、中国国际商会在各省、自治区、直辖市建立了50个地方分会、600多个支会和县级国际商会，还在机械、电子、轻工、纺织、农业、汽车、石化、商业、冶金、航空、航天、化工、建材、通讯产业、供销合作、建设、粮食、矿业、煤炭、物流等部门建立了20个行业分会，并对中国对外服务工作行业协会予以指导，全国会员企业近 7 万家。

中国贸促会、中国国际商会及其所属业务部门已经加入了许多国际组织，其中包括世界知识产权组织、国际保护工业产权协会、国际许可证贸易工作者协会、国际海事委员会、国际博览会联盟、国际商事仲裁机构联合会、太平洋盆地经济理事会、国际商会等。

8. 中国旅游协会 CTA

中国旅游协会（China Tourism Association，CTA）是由中国旅游行业的有关社团组织和企事业单位在平等自愿基础上组成的全国综合性旅游行业协会，具有独立的社团法人资格。它是 1986 年 1 月 30 日经国务院批准正式宣布成立的第一个旅游全行业组织，1999 年 3 月 24 日经民政部核准重新登记。协会接受国家旅游局的领导、民政部的业务指导和监督管理。

9. 中国展览馆协会 CAEC

中国展览馆协会（China Association for Exhibition Centers）简称中国展协，于 1984 年 6 月在国家民政部登记注册成立，是我国目前唯一的全国性展览行业组织，为国家一级社团，也是国际展览业协会（UFI）的国家级会员。业务主管单位是国务院国有资产监督管理委员会。中国展览馆协会（简称：中国展协）于 1984 年 6 月在国家民政部登记注册成立，是我国目前唯一的全国性展览行业组织，为国家一级社团，也是国际展览业协会（UFI）的国家级会员。业务主管单位是国务院国有资产监督管理委员会。中国展协主要由展览主办机构、展览场馆、展览中心、展览工程公司、展览运输公司、展览媒体、高等院校、展览科研机构以及与展览行业相关的且具有法人资格的企事业单位自愿参加组成。目前会员单位已近 300 家，分布在 29 个省、70 多个城市，其中以区域性展览协会、各行业协会名义加入的团体又包含了各自的几十家乃至上千家会员，会员单位业务范围涵盖了整个会展产业链。

10. 上海市会展行业协会 HKECIA

上海市会展行业协会（Shanghai Convention & Exhibition Industries Association，SCEIA）于 2002 年 4 月成立，由上海市从事会议、展览及相关业务的企事业单位自愿组成的跨部门、跨所有制、非营利性的行业性社会团体法人，是具有广泛代表性的新型行业协会。协会由会员单位组成，截至 2008 年 4 月，协会已有会员 457 家，会员成分已呈多元结构，基本涵盖了会展主体业务以及与之相关的业务领域。

11. 广州市会展业行业协会 GZCEIA

广州市会展业行业协会是由广州地区从事会议、展览及相关的企事业单位发起，自愿组成具有法人资格的行业性、非营利性社会团体。该行业协会在广州市登记，接受广州市协作办公室的业务指导和广州市民间组织管理局的监督管理。

该行业协会的宗旨是：遵守中华人民共和国的宪法、法律、法规和国家政策，遵守社会道德风尚。在广州市会展业管理领导小组的指导下，协助政府从事行业管理，建立行业自律机制，规范行业市场秩序，优化行业市场环境，培育国际会展品牌，保护会员合法权益，提高行业整体素质，组织行业国际交流和合作，促进广州市会展业行业的健康发展。

12. 香港展览会议业协会 HKECIA

香港展览会议业协会（Hong Kong Exhibition & Convention Industry Association，HKECIA）前身为香港展览业协会，于 1990 年 5 月由当时 10 家主要展览会主办机构创立。作为行业的喉舌，与政府及法定机构协商，促进会员的商业利益。从 1990 年 5 月开始，每隔两年，一个由 15 人组成的新执委会便由普通会员于周年大会中选出。此外本会还成立了数个事务委员会，专门负责一些特别专案及活动，如教育及培训、环境保护、策略推广及会员事务和组织海外访问团及周年晚会。

七、我国举办的和正在筹办的主要展会

1. 中国进出口商品交易会 Canton Fair

中国进出口商品交易会 China Import and Export Fair（Canton Fair for short）又称广交会，创办于 1957 年春季，每年春秋两季在广州举办，是中国目前历史最久、层次最高、规模最大、商品种类最全、国别地区最广、到会客商最多、成交效果最好、信誉最佳的综合性国际贸易盛会。为平衡外贸进出口，广交会在第 101 届，引入进口。102 届更为扶持进口发展，支持境外企业参展，并为此推出了一系列措施。

2. 昆明世界园艺博览会 Kunming World Horti-Expo 1999

1999 年昆明世界园艺博览会是认可类世博会，它设定的主题为“人与自然——迈向 21 世纪”，展期为 1999 年 5 月 1 日至 10 月 31 日，历时 184 天。会址设在昆明市北部金殿名胜风景区，占地面积 218 公顷。共有 69 个国家和 26 个国际组织参加了世博会，近 1 000 万名观众参观了世博会。这是中国首次举办的世界博览会。

3. 上海世博会 World Expo 2010 Shanghai China

上海世博会于 2010 年 5 月 1 日至 10 月 31 日在上海市中心举行。世博会的主题是“城市，让生活更美好”副主题是“城市多元文化的融合

城市经济的繁荣 城市科技的创新 城市社区的重塑”。

世博会将是上海城市发展的一个里程碑，上海作为以城市为主题的2010年世界博览会的举办城市，有着特殊的意义。上海在筹备世博会的过程中，必然会建造更多的优秀建筑，创建面向未来的住宅区，丰富城市发展的理念，完善并提升城市功能，创造城市未来发展的模式，推动中国城市化进程。

Part II 筹备会展 (Preparation for Exhibition)

Chapter 1 招展（Exhibition Invitation）

Business Situation 1

The 107th China Import and Export Fair will be held in Guangzhou, China from 15th April to 19th, 2010. China Foreign Trade Centre, the organizer of the Fair has issued exhibition invitation and Exhibitors Manual to the world possible exhibitors and buyers. The following is the Notice of Exhibitor Recruitment of International Pavilion.

第107届中国进出口交易会将于2010年4月15日—19日在广州举行。广交会举办方中国对外贸易中心开始了会展的招展工作，向全世界发出了招展函和参展信息手册等文件。以下是进口展区招展通告。

Sample

Notice of Exhibitor Recruitment of International Pavilion
进口展区招展事宜通告

For The 107th Session of China Import and Export Fair please refer to this Notice of Exhibitor Recruitment of International Pavilion of the 107th Session of China Import and Export Fair (hereinafter referred to as the Canton Fair).

现将第107届中国进出口商品交易会（以下简称广交会）进口展区招展事宜通告如下：

1. Exhibition Time 展览时间

Exhibition Time: April 15 - 20, 2010

展览时间：2010年4月15日—20日

2. Exhibition Venue 展览地点

Exhibition Venue: The International Pavilion of the Canton Fair, Pazhou Complex, China Import and Export Fair, No. 380 Yuejiangzhong Road, Guangzhou, China

展览地点：中国广州市阅江中路380号中国进出口商品交易会琶洲展馆进口展区。

3. Exhibition Space 展览面积

Exhibition Space: 15,000 sq.m. - 20,000 sq.m.

展览面积：1.5 万平方米~2 万平方米。

4. Exhibits 参展展品

The 107th session will focus on consumer goods, supplemented by industrial products. The exhibits fall into 9 exhibition subsections:

Consumer Goods

Decorations and Gifts

Foodstuffs and Agricultural Products

Machinery and Equipment

Small Vehicles and Spare Parts

Electronics, IT Products and Household Electrical Appliances

Hardware and Tools

Building Materials and Kitchen and Sanitary Equipment

Raw Materials

本届广交会进口展区以消费品类为主，工业类为辅；设立日用消费品、装饰品及礼品、食品及农产品、机械设备、小型车辆及配件、电子信息产品及家电、五金工具、建材及厨卫设备、原材料等 9 个产品区。

5. Stand Rate 展位价格

Raw Space: RMB 3,000 per sq.m.

Standard Stand: RMB 30,000 (9 sq.m. with standard facilities)

展位按光地和标准展位两类形式出租，光地展位价格为 3 000 元人民币/平方米，标准展位（9 平方米，含标准展具配置）价格为 30 000 元人民币。

To support the overseas enterprises to participate, the preferential conditions are as follows:

为支持境外企业参展，进口展区的展位价格对境外参展商给予优惠，具体为：

Exhibitors from the least developed countries listed by the United Nations will be offered stands for free. (For detailed name list, please refer to attachment 1.)

对联合国公布的最不发达国家（具体名单见附件 1）的参展商，给予免收展位费的优惠。

Exhibitors from other countries and regions will enjoy a 25% off, i. e., raw space of the International Pavilion will be RMB 2,250 yuan per s.q.m., and a single standard stand (9 s.q.m. with standard facilities) will be RMB 22,500 yuan.

其他国家和地区的参展商按定价 7.5 折优惠，即光地价格为 2 250 元人民币/平方米，标准展位（9 平方米，含标准展具配置）价格为 22 500

元人民币。

6. Application for Participation 参展申请

（1）Qualifications for Application 申请资质

All overseas enterprises which meet the requirements of Participation Provisions（see attachment 2）can apply for participation. 申请条件凡符合《参展条款》（详见附件2）的境外企业，均可申请参展。

（2）How to Apply 申请方式

Enterprises can apply directly to the China Foreign Trade Centre（hereinafter referred to as CFTC）, or apply via agents entrusted by CFTC for participation.（For Participation Application Form, please refer to attachment 3.）

企业可以直接向中国对外贸易中心（以下简称外贸中心）报名参展，也可以通过外贸中心委托的招展代理参展（参展申请表见附件3）。

（3）Standards and Organizing Principles for Agents

代理机构标准和安排原则

Those who meet the following requirements can apply to the CFTC for acting as agents for the International Pavilion of the 107th Session of the Canton Fair:

符合下列条件的机构，可向外贸中心申请作为第107届广交会进口展区招展代理：

To avoid business cross, on the basis of the ability of each agent, the China Foreign Trade Centre will segment the market and exhibit category reasonably. The validity of agent entrustment is only for the 107th session. The agency cooperation in the future will depend on the quality of the current agents and the new arrangement of the International Pavilion. The current agents will be given priority for the agency cooperation under the same conditions.

为避免交叉，外贸中心将根据各代理机构招展的能力，合理划分各自招展市场和商品范围。进口展区的委托代理招展期限仅限于第107届。今后的代理合作，将视本届代理质量以及广交会进口展区以后的相关安排情况，在同等代理条件下优先考虑。

（4）Requirements for Exhibiting Companies and Exhibits 参展企业和参展展品要求（具体内容略）

（5）Time for Stand Application 展位申请时间

The deadline for agent application is ... Upon the receipt of the application, the CFTC will decide the name list of the agents of International Pavilion of the 107th session of the Canton Fair before... and sign the Agent Agreement with them.

招展代理机构申请的截止时间为：……外贸中心收到申请后，

于……日前确定第107届广交会进口展区招展代理，并与其签订《招展代理协议》。

The deadline for stand application is February 20, 2010 Upon the receipt of the application, the CFTC will send the Notice of Stand Confirmation before February 29, 2010.

参展报名申请的截止时间2010年2月20日；外贸中心收到申请后，于2010年2月29日前发出展位确认书。

（6）Contact 联系方式（略）

Attachment 附件:

1. Least Developed Countries Listed by the United Nations 联合国公布的最不发达国家名单（略）
2. Participation Provisions 参展条款（略）
3. Application Form 参展申请表（略）

China Foreign Trade Centre 中国对外贸易中心
November 7, 2009　　2009年11月7日

Business Situation 2

The 107th American International Toy Fair will be held in Jacob K. Javits Convention Center in New York City on Feb. 14 - 17, 2010. The American Toy Industry Association Inc. is responsible for the preparation and organization of the fair. The Association has issued exhibition invitation documents at Internet website to the toy manufacturers, potential exhibitors, buyers and media all over the world. The following is the main contents of the invitation notice.

第107届美国纽约国际玩具展将于2010年2月14—17日在美国纽约贾维茨会议中心举行。美国玩具工业协会负责这次展会的筹备和组织工作。该协会通过网络向全世界玩具生产企业、可能的参展商、采购商以及媒体等相关行业发出招展信息。以下是107届玩具展招展函的主要内容。

Sample

Invitation Notice for the 107th American International Toy Fair
107届美国纽约国际玩具展招展通告

With over 20,000 attendees, 350,000 square feet of exhibit space, 100,000 products with over 7,000 never before seen in the world, 1,200 exhibitors, 1,000 global media representatives, the latest updates on Safety Legislation and what they mean for your business and four days under one roof to do an entire year's worth of business, Toy Fair is where the industry gathers.

Whether you are a buyer searching for the hottest trends, an exhibitor ready to showcase your innovative products, a trade professional wanting to discover the next great toy or a member of the media looking for the toy story of the year, Toy Fair has it all!

本届展览会展览面积35万平方英尺，展品超过10万件，其中有7 000多件是世界上从未出现过的最新产品；将有20 000多名参观者，1 200家参展商和1 000位全球媒体的代表参加。美国对玩具安全法的最新修订将对您的生意带来积极的影响。4天的展览可以为您创造全年的业务价值。

玩具展览会是玩具行业的盛会。这里应有尽有。无论您是寻求最热门趋势的买家，还是准备展示您的创新产品的参展商，无论是希望发现明年最抢手玩具的贸易方面的专业人士，还是想在展会中发现玩具领域的新闻素材的媒体，都可以在这里得到您所要的一切！

1. Show Information 展会信息

（1）What is American International Toy Fair? 美国国际玩具展简介

Toy Fair is the largest international toy trade show in the Western Hemisphere where the newest and hottest products in the children's entertainment marketplace are exhibited.

纽约玩具展是西半球最大的国际玩具贸易展，将展出儿童娱乐市场中最新、最热门的产品。

（2）When and where is the Show? 展览会时间和地点

Toy Fair 2010 will take place on February 14－17, 2010（Sunday－Wednesday）at the Jacob K. Javits Convention Center.

2010年玩具展览会将于2010年2月14—17日在贾维茨会议中心举行（星期日 — 星期三）。

（3）Where are the showroom Exhibit Sites located 展厅位置

Showroom locations throughout NYC as listed in the Exhibitor Locator Guide（available on-site）. 展厅位置可参见参展商位置指南（可上网查询）。

（4）Registration Dates/Hours 报名登记日期/时间

Noon－5:00 PM Friday, February 12

2月12日，星期五，中午12:00 — 下午5:00

Saturday, February 13, 9:00 AM－5:00 PM

2 月 13 日，星期六，上午 9:00 — 下午 5:00
Sunday, February 14, 8:00 AM - 6:00 PM
2 月 14 日，星期日，上午 8:00 — 下午 6:00

（5）Exhibit Dates/Hours 展览日期/时间
Monday, February 15　9:00 AM - 6:00 PM,
2 月 15 日，星期一，上午 9:00 — 下午 6:00
Tuesday, February 16　9:00 AM - 6:00 PM
2 月 16 日，星期二，上午 9:00 — 下午 6:00

2. Admission Policies, Fees and Documentation 入馆规定、收费和相关文件

（1）May I bring my child to the show? 可以带孩子参观展览吗？

Absolutely no one under the age of 18 (including infants and toddlers) is permitted to attend Toy Fair.

未满 18 岁的未成年人包括婴儿和幼儿都不得进入展厅。

（2）Toy Fair Fees 玩具展览会费用

- TIA Members: No charge 美国玩具业协会会员：免费
- Manufacturers' Representatives: No charge 制造商代表：免费
- $500 Non-Exhibiting Manufacturer: TIA Member — $250 / Non-member — $500

非参展制造商收费 500 美元，如是美国玩具业协会会员收费 250 美元，如果是非会员则收费 500 美元。

- Media Representatives: No charge　媒体代表：免费

（3）Who is not eligible to attend? 谁无资格参加？

Also, Who Should Attend? 究竟什么人可以参加？

- Registration is open to the trade only; Toy Fair is not open to the public. Those eligible for admission as buyers include retailers, wholesalers, importers, and buying groups. Certain categories of trade guests are also eligible for admission. Suppliers to the trade are not qualified to attend. Individuals who cannot document their direct, professional affiliation to the trade are not qualified to attend. TIA offers a specific show registration for non-exhibiting manufacturers with the goal of protecting exhibitors and their show investment.

本博览会只有贸易行业才有资格注册参加，不对公众开放。有资格参加的采购商包括零售商、批发商、进口商和采购团。某些类别的贸易客户也可以参加。贸易供应商也不能参加。任何个人，如不能提供与贸易方面相关联的直接和专业性的证明也不得参加。非参展制造商，如其目的是为了保护参展商的安全和对展览的投资利益，美国玩具业协会为他们提供特别参展登记服务。

● Suppliers to the trade including shippers, paper and packaging companies, graphic design firms, and any individual or company looking to sell their services to exhibitors.

贸易供应商包括运货商，纸张和包装公司，平面设计公司以及任何寻求为参展商出售服务的个人或公司。

● No one under the age of 18, including infants, will be admitted. Toy Fair participants will be required to show government-issued photo ID（such as driver's license or passport）upon request.

任何未满18岁的人，包括婴儿，不得进入展览场馆。要求玩具展览会参加者出示政府颁发的带照片的身份证（如驾驶执照或护照）。

● Absolutely no consumers and no one under the age of 18, including infants, toddlers, demonstrators and "consultants", will be admitted to the Javits Center exhibit halls。

任何未满18岁的人，包括婴儿、幼儿、游行示威者以及"顾问"，都不得进入贾维茨中心展览大厅。

● Unauthorized solicitation on the premises by non-exhibiting manufacturers and/or suppliers is strictly prohibited.

严禁非参展制造商/供应商在展厅进行未经授权的询价活动。

3. Show Rules 展会规则

● Exhibitors must confine their activities to their own exhibit spaces, except in the case where Show Management has made prior arrangements with official show sponsors.

除非主办方管理部门与官方指定的展览赞助商作出了提前安排，否则，参展商的任何活动都必须限制在其展品陈列范围内。

（1）Photography of exhibitors' booths is prohibited except with permission of the exhibitor.

除非得到参展商的许可，禁止在参展商展台前拍照。

（2）In compliance with New York State law, notice is hereby given that smoking is not permitted at any show site.

根据纽约州法律，禁止在任何展示地点吸烟。

（3）Those who violate any of the above rules will be escorted from the show floor and will jeopardize participation in future TIA events.

违反上述任何规定者将被带出展厅，并可能禁止参加未来玩具业协会的活动。

● Happenings at the Toy Show 展览期间的活动

There's a lot happening at Toy Fair this year — from the addition of educational seminars, learning centers and special events — all designed to maximize your time in New York and help you grow your business.

本届展览会将开展很多活动，除了增加了教育研讨会，还有学习中心以及其他特别活动，所有这些都是为了您能在纽约逗留期间充分利用时间，并帮助您拓展业务。

4. To exhibit 参展

(1) Make a Big Deal Out of Toy Fair 本届展览会提供巨大商机

Toy Fair attracts more than 13,000 buyers representing 7,000 unique retail outlets: mass merchandisers, toy and hobby stores, drug stores, department stores, grocery chains, TV shopping networks, outdoor retailers, amusement parks, warehouse clubs, gift shops, museum stores, and more. Watch a video of Joan Wyche, Buyer Relations Manager at TIA, as she talks about how great Toy Fair is.

本届玩具展览会吸引了13 000 多名买家，7 000 家独特的零售企业：大型商场、玩具和娱乐商店、药店、百货公司、连锁零售店、电视购物网络、户外零售、游乐园、仓储俱乐部、礼品店、博物馆商店等。请观看美国玩具业协会采购商关系协会经理琼·威奇女士的网上视频资料，由她讲述本届玩具展的规模。

(2) First Time Exhibitors 首次参展商

Toy Fair offers many valuable first-time exhibitor programs, all providing exhibitors with powerful means to optimize their show experience and profitability.

玩具展览会为首次参展的参展商提供了许多宝贵的项目，所有这些项目都为参展商提供了强有力的手段来优化他们的参展经验和盈利能力。

Interested in exhibiting? Fill out our Information Request Form or download the Toy Fair 2010 Space Application and Contract (PDF).

如若对参展感兴趣，请填写我们提供的信息表或下载2010 年玩具展展位申请和合同样本（PDF）。

5. Exhibitor's Education 参展商教育活动

(1) All Sessions 会议

Presentation Date: March 17, 2010 发言日期：2010 年3 月17 日

(2) Session Description 会议描述

Each February, close to 1,000 global media representatives flock to Toy Fair to report on the fun and innovative toys and playthings that will be on the wish lists of the young and young at heart in the fourth quarter.

每年2 月，全球近1 000 名媒体代表齐聚在玩具展览会现场，报道他

们发现的趣味玩具、创新的玩具以及玩具排行榜上将在第四季度开始流行的年轻人和“年轻心态”一族喜爱的玩具。

6. Media Guidelines for Exhibitors 参展商媒体指南

Each year, close to 1,000 global media representatives flock to Toy Fair to report on the hottest trends, toys and playthings found at the largest toy trade show in the Western Hemisphere.

每年，全球近1 000名媒体代表聚集在玩具展览会，报道最热门的玩具发展趋势以及在本次堪称西半球最大的玩具展中亮相的各式各样的玩具。

7. Press Room 新闻中心

• TIA provides an official Press Room space for working media to use as a home base during the show, to conduct interviews, collect exhibitor information and construct articles for publication.

玩具业协会为方便媒体工作者，为他们提供了官方新闻中心作为在展会期间的大本营，以便媒体进行采访、收集展商信息、为出版刊物撰写文章等。

• Media will have access to computer work stations with internet access where they can access and download press materials from the Virtual Press Office (VPO).

媒体可以使用带有网络接口的电脑工作站，可以访问和下载虚拟新闻办公室的新闻资料。

• Each Toy Fair exhibitor is entitled to post a free one-page profile and contact information sheet describing their company and products.

每个玩具展览会参展商可以免费邮寄一份单页的文件和联系信息表描述他们的公司和公司的产品。

8. Exhibitor FAQs 参展商常见问题解答

• Where should I find information on how to exhibit? Is my product right for Toy fair?

我应该在哪里去搜索关于如何参展的信息？我的产品适合玩具展览会吗？

• My company/product is new, and I don't have the catalog or brochure. What should I sent in for review?

我公司/产品是新研制的，我还没有产品目录和手册。我应该选送什么样的材料参加评审？

• If I submit my application, when I would be notified that my company has been accepted to exhibit?

如果我公司提交申请并获得批准参展，何时通知我公司？

- What is the size range of booths?

展台的尺寸多少？

- I'm an inventor of a new product. Is there an opportunity for me to show it at Toy Fair?

我是一项新产品的发明者。我是否有机会在玩具展上展出新产品？

- How is booth space assigned? 展位如何分配？
- When I should send in payment? 我应该在何时付款？

9. Exhibitor Search and Floor Plan 参展商搜索和平面图

- Product Zones 产品区
- Press Room 新闻中心
- Hotel, Travel and Dining 酒店住宿、旅游和餐饮
- Publication Partners 出版物合作商

10. Seminar 研讨会

- TIA to host Environmental Sustainability Seminar at Toy Fair.

玩具工业协会将在2010年玩具展上举办环境可持续发展研讨会。

Business Links

一、会展招展的基本知识

1. 会展招展的形式与流程

形式：招展通常是以招展函的形式发布招展信息，招揽目标参展商参展，上海世博会和广交会等大型展会大都通过网络发布招展函，同时发布在线参展手册以及其他相关文件来招展。网络招展已成为主要的招展形式之一。

流程：发布展会的基本情况，并向目标参展商确认。参展商准备签证资料，包括向国外组委会申请邀请函，向使馆预约签证时间等，同时也通知参展人员自己准备相关的签证资料；对参展人员的服务安排；向参展公司确认摊位的装修及样品的运输等事宜。

2. 招展函（书）的基本内容和格式

招展函是办展机构用来说明展会以招揽目标参展商参展的通告或小册子。招展函是展会进行展位营销时主要的核心资料之一，也是目标参展商最初了解展会情况的主要信息来源。

为了能使目标参展商对展会有足够的了解，并对展会作出基本的判断，招展函介绍展会的内容必须准确而全面。一般来说，招展函主要包

括以下几方面的内容：

（1）展会名称和标志、展会的举办时间和地点、办展机构名单、办展起因和办展目标、展会特色、展品范围和价格等。

（2）市场状况介绍，主要包括行业状况和地区的市场状况等。

（3）展会招商和宣传推广计划，主要包括展会招商计划、宣传推广计划、相关活动计划、展会服务项目等。

（4）参展办法，主要包括如何办理参展手续、付款方式、参展申请表和办展机构的联系办法等。

（5）各种图案，如展馆图、展馆周边地区交通图、往届展会现场图片等。如果有需要，有些招展函还对展馆作一些简要介绍。

二、参展信息手册

除了发布招展函，会展组织方还通过网络发布《参展信息手册》或《服务守则》，详细介绍会展相关信息。有的展会（如广交会）发布《参展商服务指南》，《参展信息手册》和《参展商服务指南》主要是通过网络和小册子的形式发布。

《参展信息手册》和《参展商服务指南》一般包含以下内容：

1. 前言（Preface）：表示欢迎参加展会，然后简要回顾展会历史，说明展会的目的、展品内容和展会的意义。一般都很简短。

2. 进口展区的联系信息（Contact Information of the International Pavilion of the Fair）：如负责的部门和代理机构的联系方式。

3. 展会基本信息（Brief Introduction to the Exhibition）：包括展览名称、主办单位、承办单位、展览场地、展览地点、展览日期及时间、展出内容、参展商登记时间、地点、入场办法、展位搭建、撤展时间、大会指定承建商、海外代理、撤展、展会指定刊物、展会指定信息网、展会运输代理公司、展览会指定装修代理公司、指定接待酒店相关服务。

4. 进口展区参展流程（Participation Procedures of the International Pavilion of the Fair）：即办理入馆证件（筹展证、参展商证、撤展证）、申请展位、获取展位、展位布置及展品摆放等。

5. 服务指南与服务约定（Service Guide and Stipulations）：登记服务、现场服务、特装布展施工管理约定、标准展位布展服务及约定、展品运输服务及约定、撤展服务与约定、展品网上登记、资讯服务、订房服务等。

6. 展会规则（Provisions and Regulations）：主要是安全卫生方面的规定：如安全与防火卫生保障规则、展位使用、展品管理、参展行为规则等。

7. 附件（Appendixes）：主要包括展馆位置图、交通旅游信息、水电使用收费、投诉处理等。

8. 相关表格（Relevant Forms）：参展商证申请表、筹展申请表、撤展申请表等各种申请表格。

Useful Sentences

1. 场馆选择（Choice of Venue）

（1）What would be a nice location for our automobile exhibition?
我们要举办的汽车展览选址在哪里比较合适呢？

（2）We had better start out with some place close to our target clients.
我们最好从离我们目标客户近的地方开始。

（3）It provides very easy, convenient access for show attendees, exhibitors and freight delivery.
对于参展人员，参展商和运货商来说，这个位置都非常便利。

（4）We provide our clients with a whole package of services.
我们为客户提供一系列的服务。

（5）Whichever venue best matches the criteria, bearing in mind the price range and the professional level of the venue management, should be considered.
应该考虑符合条件的场馆，同时应该考虑价格范畴和场馆管理的专业水平。

2. 介绍展会（Introducing an Exhibition）

（1）This design proposal, especially the large round sphere it incorporates echoes the scenery in Pudong.
这个设计方案，尤其是它所包含的巨大圆形球体呼应了浦东的景色。

（2）In the designing company's concept, World Expo should display a complete range of high technology.
设计公司的理念就是世界博览会应该完整地展示出高科技。

（3）The story of mankind is replete with references to fairs, not in an institutional context, but as a part of everyday social intercourse.
人类的故事中充满了对博览会的引用，这并非出于制度的影响，而是作为日常社会交流的一部分出现的。

（4）Whether a country can successfully host a world exhibition is not only a reflection of its achievements and power, but also a display of its determination and confidence to strive towards a new area.
一个国家是否可以成功地举办一届世界博览会不仅反映了它的

成就和实力，而且展示了它努力迈向一个新领域的决心和信心。

（5）The World Exhibitions are fundamentally different from ordinary exhibitions for trade and economic promotion.
世界博览会在促进贸易和经济方面与一般的展览会有着本质的区别。

3. 展览营销和广告（Exhibition Marketing and Advertising）

（1）You can expose your business by purchasing a banner ad or a link to your website.
你们可以通过购买一个横幅广告或者链接到你们的网站来增加你们公司的知名度。

（2）Association shows aren't placing the same emphasis on marketing as their independent counterparts.
单位参加的展览不像个人参加展览那么看中市场营销。

（3）In this decade, the success of a trade show will be directly related to the combined strength of exhibitors' co-marketing the show in partnership with the show organizer.
近10年来，贸易展的成功将直接与参展商和展览组织者的联手营销力度相关。

（4）The events covered a range of industries from food and health care to manufacturing and retail, but most new shows by far were technology-related, focusing on telecom, IT, the Internet and other digital applications.
这些展览活动包含了许多行业，包括食品、保健、制造业和零售业，但是到目前为止，大多数的新展览是和科技相关的，集中在电信，信息技术，因特网和其他形式的数字使用领域。

（5）Held during the three days of the fair will be various business talks, including European Food Combo, ASEAN Food Exhibition, procurement activities of China's big supermarket chains and Day of Promoting China Geographic Indication Products, which will assist you to obtain considerable benefits and establish a new commercial network.
本届洽谈会为期三天，将举办丰富的对接洽谈活动，其中包括"欧洲食品荟萃"、东盟食品展示会、中国大型连锁超市采购专场活动以及中国地理标志产品推广日活动，协助您获取可观的经贸成效，并建立新的商业网络。

Chapter 2 报名与预订展位 (Application and Booking a Stand)

Business Situation 1

Puckator Ltd. Company, one of the UK's leading importers and wholesalers of giftware, toys and home accessories, plans to participate the 107th China Import and Export Fair as an exhibitor. The marketing manager Mr. Smith calls China Foreign Trade Exhibition Company, asking for some information to make stand reservation. The China Foreign Trade Exhibition Company officer, Miss Xiao, answers all his questions.

英国 Puckator 有限公司是英国主要的礼品、玩具和家居饰品的进口商和批发商之一。该公司计划以参展商的名义参加第 107 届广交会。公司市场部经理史密斯先生打电话给中国对外贸易展览公司办公室，询问有关情况并打算预订展位。中国对外贸易展览公司办公室高级职员肖小姐接到电话，回答了对方提出的问题。

Dialogue

S = Mr. Smith　X = Miss Xiao

X: Good morning, China Foreign Trade Exhibition Company. Can I help you?

S: Yes, please. I'm Smith, the marketing manager of Puckator Ltd. Company in the UK. May I inquire something about the 107th China Import and Export Fair?

X: Of course. Anything you would like to know. Is it the first time your company participate in the Fair?

S: No, we have participated in the Fair as an exhibitor for 2 times.

X: That's great. You might remember the account number and original password to Easy Exhibitor? Go to net address *http://exhibitor.cantonfair.org.cn/en/* and sign in. Fill in the Participation Application Form online according to instruction. Then print out the approved application form with the official seal and post it to the address marked in that page.

S: Thank you. Could you please tell me something about the booth type?

X: The Canton Fair provides standard stands of unified pattern and Custom-built Stands. Basic equipments in 9 ㎡ standard stand include: three-side walls, one fascia board, one carpet, four spotlights, one F/L light, one aluminum table, four chairs, and one box of mineral water, and one telephone. Refer to the stands, on rental of raw space (minimum 18 ㎡), that exhibitor entrusts the contractor with qualification certification of the Canton Fair to set up and decorate either in the wooden structure or with materials which are different from those used in the standard stands.

S: That's useful. I think the location of a stand matters a lot. Do you have any stand with high traffic flow to recommend?

X: Yes, certainly. Besides Linear Booth, we provide Corner Booth, End-cup Booth and Peninsula Booth as well. But the price of renting them is much more expensive. And the most expensive one is Island Booth.

S: I see. Thanks a lot.

参考译文

肖小姐：早上好，中国对外贸易展览公司。有什么我可以效劳的吗？

史密斯：是的，我是英国 Puckator 有限公司的市场部经理史密斯。我想询问一些第 107 届广交会的信息。

肖小姐：没问题，我会尽力帮助您解答疑问。请问这是贵公司第一次参加广交会吗？

史密斯：不是的，我们曾经以参展商的身份参加过两届广交会。

肖小姐：好的，那么您应该还记得贵公司的广交会“易捷通”用户名和密码了？请点开“易捷通”的网站 *http://exhibitor.cantonfair.org.cn/en/*并用您的用户名以及密码登录上去，根据介绍在线填写《参展申请表》。然后把经过了审核的表格打印出来，盖上贵公司的公章，邮寄到该网页上注明的地址。

史密斯：谢谢。请问你能告诉我一些关于展位类型的信息吗？

肖小姐：广交会提供统一模型的标准摊位以及参展商自建的特装摊位。每个 9 ㎡的标准展位由 3 面围板、1 块楣板、1 块磨耗层组成。基本配置为 4 只射灯、1 支光管、1 张洽谈桌、4 张折椅、1 箱矿泉水以及 1 部电话。至于在光地展位上的、至少 18 ㎡的摊位，参展商需要授权于广交会认证过的承建商来构建装修自己的展位，构建材料可以是木质材料或者其他有别于标准摊位的材料。

史密斯：这很有用。我认为摊位的位置能对参展效果起到很大影响。你有什么客流量大的展位推荐吗？

肖小姐：有的，当然有。除了道边摊位，我们还提供角落摊位、三面开口摊位以及半岛型摊位。不过它们的价格相对来说就贵得多了。

最贵的是岛型摊位。

史密斯：我明白了，多谢。

Business Situation 2

The application for the 107th China Import and Export Fair started in November, 2009. Shenzhen Ugo Sports Shoes Co., Ltd. is planning to fill in the Booth Application Form online in the *http://exhibitor.cantonfair.org.cn/en/* for the 107th Canton Fair.

第107届广交会的报名工作已于2009年11月开始启动。深圳Ugo运动鞋有限公司通过广交会“参展易捷通”*http://exhibitor.cantonfair.org.cn/en/*在线填报《参展申请表》申请展位，准备参加第107届广交会。

第107届广交会展位申请表　Booth Application Form		
申报广交会展区代码 Booth Number(s)	申报展区名称	Booth Name(s) 展位类型 Booth Type
企业永久代码 Permanent Code	企业广交会编码 Code	
申请企业名称 Name of Company		
申请企业地址 Address of Company		
邮政编码 Zip/Postal Code		
联系部门 Contact Department		
联系人 Contact Person		
法定代表人 The legal Representative		
进出口商会会员证号 Member Number of Import and Export Chamber of Commerce	企业类型（外贸、生产、工贸、科研院所、其他）Company Type (foreign trade, manufacturing, industry and trade, scientific research institute and others)	
外资协会会员证 Member Number of Foreign-funded Enterprises Association		
进出口企业代码 Import and Export Enterprise Code	企业属性（国有、集体、私营、外资、其他）Company Property (state-owned, collectively-owned, private, foreign-funded, and others)	
上年度出口额（万美元）Exports of the Previous Year ($10,000)	海关编码 Customs Code	国家、省级奖励及数量 The Numbers of National, Provincial-level Awards

（续）

国际通行的管理体系认证或行业认证及数量 International Management System Certification and Its Number	是否列入《中国高科技出口产品目录》 Whether in《Chinese High-tech Export Products Catalog》or Not
展品名称：Name of Products	
本届申请展位数 The Current Numbers of Application for Booths	上届展位数 Numbers of the Last Stand for Booths
*是否有联营参展单位 Whether Joint Exhibitors or Not	
注：1. 本企业一经申请盖章，保证填报内容的真实性并确认已经阅读并接受《广交会出口展展位使用责任书》、《中国进出口商品交易会出口展参展须知》、《中国进出口商品交易会出口展参展商服务指南》及有关增订条款。2. 本企业申请获安排后，如企业退出参展或退回部分展位，承诺按原安排的展位数情况，缴纳全部的展位费用。	
（申请企业盖章）	（交易团盖章）
年 月 日	年 月 日
说明：	
1. 本表根据申请企业录入广交会“参展易捷通”的资料自动生成（一个展区对应一份申请表）。	
2. 本表须加盖申请企业公章，并连同相关证明材料（如上年度出口额、国家级奖励、国际通行的管理体系认证、专利、列入国家高新技术产品目录或国家科技部颁发的高新技术产品证书、海外注册商标等）一并提交给所在行政区域或系统交易团/联合交易团分团，参展申请方正式生效。 3. 如有联营（供货）单位共同参展，请在参展申请时同时提交联营单位申请资料。	

Business Links

展览会已经不是简单意义上的展示产品、推销产品、购买商品的场所。现代展览会已经快速发展为交流和获得信息的中心。参加展览会是企业整个市场拓展工作的重要组成部分，应被列入全盘市场计划之中。

参展商在确定了参展目的后，选择合适的展览会是关键。选择好之后，与主办单位取得联系，对方会传真或邮寄回报展文件。这些文件应包括展览会介绍资料、参展申请表格、参展费用、有关服务、展馆展位图、参展人员手册等。参展商应尽快填好参展表格、返回给大会主办者、并得以确认，有时参展商还要将全部或者部分展位费作为定金汇至主办者，这样展位便得到最后的确定。

1. 受理国内客商出国参展、观展申请的一般流程

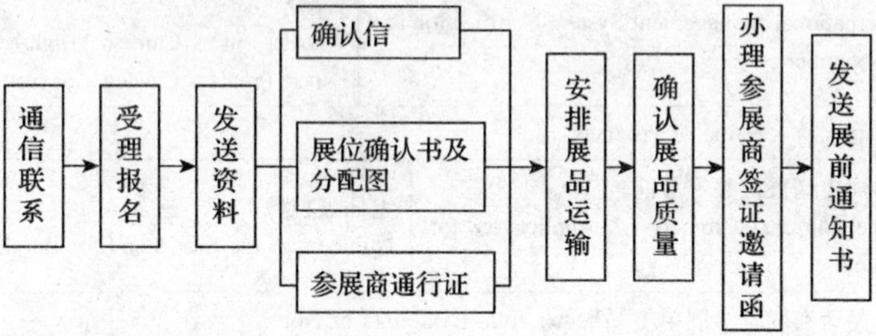

2. 参展申请程序

（以广交会为例）

Please apply according to the following instructions:（请根据以下要求进行申请：）

（1）Through agents of the Canton Fair.（通过广交会的代理人。）

（2）Direct application to China Foreign Trade Exhibition Company that is subordinated to China Foreign Trade Centre in case of absence of an agent.（如无代理人，直接向中国对外贸易展览公司申请，该公司是隶属中国对外贸易中心的。

（3）Online Application Procedures（网上申请程序）

Please do the online account registration in *Easy Exhibitor*（请通过“易捷通”进行网上账号注册）*http://exhibitor.cantonfair.org.cn/en/* Should remember the account number and original password, it is a unique ID for every applicant.（请记住账号及初始密码，因为它是能唯一确认申请人身份的标志。）

Fill in the Participation Application Form online.（请在网上填写《参展申请表》。）

Please wait for the staff to verify the validity of the information you have submitted.（请等候以确认您所提交信息的有效性。）

Please print out the approved application form with the official seal and post it to the following address. The Application Form must be received before Aug. 21, 2009.（请打印出经审批的带有公章的申请表并将其邮寄到以下地址，并要求于2009年8月21日前将该申请表寄到。）

Address（地址）:

Tel（电话）:

Fax（传真）:

3. 参展申请表的主要信息

（1）参展商信息 Exhibitor Information

公司名称（Company name），地址（Address），邮编（Zip Code），法人代表（Legal Representative），联系人（Contact Person），电话（Tel），传真（Fax），手机（Cell phone），邮箱（E-mail），网址（Website）。

（2）展位预订 Booking of Show Booths

标准展位（Standard Booth），展位数（Booth（s）），展位号（Booth Number），美元计价的展位费（The Price for the Booth in US dollars）等。

所需光地展位和特殊展位（Open（Raw）Space and Special Booth），室内还是室外（Indoor or Outdoor Booth），面积（Square Meter），价格（Price for Booth in US dollars），展品内容（Exhibits Description）

4. 展位预订的主要内容

企业参加展览会，须向组织方申请展位。大型展会一般要求通过代理公司也就是展会指定的专业机构办理展位预订，这类机构可以提供一条龙服务，也可以直接向展会组织方预订。国内企业可以参加本地区的交易团统一办理展位。参加进口展的国外企业须向由组织方指定的代理机构申报。如无代理机构，则可以通过网上申报。大多数展会都在网上公布参展申请表，以便参展企业在网上报名。

广交会公布的参展办法是：凡符合广交会参展资质标准的企业可在规定时限内通过广交会“参展易捷通 *http://exhibitor.cantonfair.org.cn/en/*”在线填报《参展申请表》，打印盖章后连同评审材料（如上年度出口额、行业自律、研发创新和自主知识产权、国际通行认证、境外商标注册、品牌荣誉、高新技术企业等）一并提交给所在行政区域或系统交易团参展组团单位，参展申请正式生效。企业在同一展区申请展位数至少为1个【标准展位面积为9 ㎡，化工产品展区按4 ㎡为1个展位，铁石制品展区按20 ㎡为1个展位，车辆（户外）展区按20 ㎡为1个展位，工程机械（棚下）展区按12 ㎡为1个展位，工程机械（露天）展区按20 ㎡为1个展位。】

5. 主办方工作

招展工作的中后期，为参展商提供的跟进服务应逐步展开。主要工作包括进一步提供展览会信息，催收参展费用，发送参展商手册，提醒进馆报到日期等。

招展人员应经常性地向参展商发出展览会的新闻简报资料《最新动态》，使参展商随时了解展览会的进展情况，让他们为参加了一个正规的展览会并受到专业的服务而感到放心。《最新动态》将会展亮点、行业反响、公司参展回应、国际参与度、招展进度、已报名参展公司简介、增值服务、同期活动、网站宣传等诸多有价值的信息传递给参展商。

对于已确认预订的申请者，招展人员要向他们催订参展合同，并发出付款通知书。只有收到了参展商的展台预订金，展会组织者才能确认其正式参展，并为他们寄发参展手册。参展手册是展会组织者为参展商进一步提供参展服务的内部工作文件，其内容详尽涵盖了参展商参展的基本信息、规章制度、参展日程安排、免费的和有偿的服务，以及服务的申请表等。收到这份参展手册后，参展商应仔细阅读，填好表格，预订服务。包括：公司简介免费刊入展览会刊，公司名称中英文楣板制作，参展胸卡制作、会刊广告的预订、住宿预订、展具租赁，展台用电/用水/用气设备租赁、展馆广告位租订、现场翻译租用、技术交流会等。

在收到参展商的服务申请表后，招展人员必须对各种表格进行整理归档，并将相关服务表格转交给服务供应商，如主场搭建商、指定展品运输商、会展旅游服务商等，以便跟进服务。

Useful Sentences

1. 参展商（Exhibitors）

(1) I'd like to sign in.
我想报名。

(2) I'd like to book a booth. Are there any left in Area B?
我想预订展位，在B展区还有剩余展位吗？

(3) Have all the end-cup booths been ordered?
所有的三面开口形展位都被预订了吗？

(4) A raw space will be fine.
一块光地就行了。

(5) Could you recommend some booths to me?
你能为我推荐一些展位吗？

2. 主办方（Organizer）

(1) I may register you online.
我可以帮您在网上注册。

(2) Let me confirm your reservation.
我再确认一下您的预订。

(3) Your booth number is...
您的展位号码是……

（4）Fill in the Participation Application Form online.
请在网上填写《参展申请表》。
（5）This is the best place for a booth.
这是搭建摊位最好的位置了。
（6）Which one would you like?
您想要哪一种摊位？
（7）We still have some Island Booths available.
我们还有一些岛型摊位。
（8）You'd better select a stand with high traffic flow.
你最好在客流密集的地方选择一个展位。
（9）Only cancellation and refund requests made in writing will be accepted.
取消参展以及退款要求必须以书面形式提出。
（10）We will send you a letter of confirmation by e-mail or fax within 5 working days.
我们将会在5个工作日内给您电邮或传真一份确认书。

3. 参展程序（Procedures for the Registration）

（1）企业确定参展，填好参展申请表并加盖公章传真或邮寄至大会组委会。
Exhibitors fax or post the application form to the preparing committee, which has been filled in and sealed.
（2）组委会收到确认申请表，参展商于10个工作日内将参展费用汇入组委会账户，并将汇款证传真至组委会以便查对。
Exhibitors remit the exhibition fee to the account designated by the committee within 10 workdays after filling in the application form, and fax the remitting evidence to the preparing committee to make a confirmation.
（3）展会安排原则是"先申请，先付款，先安排"。
The principle of arranging the booth is: "Apply first, pay first, and arrange first."
（4）会刊广告排序以收到广告费先后为准，入编截止日期为……
The ranking order of the advertisements on the catalogue will be according to the order we receive the advertisement fee. The deadline is…
（5）同时组委会将于……（日期）向参展企业寄发《参展商手册》和《进场通知书》。
Meanwhile the preparing committee will post *Exhibition Manual*, *Admission Notice* on…

Chapter 3 邀请函
(Letters of Invitation)

Business Situation 1

Shenzhen Ugo Sports Shoes Co., Ltd. has applied for participation in the 107th China Import and Export Fair which will be held from May 5th to 7th. The application has been approved by the Canton Fair Organization Committee. The company is sending invitation letters to its overseas clients and hope that they will come to the Fair for a talk and purchase its new products. The company has also told the clients its booth number in the letters.

深圳 Ugo 运动鞋有限公司申请参加 5 月 5 日至 7 日的第 107 届广交会并获得批准。公司向海外客户发出邀请，希望他们能参观广交会进行洽谈和采购，并告知了公司在广交会的展位号码。

Sample

Dear Mr. Bruce Jackson,

We should like to invite you to attend the 107th China Import and Export Fair which will be held from May 5th to 7th. Our booth number is Hall 2. 2G11 and 2. 2G12 in Pazhou Exhibition Hall.

We develop many new designs and programs this year, and I am sure there must be some kinds attracting your attention. Meanwhile, we'd like to take this opportunity to talk with you for the new business face to face.

You may see various kinds of sports shoes newly designed for both young students and adults, which are a perfect combination of comfort and the latest elements of fashion. Also you can select the most novel designs from our designs sample shelves.

Please visit our website *www. ugo. com. cn* in case you have any question.

We look forward to hearing from you soon, and hope that you will be able to attend.

Yours faithfully,

Denny Chen

P. S.

Shenzhen Ugo Sports Shoes Co., Ltd.

Company Add: ________

Tel: ________

Fax: ________

Factory Add: ________

E-mail: ________

参考译文

尊敬的布鲁斯·杰克逊先生：

我们很荣幸地邀请您参加5月5日至7日在中国广州举办的第107届中国广交会。我们的展位号是琶洲展馆2.2G11和2.2G12。

今年，我们开发出了一系列新设计的产品。我们相信一定会有产品让您满意，与此同时，我们也希望借此机会与您面对面交流，拓展我们的合作。

我们的产品中有新开发出的面向学生和成年人的运动鞋系列，该系列产品将最新的流行元素融入设计，并且穿着舒适。除此以外，我们的展厅中还有各式新产品供您选择。

我们公司的网址是 www. ugo. com. cn。期待您的关注，并欢迎您来我们的展会挑选产品。

此致

敬礼

丹尼·陈

附：

深圳 Ugo 运动鞋有限公司

公司地址：________

电话：________

传真：________

厂址：________

邮箱：________

Business Situation 2

The 107th American International Toy Fair will be held in Jacob K. Javits Convention Center in New York City on Feb. 14th – 17th, 2010. The American Toy Industry Association, Inc. is responsible for the preparation and organization of the fair. After it has issued exhibition invitation documents at Internet website to the toy manufacturers, potential exhibitors, buyers and media all over the world, the Association then sends invitation letters to the participants. Ms. Kimberly Carcone, director of the Trade Show and Event Marketing, on behalf of the organization committee, sends an invitation letter to Chenghai Toy Trading Co., Ltd. so that the company can make preparation and will obtain visa as soon as possible. The company's application as an exhibitor for participation in the fair has been accepted.

第107届美国纽约国际玩具展将于2010年2月14—17日在美国纽约雅各布K. 贾维茨会议中心举行。美国玩具工业协会负责这次展会的筹备和组织工作。该协会通过网络向全世界玩具生产企业、可能参加的参展商、采购商以及媒体等相关行业发出招展信息后，向已经获准参加展会的参展商发出邀请。美国玩具工业协会展览与活动市场部主任金伯莉·卡科恩女士代表组委会向澄海玩具贸易公司发出邀请函，以便该公司为参展作好准备并凭该邀请函尽早获得签证。澄海玩具贸易公司以参展商的身份申请参加第107届美国纽约国际玩具展，并获得批准。

Sample

Dear Ms. Dora Zhao,

I would hereby invite the members of Chenghai Toy Trading Co., Ltd. delegation totally 7 persons (listed in attachment) led by you, to come over to New York, United States for the 107th American International Toy Fair, which is to be held in New York City's Jacob K. Javits Convention Center in New York City during February 14th to 17th, 2010. Please make the necessary arrangements for your delegation to arrive in United States. During the exposition, you will stay here for 4 days. All your expenses including international air tickets, local transportation, accommodations, medical insurances and all other related expenses during your stay here will be paid by yourselves. We are looking forward to greeting you in USA very soon.

Yours sincerely,

Ms. Kimberly Carcone

Director of Trade Show and Event Marketing

参考译文

尊敬的赵女士：

兹邀请由您率领的澄海玩具贸易公司7人代表团来美国参加第107

届纽约国际玩具展。该展览将于2010年2月14—17日在纽约贾维茨会议中心举行。请您安排来美国的必要事宜。展会期间你们将在此逗留4日。所有的费用，包括国际机票、当地交通、食宿、医疗保险和其他相关费用由贵公司承担。我们期待您的访问。

此致

敬礼

金伯莉·卡科恩

美国玩具工业协会展览与活动市场部主任

Business Situation 3

Wuxi Municipal People's Government is making preparation for the work to host the "2009 China Wuxi International Conference on Service Outsourcing Cooperation", which will be held at Wuxi Taihu Hotel on Oct. 11th, 2009. The organization committee, on behalf of the municipal government, sends invitation letters to government officials, administrators, entrepreneurs and media both from home and abroad.

无锡市人民政府正筹备主办"2009中国无锡国际服务外包合作会议"。该会议将于2009年10月11日在无锡太湖饭店举行。大会组委会以政府名义向国内外的政府官员、行政管理人员、企业家和媒体发出邀请。

Sample

Invitation for 2009 China Wuxi International Conference on Service Outsourcing Cooperation

中国无锡国际服务外包合作大会邀请函

Dear Sir/Madam,

Wuxi Municipal People's Government is to host "2009 China Wuxi International Conference on Service Outsourcing Cooperation" at Wuxi Taihu Hotel on Oct. 11th, 2009.

The conference will be composed of such four sections as Keynote Speeches, Executives' Dialogue, Industrial Park Presentation, and Enterprise Interaction. In the first two sections, officials from the Ministry of Commerce will explain relevant policies and measures that support the development of the service outsourcing industry. Experts in the service outsourcing circle will elaborate on the latest development trend of the service outsourcing industry. Executives of world-famous service outsourcing enterprises will share their success stories as well as their views on the development of the service outsourcing enterprise. Wuxi Municipal Government will discuss cooperative opportunities and ways with brand name service outsourcing parks in the world. Integrating on-the-spot presentation with field visit, the Industrial Park Presentation Section will give delegations a vivid impression of Wuxi's excellent environment and its service outsourcing parks that have distinct features. The Enterprise Interaction Section will serve as a platform for the win-win cooperation between international service outsourcers and Chinese enterprises.

The conference will provide you with the information about supporting policies from the department in charge, the expertise and experience from experts, the platform for communication among peer enterprises, and great opportunities for cooperation.

We are cordially looking forward to your presence at the conference.

Wuxi Municipal People's Government

参考译文

邀请函

尊敬的先生/女士：

由无锡市人民政府主办的“2009 中国无锡国际服务外包合作会议”将于 2009 年 10 月 11 日在无锡太湖饭店举行。

此次会议将由主题演讲、高层对话、园区推介和企业互动交流四个部分组成。届时，商务部主管领导将讲解国家支持服务外包的相关政策措施。业界专家将阐述外包服务发展的最新动态和趋势，为企业提供帮助。世界著名服务外包企业的高层管理者将分享他们对服务外包企业发展的见解和成功经验。无锡市政府将与国际知名服务外包专业园区深入探讨合作的机会和途径，并通过现场演示与实地考察相结合的方式，向与会代表展示无锡独特的环境魅力。企业互动交流将由国际服务外包发包商与中国本土企业进行现场交流，为企业搭建互利合作的平台。

本次会议将带给您：主管部门支持政策的信息，专家的见识和经验，同行切磋交流的机会以及令人惊喜的合作机遇。

期待您的光临!

无锡市人民政府

Business Situation 4

Center for International Business Ethics（CIBE）has planned to host the "the Third Annual International Conference on Consumer Rights and Corporate Social Responsibility" which will be held at Beijing's Sun City on October 26th and 27th. The centre sends invitation letters to the world business, university professors and experts, and research institutes.

国际经济伦理中心计划于 10 月 26 至 27 日在北京太阳城举办 CIBE 第三届国际年会。该中心向海内外的企业界、高校教授和专家以及研究机构发出参会邀请。

Sample

Invitation for the Third Annual International Conference on Consumer Rights and Corporate Social Responsibility

第三届消费者权利与企业社会责任国际会议年会邀请函

Dear Sir/Madam,

I warmly welcome you to participate in CIBE's third annual international conference on Consumer Rights and Corporate Social Responsibility on October 26th and 27th at Beijing's Sun City. This year's conference is jointly organized by the Centre for International Business Ethics and the Research Center for Applied Ethics at the Chinese Academy of Social Science.

In the wake of serious scandals involving product safety we are firmly committed to inspire the main actors of business and society to make strong commitments in favour of the rights of every consumer. Failure to do so will be devastating, not only for businesses in China, but also for the reputation of key actors claiming to be sincerely committed to improving best practices in China.

Our conference will again invite business practitioners to enter in dialogue with scholars and people from the media and government. I am convinced that this will not be just another talk without action, but that the conference will make significant contributions and a lasting impact on companies operating in China and educational institutions.

With best wishes,

Dr. Stephan Rothlin

参考译文

尊敬的先生/女士：

热烈欢迎您参加10月26日至27日在北京太阳城举行的CIBE第三届国际年会。会议的主题是消费者权利和企业社会责任。本届年会由国际经济伦理协会及中国社会科学院应用伦理研究中心合作举办。

随着越来越多产品安全问题的出现，我们要努力促使经济和社会的主要部门做出有利于每一个消费者权益的决定。如果不这样做的话，由此带来的后果将是致命的。不仅对中国的企业是这样，而且对将真挚地为中国经济发展作出贡献的社会各界的声誉也是这样。

本次会议将再次邀请企业界人士与专家学者及来自媒体和政府部门的人士进行对话。我深信这将不会是一次没有行动的对话，会议将对中国的企业及教育机构作出重大贡献并产生深远的影响。

此致

敬礼

斯蒂芬·罗斯林

Business Links

一、会议邀请函

在国际商务活动中，向国外企业、组织或个人发出邀请，是国际会议、商贸洽谈、展览会等的必要程序，是国际商务交往的重要环节，也是国外企业、组织或个人办理出国商务旅行签证的重要依据。

通常情况下，邀请包括信息发布、回执处理、确认通知三个程序。

信息发布有的使用印刷品，包括邀请函、组织文件、会议通知等，也有的使用电子邮件或网站、公告等形式。

会议邀请函的大致内容

（1）名称和主题（Name & Theme）

（2）时间和地点（Date, Time & Location）

（3）背景说明和目的（Background & Objective）

（4）组织说明（Organization），如：主办方（Organizer）、协办方（Co-organizer）承办单位（Host）赞助单位（Sponsor）等

（5）主要议程和活动（Agenda & Activities）

（6）费用（Fee & Payment）

（7）联络方式（Contact）

（8）回执（Return Receipt or Feedback）

（9）附件（Supplement or Attachment）：附件主要包括会展活动的相关说明、规定、制度、报展注意事项、人员信息表、服务内容等相关文件

二、会展邀请函

会展邀请函与会议邀请函基本内容一致。邀请函有简易的也有比较详细的。内容主要包括：会展活动的名称、举办城市、地点、时间、背景、目的、主办机构和组织机构等。这是会展邀请函的基本格式，但是具体的内容是要根据会展的不同要求有所增删。

与会展有关的邀请函一般分为两种：一种是以会展组织方的名义向公众或参加者发出邀请，邀请函的内容要涉及会展的各项细则，这是会展招展的一部分。另一种是以展会代理商或参展商的名义向客户发出邀请。这类邀请函一般比较简单。

至于大型展会如各种博览会，由于内容丰富，所以邀请函内容也复杂得多。除了一般邀请函的基本特征外，还要写明会展活动的内容和形式、特点等，主要参加或参与对象，会展活动的相关收费标准，联络方式以及其他需要说明的事项。通常大型的展览活动涉及的内容较多，例如布展规定、进场规定、商务租赁申请等在大型展会活动邀请函中，均包括在内。有的博览会常常与研讨会等学术活动同时举行，邀请函的内容自然也复杂得多。

参展商邀请函是以参展公司名义邀请熟悉的客户来观摩会展并了解本公司产品，所以在邀请函中注明的关键内容包括展会时间地点、展位号、新产品特色及联系方式等。这类邀请函一般都很简短。

Useful Sentences

1. 邀请（Invitation）

（1）I hope that you will be able to attend.
希望您能来参加。

（2）Our company is having a reception at Grand Hotel on the evening of May 10, 2010. And I would be very pleased if you could attend.
我们公司将于 2010 年 5 月 10 日晚上在大酒店举行招待会，期待您的光临。

（3）We should like to invite your corporation to attend the 2000 International Fair. Full details on the Fair will be sent in a week.
我们想请贵公司参加 2000 国际商品交易会。关于交易会的详情我们一周内将寄给您。

(4) Our new factory will be commencing production on April 10 and we should like to invite you and your wife to be present at a celebration to mark the occasion. I look forward to hearing from you soon.
公司新厂将于4月10日开始投产，希望能邀请贤伉俪来参加新厂开工典礼。期待您的回复。

(5) We would like to invite you to an exclusive presentation of our new product. The presentation will take place at Wuzhou Hotel at 9：00 AM on April 16, 2010. There will also be a reception at 12:30 at noon. We hope you and your colleagues will be able to attend.
我公司将于2010年4月16日9时在五洲大酒店举行我公司新产品推介会。中午12点半将举行招待会。诚邀您和您的同事参加。

2. 表达感受（Expressing Feeling）

(1) It would be a great pleasure to meet you at the exhibition/trade fair.
很荣幸能在本次展会上见到您。

(2) We would very much like to have someone from your company speak at our conference.
我们将深感荣幸，得以聆听贵公司代表的讲话。

(3) As you may be aware, the mission of our association is to promote....
正如大家所知，我们大会的任务就是为了推动……的发展。

(4) I'm delighted you have accepted our invitation to speak at the Conference in Xiamen on March 8, 2010.
我很高兴您接受了我们这次在厦门会议的邀请，并将在2010年3月8日在本次会议发表讲话。

(5) The conference offers an excellent environment to meet your peers in computer science.
会议为您与计算机科学领域的同行认识提供了一个良好的平台。

3. 接受和拒绝邀请（Acceptance or Refusal of Invitation）

(1) I accept with pleasure your kind invitation to come to your college and give some lectures on *Modern American Literature* to the students of your English Department.
我很乐意接受邀请来贵院给英语系的学生教授“现代美国文学”。

(2) Many thanks for your kind invitation to dinner on July 1st, which my wife and I are very much delighted to accept.
承蒙邀请7月1日到贵府进晚餐，甚为感谢。我与我夫人极为高兴应邀赴约。

(3) Many thanks for your kind invitation to dinner party, and I am eager to see you there.
非常感谢您邀请我出席晚宴，我迫切想在那里与您见面。

(4) Thank you very much for inviting me and my wife to dinner on Tuesday, June 1st. However, I regret to inform you that owing to a previous engagement we shall not be able to come.
非常感谢您邀请本人和夫人 6 月 1 日星期二到贵府共进晚餐，但因事先有约，不能应约，极为遗憾。

(5) Many thanks for your kind invitation to your company on October 1, 2009. But I am very sorry to inform you that we are unable to come because of my previous engagement.
非常感谢您邀请我于 2009 年 10 月 1 日拜访贵公司。但很遗憾，由于事先有约，难以前来赴约。

Chapter 4 布展（Exhibition Installation）

Business Situation 1

Mr. Smith, marketing manager of Puckator Ltd. of UK is discussing something about the stand construction and designing of the stand that the company reserved with the 107th China Import and Export Fair with Mr. Liu, a designer from a stand-decorating company.

英国 Puckator 公司计划以参展商的名义参加第 107 届广交会并预定了展位。公司市场部经理史密斯先生正与广州的一家展台装饰公司的刘先生商谈有关展台搭建和装饰事宜。

Dialogue

S = Mr. Smith L = Mr. Liu

S: It's our third time attending the China Import and Export Fair. Would you please tell us something about the designing and building of the stand?

L: Yes, I'll be happy to tell you anything I know.

S: Our target customers are mid-aged men. So modernity and sobriety should be the features of our company's image.

L: So we need to get furniture such as desks, chairs and shelves which may look unique and kind of classic.

S: That's right. They will help attract our target customers.

L: And you'd better leave plenty of room for visitors on the stand.

S: Yes, at least 50% of the floor area should be left for the visitors. But how can we make our stand distinctive and noticeable?

L: You may try some bright colors and material with good texture to build the stand.

S: What you suggest is worth trying.

L: Thank you!

S: What about the height limit of the furniture?

L: The height limit is 2.5 meters and it should not extend beyond the boundaries of the sites.

S: OK, I will fax you the booth design in one or two days. When will I know the reply?

L: When the booth design gets approved, we will fax you the document as soon as possible.

S: Another point: I'd like to use some spot lights to give the stand a nice and warm atmosphere.

L: Of course.

S: When will the stand be ready before the Fair?

L: We will make it ready 3 days before the Fair opens.

S: OK, I look forward to seeing the stand.

参考译文

史密斯:这是我们第三次参加广交会了。您能和我谈谈展位的设计和搭建事宜吗?

刘先生:好的,乐意为您效劳。

史密斯:我们的目标顾客是中年男性。因此时尚庄重应该是我们公司形象的主要特征。

刘先生:那么我们配备的桌、椅、架子要独特并经典。

史密斯:好的,那样会有助于吸引我们的目标顾客。

刘先生:您的展位最好给访客预留足够的空间。

史密斯:好的,请在地面预留50%的面积给顾客。但是如何才能使我们的展位与众不同又容易被关注到呢?

刘先生:您可以使用些明亮的颜色和质地优良的材料来搭建展位。

史密斯:您的建议值得尝试。

刘先生:谢谢!

史密斯:家具的限高是多少?

刘先生:限高是2.5米,并且不可以摆放在所划定的范围之外。

史密斯:好的,这两天我就将展位设计图传真给您。我什么时候可以收到回复?

刘先生:展位设计图经批准后,我们会尽快给您回复,传真相关文件。

史密斯:还有一点,我想用些射灯给展位创造温暖美好的氛围。

刘先生:当然可以。

史密斯:展位什么时候可以完成搭建?

刘先生:广交会开幕前三天,我们可以完成搭建。

史密斯:好的,期待看到我们的展位。

Business Situation 2

Ms. Dora Zhao, assistant manager of Chenghai Toy Trading Co., Ltd. is discussing the transportation of exhibited products with an official carrier of

American International Toy Fair, 2010.

澄海玩具贸易有限公司经理助理赵女士打电话给 2010 年美国纽约国际玩具博览会的官方承运商，商谈展品运输事宜。

Dialogue

D = Dora Zhao　L = Lucy

D: I have read the information about your company, and learned that your company is an official carrier of the Toy Fair. We would like to use your company for our carrier.

L: Thank you. Your goods will be safe with us. What can I do for you?

D: We will entrust our transporter to deliver the exhibits to New York Port, where these exhibits will be transferred to you. We need the services such as customs clearance, quarantine and inspection, local transportation, storage, exhibits portage on exhibition stands and related procedures.

L: I see, that's Package Service A. Please note that relevant entrusted procedure is required in advance.

D: OK, I will. When can we transfer the exhibited products to you?

L: Any time. But if on weekends, we will charge you overtime drayage rates.

D: I see. As for rates, would you give us more preferential rates?

L: Our company offers preferential rates for ordering package service. So that's not a problem for you.

D: Good. Some of our exhibits are very delicate, and they need some special attention.

L: Yes, of course. We will have all the exhibits clearly labeled with your booth number and company name, and you'd better have them insured.

D: OK, I will. Would you please fax me the quote of your company?

L: Yes, of course. The quote includes both inbound and outbound transportation costs, duties and taxes.

D: Thanks a lot.

L: If there's anything I can do for you, don't hesitate to let me know.

D: Thanks. You are very thoughtful.

参考译文

赵女士：我从网上得知贵公司是 2010 年美国纽约国际玩具博览会的官方承运商。希望你们能做我们的承运商。

露西：谢谢。您的货物由我们运输将是安全可靠的。能为您做些什么？

赵女士：我们将委托我们的运输商把展品运到纽约港，然后在那里由你们接关。我们需要的服务有进出口通关及出入境检验检疫、国内运输、仓储、展品搬运至展位、办理相关手续等服务。

露西：我明白了，这就是我们的A套餐服务。请注意须提前办理相关委托手续。

赵女士：好的。我们什么时候能将货物交由你们接关？

露西：随时都可以。但如果是在周末，你们将需要加付加班运费。

赵女士：好的。至于费用，我们能享受优惠价格吗？

露西：我们将为预订一条龙服务的客户提供优惠的价格。因此，对您来说没有问题。

赵女士：太好了。我们有些展品是很精致的产品，需要特别小心。

露西：一定。我们会在展品包装上清楚地标注你们的公司名称和展位号。您最好给它们上保险。

赵女士：我会的。请您将贵公司的报价传真给我好吗？

露西：当然。报价包括出入境运输费、关税和税金。

赵女士：多谢。

露西：如果还有什么能帮得上您的，一定告诉我。

赵女士：谢谢。您考虑得真周到。

Business Links

在参展准备阶段，不管是国外参展商到中国参展还是中国企业到国外参展，都要经过报关、展品运输和保险、展台搭建三个主要过程。展会结束后还要负责拆卸展台。

一、报关

海关对进出境的货物的监管一般经过申报（declaration）、查验（examination）和放行（release）三个环节。报关是指进出口货物的收发货人、进出境运输工具的负责人、进出境物品的所有人或其代理人向海关办理货物、物品或运输工具进出境手续及相关海关事务的全过程。

1. 国外展品入境所需的单证有：

（1）打印的进口报关单（Printed Import Declaration Form）

（2）手写的进口报关单（Handwritten Import Declaration Form）

（3）报关委托书（Letter of Authorization for Customs Declaration Agents）

（4）展览会批文复印件（Copy of Exhibition Certification）

（5）备案登记表复印件（Copy of Registration Form）

（6）当次进口的展品清单（Bill of Imported Exhibits）

（7）内地海关及香港海关陆路进/出境载货清单（The Import or Export Land Manifest of Customs of Mainland & Hong Kong）

（8）海关监管所需的其他单证，如入境货物通关单（Import Manifest）、船运单（Ocean Bill of Lading）、空运单（AWB = Air Way Bill）、保险单（Insurance Policy）、免疫单（Quarantine）、熏蒸单（Fumigation Certificate）等。

2. 国外展品出境所需单证有：

（1）打印的出口报关单（Printed Export Declaration Form）

（2）手写的出口报关单（Handwritten Export Declaration Form）

（3）报关委托书（Letter of Authorization for Customs Declaration Agents）

（4）展览会批文复印件（Copy of Exhibition Certification）

（5）备案登记表复印件（Copy of Registration Form）

（6）当次出口的展品清单（Bill of Exported Exhibits）

（7）原出口报关单（Previous Customs Declaration Form）

（8）内地海关及香港海关陆路进/出境载货清单（Full List for Import/Export Carrying Cargo Form of Land way of Mainland & Hongkong Customs）

（9）海关监管所需的其他单证，如出境货物通关单（Export Goods Manifest）

二、展品运输

1. 展品进出口流程

（1）备齐所需单证及展品、打包、为展品投保

（2）安排运输。木质包装箱须在装运港口做熏蒸处理，并在外包加施专用标志

（3）从所在地海关出关，在展览所在地海关入关，安检

（4）运至展馆、布展。若要散发宣传品，则需将样本报海关审查

（5）展出和申报展品的处理方式：若需要回运，则填写《回运展品委托书》等表格

（6）撤展

（7）回运、转展、留购、散发或放弃

2. 展品运输服务及约定

以广交会为例。根据中国海关、出入境检验检疫机关有关规定，广交会进口展区所进口展品的进出口通关、出入境检验检疫申报，按广交

会属地管理办法，应在广州口岸办理展品相关的进口申报手续。从非展出地口岸进口的展品，应当在中国进境地口岸办理相关的转关手续。按照海关的要求，进口展区现场实施封闭式管理。筹撤展及展览举办期间，展馆范围内的展品搬运服务必须由广交会推荐的进口展区展品承运商承接。

三、展台搭建

1. 和谐（harmony）：展台是由布局（layout）、照明（lighting）、色彩（colors）、图表（charts）、展品（exhibits）、展架展具（outreach planes）等因素构成。设计时应将这些因素有机地组合成一体。

2. 简洁（concise）：照片、图表、文字说明应当明确、简洁，与展出的目标和内容无关的装饰应减少到最低程度。

3. 重点突出（to highlight focus）：展示应有中心、有焦点。

4. 主题明确（with specific theme）：一切都是围绕主题（theme），而切忌面面俱到。

5. 视觉冲击要强烈（have the eye-catching signs）：要引人注目（attractive），易于识别（easy to identify），使参观者印象深刻（impressive）。

6. 把握好观众的喜好（design from the perspective of the target audience）：从目标观众（target audience）的角度进行设计，容易引起目标观众的注意、共鸣，并留下比较深刻的印象。

7. 易于搭建与拆卸（easy to set-up & disassemble）。

8. 其他因素，如空间（space）和客流（visitor's flow）要合适，要明确预算（budget），设计一旦确定要避免更改等。

Useful Sentences

1. 展品运输（Transportation of Exhibited Products）

(1) When can we ship the exhibits to your warehouse?
我们什么时候可以把货物运送到你们的仓库？

(2) You will be subject to overtime drayage rates.
你们将需要加付加班运费。

(3) Our company will offer preferential rates for ordering package services.
我们将为预订一条龙服务的客户提供优惠的价格。

(4) We should encourage exhibitors to ask for quotes for international shipping and customs services in advance.
我们应该鼓励参展商提前向国际运输和报关公司咨询报价。

(5) Exhibitors can avoid high shipping and drayage costs with assistance

from operations managers.

参展商可以借助运营经理的帮助来避免高额的运输费用。

2. 展品保险（Insuring the Exhibited Products）

（1）This is for ensuring that all the exhibitor's plans and efforts are not reduced to a costly waste.

这是为了保证参展商的计划和努力不会白费。

（2）Most host facilities now require that the group or organization sponsoring the event buy insurance.

大多数主办单位现在都要求赞助展会的团体或者公司要购买保险。

（3）The cost of providing insurance coverage is minimal compared to the exhibitor's overall financial and legal health.

和参展商的全部财务和法律安全相比，买保险的成本是很小的。

（4）Exhibit transporter of International Pavilion is ready to carry out insurance services for import exhibits with certain charge.

进口展区展品承运商均能代办进口展品保险的有偿服务。

（5）You should directly file claim against the relevant insurance company in case of loss or damage of your import exhibits.

您的进口展品如果丢失或者损坏，请直接向您所投保的保险公司索赔。

3. 展台搭建与拆卸（Building and Dismantling an Exhibition Stand）

（1）If exhibitors employ outside contractor, they are responsible for contracting directly with the Exhibition Center.

如果参展商自己聘任其他的装修代理公司，则参展商及其装修代理公司应直接与展览中心签订合同。

（2）At least… meters clearance between existing hall walls and stands walls is required.

展馆墙壁与展台墙壁间隔至少……米。

（3）No parts of any structure may extend beyond the boundaries of the site allocated.

展台的所有部分不得超越所划定的范围。

（4）Exhibitors in raw space are responsible for providing suitable floor covering, such as carpet, for their stands.

空地的参展商必须在其展台铺设地毯等覆盖物。

（5）Double layer construction should be approved by the Organizers, and additional charges should be applied.

双层搭建必须报经主办单位批准，并按规定交纳附加费用。

(6) Passage ways in the exhibition hall must not be obstructed with packing materials, construction materials, or debris during moving in, construction of stands or removal of exhibits.
在布、撤展期间，不得将包装物品、装修材料和其他障碍物放置于公用通道上。

(7) Exhibitors who, because of operating exhibits, are likely to have substantial quantities of waste materials for removal, must inform the organizer in advance in order that the necessary arrangements can be made for which they will be charged.
参展商如因展品关系，需清理大量杂物，请提前通知主办单位，以便安排收取相关费用。

(8) Please list below the exhibit(s) exceeding 1,000kg in weight, or 5.0m in length, or 2.0m in width or 2.0m in height per single piece.
请在下表中列出重量超过 1 000 公斤或长度超过 5 米或宽度超过 2 米或高度超过 2 米的展品。

(9) Please point out the right position of the above mentioned exhibits inside your stand.
请指出上述展品在贵方展位中的位置。

(10) Please come to the exhibition ground on the first day of move-in period for moving the above mentioned exhibits or booking in advance with ... for the moving date. Your delegate(s) Mr./Ms. ... will come to the site on... (date) for supervising the moving.
请于展品入馆第一天到达展览场地监督搬运工作或者与……公司预约搬运时间。请贵方代表……先生/女士于……日到达现场监督搬运工作。

Part III 商务旅行 (Business Travel)

Chapter 1 电话邀请 (Telephone Invitation)

Business Situation 1

Miss Linda Zhang, the chief seller in Shenzhen Ugo Sports Shoes Co., Ltd., is calling Mr. Bruce Jackson, the marketing manager in Fashion Way Co., Ltd. in Canada. She invites him to the 107th China Import and Export Fair to know more about the company's newly designed sports shoes.

深圳 Ugo 运动鞋有限公司业务主管张琳达给客户加拿大 Fashion Way 有限公司的市场部经理布鲁斯·杰克逊先生打电话，邀请他参加第 107 届广交会，以便多了解公司设计的新型运动鞋。

Dialogue

L = Linda Zhang　B = Bruce Jackson　A = Office Assistant

A: Fashion Way Co., Ltd. What can I do for you?

L: This is Linda Zhang, calling from Shenzhen Ugo Sports Shoes Co., Ltd. May I speak to Mr. Bruce Jackson?

A: Wait a moment, please.

B: Hello, this is Bruce Jackson.

L: Hello, Mr. Jackson. This is Linda Zhang. I'm the chief seller in Shenzhen Ugo Sports Shoes Co., Ltd.

B: What can I do for you, Ms. Zhang?

L: Sure. In 2010, the 107th China Import and Export Fair will be held in Guangzhou in southern China. Our company will be a part of it to introduce our new products. I'm sure our products will also sell well in Canadian market. I am wondering if your company could send some representatives to the Fair.

B: I'm getting to be interested. So what is the exact time of your exhibition?

L: From May 3rd to 7th. Our booth will be 2. 2G11 and 2. 2G12 in Pazhou Exhibition Hall. I have sent you an e-mail of invitation with every detail of our exhibition.

B: Great. We'll be there, I guess.

L: Please let me know once you've confirmed your flight time. We'll be meeting you at the airport.

B: Thank you for your invitation. Goodbye, then.

L: I'm looking forward to your coming. Goodbye.

参考译文

助理：Fashion Way 有限公司。我能为您做些什么吗？

张琳达：您好。我是深圳 Ugo 运动鞋有限公司业务主管张琳达。我想找一下布鲁斯·杰克逊先生。

助理：请稍等。

布鲁斯：你好。我是布鲁斯·杰克逊。

张琳达：您好。我是深圳 Ugo 运动鞋有限公司业务主管张琳达。

布鲁斯：我能为您做些什么吗，张女士？

张琳达：是这样的，2010 年，在中国南部的城市广州将举办第 107 届广交会。届时我们公司将携新产品参展。我相信我们公司的产品在加拿大也会有很好的市场，所以我想邀请贵公司派代表到广交会来看看。

布鲁斯：我对此很有兴趣，那广交会的具体时间是哪天？

张琳达：5 月 3 日至 5 月 7 日。本公司的展位号是琶洲展馆 2.2G11 和 2.2G12。我已经给您发了一份邀请函，展览的相关内容都在上面。

布鲁斯：好极了。我想我们会去的。

张琳达：请及时告知确认后的航班，我们会去机场接您。

布鲁斯：谢谢你的邀请。再见。

张琳达：期待您的到来。再见。

Business Situation 2

Ms. Kimberly Carcone, the director of Trade Show and Events Marketing Committee of American Toy Industry Association Inc., is calling Ms. Sun, manager of Chenghai Toy Trading Co., Ltd. to invite her to take part in the International Toy Fair in New York, which will be held in February 14th to 17th, 2010 as planned.

美国玩具工业协会贸易展览与活动策划委员会主任金伯莉·卡科恩代表主办方美国玩具工业协会，打电话给澄海玩具贸易有限公司总经理孙女士，邀请她参加 2010 年 2 月 14—17 日举行的纽约国际玩具博览会。

Dialogue

K = Kimberly Carcone S = Lisa Sun

K: Hello, this is Kimberly Carcone calling from America. May I talk to Ms. Lisa Sun, the general manager of your company?

Office Assistant: Hold on, please.

S: Hello, this is Lisa Sun. How may I help you?

K: Hello, this is Kimberly Carcone. I'm the director of Trade Show and Events Marketing Committee of American Toy Industry Association Inc. I'm inviting your company to attend our exhibition next year, the New York International Toy Fair.

S: That's great. I know this exhibition, and we've sent our products there this year, and got good responses. So next year, right? Still in February?

K: Yes, from 14th to 17th. I've sent you an e-mail about the details as well as a formal letter of invitation. Since this won't be the first time that you attend the Fair, I guess you must have already known that you'd better book the booths in advance so that you may get the better promotion of your products.

S: Yes, I know that. Thank you for your advice, though. We will get our new products ready and make every preparation for the Fair.

K: OK, then, we'll be glad to see you and your products in New York next year.

S: Thank you. Goodbye.

K: Goodbye.

参考译文

金伯莉：您好，我是金伯莉·卡科恩，从美国打来的。我想找贵公司总经理孙女士。

办公室助理：请稍等。

孙经理：你好，我是莉萨·孙。请问有什么事吗？

金伯莉：您好，我是美国玩具工业协会贸易展览与活动策划委员会主任金伯莉·卡科恩，我想邀请贵公司参加我们明年的展会，纽约国际玩具博览会。

孙经理：太好了，我知道这个展会，我们今年就参加了，而且反响不错。那么明年也是在2月份吗？

金伯莉：是的，14号到17号。我给您发了一封邮件，包括一份正式的邀请函和相关细节。既然这不是贵公司第一次参加，我想您可能已经知道提前预订展位会对贵公司产品的推广更加有利的。

孙经理：我知道，不过还是谢谢你的提醒。我们会开发出更新的产品，为这次博览会作好准备。

金伯莉：那好，希望明年在纽约可以再次见到贵公司的产品展出。

孙经理：谢谢。再见。

金伯莉：再见。

Business Links

1. 电话邀请

除了书面邀请外，在实际交际中，口头邀请也是很常用的。口头邀请主要是指打电话或当面以口头的形式进行邀请。口头邀请的适用范围很广，不仅可以用于邀请某人参加某一重要活动，请人赴宴等较大的事，也可以用于像请人喝茶，出去散步等较小的事。由于电话邀请通常是一种比较随便，非正式的邀请，所以它往往也没有固定的格式，其遣词造句也比较随意，且往往受邀请和被邀请人的身份、地位的影响而有所变化。

在本章中，因为是商业活动的邀请，所以邀请电话实际上是作为邀请函以外的一种附加方式，对于邀请的具体内容和反馈还是应该以邀请函及回执为主。

2. 邀请的接受和拒绝

收到诸如展览会、会议或其他活动的邀请，可以用书面或口头表示接受或者拒绝，但一定要遵循一定的礼节，注意表达方式。一般都要在开头部分表示谢意，比如先打招呼，说句客套话，然后再进入主题。这是电话英语或者是英语会话的一般顺序。

Useful Sentences

1. 寒暄问候（Greetings During a Call）

(1) Hello.
您好。

(2) This is Den Smith.
我是丹·史密斯。

(3) Who is that?
请问您是哪位?

(4) May I have your name, please?
可以问一下您的姓名吗？
(5) Beijing Trading Company. May I help you?
北京贸易公司。需要我帮忙吗？

2. 请人接电话（Asking to Speak to Somebody）

(1) Is Jack Smith in?
杰克·史密斯在吗？
(2) Hello! Is Jack there?
您好！是杰克吗？
(3) May I speak to Tommy? It's urgent.
我找汤米，有急事。
(4) Please connect me with Mr. Zhang.
请给我转接张先生。
(5) Is Ms. Clark available?
克拉克女士在吗？

3. 同意或拒绝（Positive Answers or Negative Answers）

(1) OK, I'll just put you through.
好的，我这就给您转接。
(2) Yes. Speaking, please.
是的。我就是，请说。
(3) I'm sorry, he's not in the office now.
很抱歉，他现在不在办公室。
(4) I'm sorry, but he's in Shanghai on business.
抱歉，他去上海出差了。
(5) Can I take a message for him?
要我转告他吗？

4. 发出邀请（Making an Invitation）

(1) I'd like to invite you to attend…
我想邀请您参加……
(2) Will you be available next week?
您下周有空吗？
(3) I am wondering if you can come and give a speech at the opening ceremony.
不知道您能否来参加开幕式并讲话？
(4) I'm looking forward to your coming.
期待您的到来。

(5) Please let us know your arrival time, so we can meet you at the airport.
请告知到达时间，我们好去机场接您。

5. 其他邀请用语（Other Expressions of Invitation）

(1) Are you interested in going dancing tonight?
今晚有没有兴趣去跳舞？

(2) Would you like to go shopping with me this weekend?
这个周末想跟我去逛街吗？

(3) How about going to see a movie with me tonight?
今晚跟我去看场电影如何？

(4) I'm inviting you to my birthday party.
我邀请你参加我的生日派对。

(5) Hey, do you want to check out a band this Saturday night?
喂，这个星期六晚上要不要去看一个乐团表演？

(6) I'm thinking about going to KTV with my co-workers tonight. Wanna come?
我想今天晚上跟同事去 KTV。你要来吗？

(7) Are you free tomorrow night? I'm wondering if you're free for dinner.
你明天晚上有空吗？我想知道你有没有空一起吃晚饭。

(8) Are you up for a barbecue this weekend?
要不要这个周末去烤肉？

(9) Do you have any special plans for the weekend? Maybe we can go climbing. How does that sound?
这个周末有没有什么特别的计划？或许我们可以去爬山。你意下如何？

(10) Why don't we go get some tea?
我们何不一起去喝茶？

6. 其他接受邀请用语（Other Positive Answers）

(1) Yes, it's very kind of you.
好，太感谢你了。

(2) I'd very much like to. Thank you.
我很愿意，谢谢你。

(3) I'd like /love/ be glad to…
我很愿意/喜爱/高兴……

(4) That'll be very nice.
那太好了。

（5）With pleasure.
我很乐意。

7. 其他拒绝邀请用语（Other Negative Answers）

（1）I'm afraid I can't come.
恐怕我不能来。

（2）I'm sorry. I can't come.
对不起，我不能来。

（3）I'd like to, but my mother is ill.
很愿意去，但我母亲生病了。

（4）I'd very much like to, but I've already had plans for tonight.
我很愿意去，但我今晚已另有安排了。

（5）I wish I could. but I've promised to show Tom around.
我希望能去，但我已答应带汤姆到处转转。

Chapter 2　预订机票和房间 (Booking Tickets and Rooms)

Business Situation 1

Mr. Bruce Jackson and his assistant manager Mr. Bill Jones are going to Guangzhou for the 107th China Import and Export Fair. Bruce calls the local travel agency to reserve two return air tickets to Guangzhou and book a double room for their stay in Guangzhou.

布鲁斯·杰克逊先生和经理助理比尔·琼斯先生将去广州参加107届广交会。布鲁斯给当地旅行社打电话预订两张飞往广州的往返机票，并为他们在广州预订一个双人间。

Dialogue

B = Bruce Jackson　C = Clerk

C: Hello, this is Toronto Travel Agency. Can I help you?

B: Yes, sir. I would like to reserve two air tickets.

C: OK. Where to?

B: From Toronto to Guangzhou, China.

C: When do you plan to leave?

B: April 30th, that's three days before China Import and Export Fair.

C: Just a minute, please. Let me check. There is no direct flight to Guangzhou. Flight AC031 departs at 14:55 and arrives at Beijing at 16:05 the next day. Then you need to change to another flight. Flight CA1309 departs from Beijing at 18:00 and arrives at Guangzhou at 21:00. May I book two tickets for you?

B: Yes, please. That's OK for my schedule.

C: One-way or round trip?

B: Round trip, please.

C: Economy or executive?

B: Economy, please. How much are the tickets?

C: That's Canadian $7,913 for one round-trip ticket including the base fare and taxes and fees. For two tickets, that's Canadian $15,826.

B: OK. How shall I pay my air tickets?

C: You can visit our travel agency to pay your air tickets or you can pay us by e-banking, or by check.

B: Well, I may visit your travel agency.

C: May I know your name and telephone number, please?

B: Bruce Jackson.

C: How do you spell it please?

B: B-R-U-C-E, Bruce; J-A-C-K-S-O-N, Jackson. And my telephone number is 5689235. By the way, are the tickets confirmed?

C: No. You have to confirm them three days before the departure.

B: Thank you.

C: Just a minute, I have booked the tickets for you. Anything else?

B: I would like to book a double room near the Pazhou Complex, Guangzhou.

C: Yes, sir. The Garden Hotel is a five-star hotel near the Pazhou Complex. It's 15 minutes' drive from the hotel to the Pazhou Complex.

B: What are the rates for a double room?

C: The room rates are $200 for a double room including breakfast and service charge.

B: Well, it's acceptable.

C: How long will you stay there?

B: About eight days. From May 1st to May 8th.

C: Yes, I have booked you a double room at the Garden Hotel from May 1st to May 8th.

B: Thank you very much.

C: Have a good journey.

参考译文

职员：您好，多伦多旅行社。需要我帮忙吗？

布鲁斯：是的，先生。我想预订两张机票。

职员：好的，您要飞往哪里？

布鲁斯：从多伦多飞往中国广州。

职员：您计划何时出发？

布鲁斯：4 月 30 日，广交会的前三天。

职员：请稍候。让我看一下。没有飞往广州的直达航班。AC031 航班 14：55 起飞，次日 16：05 到达北京。然后您需要换乘另一架班机。CA1309 航班于 18：00 从北京起飞，21：00 抵达广州。要为您订两张票吗？

布鲁斯：好的，符合我的行程。

职员：您要订单程机票还是往返机票？

布鲁斯：请给我订往返机票。
职员：经济舱还是商务舱？
布鲁斯：经济舱。多少钱？
职员：每张往返机票 7 913 加元，包括基本票价和所有税费。两张机票是 15 826 加元。
布鲁斯：好的。我如何付款呢？
职员：您可以来我们旅行社付款，也可以通过网上银行或者用支票付款。
布鲁斯：好的，我会去你们旅行社的。
职员：您能留下您的姓名和电话吗？
布鲁斯：布鲁斯·杰克逊。
职员：请您拼一下，好吗？
布鲁斯：B-R-U-C-E, Bruce；J-A-C-K-S-O-N, Jackson。我的电话是 5689235。顺便问一声，机票确认了吗？
职员：没有。您要在出发前三天确认机票。
布鲁斯：谢谢。
职员：请稍候，我已经为您预订了机票。还能为您做些什么？
布鲁斯：我想预订广州琶洲展馆附近的酒店，要一个双人间。
职员：好的，先生。花园酒店位于琶洲展馆附近，是一家五星级酒店。距琶洲展馆有 15 分钟的车程。
布鲁斯：一个双人间房费是多少？
职员：房费是 200 美元，含早餐和服务费。
布鲁斯：嗯，还能接受。
职员：您要住多久？
布鲁斯：大约 8 天。从 5 月 1 日到 5 月 8 日。
职员：好的，我给您预订了花园酒店的一个双人间，时间从 5 月 1 日到 5 月 8 日。
布鲁斯：非常感谢。
职员：祝您一路顺利。

Business Situation 2

Ms. Dora Zhao, the assistant manager of Chenghai Toy Trading Co., Ltd. is the head of the delegation of 7 people attending the New York Toy Fair in 2010. They have already bought flight tickets from Guangzhou to New York. Now Dora Zhao, phones the Global Travel Agency in New York to make a reservation for seven return air tickets from Los Angeles to Shanghai Pudong Airport, and she also books hotel rooms close to Jacob K. Javits

Convention Center for their stay in New York.

澄海玩具贸易有限公司经理助理赵女士担任 2010 年美国纽约国际玩具博览会 7 人参展团团长。他们已经购买了从广州飞往纽约的机票。现在多拉·赵打电话给纽约环球旅行社，预订 7 张由洛杉矶返回上海浦东机场的机票，同时她要求预订纽约雅各布 K. 贾维茨会议中心附近的酒店房间。

Dialogue

D = Dora Zhao　C = Clerk

C: Hello, the Global Travel Agency. Can I help you?

D: I'd like to make a reservation from Los Angeles to Shanghai.

C: Yes, madam. Which airport? Hongqiao Airport or Pudong Airport?

D: Pudong Airport, please. It's more convenient for us.

C: When is your departure?

D: We are coming for the American International Toy Fair, then we would visit Chicago. After that it's a journey to the west. Yes, it should be February 26th.

C: OK, February 26th. One person?

D: No, there are seven of us, seven adults.

C: Just a moment, please. Flight M1630 departs at 15:26 and arrives at Pudong Airport at 18:53 the next day by way of Honolulu.

D: How long is the layover in Honolulu?

C: About 40 minutes. It depends.

D: Do you have any direct flight?

C: Sorry, all the direct flights are fully booked.

D: OK, that's fine. Can we have any discount?

C: I'm afraid you can't. It's the busy season. Do you want to go first class or economy?

D: Economy class would be fine.

C: That's US $2,200 including the ticket, taxes and fees for each person. It comes to $15,400 for seven people. May I know your name, please?

D: Yes, Dora Zhao. I'll fax you the copies of our passports as soon as possible. And would you please reserve three double rooms and a single room from February 13th to 17th, at a hotel near Jacob K. Javits Convention Center?

C: Yes, madam. Just a minute. What about Golden Time Hotel? It's a three-star hotel and 15 minutes' drive away from the Center.

D: What are the room rates?

C: It's $150 for the single room and $200 for the double room including service charge.

D: That's fine.

C: OK, I have booked you one single room and three double rooms at Golden Time Hotel. Anything else?

D: No, thank you very much.

C: Please call us again for any future reservation.

D: OK. Goodbye.

C: Goodbye.

参考译文

职员：您好，环球旅行社。需要我帮忙吗？

赵女士：我想预订从洛杉矶飞往上海的机票。

职员：好的，女士。到达哪座机场？虹桥机场还是浦东机场？

赵女士：浦东机场。那里对我们更方便些。

职员：你们何时出发？

赵女士：我们来参加美国纽约国际玩具博览会，然后我们将参观芝加哥，之后去西部旅游。应该是2月26日离港。

职员：好的，2月26日。是1个人吗？

赵女士：不，我们一共7个人，7个成人。

职员：请稍候，M1630号航班15:26离港，经由檀香山，于次日18:53抵达浦东机场。

赵女士：在檀香山停留多久？

职员：大约40分钟，具体视情况而定。

赵女士：你们有直达航班吗？

职员：对不起，所有的直达航班已被预订一空。

赵女士：好的，没关系。我们能享受折扣吗？

职员：对不起，没有折扣。现在是旺季。您要头等舱还是经济舱？

赵女士：经济舱就行。

职员：每人2 200美元，包括机票和税费。7人总计15 400美元。您能留下姓名吗？

赵女士：好的，多拉·赵。我会尽快把我们的护照复印件传真给你们。此外，你能给我预订雅各布K. 贾维茨会议中心附近的酒店吗？2月13日到2月17日，三个双人间和一个单人间。

职员：好的，女士。请稍候。黄金时代酒店怎么样？它是一家三星级酒店，距会展中心有15分钟的车程。

赵女士：房费是多少？

职员：单人间每晚150美元，双人间每晚200美元，含服务费。

赵女士：可以。

职员：好的，我已经为您预订了黄金时代酒店的一个单人间和三个双人间。还有什么能为您效劳的吗？

赵女士：没有了，非常感谢。

职员：如果您还有任何预订，请与我们联系。

赵女士：好的。再见。

职员：再见。

Business Links

1. 预订机票

在国外买飞机票可以直接从各旅行社购买，也可以通过航空公司购买。每个旅行社所卖机票的价格尽管都是随着季节的变化而变化，但旅行社间的价格也有很大的差异，有时还可以讨价还价。在买机票前，要多看些报纸或上网浏览信息，对比各家的票价，再打电话咨询。通常在淡季（a slack season）会有折扣。在旺季（a busy season）折扣较少或没有折扣。另外，买机票时，要问清楚你所买的机票是否含有城市噪声费、机场税等额外费用，并随身带好所交额外费用的收据，以免到机场时遇到麻烦。

在国外预订的机票的时间可长可短，长的可以达到一年以上，所以机票一般都是未经确定的不定期机票（open-end ticket），在出发的前几天必须确认机票，这时机票才有效。

2. 订房服务

旅行社还提供订房服务，在预订酒店之前，应上网了解该酒店的一切情况，诸如地理位置、硬件设施、服务项目，是否提供免费早餐等。既不要盲目使用有偿服务，也不要错过应有的免费服务。部分酒店收取的费用中除了房费还包括15%的服务费。到达目的地之后，到酒店的前台提供订房时的相关信息即可入住。

3. 住房选择

（1）商务酒店

酒店会根据营业旺季、平季和淡季的不同，推出不同的价格策略。如果赶上大型的会议或展览，价格也会随行就市上涨。商务旅行者应该根据自己公司的实力和形象，来选择相应档次的酒店入住。

很多商务酒店为商务人士量身定做了行政楼层，其房价里面一般包含了很多优惠甚至免费的服务，硬件设施比普通楼层的要好。

（2）汽车旅馆

廉价汽车旅馆采用标准化的建造模式，内部省掉了一切顾客不需要的设施和豪华装饰，以减少成本费用，以最低的价格向驾车的商务旅行者和度假家庭提供廉价的住宿服务。

（3）酒店式自助公寓

酒店式自助公寓（也可称为家庭旅馆）是一种新兴的短期居住方式。房屋设施齐全舒适，房内使用面积比同等宾馆的大，价格只是同级宾馆的几分之一。非常适合商务考察、因公出差的自助人士居住。

Useful Sentences

1. 机票预订或取消预订（To Make or Cancel a Reservation for Air Tickets）

（1）I'd like to make a reservation to Los Angeles on June 6th.
我想预订一张6月6日飞往洛杉矶的机票。

（2）Do you have any direct flight?
有直达的航班吗？

（3）Please put me on the waiting list.
请把我加到等候者名单中。

（4）Flight M3630 arrives at Bangkok Airport at 22:53 the next day by way of Honolulu.
M3630航班经由檀香山于次日22:53抵达曼谷机场。

（5）I'd like to cancel my reservation on Flight AC067 to London on the 12th. My name is Wang Lin.
我想取消12号飞往伦敦的AC067航班的预订。我叫王林。

2. 询问目的地和出发时间（To Ask about the Destination and Departure）

（1）Where do you wish to go/fly?
您要飞往哪里？

（2）What's your destination?
您的目的地是哪里？

（3）When is your departure?
您何时出发？

（4）Which is the departure terminal for United Airlines?

请问联合航空是在哪栋航站楼候机？

3. 询问价格和税费（To Ask about the Prices and Taxes）

（1）How much is a one-way ticket to Toronto?
一张飞往多伦多的单程机票多少钱？

（2）The total is $2,655.26, including $1,986 for the base fare, and $669.26 for the taxes, fees and charges.
基本票价 1 986 美元，各种税费 669.26 美元，总计 2 655.26 美元。

（3）May I have any discount?
有折扣吗？

（4）Yes, we can offer you 10% discount.
有的，我们可以给您打 9 折。

（5）Since you are travelling during the busy season, the price is a little higher.
因为您出行的日期是旺季，所以票价会高一些。

4. 预订房间（Booking Rooms）

（1）Good morning, White Swan Hotel. Can I help you?
早上好，白天鹅酒店。需要我帮忙吗？

（2）I'd like to make a reservation for 5 nights from July 5th to 9th.
我想预订从 7 月 5 日至 7 月 9 日共 5 晚的住宿。

（3）How many in your party?
你们有多少人？

（4）What kind of rooms would you like to have, single or double?
您想要什么样的房间，单人间还是双人间？

（5）How much /What are the room rates?
房费是多少？

Chapter 3 入境通关 (At Customs and Immigration)

Business Situation 1

After their arrival at Baiyun Airport, Guangzhou, Mr. Bruce Jackson and Mr. Bill Jones now approach customs. They are going to pass through customs and are ready to answer the customs officer's questions.

到达广州白云机场后，布鲁斯·杰克逊先生和比尔·琼斯先生向海关走去。他们即将通关，并准备好了回答海关官员的问题。

Dialogue

B = Bruce Jackson C = Customs Officer

C: Good morning, sir. May I see your passport and visa?

B: Good morning. Here you go.

C: Your Declaration Card and Health Certification, please.

B: Here you are.

C: What's the purpose of your visit to China, for sightseeing or on business?

B: On business. I'm here participating in the 107th Canton Fair.

C: How long are you going to stay in Guangzhou?

B: About 7 days.

C: Where are you going to stay in Guangzhou?

B: The Garden Hotel.

C: Do you have anything to declare?

B: No, I just brought with me some daily necessaries and documents.

C: OK. How much money have you taken with you?

B: About 4,000 Canadian dollars.

(*After checking, the customs officer stamps Bruce's passport and returns it.*)

C: OK, you are clear to claim your luggage. Go along with the walkway leading up to Terminal, Luggage Department, then pass through "Nothing to Declare" aisle to the main airport building please.

(*Bill goes through the same procedures.*)

C: Welcome to China. Have a nice trip!

B: Thank you.

参考译文

海关官员：早上好，先生，请出示您的护照和签证。
布鲁斯：早上好，给您。
海关官员：请出示您的申报表和健康证明。
布鲁斯：给您。
海关官员：您此次中国之行是为了观光还是商务旅行？
布鲁斯：是来商务旅行的。我们是来参加第 107 届广交会的。
海关官员：您打算在广州待几天呢？
布鲁斯：预计 7 天。
海关官员：您将住在广州哪里呢？
布鲁斯：花园大酒店。
海关官员：您有什么需要申报的吗？
布鲁斯：没有，我只带了些日用品和文件。
海关官员：好的。您带了多少现金呢？
布鲁斯：大约 4 000 加元。
（一番检查之后，海关官员把布鲁斯的护照盖好章并递回给他。）
海关官员：好了，您可以入关并领取行李了，首先，走到航空集散站领行李处，然后经“无申报”通道到机场主楼。
（比尔经历了同样的程序。）
海关官员：欢迎你们来到中国，祝你们此次旅行愉快。
布鲁斯：谢谢。

Business Situation 2

Ms. Dora Zhao and her 6 colleagues come to the counter for foreigners after the plane lands at the New York International Airport, and line up to accept the questioning and checking passports from the customs officer and fill out the Declaration Card, claim their baggage.

飞机在纽约国际机场着陆后，赵女士和她的 6 位同事来到外籍人士柜台，排队接受海关官员的询问和护照检查，并且填写了申报表，然后领取了行李。

Dialogue

C = Customs Officer　D = Dora Zhao

C: Good morning, madam. May I see your passport and visa?
D: Good morning. Here you go.

C: Your Declaration Card and Health Certification, please.

D: Here you are.

C: What's the purpose of your visit to New York City, for sightseeing or on business?

D: On business. We are here to take part in the 107th American International Toy Fair in New York City's Jacob K. Javits Convention Center. This is an invitation letter. (*She shows the invitation letter to customs official. Things will be easier because of an invitation letter.*)

C: How long are you going to stay in New York?

D: About 5 days.

C: Where are you going to stay in New York City?

D: The Golden Time Hotel.

C: Do you have anything to declare?

D: No, I just brought some daily necessities, and samples of our company's toys.

C: OK. How much money have you taken with you?

D: RMB 130,000 yuan.

(*After checking, the customs officer stamps Ms. Zhao's passport and returns it.*)

D: Where shall we claim our luggage?

C: First of all, please go along with the walkway leading up to Terminal, Luggage Department, according to the instructions or notices on the computer screen to find your flight number. Then, check carefully the numbers of your baggage, because a lot of suitcases look exactly the same, finally pass through "Nothing to Declare" aisle to the main airport building please.

(*Ms. Zhao's 6 colleagues go through the same procedures.*)

C: Welcome to the United States. Have a nice trip!

D: Thank you.

参考译文

海关官员：早上好，女士。请出示您的护照和签证。

赵女士：早上好，给您。

海关官员：请出示您的申报表和健康证明。

赵女士：给您。

海关官员：您此次来纽约是为了观光还是商务旅行？

赵女士：是来商务旅行的。我们是来参加在纽约贾维茨会议中心举行的第107届纽约国际玩具博览会的。这是邀请函。（她随即将邀请函递给了海关官员，有了邀请函处处容易通过。）

海关官员：您打算在纽约待几天呢？

赵女士：预计5天。

海关官员：您将住在纽约哪里呢？

赵女士：黄金时代大酒店。

海关官员：您有什么需要申报的吗？

赵女士：没有，我只带了些日用品和我公司玩具的样品。

海关官员：您带了多少现金呢？

赵女士：130,000元人民币。

（一番检查之后，海关官员把赵女士的护照盖好章并递回给她。）

赵女士：请问我们在哪里领取行李呢？

海关官员：首先，根据走道里的指示走到航空集散站领行李处，依信息显示屏找到自己班次的行李招领台，然后仔细确认您的行李箱号牌，因为很多的行李箱从外观看是一模一样的，最后经“无申报”通道到机场主楼。

（赵女士的6位同事经历了同样的程序。）

海关官员：欢迎你们来到美国，祝你们此次旅行愉快。

赵女士：谢谢。

Business Links

1. 外国人进入中国国境

参展商首先应办好审批手续，报经上级主管部门批准后，通知外国人办理进入我国的签证，并将邀请函电发给外国人所在国的驻外使领馆，作为该外国人办理签证的依据。申请中华人民共和国签证的外国人需提交有效的普通护照或代替护照的旅行证件，回答被询问的有关问题，填写完整的外国人签证申请表一份，提交一张近期二寸正面免冠照片，根据申请来中国的事由提交相关证明。目前，我国根据外国人来华的身份和所持的护照的种类，分别发放外交签证、礼遇签证、公务签证和普通签证四种签证。一般外国人来中国持普通签证。为便于管理，中国普通签证分为九种，采用不同的汉语拼音字母加以标示。由于展会时间通常较短，来华参加商展的外国人大多申请普通签证中的L签证，即旅游签证。

在中国办理有关入境手续有三关，即卫生检疫、证照查验和海关检查。从入境边检开始，经卫生查验，接着取行李至海关检查，按顺序办理。中国海关官员会根据接受检查的人员身份使用中英文，在回答问题的时候，应大方坦诚，据实回答。

2. 外国人进入美国国境

进入美国海关，须填写两份表格，一份是美国出入境证明单（I-94）（详见附录），一份是美国海关申报单（详见附录）。美国的海关官员会检查这两份表格并最后决定您是否可以进入美国以及能在美国停留的时间。请千万保管好，并随时携带I-94表，尤其在临时离开美国国境的时候，否则无法再度返回。外国人搭机抵达美国国境，必须在最先着陆的机场办理入境手续，接受移民官及海关官员的检验。前者检查旅客资格，即是否可以入境；后者查验旅客的行李是否应缴关税，或是否携带违禁物品。

3. 绿色通道和红色通道

在实施双通道制的海关现场，进出海关的通道分为“红色通道”（“Goods to Declare” channel or red channel）和“绿色通道”（“Nothing to Declare” channel or green channel）两种。

“红色通道”也称“申报通道”（亦称“应税通道”），是指须经过海关检查和检验手续后，方可放行的通道。选择红色通道的旅客，须向海关出示本人证件和《进出境旅客行李物品申报单》。海外游客进入中国境内，一般须经“红色通道”，事先要填写《旅客行李申报单》向海关申报，经海关查验后放行。申报单上所列的自用物品，海关加上“△”记号的，必须复带出境（例如录音机、照相机、摄像机等）。外国游客不准代他人携带物品进出境。海外游客来中国旅行，可携带旅程中需要的，数量合理的自用物品。

从海外回程的中国游客入境时，须向口岸边防检查站交验有效护照或其他有效证件以及出境时经海关签章的旅客行李申报单。游客在海外购买了音像制品和印刷品的，也需申报和交验。若藏匿不报，海关将按规定处理。

“绿色通道”亦称“免税通道”。凡持有中国主管部门给予外交礼遇签证护照的外籍人员或海关给予免验礼遇的人员，可选择“绿色通道”通关，但需向海关出示本人证件和按规定填写申报单据。

不明海关规定或不知如何选择通道的旅客，应选择红色通道通关。

Useful Sentences

1. 移民局官员的检查和询问（Checking and Questioning from Immigration Official）

(1) May I see your passport?

能看看您的护照吗？

（2）What's the purpose of your visit?
您此次来访的目的是什么？

（3）What's the purpose of your travel in Guangzhou?
您此次广州之行的目的是什么？

（4）How long will you be staying in China?
您打算在中国待多长时间？

（5）Where are you staying?
您住在哪儿？

2. 海关官员的检查和询问（Checking and Questioning from Customs Official）

（1）Anything to declare?
您有什么需要申报的吗？

（2）Would you mind opening this suitcase for inspection?
能打开您的行李箱检查一下吗？

（3）How much money do you have with you?
您随身携带了多少现金？

（4）You'll have to pay duty on this.
您必须为这项物品缴付税金。

（5）You are all clear. /You've got through the customs. /You are through.
您可以通关了。

3. 领取行李（Claiming the Luggage）

（1）Where shall we claim our luggage?
我们在哪儿领取行李呢？

（2）Show your numbers of luggage, please.
请出示您的行李箱号牌。

（3）Do you have anything to consign for shipment?
您有什么需要托运的吗？

（4）I want to consign this huge suitcase.
我想托运这个大行李箱。

（5）Check carefully the numbers of your baggage, because a lot of suitcases look exactly the same.
请注意确认您的行李箱号牌，因为很多行李箱看上去是一模一样的。

Chapter 4 外币兑换服务 (Foreign Currency Exchange Service)

Business Situation 1

Mr. Bruce Jackson wants to exchange some Canadian currencies into RMB. Now he is in the money exchange office at the Baiyun Airport. He wants to know the exchange rate, and the way to his hotel.

布鲁斯·杰克逊先生想把一些加拿大货币兑换成人民币。因此，他来到了白云机场的外币兑换处。他想知道现在的外币兑换率以及如何到达他所住的酒店。

Dialogue

B = Bruce Jackson C = Cashier

C: May I help you, sir?

B: Yes, I'd like to change 5,000 Canadian dollars into Chinese RMB. What's the exchange rate?

C: It's 100:636.38. May I have your passport?

B: Here it is.

C: Would you kindly sign the exchange form, giving your name and address?

B: OK.

C: What denominations would you like?

B: Please give me 100 yuan and 50 yuan paper notes, and the rest in small change.

C: Fine, please wait a moment. Here you are. Please count it now.

B: Exactly right. Thank you. By the way, do you know the Garden Hotel?

C: Yes, I know. It's one of the best hotels in Guangzhou.

B: Then would you mind telling me how to get to this hotel?

C: Sure. You can take the airport express shuttle No. 5 to Haizhu Square, then transfer to underground railway No. 2, and get off at Pazhou Station. After about 10 minutes of walking, you'll see it. However, if you are in a hurry, taking a taxi may be the best and most convenient choice.

B: Is it far away from the International Exhibition Center?

C: No, it's easy to get there.

B: I see. Thanks a lot.

C: You are welcome.

参考译文

收银员：您有什么需要帮忙的吗？

布鲁斯：我想将5 000加元兑换成人民币。请问今天的汇率是多少？

收银员：今日加元对人民币的汇率是100：636.38，请给我您的护照。

布鲁斯：给您。

收银员：请您在这张兑换单上填写您的姓名和地址好吗？

布鲁斯：好的。

收银员：您需要兑换多大面额的人民币呢？

布鲁斯：请帮我分别兑换成100元和50元的纸币，其余是小面额的就行了。

收银员：好的，请稍等。给您钱，请您点一点。

布鲁斯：完全没问题，谢谢，顺便问一下，您知道花园大酒店吗？

收银员：我知道，那是广州最好的酒店之一。

布鲁斯：那您能告诉我去这家酒店该怎么走吗？

收银员：当然没问题，您可以乘坐机场5号快巴到海珠广场，然后转乘到2号地铁，在琶洲站下，再步行10分钟，您就能看到这家酒店了。但如果您很赶时间的话，打车去对您来说是最便捷的方式了。

布鲁斯：那这家酒店离国际展览中心远吗？

收银员：不远，到那儿很方便的。

布鲁斯：我明白了，谢谢您。

收银员：不客气。

Business Situation 2

Ms. Dora Zhao is in the New York International Airport. She wants to exchange some RMB into US dollars, now she is in the currency exchange office at the New York International Airport.

赵女士在纽约国际机场。她想把一些人民币兑换成美元。现在，她正在纽约国际机场的外币兑换所。

Dialogue

C = Cashier D = Dora Zhao

C: May I help you?

D: Yes, I'd like to change some Chinese RMB into 15,000 dollars. What's the exchange rate today?

C: It's 683.15: 100. Please give me RMB 102,472.5 yuan and your passport.

D: Here it is. And what are the service charges?

C: 10 US dollars.

D: OK, and can I have the receipt for the service charges?

C: No problem. Would you kindly sign the exchange form, giving your name and address?

D: Sure.

C: What denominations would you like?

D: Please give me 100 dollars and 50 dollars paper notes, and the rest in small change.

C: Fine, please wait a minute. Here you are. 15,000 dollars minus 10 dollars service charges, totally, 14,990 dollars, and the receipt here. Please count it now.

D: Exactly right. Thank you. By the way, do you know the Golden Time Hotel?

C: Yes. It's a three-star hotel.

D: Then would you mind telling me how to get to this hotel?

C: No problem. You can take a taxi to the hotel directly. This is the best and most convenient choice for you.

D: Is the hotel far away from New York City's Jacob K. Javits Convention Center?

C: No, it's only 15 minutes' drive away from the Center.

D: I see. Thanks a lot.

C: You are welcome.

参考译文

收银员：有什么需要帮忙的吗？

赵女士：我想用人民币兑换15000美元。请问今天的汇率是多少？

收银员：今日汇率是683.15人民币兑换100美元，请给我102 472.5元人民币和您的护照。

赵女士：给您，请问手续费是多少呢？

收银员：10美元。

赵女士：好的，您能给我手续费的发票吗？

收银员：好的，没问题，请您在这张兑换单上填写您的姓名和地址。

赵女士：好的。

收银员：您需要兑换多大面额的美元呢？

赵女士：请帮我分别兑换成100美元和50美元的纸币，其余是小面额的就行了。

收银员：好的，请稍等。15 000美元减去10美元的手续费，剩余总计14 990美元，这是发票，给您，请您点一点。

赵女士：完全没问题，谢谢，顺便问一下，您知道黄金时代大酒店吗？

收银员：知道。这是一家三星级大酒店。

赵女士：那您能告诉我去这家酒店该怎么走吗？

收银员：没问题，您可以直接打车去，这对您来说是最便捷的方式了。

赵女士：那这家酒店离纽约贾维茨会议中心远吗？

收银员：不远，离会议中心只有15分钟的车程。

赵女士：我明白了，谢谢您。

收银员：不客气。

Business Links

1. 出境外币兑换

(1) 购汇

出国前兑换好外币是很重要的，如果您有出国旅游、留学、探亲和商务考察等需求时，您可以持人民币在由中国人民银行批准进行外币兑换业务的银行或兑换点，兑换成所需的外币，以方便在境外使用。中国银行提供17种货币供您选择（具体币种以各地中国银行营业网点提供的信息为准）。购汇后可直接办理境外汇款（包括电汇和银行汇票）、旅行支票以及银行卡。境内居民个人购汇实行年度总额管理，年度总额为每人每年等值50 000美元。如您在年度总额内购汇，凭本人真实身份证明并向银行申报用途后即可办理购汇。如超过年度总额购汇，银行按外汇管理规定审核您的真实需求凭证后即可办理购汇。

(2) 了解出境当地货币情况

在出境参展之前，最好要先了解出境地货币使用情况。比如在欧洲的大部分国家，欧元是通用货币，因此如果参加的是欧洲国家展会，身上当然要有欧元傍身。但在新西兰除了可以使用新西兰元之外，有些商场也可以接受澳元和美元支付。在俄罗斯也相似，一般是用美元和欧元兑换成卢布来使用，但也有一些商店接受用美元或欧元直接消费。

(3) 减少兑换次数

一般来说，兑换目的地国家货币时应当避免多次兑换，以减少因多次兑换而产生的货币损失。如果需要的外币量不多，可以先在国内银行兑换所需的外币。

(4) 不要只兑换成一种货币

以前人们出境前会提前将所有携带的货币都兑换成美元，因为美元在许多国家都是通用的，到目的地后还可以用美元来兑换当地货币使用。

不过，由于近年来美元整体态势疲软，美元汇率下滑导致美元越来越不“值钱”了，因此如果在国内就用人民币都换成美元，再到国外去用相对低的汇率换成其他货币，那么总体来说其实很不划算。因此，参展商可以先参考一下目的地货币的汇率，考虑如何盘活自己手头上拥有的币种。

一般来说，出境参展时需要携带大量货币，而对于参展商来说，有四种选择：旅行支票、国际信用卡、银行汇票以及现钞。但是由于各国法律规定不同，建议以前三种方式任意组合加上携带一定量的现钞，安全又稳妥。但是为了减少因多次兑换产生的货币损失，兑换目的地国家货币时应当避免多次兑换，并且应到本国或者目的地国家当地正规外币兑换机构办理。

2. 入境人民币兑换

参展商手中持有外币需要兑换成人民币的，可凭本人有效证件办理。我国合法提供外币兑换服务的机构有：机场外币兑换处、居住酒店的外币兑换处、中国银行各分行以及办理人民币业务的外国银行。经银行职员鉴别外币币别、真伪、流通情况并清点金额无误后，按要求逐项清楚填写《外币兑换水单》，其内容包括姓名、地址、护照号码、外币种类、兑换数量等，经参展商签字后，由银行职员根据外汇牌价（兑入外币使用现钞买入价）折算成人民币付予客户。

Useful Sentences

1. 外币兑换 (Foreign Currency Exchange)

(1) Can you change US dollars to RMB?
您能把这些美元换成人民币吗?

(2) I want to exchange my US dollars into Chinese money.
我想把我的这些美元换成人民币。

(3) we are at your service.
竭诚为您服务。

(4) What currency would you like to exchange?
您想兑换成哪一种货币呢?

(5) Please fill out the exchange form first.

请您先填写兑换单。

2. 询问汇率（Asking for the Exchange Rate）

(1) What's the exchange rate for RMB to Euros?
人民币兑欧元的汇率是多少？

(2) The current rates are displayed to your right, sir.
先生，当前的汇率展示于您的右侧。

(3) What is the exchange rate today?
今日的汇率是多少？

(4) The exchange rate today is 6.8334 yuan to one dollar.
今日人民币兑美元的汇率是6.8344:1。

(5) Could you help me exchange some Chinese RMB into dollars?
您能帮我把这些人民币兑换成美元吗？

3. 询问币值（Asking for the Denomination）

(1) Could I have the bills in smaller denominations, please?
我可以将这些纸钞换成更小的面额吗？

(2) I need 300 yuan in 100 yuan notes.
我需要将这300元换成每张100元面额的纸币。

(3) What denominations would you like?
您需要兑换多大面额的？

(4) Please give me 100 yuan and 50 yuan paper notes, and the rest in small change.
请帮我兑换成100元和50元面额的纸币，其余的换成小面额的零钱。

(5) What are the exchange service charges?
请问兑换手续费是多少呢？

4. 询问如何到达目的地（Asking for How to Reach the Destination）

(1) Excuse me, could you tell me how to get to the restaurant?
请问，您能告诉我如何找到这家饭店吗？

(2) Where is the closest China Bank?
请问离这儿最近的一家中国银行在哪儿？

(3) Do you know the way to the airport?
您知道去机场怎么走吗？

(4) How do I get to the post office?
要去这家邮局我该怎么走？

(5) Make a right, pass two stop signs and you will run into it.
先向右走，经过两个指示停止的路标，你就找到了。

Chapter 5 入住酒店（Check In）

Business Situation 1

Mr. Bruce Jackson and Mr. Bill Jones arrive at Guangzhou Airport. They take a taxi to the Garden Hotel and check in at the front desk. He goes through the formalities at the front desk and asks the information about the restaurant and business center.

布鲁斯先生和比尔先生到达了广州机场，然后乘出租车来到所预订的花园酒店，在前台登记入住。他办理入住手续并询问有关餐厅和商务中心的信息。

Dialogue

B = Bruce Jackson R = Receptionist

R: Good evening. Can I help you?

B: Yes. Do you have a reservation for Bruce Jackson?

R: Just a moment, please. I'll check. Oh, yes. Is that Mr. Bruce Jackson from Toronto?

B: That's right.

R: Would you please show me your passports?

(*Bruce and Bill hand their passports to the receptionist.*)

B: Here you are.

R: Thank you. You have booked a double room for eight nights.

B: Yes, from today to May 8th. We'd like to have a room with a beautiful view if possible.

R: Let me see... Yes, you can have Room 1208. It's in the back, facing the back garden. Our back garden is featured with Lingnan garden characteristics, with waterfalls and rockeries.

B: That's great. Thank you.

R: My pleasure. Any other special requests?

B: Oh, yes. We'd like a wake-up call, please.

R: And what time will that be?

B: Seven o'clock in the morning.

R: I got it. We ask a deposit of RMB 1,000 yuan, Mr. Jackson.

B: In cash? Do you accept a Visa card for the deposit?

R: Sure, that'll do.

B: Good. Is breakfast included?

R: Yes, it is. Breakfast is served from 7:00 AM to 9:30 AM. The restaurant is upstairs, on the second floor. The French restaurant is on the third floor. It offers the finest French and Continental cuisine.

B: Thanks. By the way, where is the Business Center?

R: The Business Center is located on the fourth floor. Business hours are from 7:00 AM to 11:00 PM. The service includes Fax, IDD telephone, Secretarial & Translation Service, Wireless & Broadband Internet, Photocopying Printing, Personal Computer, Equipment Rental and so on.

B: Thank you so much. It's very kind of you.

R: Not at all. Anything else I can do for you?

B: No.

R: Here are your passports and this is the magnetic card to your room 1208. Have a nice stay.

B: I will. Thanks.

参考译文

接待员：晚上好。需要我帮忙吗?

布鲁斯：是的。有布鲁斯·杰克逊名下的预订吗?

接待员：请稍候。让我看看。哦，是的，您是来自多伦多的布鲁斯·杰克逊先生吗?

布鲁斯：是的。

接待员：请您出示护照好吗?

（布鲁斯和比尔将护照交给接待员。）

布鲁斯：给您。

接待员：谢谢。您预订了一个八晚的双人间。

布鲁斯：是的，从今天到5月8日。我想要一个风景秀丽的房间。

接待员：让我查一下……好的，您可以住1208号房间。它在后面，面对后花园。我们的后花园是岭南特色园林，有瀑布和假山。

布鲁斯：太棒了。谢谢。

接待员：乐意为您效劳。还有什么特别要求吗?

布鲁斯：哦，是的。我们想要个叫醒服务。

接待员：您要什么时间叫醒呢?

布鲁斯：早上7点。

接待员：明白了。杰克逊先生，我们要求预交1 000元押金。

布鲁斯：现金吗？你们接受维萨卡支付押金吗?

接待员：当然可以。
布鲁斯：好的。房费含早餐吗？
接待员：是的。早上7点至9点30分供应早餐。餐厅在楼上，二楼。法式餐厅在三楼，提供最好的法式和欧洲大陆风味餐饮服务。
布鲁斯：谢谢。顺便问一声，商务中心在哪儿？
接待员：商务中心在四楼。营业时间从早7点至晚11点。服务包括传真，国际长途直拨电话，秘书翻译服务，无线宽带网络，影印，个人电脑和设备租用等。
布鲁斯：非常感谢。您真是太好了。
接待员：不用谢。还能为您做些什么？
布鲁斯：没有了。
接待员：这是你们的护照和1208号房间的磁卡。祝你们入住愉快。
布鲁斯：好的。谢谢。

Business Situation 2

Ms. Dora Zhao and her colleagues arrive at New York Airport. They take a taxi to the Golden Time Hotel and check in at the front desk. She goes through the formalities at the front desk and asks about the information about the restaurant and business center.

赵女士和她的同事抵达纽约机场。他们乘出租车来到所预订的黄金时代酒店，在前台登记入住。她办理入住手续并询问有关餐厅和商务中心的信息。

Dialogue

R = Receptionist D = Dora Zhao

R: Good evening. Can I help you?

D: Yes. Do you have a reservation for Dora Zhao?

R: Just a moment, please. Let me check. Oh, yes. You booked two double rooms and a single room for five nights.

D: I'm afraid there's a mistake. I asked three double rooms and a single room, not two double rooms.

R: Let me see. I'm terribly sorry, madam. It's a mistake. You have booked three double rooms and one single room from today to the 17th. They are Room 1621, 1622, 1623 and Room 1635. Room 1635 is a single room. We ask a deposit of $800, Ms. Zhao.

D: That's fine. Do you accept a Visa card for the deposit?

R: Yes, that'll do. May I see your passports?

D: Here you are.

(*Ms. Zhao and her colleagues show their passports to the receptionist.*)

R: Thank you. Here are the magnetic cards and your passports. The restaurant is on the second floor. Is there anything I can do for you?

D: Yes, where is the Business Center?

R: The Business Center is located on the third floor. Business hours are from 7:00 AM to 10:00 PM. The service includes Fax, IDD telephone, Wireless & Broadband Internet, Printing, Equipment Rental, Meeting Room Rental and so on.

D: That's great. By the way, how do we get to Jacob K. Javits Convention Center?

R: You can take the subway or taxi there. The subway station is just outside our hotel on the right. But for the American International Toy Fair, we offer free shuttle bus service for our guests from 8:00 AM to 8:00 PM. You can take the bus at the porch. And here is a timetable for the shuttle bus.

D: Thank you very much. You are so thoughtful.

R: Thank you. Anything else I can do for you?

D: No.

R: Have a nice stay.

D: Yes, I will.

参考译文

接待员：晚上好。需要我帮忙吗？

赵女士：有多拉·赵名下的预订吗？

接待员：请稍候。让我看看。哦，是的。您预订了两个双人间和一个单人间，一共五晚。

赵女士：恐怕弄错了吧。我要了三个双人间和一个单人间，不是两个双人间。

接待员：让我看看。非常抱歉，女士。您是预订了三个双人间和一个单人间，从今天一直到17号。为您准备了1621，1622，1623和1635号房间。1635是一个单人间。赵女士，请您预交800美元押金。

赵女士：好的。你们接受维萨卡支付押金吗？

接待员：好的，可以的。我能看看你们的护照吗？

赵女士：给你。

(赵女士和她的同事向接待员出示护照。)

接待员：谢谢。这是磁卡和你们的护照。餐厅在二楼。还能为您做些什么?

赵女士：请问商务中心在哪儿?

接待员：商务中心在三楼。营业时间从早 7 点至晚 10 点。服务包括传真，国际长途直拨电话，无线宽带上网，打印，设备租用，会议室租用等。

赵女士：太好了。顺便问一声，去雅各布 K. 贾维茨会议中心的路怎么走?

接待员：您可以乘坐地铁或出租车。地铁站就在我们酒店大门外的右侧。但我们酒店免费为客人提供往返汽车，方便他们参加美国国际玩具博览会。时间从早 8 点至晚 8 点，您可以在门廊处搭乘往返汽车。这是往返汽车的时刻表。

赵女士：多谢。你们考虑得太周到了。

接待员：谢谢。还能为您做些什么?

赵女士：没有了。

接待员：祝您入住愉快。

赵女士：好的。

Business Links

国外酒店

国外酒店的住宿费用都很高，有些旅馆稍便宜一些，酒店业发展至今，真可谓名目繁多，应有尽有。由于历史的演变，传统的沿袭，地理位置与气候条件的差异，酒店用途、功能、设施的不同，世界各地的酒店五花八门。按照传统分类法，酒店可分为四种类型：

1. 商业性酒店（Commercial Hotel)。一般来讲，这类酒店都位于城市中心，商客居住的时间大都在星期一至星期五，这是从事商业活动的时间。在周末，也就是在星期六和星期天是商业性游客的假日，因此很少来酒店订房、居住和办公。世界国际酒店集团所属的酒店，绝大多数是商业性酒店，他们根据旅游市场的需求比例，建造各种类型的酒店。如纽约希尔顿酒店（Hilton Hotel, New York)、芝加哥凯悦酒店（Hyatt, Chicago)、华盛顿万豪（Marriott，Washington)、日本东京帝国酒店(Imperial Hotel，Tokyo）等都是典型的商业性酒店。

2. 长住式酒店（Residential Hotel)。主要为商客的一般性度假提供公寓生活，它被称之为公寓生活中心。长住式酒店主要是接待常住客人，这类酒店要求常住客人先和酒店签订一项协议书或合同，写明居住的时间和服务项目。

3. 度假性酒店（Resort Hotel）。主要位于海滨、山城景区或温泉附近。最突出最重要的项目便是它的康乐中心，因为它主要是为度假游客提供娱乐和度假场所。

4. 会议酒店（Convention Hall）。是专门为各种从事商业、贸易展览会、科学讲座会的商客提供住宿，膳食和展览厅、会议厅的一种特殊型酒店。会议酒店内设有大小规格不等的会议室、谈判间、演讲厅、展览厅等。

此外，有的旅馆稍便宜一些，像汽车旅馆（Motel）目前在高速公路交流道附近很多，建筑成凹形，楼下停车，楼上是客房，设有餐厅，专门为开车旅客提供休息、住宿场所。青年旅馆（Youth Hotel）、招待所（Hotel）等是为青年旅游者或大学生开办的旅馆，也比较便宜。

酒店客房通常有单人间（single room），双人间（double room）和套间（suite）。入住时间通常是下午 2 点后，退房时间通常是在中午 11 到 12 点之前。酒店提供的服务通常有预订房间（advance reservation）、应接服务（bell service）、叫醒服务（wake-up service）、订票（ticket service）、换钱（exchange money）、洗衣服务（laundry service）、客房服务（room service）、商务中心（business center）等。有的酒店还内设邮局和银行。

星级酒店的服务很周到，例如有人帮你拿行李，领你到房间，这时你要给服务员小费，以示感谢，因此要随身带些零钱。有的酒店规定，不许服务员收小费。如果你给小费，服务员会告诉你在房费中已包括小费。

Useful Sentences

1. 迎接客人（Greet the Guests in a Hotel）

(1) Good morning, sir.
先生，早上好。

(2) Good afternoon.
下午好。

(3) Good evening, madam.
女士，晚上好。

(4) Have a nice stay.
祝您入住愉快。

(5) Yes, I will. Thank you.
好的，谢谢。

2. 预订房间（Talk about Reservations in a Hotel）

（1）Good afternoon, I have made a reservation for a double room.
下午好，我预订了一个双人间。

（2）I have made a reservation for our delegation for 3 nights' stay. My name is Jefferson.
我为我们的代表团预订了三晚的房间。我叫杰斐逊。

（3）I'm sorry. All our rooms are occupied.
对不起。我们所有的房间都已客满了。

（4）Good evening. I've just made a reservation for 2 nights through Rome Travel Agency. My name is Jackson White.
晚上好。我通过罗马旅行社订了一个两晚的房间。我叫杰克逊·怀特。

（5）Good afternoon. Do you have a reservation for Mr. Simpson?
下午好。有辛普森先生预订的房间吗？

3. 谈论房间（Talk about the Rooms）

（1）I'd like to have a room with a bath.
我要一个带浴室的房间。

（2）Could you let me have a quiet room if possible, not too near the street?
如果有可能的话，您能给我一个别太靠近马路的安静的房间吗？

（3）May I have a room with an ocean view?
我能要一间海景房吗？

（4）You can have Room 1219. You can hear the sea breeze at night.
您可以住 1219 号房间。晚上您能听到海风轻拂。

（5）Oh, I'm sorry. All the single rooms are taken. But we happen to have a suite available, with a living room and a kitchenette.
哦，对不起。所有的单人间都已经客满。但我们正巧还有一个套间，带有一个起居室和一个小厨房。

4. 谈论酒店服务（Talk about the Service at the Hotel）

（1）The Business Center is on the 2nd floor. The business hours are from 7:00 AM to 11:00 PM.
商务中心在二楼。营业时间从早 7 点至晚 11 点。

（2）Breakfast is served from 7:00 AM to 11:00 AM. Lunch is from 12:00 AM to 3:00 PM, and dinner from 6:00 PM to 9:30 PM.
早餐是从早 7 点至上午 11 点。午餐是从中午 12 点至下午 3 点，晚餐是从下午 6 点至晚上 9 点 30 分。

（3）You can get room service on the phone by dialing 666.
您可以拨打电话 666，得到客房服务。
（4）We'd like a wake-up call, please.
我们想要叫醒服务。

5. 办理结账（Check out of a Hotel）

（1）We are here to check out. Here is the key.
我们要结账。这是钥匙。
（2）I wonder if you accept traveler's checks.
我想知道你们是否接受旅行支票。
（3）Here is a check for $300, and you can keep the change.
这是 300 美元的支票，不用找零。
（4）Have you used any hotel service since breakfast?
吃过早饭后您还用过宾馆的服务吗？
（5）Have a nice trip home.
祝您归途愉快.

Chapter 6 问路（Asking for Directions）

Business Situation 1

After Mr. Bruce Jackson checks in at the hotel, he leaves his luggage there. Now he wants to visit Pazhou Complex for the decoration of his booth, and then he wants to visit the downtown area to see the shoe business there. But he doesn't know his way around yet, so he asks a clerk of the hotel for directions.

布鲁斯·杰克逊先生办理好入住手续之后，他把行李留在酒店。现在，他想去琶洲展馆看看，确定摊位的装修，之后要去市中心看看广州的鞋业情况。但是他不认识路，他向酒店的职员问路。

Dialogue

B = Bruce Jackson C = Clerk R = Receptionist

B: Excuse me, could you tell me how I can get to Pazhou Complex?

C: Yes, our hotel offers the shuttle bus. You can also take the subway there.

B: Where is the subway station?

C: Walk out of the gate and walk north. Turn right at the first crossing, and it's about 200 meters on your right.

B: Walk north, turn right at the first crossing, and it's about 200 meters on the right.

C: Yes, that's right. You can't miss it.

B: Do I need to get a transfer?

C: Yeah. First, you should take Line 4. Get off at Wanshengwei interchange station, and take Line 2 to Pazhou subway station.

B: Thanks a lot.

C: My pleasure. Is there anything else I can do for you?

B: Yes. I'd like to visit the downtown area. But where is the downtown area?

C: The downtown area is around Beijing Road. The subway Line 2 will take you there.

B: Thank you very much.

C: Don't mention it.

(*Bruce arrives at Pazhou Complex, and he wants to find an ATM to withdraw some cash.*)

B: Excuse me, where can I find an ATM ?

R: The ATMs are not on this floor. They are on the second floor.

B: The second floor? I'd better take the elevator.

R: When you come out of the elevator, go left. They are at Section B2.

B: Thank you.

R: Is there anything else that I can do for you?

B: Yes, by the way, how can I get to the downtown area?

R: You can take the subway to get there. Take Line 2 and get off at Gongyuanqian Stop. Then you can go to Beijing Road, where there are all kinds of department stores and shops.

B: Thank you very much.

R: Any time.

参考译文

布鲁斯：打扰了。请问如何去琶洲展馆？

职员：我们酒店提供往返汽车服务。您也可以乘地铁去那里。

布鲁斯：地铁站在哪儿？

职员：出大门往北走。在第一个十字路口向右拐，走大约200米，在您的右手边。

布鲁斯：往北走，在第一个十字路口向右拐，走大约200米，在右手边。

职员：对的。您不会找不到的。

布鲁斯：我需要换乘吗？

职员：是的。首先，您乘坐4号线至万胜围换乘站，然后坐2号线至琶洲地铁站。

布鲁斯：多谢。

职员：乐意为您效劳。还能为您做些什么吗？

布鲁斯：是的。我想去市中心看看。但是市中心在哪儿？

职员：市中心在北京路一带。地铁2号线可到。

布鲁斯：非常感谢。

职员：不用谢。

（布鲁斯到达了琶洲展馆，他想找自动取款机取些现金。）

布鲁斯：请问，哪儿有自动取款机？

接待员：自动取款机不在这层楼。在二楼。

布鲁斯：二楼？我最好走自动扶梯。

接待员：走下扶梯，向左走。它们在B2区。

布鲁斯：谢谢。

接待员：我还能为您做些什么吗？

布鲁斯：是的，顺便问一声，我怎么去市中心？
接待员：您可以乘地铁去市中心。乘地铁 2 号线在公元前站下车。然后去北京路。那里百货商店和各类商店云集。
布鲁斯：非常感谢。
接待员：随时都愿效劳。

Business Situation 2

Ms. Dora Zhao and her colleagues leave their luggage at the hotel and visit Jacob K. Javits Convention Center. After that, they would like to visit some toy shops at downtown. But they don't know their way around yet, so Dora asks the receptionist for directions.

赵女士和她的同事们把行李留在酒店并参观雅各布 K. 贾维茨会议中心。之后，他们还将去市中心的玩具商店参观。但是他们不认识路，于是，赵女士向接待员问路。

Dialogue

D = Dora Zhao　R = Receptionist

D: Excuse me, how can I get to the downtown area?
R: You mean the shopping center?
D: Yes. We'd like to visit the shopping center. How can I get there?
R: You can go to the Macy's. It's about 20 minutes' walk.
D: But I'm new here. I don't know my way around yet.
R: Walk along the 34th Avenue, I mean walk southeast. It's about four or five blocks ahead.
D: Thank you very much. Can we take a bus?
R: Yes. You can take M34 outside our center. Get off at West 34 St. at 7th Avenue and Macy's is just across the road.
D: Thanks a lot.
R: My pleasure. The public transportation fare is \$2. Buses accept MetroCards and exact change fares.
D: MetroCards?
R: Yes, they are available in our center and local shops.
D: Thank you very much. You are so thoughtful.
R: It's my pleasure.
(*After visiting the Macys, Ms. Zhao and her colleagues hope to visit another*

department store, Bloomingdales.)

D = Dora Zhao C = Clerk

D: Excuse me, could you tell me how I can get to the Bloomingdales?

C: There are several Bloomingdales in our city. Which one do you want to visit?

D: What about the closest one?

C: There is a Bloomingdales at Broadway Street, and you can walk along Broadway Street.

D: Great! How can we get there?

C: Walk along this road, and take the first turning on your right. You can see 34th St. — Herald Sq. Station. Take the subway W, and get off at Prince St. Station. The Bloomingdales is just one block southwest.

D: Thanks a lot.

C: You are welcome.

参考译文

赵女士：请问，去市中心怎么走？

接待员：您是说购物中心吗？

赵女士：是的，我们想去购物中心看看。怎么去呢？

接待员：您可以去梅西百货公司。步行20分钟左右可到。

赵女士：可我是外来的，还不认识路呢。

接待员：沿着34号大街朝东南走，大约四五个街区就到了。

赵女士：非常感谢。我们能乘公共汽车吗？

接待员：可以。你们可以在会展中心外乘坐M34路公共汽车，到西34大街和第7大道的路口下车，梅西百货公司就在马路对面。

赵女士：多谢。

接待员：乐意为您效劳。公交车费是2美元。公共汽车接受地铁卡和现金，但不找零。

赵女士：地铁卡？

接待员：是的。我们中心和当地的商店都有售。

赵女士：非常感谢。您为我们考虑得真周到。

接待员：乐意为您效劳。

（参观梅西百货公司之后，赵女士和她的同事去另一家百货商店布鲁明岱尔）。

赵女士：请问，您能告诉我怎么去布鲁明岱尔吗？

职员：我们市有好儿家布鲁明岱尔。您要去哪一家呢？

赵女士：最近的一家在哪儿？

职员：在百老汇街有一家。您还可以在百老汇逛逛。

赵女士：太好了！请问怎么走？

职员：沿着这条路一直往前走，在第一个路口向右拐。您就能看到 34 大街的赫拉德广场站。坐 W 路地铁，在王子街站下。再向西南走一个街区，布鲁明岱尔就到了。

赵女士：多谢。

职员：不用谢。

Business Links

国外许多城市优先发展公共交通，特别是地铁、轻轨等大运量快速轨道交通方式。城市间的多种交通方式统一规划，协调发展。许多国家的大城市规模庞大，道路交通复杂，因此一份地图是必不可少的，在商务旅行时了解西方国家的交通信息将更有利于自己的出行。

1. 西方公交

在一些西方国家，有的整条路上就只有一路公交车来回行驶。例如在加拿大的温哥华，有一条大街叫“41 大道”，在这条道上运营的公交车只有 41 路公交车。在澳大利亚，为了使巴士专用车道更加容易辨认，也为了帮助司机不至于走错路线，巴士专用道的地面全被涂成了红色。在美国，公交专用道设在黄线左侧。纽约的公共汽车东西向行驶，乘公交车较方便，每隔一个大道都设有站牌。票价与地铁同为计次收费，每次 2 美元。下车前要先拉铃，前方会出现“停车”标志。若需转乘其他公车，上车时先向司机索取转乘券，就可以免费转乘。

在德国，很多城市还保留着有轨电车。车站上都有行车的时刻表和交通图表，非常准时，出行者可以对照使用。

英国伦敦道路较狭窄复杂，并不适合商务旅行者开车旅行。伦敦公共交通是由地铁、巴士、有轨电车、轻轨、长途汽车、火车和轮渡构成的完善系统。地铁虽然外表有点旧，但路标清晰，四通八达。

比利时首都布鲁塞尔的公共交通主要以有轨电车为主。公共汽车、有轨电车和地铁构成了城市主要干线和公共交通网络。在部分地铁站旁设置城市自行车交换点，提供专门的自行车，用车人可以自动存取。

2. 乘车旅行注意事项

无论乘火车、公交车还是地铁，上车前一定要问清楚该车是否到你要去的地方，中途是否需要换车，在哪个站换。搭乘公共交通车辆时要注意自己的钱物，留心车内的动静。如发现异常，赶快告诉司机，自己不要随便介入。

等车时要和其他搭客站在一起，不要太靠近地铁站台或马路，以保证安全。如果是夜晚，一定要在灯光明亮和有人的地方等车。上车后假如乘客稀少，要尽量坐在靠近司机的地方。下车的站和回家的路尽可能选择人多灯亮的地方。

出门旅行要照看好自己的东西，不要交给不认识的人看管，也不要随便答应给不认识的人带东西或托运行李。

注意公众场合不要大声讲话，排队时要与前面的人保持一定距离。遵守交通秩序，特别是过马路时要遵守行人信号灯指示。

3. 国际驾照

只要持有国际驾照和信用卡，即可很方便地在机场、宾馆等公共场所租到车，租金远远低于乘出租车的费用。国际驾照上有 8 种语言——英语、法语、西班牙语、俄语、阿拉伯语、汉语、德语和日语。为驾车者和警察克服了因语言障碍而带来的困难。国际驾照在《联合国道路交通公约》的所有签字国有效。

无论您是商务旅行、度假还是度蜜月，国际驾照都可以为您带来极大的方便，并且可以托管和租用汽车。万一您的护照遗失或被窃，国际驾照还可作为身份证明的有效证件。

4. 纽约的交通

（1）纽约的地铁

纽约的地铁四通八达，也许是全世界最发达的地铁系统，26 条地铁路线将拥有 1 000 多万人口的纽约市连为一体。地铁线路名称分别用英文字母 A、B、C 和阿拉伯数字 1、2、3 等来标明，并且在车厢以及地铁图上面使用不同的色彩标示。在纽约市区内的各个旅游问讯处，还提供一种折叠起来就像一张地铁卡大小的地铁图，这种小小地铁图有时候也可以在当地的银行里面免费获得。

（2）纽约的出租车

2004 年 5 月纽约出租车提价，达到目前起价 2.5 美元，然后每行驶 0.2 英里（约 320 米），或等候 2 分钟加收 40 美分的水平，小费需付 10%—15%。提价引起了一些市民的抱怨，客运量有所减少，但纽约的出租车收费在全美仍属最便宜之列。

Useful Sentences

1. 问如何到达某处（To Ask How to Get Somewhere）

(1) Excuse me, could you tell me where the baggage claim area is?
请问在哪儿取行李？

(2) Excuse me, could you tell me which way the Foreign Trade Building is?
请问去世贸大楼往哪边走?
(3) Excuse me, which is the way to the May Flower Hotel?
请问去五月花酒店怎么走?
(4) Excuse me, how can I get to the downtown?
请问我怎么去市中心?
(5) Excuse me, where is the Rainbow Restaurant?
请问，彩虹饭店在哪儿?

2. 指路 (To Give Directions)

(1) It's downstairs. 在楼下。
(2) It's that way. 往那边走。
(3) Go along this road for two blocks. Then turn left on the Smith Street.
沿着这条路走过两个街区。然后在史密斯街向左转。
(4) Walk along this road, and take the first turning on your right.
沿着这条路一直往前走，在第一个路口向右拐。
(5) The building is about fifty meters down the road on your left.
大楼就在你的左边沿着马路大约 50 米的地方。
(6) Go one block west, turn north and it's on your left.
往西走一个街区，转向北，它就在你的左边。
(7) Go straight along the road till you come to the corner, then make a left turn.
沿这条路一直往前走到拐角地方，然后向左转。
(8) You should take No. 1 subway.
你得乘地铁 1 号线。
(9) You can take a No. 5 bus from here, but then you'll have to walk about five minutes.
从这儿你可以坐 5 路车，不过下车后你还得走大约 5 分钟的路。
(10) It's opposite the cinema. You can't miss it.
在电影院对面。你不会找不到的。

3. 乘公共交通旅行 (To Travel by Public Transportation)

(1) Excuse me, does this bus go to the park?
请问这车开往公园吗?
(2) Which bus should I take to the museum?
乘哪路公共汽车可以去博物馆?
(3) Does the subway go to the downtown area?

这条地铁是开往市中心的吗？

(4) Can you tell me the way to the subway station?

请问去地铁站怎么走？

(5) Excuse me, how do I change buses to go to the beach?

劳驾，去海滩我该怎么换车？

4. 表达感谢（To Express Gratitude）

(1) Many thanks. / Thanks a lot.

多谢。

(2) Thank you for everything.

太谢谢您啦。

(3) It's most thoughtful of you.

您真是想得太周到了。

(4) Don't mention it.

没什么。/不用谢。

(5) It's a pleasure.

很高兴能为您效劳。

Chapter 7 告别宴会 (Farewell Party)

Business Situation 1

Denny Chen invites Bruce Jackson and Bill Jones to a dinner party in a restaurant. First, Mr. chen proposes a toast, then Linda Zhang introduces the information about Chinese cuisine to them. Finally, Bruce expresses his gratitude.

陈先生在酒店宴请布鲁斯·杰克逊和比尔·琼斯。先由陈先生作祝酒词，然后由张琳达女士介绍中国菜，最后布鲁斯表达感谢。

Dialogue

D = Denny Chen	L = Linda Zhang	B1 = Bruce Jackson	B2 = Bill Jones

D: Mr. Bruce Jackson and Mr. Bill Jones, it's my great honor to have you all here this evening. On behalf of Shenzhen Ugo Sports Shoes Co., Ltd., I'd like to extend our sincere thanks for the close cooperation and kind support you have given us. Now I will propose a toast: To the success of the fair! To our friendship and cooperation! To the health of everyone here! Cheers!

B1: Thank you so much. Cheers!

B2: OK. Bottoms up!

L: Cheers!

B1: Linda, this is our first visit to China. To tell the truth, I have no idea of the Chinese food. Do you, Bill?

B2: I'm afraid I don't either. Linda, could you give us a brief description of the Chinese food?

L: Yes. The Chinese food can be divided into eight styles. They are Shandong style, Sichuan style, Cantonese style, Fujian style, Jiangsu style, Zhejiang style, Hunan style and Anhui style.

B1: What are the different features of them?

L: Shandong food is known for its excellent seafood dishes and delicious soup. Sichuan food is strong and hot. Fujian food is characterized by light tastes, slightly sweetness and sourness. Jiangsu food is distinguished for exquisite ingredients, freshness. Zhejiang food is light, highly finished. Hunan food is known for sourness and spicy dishes. Anhui food pays great attention to nutritious food. This restaurant is famous for its Cantonese food.

B2: Would you tell us its feature?

L: Cantonese food is the most popular style outside China. Cantonese cuisine originates from the region around Canton (Guangzhou) in southern China's Guangdong province. Well, it pays much attention to the freshness, tenderness and smoothness of the dishes. The Cantonese food is light.

B1: That's great!

L: Unlike other Chinese cuisines, the Cantonese usually serve soup before a meal. The soup is usually a clear broth prepared by simmering meat and other ingredients, and cooked on mild fire for hours. Cantonese normally only consume the liquid in the pot, the solids are usually thrown away.

B1: Well, I think we shall try the soup first.

D: OK, please have a try!

B1: En. Nice!

B2: Linda, how about this dish? What is it?

L: That's Blanched Chicken. It is a famous dish in Guangzhou.

B1: That sounds nice.

L: And those are some vegetable dishes. Fried Mushrooms and Bamboo Shoots and Bean Curd with Hot Pepper.

B1: That is very good.

D: OK, let's toast ever-lasting peace.

B2: Cheers!

L: Cheers!

B1: OK, cheers! Thank you. We really enjoy the delicious food and excellent wine. Also, the music is perfect. I enjoy meeting and talking to you and sharing the time together. As we say, well begun is half done. I hope we would maintain this good relationship and make next year another great one together!

D: I hope so too. Thank you!

参考译文

陈经理：布鲁斯杰克逊先生和比尔琼斯先生，今天两位能参加这个晚宴，我们深感荣幸。我谨代表深圳 Ugo 运动鞋有限公司向各位给予我们的密切合作与热心帮助表示衷心感谢。现在请允许我提议：为交易会的圆满成功，为我们的友谊与合作，为在座各位的健康，干杯！

布鲁斯：谢谢！干杯！

比尔：干杯！

张琳达：干杯！

布鲁斯：琳达，这是我们第一次来中国，说实话，我对中国饮食一点也不了解，你呢，比尔？

比尔：我也不知道，琳达，你能给我们简要地介绍一下吗？

张琳达：好啊，中国菜主要分为八个菜系，山东菜、四川菜、广东菜、福建菜、江苏菜、浙江菜、湖南菜和安徽菜。

布鲁斯：它们有什么分别吗？

琳达：山东菜以精制海鲜菜和鲜汤著名。四川菜很辣。福建菜的特点是清淡、微甜和酸。江苏菜选料精细，味道新鲜。浙江菜清淡，重烹调手法。湖南菜以酸和辣著名。安徽菜注重营养。这家餐厅是做广东菜的，很出名。

比尔：你能说说它的特点吗？

张琳达：广东菜在国外非常受欢迎，广东菜起源于中国南方的广东省，主要以广州为中心，以鲜、嫩、滑为特色，味道比较清淡。

布鲁斯：不错！

张琳达：与其他的菜系不同的是，广东人通常在用餐之前要喝汤，这种汤通常都是用肉和其他配料一起用文火长时间熬熟的，广东人只喝汤，不吃里面的配料。

布鲁斯：好的，我想我们应该也先尝尝汤。

陈经理：好啊，请尝尝！

布鲁斯：嗯！美味！

比尔：琳达，这是什么菜啊？

张琳达：那是白斩鸡，在广州非常有名的一道菜。

布鲁斯：听起来不错！

张琳达：还有这些是蔬菜类。香菇炒笋尖、麻辣豆腐。

布鲁斯：很好！

陈经理：让我们为永远和平再干一杯！

比尔：干杯！

张琳达：干杯！

布鲁斯：干杯！谢谢！菜很美味，酒也很棒，我们非常喜欢。当然，这里的音乐也很不错，我很高兴能与你们会面并洽谈，也很享受和你们一起度过的这段时间，正如我们说的，好的开始就是成功的一半，希望我们能维持这种友好的合作并努力在明年争取更好的合作。

陈经理：我也是，谢谢！

Business Situation 2

Ms. Kimberly Carcone, director of Trade Show and Events Marketing Committee, on behalf of American Toy Industry Association Inc., invites Chenghai Toy Trading Co., Ltd. to join the American International Toy Fair in New York. And they hold a banquet in Jacob K. Javits Convention Center. Mr. Dai, vice president of the project department of Chinese Toy Industry Association, joins in the party, together with all Chinese exhibitors. Carter Keithley, president of the Toy Industry Association, shows their gratitude to all the participants, especially to the performance and achievements. He hopes to strengthen co-operation between American and Chinese exhibitors. Mr. Dai also expresses his gratitude to the organizers and congratulation on the success of the fair.

美国玩具工业协会举办宴会，宴请各国参展商。美国玩具工业协会贸易展览与活动策划委员会主任金伯莉·卡科恩女士代表主办方邀请澄海玩具有限公司参加宴会。中国参展组织机构、中国玩具协会会展项目部副主任戴先生带领所有中国参展商参加了宴会。宴会在雅各布 K. 贾维茨会议中心举行。美国玩具协会主席卡特·吉时利代表主办方对各国参展组织机构和参展商以及前来采购的企业表示感谢，特别对中国参展商在会展期间的表现以及所取得的成绩表示祝贺。并希望中美玩具界加强合作。戴先生也对主办方的努力表示感谢并对这次展会的成功举办表示祝贺。

Dialogue

C = Carter D = Dai

C: Ladies and gentlemen, I wish to express my gratitude to you for your generous support and great effort exerted in this fair. I could hardly express my joyfulness about the victory of the cooperation, which you are quite aware of. I will certainly thank you widely, my friends. And I also want to take this opportunity to thank our Chinese guests for their close cooperation and kind support. The fair is more than a business event. It promotes friendship as well as trade. Now, may I propose a toast: To the success of the fair.

D: Cheers!

D: Congratulations! This fair is so successful!

C: Thank you. Of course, I want to show my great gratitude to our Chinese friends. And meantime I'd like to congratulate your success in this fair too. Your job was so excellent.

D: Thank you! However, all of our success relies on your perfect arrangements and cooperation. I'd also like to show my sincere thanks to Ms. Kimberly Carcone. This is a very successful and nice fair.

C: We also need further development. Wish our two countries would strengthen the cooperation and produce more fine and inexpensive toys.

D: You bet. Now let's drink to our further cooperation.

C: OK, cheers!

参考译文

卡特：女士们、先生们，我向你们在这次交易会中所付出的巨大的努力和给予的大力支持表示衷心的感谢。我难以用言语表达对于这次大会的成功举办我有多么的开心，这一点相信大家都知道。感谢每一个人，谢谢！当然我还想借此机会向我们的中国客人的密切合作与热心支持表示衷心的感谢。交易会不仅仅是商业活动，它不但促进贸易，而且促进友谊。现在请允许我提议：为交易会的圆满成功干杯！

戴经理：干杯！

戴经理：恭喜恭喜！大会很成功啊！

卡特：当然。也要感谢你啊，我们的中国客人！你们在这次交易会上也是大获成功啊。你们做得好！

戴经理：谢谢！当然，我们的成功也是依靠您的完美的安排和协助啊！还要感谢金伯莉·卡科恩女士，很感谢你们！这次交易会办得非常好，非常成功。

卡特：我们日后还需要进一步地发展。希望我们两国之间可以加强合作，做出更物美价廉的玩具产品。

戴经理：当然！让我们为以后的合作干杯！

卡特：干杯！

Business Links

1. 告别晚宴和招待会

在会展活动过程中还有一个很重要的环节，就是活动结束时东道主要宴请与会代表或重要嘉宾和客商。其主要形式有招待会、告别晚宴等。

（1）告别晚宴对于所有的会展活动来说，可以起到画龙点睛的作用。通过独特的主题策划、空间艺术设计，为客户营造浓郁的宴会氛围。为宴会赋予鲜明文化背景与独特民族风格，明确体现活动宗旨与特色。

（2）招待会是一种常为表示隆重或正式欢迎的社交集会。通常具有娱乐或取乐性。

2. 正式场合用餐礼仪

（1）就座时，身体要端正，胳膊肘不要放在桌面上，不可跷足，与餐桌的距离以便于使用餐具为佳。餐台上已摆好的餐具不要随意摆弄。将餐巾对折轻轻放在膝上。

（2）使用刀叉进餐时，从外侧往内侧取用刀叉，要左手持叉，右手持刀。切东西左手拿叉按住食物，右手执刀将其锯切成小块，然后用叉子送入口中。使用刀时，刀刃不可向外。进餐中放下刀叉时，应摆成"八"字形，分别放在餐盘边上。刀刃朝向自身，表示还要继续吃。每吃完一道菜，将刀叉并拢放在盘中。要记住：任何时候，都不可将刀叉的一端放在盘上，另一端放在桌上。

（3）喝汤时不要啜，吃东西时要闭嘴咀嚼。不要咂嘴发出声音。如汤菜过热，可待稍凉后再吃，不要用嘴吹。喝汤时，用汤勺从里向外舀，汤盘中的汤快喝完时，用左手将汤盘的外侧稍稍翘起，用汤勺舀净即可。吃完汤菜时，将汤匙留在汤盘（碗）中，匙把指向自己。

（4）进餐时应与左右客人交谈，但应避免高声谈笑。不要只同几个熟人交谈。如不认识左右客人，可向其自我介绍。别人讲话时不可搭嘴插话。

Useful Sentences

1. 祝酒词（Toasts）

（1）Cheers!
干杯！

（2）Bottoms up!
干杯！

（3）Let's drink a toast.
让我们干杯！

（4）We'll drink your health.
为您的健康干杯！

（5）Let's get our minds off of work and have a good time. /Let's forget about work and have some fun.
让我们忘记工作好好享受一下！

（6）Now, I'd like to propose a toast: To your health, and to the health of all gathered here.

现在我提议：为您的健康，为所有在座各位的健康，干杯！

2. 介绍菜肴（Introduce Chinese Dishes）

(1) Chinese cuisine has so much color, flavor and taste.
中国烹饪色、香、味俱全。

(2) This restaurant is famous for its roast duck. It is well known all over the world.
这家饭店以烤鸭著称。中国烤鸭世界闻名。

(3) There are dozens of ways to do the dish in Chinese cuisine. Take fish, you can have it fried, stewed, steamed, smoked or sautéed.
中国菜有许多做法。比方说鱼，可以煎、煨、蒸、熏，还可以炒。

3. 表达感谢（Show Gratitude）

(1) Thank you for your time and consideration again.
再次感谢您的时间和考虑。

(2) Thanks for coming all the way over here.
谢谢您不远万里专程跑一趟。

(3) We are deeply grateful for your support.
我们深深感谢您的支持。

(4) This is for all the things that you have done for me.
这是为了感谢您为我所做的一切。

(5) I really appreciate your help.
我真的非常感谢您的帮助。

4. 良好祝愿（Good Wishes）

(1) Have a good time！祝你们玩得愉快！

(2) Have a nice evening！祝你晚上愉快！

(3) Happy birthday！生日快乐！

(4) Merry Christmas！圣诞快乐！

(5) May you succeed！祝你成功！

5. 告别（Part or Say Good-bye）

(1) Wish you a very pleasant journey home！Have a good journey！
祝您归途愉快！一路顺风！

(2) Thank you very much for everything you have done for us during your stay in China.
谢谢您在中国期间为我们所做的一切。

(3) It is a pity you are leaving so soon.

很遗憾您这么快就要离开。

(4) I'm looking forward to seeing you again.

希望再次见到您。

(5) I'll see you at the airport tomorrow morning.

明天上午我在机场见您。

Chapter 8 餐馆用餐 (At the Restaurant)

Business Situation 1

Bruce Jackson and Bill Jones come into a Chinese restaurant to have a taste of the local food after the success of the business.

布鲁斯·杰克逊和比尔·琼斯在成功拿到订单后决定好好慰劳自己。于是他们走进一家中国餐厅，打算放松一下，尝尝美味地道的中国菜。

Dialogue

B1 = Bruce Jackson	B2 = Bill Jones	W = Waiter

W: Good evening, sir. Here is our menu. Would you like something to drink before you order?

B1: Yes. Mineral water, please.

W: OK. Are you ready to order now, or should I come back later?

B2: No, we are still looking at the menu. Maybe you could recommend something for the main courses. We don't know much about Chinese food. What do you recommend?

W: We have all kinds of Chinese food and wine at your choice. I can recommend our special dishes. Double-cooked Pork, Mapo Bean Curd. Our chef's special today is Plain Steamed Crabs. They really taste good. I'm sure you'll like them.

B1: Sounds great! We'll take them and a Salad.

W: So, you want Double-cooked Pork, Mapo Bean curd and Plain Steamed Crabs and a Salad. What would you like to drink?

B1: Do you have a wine list?

W: Yes. Here you are. We have mineral water, Coke, tea and Chinese Qingdao beer and Maotai.

B2: What is Maotai?

W: Maotai is the best liquor in China. It's strong liquor made from sorghum grain, but it doesn't go to the head as most liquor does.

B2: Is anything else besides Maotai?

W: If you prefer something milder, there is rice wine.

B2: That sounds fine. We'll take the rice wine.

W: OK. Just a moment, please.

(*Serving the dishes*)

W: Here is the Plain Steamed Crabs.

B1: What are these monsters?

W: Monsters? No, they are fresh water crabs from the East Lake. They may look ugly. But you will love them because they taste very good.

B1: Really? Could you tell me how they are prepared?

W: Well, they are steamed. Put some water in a pot and put the tied crab onto a meshed frame above the water. Boil the water for about twenty minutes, and the crabs are ready to be served.

B2: How do I eat them?

W: Break the shell with your teeth. Then dip the meat in a mixture of soya sauce, vinegar and sliced ginger.

B2: I see… Oh, very nice. Well, are they in season now?

W: No, according to the saying "In the 9th month of the lunar calendar, eat female crabs, and in the 10th month, eat male ones."

B2: It's said that some people in China Hong Kong and China Macau have complained against the Chinese mainland exporters for making the smaller crabs much more expensive than the bigger ones.

W: As regards the taste, the smaller female crabs are better than the male crabs. But the claws of the bigger male crabs are much better than those of the female crabs.

B2: That's right. River crabs are always preferable. Their delicious taste is a popular favorite.

W: So, you enjoyed the crabs.

B2: Oh, yes, very much. The crab dish was very delicious. I like them very much. Besides, your service is excellent. Thank you.

W: It's very kind of you to say so. Now your second dish is coming.

参考译文

侍应：晚上好，先生！这是我们的菜单，请问在点菜前要先喝点什么吗？

布鲁斯：好的，矿泉水。

侍应：好的，先生现在点菜吗，还是我等会儿再来？

布鲁斯：不用，我们正在看菜单，你有什么好推荐吗？我们对中国菜不是很了解。

侍应：我们有各式各样的中国菜和酒供应，我们的特色菜有回锅肉，麻婆豆腐。我们主厨今天的特色菜是清蒸螃蟹。这道菜真的很好，我想你们一定会喜欢的。

布鲁斯：听起来不错，就点它们了，外加一份沙拉。

侍应：好的，你们点了回锅肉、麻婆豆腐、清蒸螃蟹和一份沙拉，你们要喝点什么吗?

布鲁斯：你们有酒单吗?

侍应：有，给您。我们有矿泉水、可乐、茶、青岛啤酒和茅台。

比尔：茅台是什么?

侍应：茅台是中国最好的酒，它是用高粱酿造出来的烈酒，但喝了以后不上头。

比尔：除了茅台还有什么?

侍应：如果您不想要这么烈的酒，可以试试米酒。

比尔：好啊，尝尝吧!

侍应：好的，请稍等!

(上菜)

侍应：这是你们的清蒸螃蟹。

布鲁斯：这些怪物是什么啊?

侍应：怪物?不是，它们是新鲜的东湖淡水螃蟹。也许看上去不怎么样，但你们尝了之后会喜欢，味道很不错。

布鲁斯：是吗?你能讲讲它们是怎么做的吗?

侍应：哦，它们是蒸出来的。在锅里放些水，再把绑好的螃蟹放在蒸架上，然后蒸20分钟就可以吃了。

比尔：我们怎么吃呢?

侍应：咬碎外壳，再放到酱油、醋和姜丝做的味碟里蘸一下。

比尔：哦，我知道了……嗯!味道不错!现在是螃蟹的上市时间吗?

侍应：不是，老话说“农历九月吃母蟹，农历十月吃公蟹。”

比尔：据说中国香港和中国澳门的居民常抱怨内地商人常常把小螃蟹卖得比大的还贵。

侍应：从味道上来说，小母蟹的确比公蟹要好，但大公蟹的蟹钳比母蟹的肉多。

比尔：那倒是。河蟹一直都很受欢迎，它的味道很合大众口味。

侍应：那您也喜欢这道菜了。

比尔：是的，非常喜欢。味道很好。你的服务也很好，谢谢。

侍应：谢谢您这么说。哦，您的第二道菜来了。

Business Situation 2

Chenghai Toy Trading Co., Ltd. participates in the 2010 American

International Toy Fair in New York. And after they sign the contract successfully, they want to try the western food. Now they enter a restaurant.

澄海玩具贸易有限公司参加2010年纽约国际玩具博览会，完成了预订的签约任务，准备尝尝正宗的西餐，他们走进一家餐馆。

Dialogue

A = Anna Zhang　D = Dai　W = Waiter

W: Good evening. Will it be a table for four, sir?

D: Yes. I'm Dai. I made a reservation for six people at 7:15, and two more people are on their way.

W: I have your reservation, Mr. Dai. The table will be ready for you at 7:15. It's just 7:00 o'clock. Would you care to have a drink in the bar in the meantime? The bar is to your right. Shall I ask your friends to join you there?

D: That's fine.

(*The other couple arrives.*)

W: Good evening! Is it Mr. Dai's party?

A: Yes, we are.

W: They're in the bar, sir. It's to the right.

W: Your table is ready, Mr. Dai. Would you please come this way?

A: Thank you.

W: Would you take your seats, please, ladies and gentlemen? (*He pulls out the seats for them and they sit down.*) Do you care for anything to drink before you order?

D: No, thank you. I think we'll skip the aperitif and order straight away.

W: OK, here are the menus.

D: Now let's see...

(*After waiting for a few minutes*)

W: Are you ready to order now?

D: No, we are still looking at the menu. Maybe you could recommend something for the main course.

W: Certainly. The T-bone steak is very good. I would suggest you try that.

D: That's a good idea. I love beefsteaks. I'll have the T-bone Steak.

W: What kind of potatoes would you like to go with it?

D: Baked, please.

W: And what will your vegetable be?

D: I'll have the carrots and broccoli.

W: And what would you like for appetizer?

D: I'll have the salad and the baked salmon.

W: And would you like dessert or cheese?

D: Dessert.

W: What can I get you for dessert?

D: I'll take the ice cream, strawberry ice cream.

W: Thank you.

参考译文

侍应：晚上好，要四人桌吗？

戴经理：是的，我姓戴，我订了一张六人桌，7点15来用餐，另外还有两人在路上。

侍应：是的，有您的预订，是7点15分的。现在是7点，您请在吧台先喝杯东西等一下。我待会儿叫您的朋友到吧台找您好吗？

戴经理：当然，好的。

(另外两人到了。)

侍应：晚上好，请问你们是和戴先生一起的吗？

张：是的。

侍应：他们在吧台，请往右边走。

侍应：您好，戴先生，你们的位子好了，请这边走。

戴经理：谢谢！

侍应：女士们、先生们请坐。请问你们点菜前要喝点什么吗？

戴经理：不用了，我想我们就不要开胃酒直接点菜吧。

侍应：好的，这是菜单。

戴经理：好的，让我们先看看……

(几分钟过后)

侍应：请问您现在可以点菜了吗？

戴经理：不行，我们还在看菜单，你有什么好介绍吗？

侍应：当然有，今天的T骨牛排很好。我建议你们尝尝。

戴经理：不错，我喜欢牛排，来一份吧。

侍应：你喜欢西红柿怎样做来搭配牛排呢？

戴经理：烤的。

侍应：您想要搭配什么蔬菜呢？

戴经理：胡萝卜和花椰菜。

侍应：您想要什么开胃菜呢？

戴经理：沙拉和烤鲑鱼。

侍应：您是要甜点还是奶酪？
戴经理：甜点吧。
侍应：您要什么甜点？
戴经理：冰淇淋，草莓冰淇淋。
侍应：谢谢。

Business Links

1. 国外的饮食

（1）法式菜：选料广、精、鲜。对原料的要求比较严格，讲究原汁原味，追求鲜嫩，喜欢用酒做调料。

（2）美式菜：美国人生活习惯比较随意。大都不喜欢喝茶，而喜欢喝加冰的凉开水和矿泉水。还喜欢用水果做菜，对甜食很讲究，如各种布丁、苹果派等。

（3）非洲菜：说到非洲美食，首先必须得提水果。非洲的水果很美味，这可能是所有来非洲的外国人对于非洲美食最能统一的观点了。非洲的水果主要有香蕉、菠萝、西瓜、芒果、橙这五种，还有柚子、油梨果、杨桃等。菜肴多数就是番茄、土豆、洋葱、南瓜、包菜等，样式不多。鱼、虾和蟹在近海的非洲国家可以说是应有尽有。

（4）自助餐：自助餐（buffet），有时亦称冷餐会，它是目前国际上所通行的一种非正式的西式宴会，在大型的商务活动中尤为多见。它的具体做法是：不预备正餐，而由就餐者在用餐时自由随意地选择食物、饮品，然后或立或坐，与他人或是独自用餐。自助餐之所以称为自助餐，主要是因为用餐时用餐者可以自己动手，自己帮助自己，在既定的范围之内选用菜肴。至于它又被叫做冷餐会，则主要是因其提供的食物以冷食为主。当然，也会适量地提供一些热菜，或者提供一些半成品由用餐者自己进行加工。如今，自助餐已不局限于各种宴会，在生活节奏日益加快的今天，到经济实惠的自助餐馆大快朵颐，已成为人们休闲聚友的首选之一。

2. 如何给小费

在餐厅用餐，如果账单已加收一成的服务费，小费可以不用给。若是未加收服务费，就要看顾客自己的感觉。如果觉得服务不错，可以多给一点。许多人常将费用取一个最接近整数的值，将钱留在账单内，然后离去，服务生就知道多出来的是小费。切记，给小费时，千万不要给一堆零钱，以免给人施舍的感觉。

Useful Sentences

(1) — Oh, it is really a nice place to dine. Would you like an aperitif before you order?
哦，这真是个用餐的好地方，在你点菜前要不要来杯开胃酒？
— No, I think I'd like to order straight away.
不用了，我想直接点菜吧。
— OK.
好的。

(2) — Have you ever had Chinese food before?
你以前吃过中国菜吗？
— No, I haven't. Back home, my friends talk all the time about Chinese food.
没有，从中国回去的朋友一直在聊中国菜。
— They serve different styles of Chinese food here. But I'm not sure which style you prefer?
这里提供各种风味的中国菜，但我不知道你喜欢哪类菜？
— I have no idea, I'm in your hands.
我不知道，听你的。
— I think Mapo Tofu is quite special.
我觉得麻婆豆腐很特别。
— All right. I'll have it.
好的，就点它了。

(3) — What's your impression of China now?
你现在对中国的印象是怎样的？
— It's definitely different from what we had heard before we came.
和我们来之前听说的完全不一样。
— I'm glad you have enjoyed your stay in China.
你们在中国玩得很愉快我很高兴。

(4) — I am not familiar with French food. Would you mind giving me some suggestions?
我对法国菜不是很熟，可以给我一点建议吗？
— What is your house specialty?
请问你们的招牌菜是什么？
— Our roast chicken is very good.
我们的烤鸡很有名。

(5) — I would like a lamb chop.

我要一份小羊排。

— How would you like your lamb chop?

请问要几分熟？

— I would like to have my steak rare/medium/medium-well/well-done.

要三分/五分/七分/全熟。

（6）Would you care for anything to drink?

Will you be ordering anything from the bar?

Would you like to see our wine and spirits list?

您要喝点什么吗？

（7）Are there any dishes that the chef recommends today?

Is there a special of the day?

Do you recommend any particular dish?

Is there a house specialty today?

今天有什么特色菜吗？

（8）May I have another look at the menu, please?

I would like to see the menu again, please.

我想再看一下菜单，好吗？

（9）Please pack/box up the leftovers for me.

I would like to take the leftovers home with me.

May I have a doggie bag, please?

请帮我把剩菜打包。

（10）Check, please.

Please give me the bill.

May I have the check, please?

Would you please bring us the check?

我要结账。

I'd like the receipt.

May I have a receipt, please?

麻烦开一下收据。

Is a service charge included?

Does this include the service charge?

请问含服务费吗？

A 15% service charged is automatically added to the bill.

账单已内含 15% 的服务费。

Chapter 9 观光与购物 (Sightseeing and Shopping)

Business Situation 1

Denny Chen, together with other five guests, has just gone around Guangzhou city by car and now is visiting Bai Yun Mountain. Linda Zhang is showing them around and introducing the information of the mountain. Meanwhile, Chen also tells them there will be a banquet for them tonight.

陈经理一行五人先参观了一下市区，张琳达小姐简要介绍了市区的主要景点，然后来到了广州白云山风景区，介绍了白云山景区。陈经理另外告知晚上为他们设了酒宴。

Dialogue

Z = Linda Zhang　B = Bruce　D = Denny Chen

B: Well, Guangzhou is so beautiful!

Z: Yes, Guangzhou is the biggest city in South China and one of the most important cities in Guangdong Province. Guangzhou has a long history of about 2,100 years. It is about the age of Rome, the famous city in Italy. The population of Guangzhou is more than 7,000,000. In the centre of the city, the streets are very noisy and crowded. It isn't cold there in winter, but it is quite hot in summer. February is the coldest month and August is the hottest month. Guangzhou is a very beautiful city. You can see green trees and flowers all the year round. There are many interesting places to visit. There are a lot of parks, temples and museums. The things in the shops are often quite cheap, so people like going shopping there.

B: OK, now we are in the Baiyun Mountain. But Miss Zhang, why people call it "Baiyun" Mountain? What does "Baiyun" mean in Chinese?

Z: In Chinese, Baiyun Mountain is translated literally to White Cloud Mountain, since white clouds often encircle the peaks when the sun is shining. Combined with the famous Pearl River, people usually say "Pearl River and White Clouds" to praise Guangzhou.

B: Oh, I see.

Z: Baiyun Mountain belongs to the end section of the Jiulian Mountain

Range, Which is called the Dayu Mountain Branch. It is located seventeen km from Guangzhou. Baiyun Mountain consists of over 30 peaks and has a mountain area of 28 sq. km, which is equal to the total area of Macao. The highest peak, Moxing Peak, is 382 meters and the highest summit in Guangzhou.

B: That's cool! Can I climb to the top of it?

Z: Of course you can, if you have time and courage. Meanwhile, White Cloud Mountain is an ideal place for people to unwind and forget their cares. The park is divided into six areas that are popular with visitors: Bright Pearl Building Park, Bird Spring Valley Park (Mingchun Valley), Santailing Park, Luhu Park, and the Fei'eling Park. Yuntai Garden, a bright pearl in the crown of White Cloud Mountain, is located in Santailing Park, and is an enormous garden filled with all kinds of blooming flowers and trees. After seeing this site, it comes as no surprise that Guangzhou is known as the City of Flowers.

B: That's great! We love flowers and trees.

Z: There is also a Sculpture Park, located in Fei'eling, and covering an area of 46 hectares (113 acres). It was built according to the fashion trends of the times, which was to use modern languages in sculpture. Visitors will also find the biggest natural birdcage in China, which is perfect for enjoying all kinds of birds. It is called Bird Spring Valley Park. Here visitors can stroll by the river and mountains, enjoying the birds. Luhu Park is famous for Jinye Pond. The lake is so clear that the beautiful sights surrounding the lake are perfectly reflected in the water, like a brilliantly drawn picture.

B: Since this scenic area is so large, how does your government protect its environment?

Z: Recently, the Baiyun Mountain Scenic Spot Management Bureau has been established to protect it. Baiyun Mountain has been constructed to be a large-scale national Chinese scenic area and one of the first groups of the prestigious AAAA Tourist Spot.

B: Oh, that's great!

D: Well, do you have any plans this evening, Bruce? We would like to have the pleasure of inviting you to dinner.

B: That's very kind of you! OK, we'd be delighted to come.

参考译文

布鲁斯：啊，广州真是个美丽的地方！

张琳达：是啊，广州是中国南方最大的城市也是广东省最重要的城市之一。广州有着悠久的历史，有2 100多年了。相当于意大利的名城罗马了。广州市人口700多万。在市中心的街道非常热闹拥挤。这里的冬天不冷，但是夏天很热。二月最冷，八月最热。广州的美还在于它一年四季都繁花似锦，绿树环绕。在这里有很多花园、寺庙和博物馆等有趣的地方可以参观游览。物价也不是很高，所以这里的人也很喜欢购物。

布鲁斯：啊，我们到白云山了，张小姐，为什么人们叫它“白云山”呢？“白云”在汉语里是什么意思呢？

张琳达：在汉语里白云是指“白色的云”的意思。因为每当太阳初升的时候，这座山就被白云环绕，和珠江一体。人们常用“珠江白云”来形容广州。

布鲁斯：哦，是这样啊，我明白了。

张琳达：白云山位于九连山脉尾部，叫大禹山分支。位于广州市北部，距市区约17公里。景区内有30多座山峰，占地面积28平方公里，相当于整个澳门的面积。景区内最高峰为摩星岭，海拔382米，也是广州的最高点。

布鲁斯：酷！那我们可以爬上去吗？

张琳达：那当然了，只要你有时间和勇气。与此同时，白云山还是让你忘记烦恼和放松心情的很好的地方。整个园区分成六个部分：明珠楼、鸣春谷、三台岭、麓湖、飞鹅岭和摩星岭，深受游客的喜爱。云台花园是白云山上一颗闪亮的明珠，位于三台岭，是一个花团锦簇的大花园，到了那里你就不会奇怪为什么广州被称为花城了。

布鲁斯：太好了，我们很喜欢花草树木。

张琳达：另外，在飞鹅岭还有个大的雕塑园占地46公顷，它是根据当时的时尚趋势而设计的，被认为是现代语言在雕塑艺术中的体现。在这里我们还可以看到中国最大的自然鸟笼，一边徜徉于青山绿水，一边欣赏各种各样的鸟。麓湖公园因金叶池塘出名。湖水清澈倒映着周围的景致，犹如一幅美丽的风景画。

布鲁斯：这个景区的面积这么大，政府部门是怎么来保护它的环境呢？

张琳达：最近，成立了白云山景区管理局。景区已经被建设成国家级的大规模景区，并已列为我国最早的一批4A级景区。

布鲁斯：哦，那不错。

陈经理：布鲁斯，今晚你们有什么安排吗？我们想邀请你们参加晚宴。

布鲁斯：你们真是太好了，好的，我们很乐意参加。

Business Situation 2

Miss Anna Zhang, the manager of Chenghai Toy Trading Co., Ltd. phones the Global Travel Agency at New York to ask some information about the sightseeing in New York City. They want to take a city pass and visit the Metropolitan Museum of Art, the United Nations, Ground Zero and Statue of Liberty etc.

澄海玩具贸易有限公司业务部经理张安娜打电话给纽约环球旅行社，询问有关参加旅行团游览纽约市的事宜。他们借来纽约的机会，准备参观纽约的市容市貌，如大都会博物馆、联合国大厦、“9·11”事件遗址、自由女神像等。

Dialogue

C = Clerk　A = Anna Zhang

C: Hello, the Global Travel Agency. Can I help you?

A: I'd like to get some travel information of New York.

C: Yes, madam. How many people are there in your group?

A: Seven.

C: How long will you stay in New York?

A: We are coming for the American International Toy Fair. And we have finished it. Now we have one day to get a city pass. We want to visit the Metropolitan Museum of Art, the United Nations, Ground Zero and Statue of Liberty. Can you arrange a tour for us?

C: OK, then I suggest that you would take a circle-line around the Manhattan. That will only take you one day to go around the center of the city.

A: How about the fee?

C: Just a moment, please. 39 dollars for each adult. Do you have any children with you?

A: No, we don't have children with us.

C: OK. This 39-dollar includes the bus fee, the admission fee to the scenic spots and good guide service, while it doesn't include the lunch, tip and your carfare from your hotel to the bus station.

A: I see. We'll leave everything up to you, then.

C: My pleasure. If there should be any changes, I'll let you know in time.

A: OK, that's fine. Can we have any discount?

C: I'm afraid you can't. It's the busy season. May I have your name and number please?

A: Of course. My name is Anna Zhang and my number is 3332569.

C: OK, thank you. I'll call you later. Goodbye.

A: Goodbye.

参考译文

职员：您好，环球旅行社。需要我帮忙吗?

张安娜：我想了解一些关于在纽约旅游的信息。

职员：好的，女士。你们一行多少人呢?

张安娜：七个。

职员：你们在纽约待多久?

张安娜：我们是来参加美国纽约国际玩具博览会的，现在结束了。我们有一天的时间，准备参观纽约的市容市貌，如大都会博物馆，联合国大厦，“9·11”事件遗址，自由女神像等。你能帮我们安排一下行程吗?

职员：好的，这样的话我建议你们可以采用曼哈顿环岛游的方式。只需要一天的时间便可游览市中心。

张安娜：费用是多少呢?

职员：请稍候，每个成人费用为39美元，你们中有儿童吗?

张安娜：不，没有。

职员：好的。这39美元包括车费、景区门票费和优质导游服务费，但不包括午餐、小费和从宾馆到车站的车费。

张安娜：好的，一切全拜托你们了。

职员：我们很荣幸。好，如果安排上有什么变化我们会及时通知你们。

张安娜：好的。我们能享受折扣吗?

职员：很抱歉，现在是旺季，没有折扣。您能留个联系电话吗?

张安娜：当然。我叫张安娜，我的电话是3332569。

职员：好的，谢谢您。再联系，再见。

张安娜：再见。

Business Links

1. 商务旅游活动

旅游活动是商务活动的一个重要环节。在签约前后，陪同客商观光旅游可以加深外国客商对我国的了解，增进感情等。我国企业人士到海外，也多会利用难得的机会，在国外观光旅游，以便对该国的文化风俗有更深的了解，放松心情等。从内涵来看，商务旅游活动具有以下几个特点：

（1）国际化的商务旅游是跨国的经济活动，从现在来说，这一特点体现得越来越充分。

（2）国际化的商务旅游是跨文化的活动，所以我们如果只从经济角度来理解商务旅游是不全面的。在这个过程之中是各种文化的碰撞，也是各种文化的交流。商务旅游文化差异，在这个过程里也体现得越来越充分。所以把握文化差异对商务旅游非常重要。

2. 国外旅游购物技巧

（1）折扣季前后各有优缺点，把握好购物时机

到国外购买时尚名品是每个出国旅客的想法，尤其是在折扣期间，每年圣诞节过后4～6个礼拜就是一年一度的秋冬时装打折时期，此时，商店通常从7折开始，到元旦过后便直下5折，加上各地放年假的原因，吸引来大量的游客。旅游旺季期间虽然可以买到较便宜的东西，但同时旺季带来的连锁效应使得机票、酒店住宿费比平常高，而且旅游景点及购物商场到处很拥挤。反购时装上市的季节都是旅游淡季，机票、酒店住宿费相对也较便宜。虽然买到的东西较贵，但与机票及酒店住宿费整体核算，还是很划算的。

（2）勿忘办理退税，享受再打一次折扣

虽然欧洲是高税费的国家，但是外国旅客不需负担高昂的税费，所以购物可以办理退税。退税额大约在12%～18%之间。若扣除手续费，约可拿到11%～15%的退款，如此一来等于再打一次折扣，很划算。

Useful Sentences

1. 介绍景点（Introduce the scenic spot to the tourists）

（1）Look, that is an exotic pine. You see, it has stretched its boughs to welcome us.

看，那棵奇松，正向我们伸展枝叶欢迎我们呢。

（2）On Baiyun Mountain, towering cliffs are everywhere, and every cliff has its pines and each pine has its unique postures.

白云山到处都是险峰，每个险峰上都有奇松，每棵奇松都有自己独特的身姿。

（3）According to the legend, white clouds often encircle the peaks when the sun is shining in autumn.

传说秋天太阳出来的时候白云会环绕着山峰。

（4）Guangzhou is a long-history city, and it was founded in the Qin &

Han Dynasties 2,220 years ago, but Baiyun Mountain was well-known for its nice scenery even earlier than the foundation of Guangzhou City.

广州有悠久的历史，建立于2 200年前的秦汉时期，但白云山因其美丽的景色闻名于世的时间比广州城的建立还要早。

(5) Luhu Lake is the biggest man-made lake and a public multi-function park in Guangzhou. Here you may enjoy culture, leisure entertainment, sports exercises, delicious foods etc.

麓湖是广州最大的人工湖，也是一个多功能的公园。这里集文化、娱乐、健身和美食为一体。

2. 购物 (Shopping)

(1) — Where are the women's clothes? You know, most ladies are interested in clothes. I'm not an exception.

哪儿是女装部？你知道，大多数的女性都对服装感兴趣。我也不例外。

— It is on the third floor. There are different kinds of new fashions there.

在三楼。那儿有很多新款呢。

(2) — How much is it?

多少钱？

— 300 dollars.

300美元。

— Well. It is too much. Can you give me a discount?

太贵了。能给我打折吗？

— I'm afraid I can't. Our prices are all set in this department.

不可以，我们的价格是百货商场统一定的。

— OK, I'll take it. Please wrap it up for me.

好吧，就买它了。请帮我包起来。

(3) — How can I help you?

我能为您服务吗？

— Yes, I would like to look at some of your products.

是的，我想看看你们的商品。

— Did you have anything specific in mind?

你有什么具体想买的吗？

— No, do you have any good ideas?

没有，你有什么好建议吗？

(4) — How much is the membership fee?

会员费是多少呢？

— I'm not sure.

我不确定。

— But if you are only going to stay a year, I don't think Price Club is good to join.

不过如果你只待一年，加入俱乐部并不划算。

— They have great deals occasionally.

有时他们会有很棒的促销。

— They are very good for people who like to buy new things all the time.

对那些总是想买新产品的人而言是划算的。

（5）— Where is the fitting room? I don't see it.

更衣室在哪里？我没看到。

— The fitting rooms are over there.

更衣室在那里。

3. 邀请（Make Invitations）

（1）Do you have any plans tomorrow evening?

明天晚上您有什么安排吗？

（2）Are you doing anything special on Friday evening?

星期五晚上您有什么事情吗？

（3）Are you free on Wednesday afternoon?

星期三下午您是否有空？

（4）No, I've nothing planned.

没有，没什么安排。

No, I haven't made any plans.

没有，没什么计划。

No, nothing in particular.

没有，没什么特别的事。

（5）We're very glad you could come.

您能来，我们非常高兴。

We're so happy you could make it.

您能赶来，我们非常高兴。

Everyone's happy you are able to come.

您能来，大家都很高兴。

4. 观光（Sightseeing）

（1）— Good evening. It's nice to be here.

晚上好，很高兴能到这儿来。

— We're glad you could come.

您能来，我们很荣幸。

(2) — I've been looking forward to seeing all of you. It seems there are a lot of people here tonight.

我一直期待着见到各位。看起来今晚这里宾客满座。

— Yes. Let's go over to meet some of them.

是的，让我们过去结识几位。

(3) — We'd like to take a one-day sightseeing tour around the city. What would you advise us to see here?

我们想城市观光一日游。您建议我们游览什么呢?

— Fine, I can recommend you a popular plan.

好的，我会推荐一个很受欢迎的游览计划。

(4) — How long does the tour take?

这次观光会花多长时间?

— About eight hours.

大概 8 小时。

(5) — Good afternoon. I've come to talk about the itinerary for our trip. Can you spare me some time?

下午好。我来谈谈我们旅游行程的事。请问您有时间吗?

— Sure.

当然有时间。

— How many scenic spots will we visit tomorrow?

明天我们会游览几个景点啊?

— Three.

3 个。

Part IV 参加会展 (Attending Exhibition)

Chapter 1　办理采购商证手续 (Go Through Purchaser's Formalities)

Business Situation 1

Mr. Bruce Jackson is the marketing manager of Fashion Way Co., Ltd. in Canada. He's visiting the 107th China Import and Export Fair with his assistant Mr. Bill Jones. Mr. Bruce Jackson goes through purchaser's formalities at Pazhou Complex and then calls Miss Linda Zhang for an appointment.

布鲁斯·杰克逊先生是加拿大 Fashion Way 公司的市场部经理。他与他的助理比尔·琼斯先生一同来参加第 107 届中国广交会。布鲁斯先生在广交展琶洲展馆办理采购商手续，之后打电话给张琳达商定见面时间。

Dialogue

C = Clerk　B = Bruce　L = Linda Zhang

C: Good morning! What can I do for you?

B: Good morning! We are purchasers from Canada. What should we do to apply for the Overseas Buyer's Card?

C: First of all, please fill in the application forms.

B: Thank you.

C: Do you have personal photos?

B: Sorry, we don't.

C: In that case, you have to have your photos taken over there.

B: OK.

(*Ten minutes later*)

B: Miss, our photos are ready.

C: May I see your application forms, ID cards, overseas passports as well as your business cards?

B: Sure. Here you are.

C: Thanks! By the way, do you have an invitation card?

B: Yes, an exhibitor sent us one.

C: That's good. Thus you don't have to pay for the buyer's cards.

B: Great!

(*After having the buyers' cards made, Mr. Bruce Jackson called Miss Linda Zhang.*)

L: Hello! This is Linda Zhang speaking.

B: Hello! This is Bruce Jackson from Fashion Way Co., Ltd.

L: Hi, Mr. Jackson! Are you in China?

B: Yes, just outside of the Complex. I would like to visit your booth today. Would it be possible to see your sales manager?

L: Welcome! Our booth No. is 22. C30. on the second floor. Our sales manager and I will be right here waiting for you.

B: OK. See you soon. Bye!

L: Bye!

参考译文

职员：早上好！能为您做些什么？

布鲁斯：早上好！我们是加拿大的采购商。请问如何办理海外采购商证？

职员：首先，请填写这些申请表。

布鲁斯：谢谢。

职员：你们有个人照片吗？

布鲁斯：对不起，没有。

职员：那么，请到那边拍摄照片。

布鲁斯：好的。

（十分钟后）

布鲁斯：我们的照片好了，小姐。

职员：请出示你们的申请表、身份证、海外护照和名片。

布鲁斯：好的，给你。

职员：谢谢！请问您有邀请函吗？

布鲁斯：是的，有位参展商给我们发了一份。

职员：好的。那您不用为采购商证交费了。

布鲁斯：太好了。

（采购商证制作好后，布鲁斯·杰克逊先生给张琳达小姐打电话。）

张琳达：您好！我是张琳达。

布鲁斯：您好！我是 Fashion Way 公司的布鲁斯·杰克逊。

张琳达：您好，杰克逊先生！您在中国吗？

布鲁斯：是的，我就在展馆外面。今天想来您的展位看看。能见到您的销售经理吗？

张琳达：欢迎您！我们的展位号是二楼的 22. C30。我和我们的销售经理会在这儿等您。

布鲁斯：好的。再见！
张琳达：再见！

Business Situation 2

Ms. Dora Zhao, the assistant manager of Chenghai Toy Trading Co., Ltd., goes through the formalities and asks about the procedures of the 107th American International Toy Fair and the location of her company's booth at the Convention Center. She gets the materials for the fair.

澄海玩具贸易有限公司经理助理赵女士正在会议中心咨询有关第107届美国国际玩具博览会的程序等问题，办理有关手续，询问博览会的具体安排、本公司展柜的具体位置，索要资料等。

Dialogue

C = Clerk D = Dora Zhao

C: Good morning! Can I help you?
D: Good morning! We are exporters from China. What should we do for the registration?
C: Have you filled in the forms at our website?
D: Yes, we have filled in the forms online.
C: OK, may I know your name please?
D: Dora Zhao. D-O-R-A, Z-H-A-O.
C: Let me check. Ah, it's here. Your company has registered online. May I see your passports, please?
D: Yes, here you are.
C: Thank you. We have printed your forms. Do you have personal photos?
D: Yes, here you are.
C: Here are your passports and Attendee's Cards. Anything else?
D: May I know the arrangement of the fair?
C: Certainly, here's the brochure for the 107th American International Toy Fair. It includes the arrangement of the fair and the booth number of each company. And your company's booth is at 3B on level three.
D: By the way, it's the first time for our company to attend the Toy Fair here, and we are not familiar with the service here.
C: Our convention center welcomes all the guests from the world and we know the attendees may not know the service here. Therefore, we printed

The Javits Tool Kit for you. It introduces all the service here, including electricity, cleaning, telecommunications, booth catering, Business Center, banking service, advertising and so on.

D: That's great.

C: To place your order, call toll-free 1-877-4 JAVITS (452-8487), or go online to: *www.JavitsCenter.com*, or use the simple order forms at the back of this catalog. If you need additional information or assistance during your show, just stop by our conveniently located Exhibitor Service Desk anytime during move-in and during show hours.

D: Thank you very much.

C: It's my pleasure.

参考译文

职员：早上好！需要我帮忙吗？

赵女士：早上好！我们是来自中国的出口商。我们如何登记？

职员：您在我们的网站上填写了相应的表格吗？

赵女士：是的，我们已经在线填写了。

职员：好的，请问您的姓名叫什么？

赵女士：多拉·赵。D-O-R-A, Z-H-A-O。

职员：让我看一下。啊，在这里。您的公司已经在线登记了。我能看看您的护照吗？

赵女士：好的，给你。

职员：谢谢。我们已经打印了您的表格。您有个人照片吗？

赵女士：有，给你。

职员：这是您的护照和您的参展商证。还能为您做些什么？

赵女士：我想了解一下展会的安排，好吗？

职员：当然可以，这是107届美国国际玩具博览会的手册。里面包括展会安排和每家公司的展位号。您的公司在三楼3B区。

赵女士：顺便问一下，这是我们公司第一次参加这里的玩具展，我们对这里的服务不太熟悉。

职员：我们会展中心欢迎来自世界各地的客人，我们也知道参展商可能不了解这里的服务。因此我们印制了"贾维茨工具包"。它介绍了这里所有的服务项目，包括电力、清洁、远程通信、展位餐饮服务、商务中心、银行服务、广告等。

赵女士：太好了。

职员：如果您需要预订，请拨打免费电话1-877-4 JAVITS (452-8487)，或登录www.JavitsCenter.com，或填写目录后的订单表格进行预订。如果您在会展期间还需要信息咨询及其他的服务，可以到就近的展商服务台咨询。

赵女士：多谢！

职员：乐意为您效劳。

Business Links

1. 会展参展流程

（1）参展企业与主办方联系，确定展位的面积和位置。

（2）填写展位申请表，并签字盖章。然后传真或邮寄至主办方。主办方盖章回传。双方各保留备份。主办方应及时给参展企业开展位费的发票。

（3）参展企业参照合同的截止日期付清展位款项。

（4）主办方给参展企业发送技术手册和市场手册，参展企业填写完成后及时寄回给主办方。市场手册（Marketing Manual），简称 MM，需要填写的内容包括客户基本信息（客户的基本信息将刊登在会刊上。）、翻译预订等。技术手册（Technical Manual），简称 TM，需要填写的内容包括额外展具的租赁、客户楣板信息、技术支持等。主办方收到文件后及时给参展企业开出服务发票。

（5）参展企业参照合同的截止日期付清服务款项。

（6）参展企业在确认展位后，若非经组委会同意，不得撤销参展申请。否则根据合同要求交纳赔偿金。

2. 办理海外采购商证

国外采购商在进入展厅之前必须先申办海外采购商证。海外采购商证可以在多届展会中循环使用。办证时须提供个人有效证件（个人有效身份证件包括：外国护照，华侨身份有效证件或有一年以上境外有效工作签证的中国护照，港、澳回乡证或身份证，台胞证）和个人近期证件照（规格为 5cm×4cm）。

3. 参展注意事项

（1）参展技巧：展览开幕前一定要与主办方或其他展会代理积极沟通。产品的运输和签证事宜一定宜早不宜迟。按时递交相关资料，准备展品运输。各种文件的填写必须准确、完整，以防在展前出现问题无法解决。

（2）展位设计：合理采用照明来突出展品的效果。展品的摆设要醒目，切忌凌乱，可以利用一些图片和饰物突出展品。除标准搭建外，参展商可以委托组委会或选择由组委会指定的展台搭建商制作特装展台，参展商需与搭建商落实展台设计、装修等相关事宜，并在展前商议布展活动安排。

（3）名片收集：携带足够多的名片，积极与买家交换名片。现场搜集展览相关资料：如展览会刊、参展商手册、宣传广告、竞争对手的宣传资料和主办方的调查表等。

（4）做好前期投入：对参展人员最好进行一个短期的培训，可以显著提高展览的效果。如果有可能，可以在会刊上刊登一些广告或者在展馆的广告牌上、宣传牌上印上产品的商标，也可以使观众在最短的时间内了解您的公司。

（5）展后安排：联系展会上对产品感兴趣的客户，给客户寄送产品目录和相关资料。与主办方联系，表达对展览的看法，提出意见。评估参展情况，是否达到预期目标。核算参展费用。总结参展经验，为下次参展作准备。展会后多与主办方沟通，了解市场最新动态及资讯。

Useful Sentences

1. 寒暄（Greeting）

（1）What can I do for you?
我能为你们做些什么？

（2）We want to apply for the overseas buyers' cards.
我们想申请办理海外采购商证。

（3）Can I help you?
需要我帮忙吗？

（4）I hope you will enjoy your stay with us.
希望您将在我们宾馆过得愉快。

（5）I hope you have enjoyed your stay with us.
希望您在我们宾馆过得愉快。

2. 报名登记（Registration）

（1）Excuse me, what should I do to apply for the credit card?
请问，申请信用卡需要办理什么手续？

（2）Firstly, please fill in the application form.
首先，请填写申请表。

（3）I want to check in, please.
请帮我登记入住。

（4）May I see your ID Card?
请出示您的身份证。

（5）May I see your passport?
我能看看您的护照吗？

(6) How long are you planning to stay in China?
您打算在中国待多久?

(7) What should we do for the registration?
我们如何登记?

(8) Have you filled in the forms at our website?
你们在我们的网站上填写表格了吗?

(9) Here are your passports and attendee's cards.
这是你们的护照和参展商证。

(10) Here's the brochure for the Food Fair.
这是本次食品展会的手册。

3. 打电话预约（Call to Make an Appointment）

(1) Would it be possible to see Mr. Chen sometime this week?
本周我能见到陈先生吗?

(2) I'd like to meet you the day after tomorrow.
希望后天能见到您。

(3) I'd like to talk to you about the new product.
我想与您谈谈新产品。

(4) I'd like to make an appointment with Mr. Chen.
我想约陈先生见面。

(5) May I make an appointment?
我能预约一下吗?

(6) I'd like to arrange a meeting to discuss our new order.
我想安排一个会议来讨论我们的新订单。

(7) Let's fix the time and the place of our meeting.
让我们定下会议的时间和地点。

(8) Can we make it a little later?
我们可以把时间推后一点吗?

(9) Do you think you could make it on Monday afternoon? That would suit me better.
可以定在星期一下午吗? 那对我来说可能更好。

(10) Would you please tell me when you are free?
请告诉我您何时有空?

4. 打电话取消预约（Call to Change an Appointment）

(1) I'd like to cancel my appointment with Mr. Scott.
我想取消我与斯科特先生的约会。

(2) Something urgent has come up. Could I postpone our appointment?
我突然有急事。能否推迟我们的约会?

(3) May I ask you to postpone the meeting until the day after tomorrow?
请您把会议推迟到后天好吗?

(4) I'm afraid I have to cancel my appointment.
恐怕我得取消预约。

(5) Will you change our appointment tomorrow at 10:00 to the day after tomorrow at the same time?
您可以把我们明天10点的约会改到后天相同的时间吗?

Chapter 2 商务会议（Business Meeting）

Business Situation 1

Mr. Denny Chen, sales manager of Shenzhen Ugo Sports Shoes Co., Ltd., and Miss Linda Zhang, chief seller of Shenzhen Ugo Sports Shoes Co., Ltd., are to hold a product showing meeting. Mr. Bruce Jackson, marketing manager of Fashion Way Co., Ltd. and Mr. Bill Jones are going to attend the product show meeting held by Shenzhen Ugo Sports Shoes Co., Ltd.

深圳 Ugo 运动鞋有限公司销售部经理陈先生和业务主管张小姐主持了公司的产品发布会。Fashion Way 公司的布鲁斯·杰克逊先生和比尔·琼斯先生参加了该发布会。

Dialogue

B = Bruce Jackson	W = Woman	D = Denny Chen	L = Linda Zhang

B: Excuse me. My name is Bruce Jackson. This is Mr. Bill Jones.

W: Have you pre-registered?

B: Yes, we have.

W: Oh, I got it. Here are your conference badges, your registration packets including a conference program, a map of Guangzhou, nearby restaurant information and other related materials.

B: Thank you very much.

W: You are welcome. By the way, conference papers are available on that long table across the hall on a first-come, first-service basis, and you'll find free coffee and freebies in the lounge behind you. The product introducing meeting begins in about half an hour in the Show Room.

B: Thank you very much.

(*About half an hour later*)

D: Ladies and gentlemen, may I have your attention, please? My name is Denny Chen, sales manager of Shenzhen Ugo Sports Shoes Co., Ltd. I am honored to chair this morning's meeting. It's my great pleasure this morning to welcome you, the distinguished guests from all over the world, to our product show meeting in the international fair. Miss Linda

Zhang, chief seller of our company, will be responsible for this morning's conference. She will review our accomplishment in the field of shoes manufacturing and introduce our fashionable shoes in detail. And she will introduce where our company will lead in the future. And now here comes Linda Zhang.

(*Applause*)

L: Good morning, ladies and gentlemen, and Mr. Chairman. Thank you for that kind introduction and let me also take this opportunity to present our company and introduce our new products to all of you here. We specialize in sports shoes for many years. Our company is one of the leaders in the shoes industry and we provide a unique collection of shoes for markets both at home and abroad. What I'd like to say is that we have just brought out some new models. It's a choice of variety of shoes which you can get nowhere other than from us... And finally, we have been on good terms with many of you. And of course, some of you are new here but that makes no difference. So, to you, we will not only make concessions in price, but also offer good commissions. This is our overall philosophy in doing business. I'm sure the commission we offer is really favorable. Here are our brochures and quotations, and you can have a closer look at them. If you have any question, just come to me.

参考译文

布鲁斯：对不起，我叫布鲁斯·杰克逊。这位是比尔·琼斯。

女士：你们预先报名了吗？

布鲁斯：是的，报过名了。

女士：啊，是的，那么这是您的胸牌和大会文件袋，其中有会议安排，广州地图，附近的宾馆分布图和其他会议相关材料。

布鲁斯：非常感谢。

女士：不用客气。顺便说下，会议材料在大厅对面的长桌上，先到先拿。在您身后的休息室里有免费供应的咖啡和赠品。产品介绍会议大约半小时后在会议室举行。

布鲁斯：非常感谢。

（大约半个小时后）

陈经理：先生们、女士们。请注意了。我是丹尼·陈，是深圳 Ugo 运动鞋有限公司的销售经理。今天上午的会议将由我主持。很高兴欢迎世界各地的嘉宾，来参加我公司在国际会展的产品发布会。今天早上的主要发言者是张琳达小姐，她是我们公司的销售主管。首先将为大家回顾我们公司在运动鞋制造业领域所创下的成绩，然后详细介绍我公司新款鞋，而且她会为大家介绍我公司的开拓方向。现在请张小姐发言。

（掌声）

张琳达：先生们、女士们、尊敬的主席，上午好。首先，我感谢主席和大家给我这次展示公司及介绍公司新产品的机会。我公司专业从事运动鞋业制作已有多年历史，现已成为运动鞋业的佼佼者，生产出深受国内外市场欢迎的各类特色运动鞋。我今天特意带来了一些我公司的新开发的鞋款。这些款型是我公司独家研发拥有的……最后，我公司已和许多来宾有融洽的合作关系，当然在座的也有些新面孔，但是没有关系。对各位来宾，我公司不仅在价格上有优惠，而且提供丰厚的佣金。这些是我公司宣传手册和报价，你们可以仔细看一下。有疑问的话，可以问我，我很乐意为大家服务。

Business Situation 2

Ms. Dora Zhao, Mr. Frank Li and Miss Anna Zhang, on behalf of Chenghai Toy Trading Co., Ltd. attend the opening ceremony of the 107th American International Toy Fair. After entering the exhibition hall, they meet and chat with their clients. On the opening ceremony, Mr. Carter Keithley, president of the Toy Industry Association makes a brief opening speech. Then Ms. Kimberly Carcone, director of Trade Show and Event Marketing, gives a brief introduction to the American International Toy Fair. Ms. Julie Livingston, Senior Director of Public Relations makes a closing speech.

澄海玩具贸易有限公司参展代表赵女士、李先生和张小姐等参加了第107届美国玩具展开幕式。他们进入会场后，与有些客户进行了对话。美国玩具工业协会主席卡特先生作了简短的讲话。美国玩具工业协会所属的贸易展览与活动策划委员会主任金伯莉·卡科恩女士对此次博览会的基本情况作了简要介绍。公关部主任朱莉娅·利文斯顿女士作了大会总结。

Dialogue

W = Woman	F = Frank Li	D = Dora Zhao
A = Anna Zhang	G = George Johnson	C = Carter Keithley
K = Kimberly Carcone	J = Julie Livingston	Ch = Chairman

W: Do you have an invitation letter?

F: Yes, right here.

D: Here is mine.

A: It's right here.

W: Thanks. Please come in.

(*Three minutes later, at the exhibition hall*)

A: Hi, George.

G: Hi, Anna. I hope this fair will be productive.

A: So do I. We cooperated with each other very well in the previous years, right?

G: Yes, we do appreciate for your effort in our pleasant cooperation. Shall we begin with a review of last time?

A: Yes, I would like a refresher.

(*Several minutes later*)

Ch: Ladies and gentlemen, allow me to call this meeting to order. The opening ceremony would start soon. Please get yourself seated. Thank you.

(*The opening ceremony will now begin.*)

Ch: Now I have the honor to call upon Mr. Carter Keithley, president of the Toy Industry Association.

C: Ladies and Gentlemen, good morning. It is really a great honor and pleasure for me to attend and speak at the opening ceremony of American International Toy Fair. Now, I have the pleasure to declare the 107th American International Toy Fair open. On behalf of Toy Industry Association, I extend my warmest welcome to all distinguished guests present here. And I wish the fair a complete success!

(*Applause*)

Ch: Ladies and gentlemen, distinguished guests, now, on this special occasion, Ms. Kimberly Carcone, director of Trade Show and Event Marketing will make a brief introduction to the fair. And now I give you Ms. Kimberly Carcone.

(*Applause*)

K: Ladies and gentlemen, good morning! I feel greatly honored to make a speech at the opening ceremony of American International Toy Fair. It is my privilege, on behalf of Toy Industry Association, to bid our distinguished guests a hearty welcome. The American International Toy Fair is one of a few major toy industry trade shows held around the world. The show is the largest toy trade show in the Western countries. It is held annually in mid-February in Jacob K. Javits Convention Center and is open to the toy trade only. It is staged by the Toy Industry Association. In 2008, more than 1,500 manufacturers, distributors, importers and sales agents from 30 countries exhibited their toys and entertainment products in over 300,000 square feet (28,000 m^2) of exhibit space.

We wish everyone achieve a great success on today's fair!

(*Applause*)

J: Thank you! Thank you all for coming and taking part in our fair. And this fair provides me with such an excellent opportunity to meet old friends and make new ones. For what we have already been able to do in cooperation, I give you my sincere thanks. On behalf of the sponsors, I wish to apologize for any inconvenience to any of the participants, especially the foreign guests. They may have had to suffer in connection with hotel accommodations, meals, or transportation. At last, wish our fair a success!

参考译文

女士：你们有邀请函吗？

李先生：有，在这里。

赵女士：这是我的。

张安娜：我的在这儿。

女士：谢谢！请进！

（三分钟后，在展厅）

张安娜：你好！乔治。

乔治：你好！安娜，我希望这次展会能给我们带来收获。

张安娜：我也希望这样。我们多年来合作得相当愉快，对吧？

乔治：是啊。我们非常感谢你们为顺利合作所作的不懈努力。要不我们从回顾上次合作开始？

张安娜：好的。我也想要回顾一下。

（几分钟后）

主持：女士们、先生们，请就位，开幕式即将开始。谢谢！

（开幕式开始）

主持：现在我很荣幸地请美国玩具工业协会主席卡特·吉时利先生讲话。

卡特：女士们、先生们，上午好。本人很荣幸也很高兴能够参加美国国际玩具展开幕式并且讲话。现在我很高兴地宣布第107届美国国际玩具展开幕！我谨代表玩具工业协会，对在座的各位贵宾表示最热烈的欢迎。预祝展会圆满成功！

（掌声）

主持：女士们、先生们，各位贵宾，在这个特别的时刻，我们欢迎贸易展览与活动策划委员会主任金贝莉女士对此次博览会的基本情况作简要介绍。诚请金贝莉女士讲话。

（掌声）

金伯莉：女士们、先生们，上午好！我很荣幸能够在美国国际玩具展开幕式上讲话。我谨代表玩具工业协会对各位来宾表示最诚挚的欢迎！美国国际玩具展会是西方第一大玩具贸易展会，也是世界级大型玩具博览会之一。它由美国玩具工业协会承办，每年2月中旬在纽约雅各布 K. 贾维茨会议中心举办。2008 年，来自 30 多个国家，超过 1 500 家制造商、销售商、进口商和销售代理商，在面积达 300 000 平方英尺（28 000 平方米）的展厅里展示了各式各样的玩具娱乐产品。我们祝各位在这次的展会上取得巨大成功！

（掌声）

朱莉娅：谢谢！感谢大家不辞辛苦地来参加此次展会。这次展会为我与各位新老朋友相聚提供了宝贵的机会。我对我们大家一直以来的愉快合作表示真诚地感谢！我谨代表主办方，对各位来宾，尤其是外国来宾，在酒店住宿、就餐和交通方面遇到的诸多不便，表示我们深深的歉意。最后，预祝本次展会圆满成功！

Business Links

1. 商务会议形式

一般的商务会议形式有项目会议（project meeting）、预算会议（budget meeting）、业务洽谈会（business negotiation）、订货会（order fair）、采购会（commodity fair）、新产品推广会（new product promotion）、集团公司董事会（board meeting）、客户联谊会（customer banquet）、行业研讨会（trade seminar）以及新闻发布会（press conference）等。

2. 参加会议时的注意事项

（1）开会时尽量选择靠近老板的位置

开会时，除非座位已事先安排，否则宜选择靠近老板或实权者的座位。这是团队精神的体现。

（2）开会时避免选择靠门窗的位置

因为门口是出入必经之地，人员的出入会打断你的发言，从而削弱你发言的分量。而且窗口的位置和名画或令人感兴趣的物品旁边的位置，容易使别人分散对你的注意力，不是好位置，宜避而远之。

3. 推广新产品

在商业会议中，通常采用新闻发布会（press conference）和产品发布会（product show meeting）等会议形式来宣传推广新产品。

4. 产品介绍会或产品发布会注意事项

产品发布会的目的是使新产品面市、达成销售意向。类似于订货会。新闻发布会一般针对对于企业意义重大，媒体感兴趣的事件举办。行业组织或政府举办的大型展览或会议，都会在筹备初期举办一次新闻发布会，以此来吸引更多的参展商和观展人员。我国对新闻发布会是有严格申报、审批程序的。对企业而言，没有必要如此繁琐，所以避免使用“新闻发布会”的字样而直接把发布会称为“信息发布会”或“媒体沟通会”即可。

在展会活动中，参展单位可以针对公司特点来召开产品发布会，类似于订货会。

5. 发布会的筹划

一般来说，发布会的筹划包括7大部分：

（1）活动策划与主题确定

发布会名字会印在关于新闻发布会的一切表现形式上，包括请柬、会议资料、会场布置和纪念品等。在选择新闻发布会的标题时，一般需要说明发布会的主旨内容，如：“某某企业2010新品信息发布会”。

（2）节目策划与议程安排

（3）资料准备

（4）同与会人员的邀请、沟通与确定

选择与会人员：事先发会议通知和议程，发出会议通知的同时必须明确会议主席、演讲人和会议日程安排。

（5）时间、场地落实与场景布置

时间、地点：包括开会日期、地点、开会时间长短。

设备：会议厅容纳人数、主席台的大小、投影设备、电源、布景、领夹式麦克风、远程麦克风。

（6）产品展示、演示与信息发布

提供给媒体的资料，一般以广告手提袋或文件袋的形式，整理妥当，按顺序摆放，再在新闻发布会前发放给新闻媒体，顺序依次应为：媒体通行证、会议议程、新闻通稿、演讲发言稿、发言人的背景资料介绍（应包括头衔、主要经历、取得成就等）、公司宣传册、产品说明资料、有关图片、纪念品（或纪念品领用券）、企业新闻负责人名片、空白信笺和笔。

（7）现场气氛控制

在发言人进行发言以后，有一个回答记者问的环节，现场气氛的控制需要较高的技巧。

6. 产品介绍会内容

（1）欢迎词

（2）公司介绍

（3）产品介绍、展示

（4）提供报价

（5）公众发言

（6）感谢词

Useful Sentences

1. 仪式致辞（Ceremonial Address）

（1）On the occasion of this opening ceremony, I would like to express my appreciation to the host for this opportunity to address the meeting on the topic of financial crisis.
值此大会开幕之际，我为能有机会就金融危机问题进行发言，向东道主致以谢意。

（2）It gives us a feeling of special joy to have the opportunity of entertaining our distinguished guests from India.
我们特别高兴能有机会招待我们的印度贵宾。

（3）We have prepared a humble welcome dinner to celebrate our friendly cooperation. I'd like to take this opportunity to express our sincere thanks to all the guests present here.
为庆祝我们的友好合作，我方准备了简单的欢迎宴会。我想借此机会对各位来宾表示诚挚的谢意。

（4）On behalf of the sponsors, I wish to apologize for any inconvenience to any of the participants, and especially the foreign guests, may have had to suffer in connection with hotel accommodation, meals, and transportation.
对于所有参加者，尤其是外国客人，由于旅馆的膳宿设备、餐点、交通所造成的诸多不便，本人谨代表主办方表示歉意。

（5）I'd like to end my speech. Thank you for your attention.
我的发言到此结束，谢谢各位。

2. 会议开始与介绍议程（Opening and Introducing the Procedures）

（1）Good morning/afternoon everyone. If we are all here let's get started/start the meeting/start.

早上/下午好！既然各位已就座了，就开始开会吧！

（2）We're pleased to welcome（name of participant）.

很高兴欢迎（人名）。

（3）So let's start with… /I'd suggest we start with…

让我们开始……/我建议我们开始……

（4）I think that takes care of the first item. Shall we leave that item?

我想第一项议题已讨论得很详细了，这项讨论就此结束吧？

（5）I'd like to hand over to（name）who is going to lead the next point.

我想让（人名）来主持下一项议题。

3. 总结与结束会议（Summarizing and Closing the Meeting）

（1）Before we close today's meeting, let me just summarize the main points.

在结束今天的会议之前，我来总结下会议主要议点。

（2）Right it looks as though we've covered the main items. If there are no other comments, I'd like to wrap this meeting up.

看起来我们已经涉及了主要议题。如果没有别的意见的话，我想宣布本次会议到此结束。

（3）I would like to conclude my speech with my best wishes to all distinguished guests here.

在结束讲话之际，我向在座各位嘉宾致以最美好的祝福。

（4）The meeting is finished we'll see each other next time.

会议到此结束，我们下次会议再见！

（5）In conclusion, I would like to express my wish to meet you again at our next meeting. Thank you for your attention!

最后，我希望我们能够在下次会议再度相会。谢谢各位的参加！

Chapter 3 在展厅 (At the Exhibition Hall)

Business Situation 1

Mr. Bruce Jackson, marketing manager of Fashion Way Co., Ltd., is visiting the booth of Shenzhen Ugo Sports Shoes Co., Ltd. Mr. Bill Jones, assistant manager goes with him. Miss Linda Zhang, chief seller of Shenzhen Ugo Sports Shoes Co., Ltd. is greeting them.

Fashion Way 公司的市场部经理布鲁斯·杰克逊先生和经理助理比尔·琼斯先生来到了深圳 Ugo 运动鞋有限公司的展位。该公司的业务主管张琳达小姐前来迎接。

Dialogue

L = Linda Zhang B1 = Bruce Jackson B2 = Bill Jones

L: If I'm not mistaken, you must be Bruce from Toronto.

B1: Yes, I'm Bruce Jackson. Here is my card.

L: Pleased to meet you, Mr. Jackson. I'm Linda Zhang, chief seller of Shenzhen Ugo Sports Shoes Co., Ltd. Our sales manager, Mr. Denny Chen asked me to meet you because he is chairing a meeting at this moment. He sends his warmest regards.

B1: Oh, nice to meet you, Miss Zhang.

(*They exchange their calling cards.*)

L: How was your flight?

B1: The flight was smooth, and the service was good. Things couldn't have been better.

L: Is this your first trip to China? How did you find Guangzhou?

B1: Actually, I have been in China before, but this is my first time in Guangzhou. It's a beautiful city. I like it very much. I also love the architecture here. It's stunning.

L: Yes, Guangzhou is a very beautiful city indeed. I hope you'll have a pleasant stay.

B1: Thank you!

L: Is that the assistant manager over there?

B1: Yes, it is.

L: I haven't met him yet.

(*Mr. Bill Jones approaches them.*)

B1: Linda. I would like you to meet my assistant manager, Bill Jones. Bill, this is Linda Zhang.

B2: Hello, Ms. Linda Zhang.

L: Linda, please. "Ms. Linda Zhang" makes me sound so ancient.

B2: Fine, Linda. And I'm Bill. You see, we are all very excited to be here in China. We are looking forward to working with you.

L: So am I. I want to extend my personal earnest welcome to all of you and sincerely hope that your visit here will be rewarding.

B1 and B2: Thank you!

L: Well, to start the ball rolling, may I introduce our products to you?

B1 and B2: Great! Thanks!

参考译文

张琳达：没错的话，您应该是来自多伦多的布鲁斯吧？

布鲁斯：没错，我是布鲁斯·杰克逊。这是我的名片。

张琳达：很高兴见到你，杰克逊先生。我是深圳 Ugo 运动鞋有限公司的销售主管张琳达。我们销售经理此时正在主持一个会议，所以我在这里迎接你们。他要我先代他向你们致意。

布鲁斯：非常高兴见到你，张小姐。

(双方互换名片。)

张琳达：空中旅行怎么样？

布鲁斯：一路很顺利，服务很周到，一切都再好不过了。

张琳达：这是您第一次来中国吗？您觉得广州这个城市怎么样？

布鲁斯：其实我来过中国，不过，这是我第一次到广州。这是座很美丽的城市，我很喜欢。我很喜欢这里的建筑，很迷人。

张琳达：是的。广州的确很漂亮。希望您在这里过得愉快！

布鲁斯：谢谢！

张琳达：那位是您的经理助理吗？

布鲁斯：是的。

张琳达：我还没见过他呢。

(比尔·琼斯正走近他们。)

布鲁斯：琳达，我想给你介绍下我的助理经理比尔·琼斯。比尔，这位是张琳达。

比尔：您好！张琳达女士。

张琳达：叫我琳达就可以了。"张琳达女士"听起来有点生分了。

比尔：好的，琳达。你就叫我比尔好了。你知道，我们都很兴奋能来广州。期待与你的合作。

张琳达：这也是我的愿望。对诸位的来访，我本人表示诚挚的欢迎，并衷心祝愿你们取得圆满的成功。

布鲁斯和比尔：谢谢！

琳达：那么就从介绍我们的产品开始吧？

布鲁斯和比尔：太好了！谢谢！

Business Situation 2

Mr. Mark Schultz and Ms. Carolyn Cardinal from Irwin Toy Inc. come to the booth of Chenghai Plastic Toy Trading Co., Ltd. . Miss Anna Zhang, chief seller of Chenghai Toy Trading Co., Ltd. is greeting them.

美国 Irwin 玩具公司市场部经理马克·舒尔茨先生和销售部经理卡罗琳·卡迪纳尔女士，来到澄海玩具贸易有限公司的展柜前。业务主管张安娜小姐上前迎接。

Dialogue

M = Mark Schultz	C = Carolyn Cardinal	A = Anna Zhang	F = Frank Li

A: Hi, Ms. Carolyn Cardinal.

C: Hi, there. I'm so happy to see you again, Anna. I'd like you to meet Mr. Mark Schultz, our marketing manager.

A: How do you do?

M: It's a pleasure to meet you, Anna.

A: May I introduce my colleagues to you? This is Ms. Dora Zhao, our assistant manager. This is Mr. Frank Li, our sales manager.

F: How do you do, Mark.

M: How do you do.

D: I am very glad to meet you, Mark and Carolyn.

(*They shake hands and then exchange their calling cards.*)

A: Mr. Mark Schultz, you know, I've heard a lot about you.

M: Really? I hope it's not anything bad about me.

A: Not at all. You are very popular. Everything I've heard has been good! So you're the one responsible for those outstanding sales figures I've seen.

M: Thank you. You flattered me. I must say I have a great team. You see, I am here because your toys are really appealing to me. We're happy to see that the goods here are similar to the catalogues and the samples we received from your company. These items are most saleable in our market. By the way, in your product showing meeting and press conference, your products, presentation, and hospitality really impressed me.

A: Thank you! I'm very glad to hear that. By the way, we have a lot of new toys on display. Would you like to have a look at them? Any question, please feel free to let me know.

C and M: Thank you!

A: You are welcome!

(*Several minutes later*)

M: What a spacious showroom! I wonder if you have the time to show me around your showroom.

A: Yes, it is a great showroom. It is divided into three sections. In this section, we can see newly modified models. Well, the toys on the right are electronic toys and intellectual toys, suitable for children from the age of five and upward. They are cute, aren't they? It's a choice of variety of toys which you can get nowhere other than from us. And here on the left are plush stuffed toys. Teary bears, Mickey Mouse, Snoopy, deer, sheep, tigers, pandas, and whatever you name. Don't you think they are lovely? Our products are very popular in many parts of the world, because we are very particular about the quality of the toys. If you have a closer look at them and you know I'm telling the truth.

M: I'm looking for some electronic toys — something nice, but not too expensive. Would you recommend some to me?

A: I'd love to. Here are our new or modified models. Now I would like to recommend specially a new model of racing cars to you. You press this button and it starts to go. You see it's now turning around the corner. And it can reverse and change its routes and directions. It is very easy to operate. The thing you only have to do is to press the green buttons here. And I have something more interesting to show, a toy plane. It is a remote control plane. We have two buttons to control the movement and altitude. It also has two selectable speed controls. The most exciting thing about it is its skillful maneuver. When it flies to a certain height, it can do trick flying. It's a shame that I can't show you how it works here in this showroom. All boys love it, and of course many girls love it, too.

M: What's the price of this racing car?

A: This racing car costs US $20. Now, we also offer good commissions. We can allow you an eleven percent commission for an order exceeding \$10,000 and 15 percent for an order over \$30,000. I'm sure the commission we offer is really very favorable.

M: Anyway, I was greatly impressed by your showroom, and we'll study your catalogues further and let you know our decision as early as possible.

A: Thank you. I look forward to your early reply.

参考译文

张安娜：您好！卡罗琳·卡迪纳尔女士。

卡罗琳：您好！很高兴再次见到你，安娜。我想介绍我们的市场部经理马克·舒尔茨先生给您认识。

张安娜：您好！

马克：安娜，很荣幸认识您。

张安娜：请允许我介绍我的同事们给您认识。这位是我们公司的经理助理赵女士，这位是我们的销售经理李先生。

李先生：您好！马克。

马克：您好！

赵女士：很高兴认识你们，马克，卡洛琳。

（互相握手并交换名片。）

张安娜：马克·舒尔茨先生，久闻您大名哦。

马克：真的吗？希望您听说的不是我的坏事。

张安娜：根本不是什么坏事。您非常受欢迎。我所听说的都是很好的事情。您取得了很突出的销售业绩呢。

马克：谢谢！您过奖了。那是因为我们优秀团队的努力。现在我在这里是因为贵公司的玩具特别吸引人呢。我们很高兴贵公司展示的产品和贵公司寄给我们的产品目录和样品非常相似。那些产品在我们的市场很畅销。另外，在贵公司产品展示会和新闻发布会上，贵公司所展示的产品、展示方式，还有友好热情真的让人很难忘。

张安娜：谢谢！很高兴您能这么说。顺便说一下，我们还展示了很多新玩具。来看一看吗？如果你们有什么问题，尽管来问我。

卡罗兰和马克：谢谢！

张安娜：不客气。

（几分钟后）

马克：展示厅真大啊！不知道你有时间可以带我参观一下吗？

张安娜：我们的展示厅很大，分为三部分。在这个展厅，我们可以看到很多新开发的产品。请看我右手边的玩具，这些玩具是电子玩具和智力开发玩具，适合五岁以上的儿童玩。很可爱，对吧？

这些新款质量上乘，在别的地方根本买不到。

左手边这里是长毛绒填充玩具。玩具熊、米老鼠、史奴比、鹿、绵羊、虎、熊猫，什么都有。它们很可爱吧？我们的产品在世界很多地方深受欢迎，因为我们非常重视玩具的质量。如果你们仔细看，就知道我说的都是实话。

马克：我想看看你们的电子玩具，要质量好点的，但是价格不要很贵。你能给我推荐几种吗？

张安娜：当然可以。这些是我们新推出的或者改进型的款式。现在，我想特意给你们推荐一款新型赛车。你按一下这个按钮，它就动起来了。你看，现在它在墙角拐弯了。而且，它还可以倒车，变换线路和改变方向。操作起来也非常方便，只要按这几个绿色按钮就行了。接下来，我要给你们展示一件更有趣的玩具，一架玩具飞机。这是个遥控玩具，上面有两个按钮控制运动和飞行高度，它还有两个调速装置。而这个玩具最让人兴奋的是：它可以做特级动作。很可惜我不能在展室里给你们演示。所有的男孩子都喜欢这个玩具；当然，很多女孩子也喜欢。

马克：这个电动玩具车价格怎样？

张安娜：这种电动玩具车 20 美元。现在，我们提供丰厚的佣金，如果订货量超过 10 000 美元，我们给 11% 佣金；超过 30 000 美元，佣金将达到 15% 。我可以说，我们的佣金真的非常优厚了。

马克：你们的展室给我留下了很深的印象。我们将对你们的产品目录作进一步的研究，也会尽早通知你们我们的研究决定。

张安娜：谢谢！我期待早日得到你们的回复。

Business Links

1. 展会上接待客户步骤

（1）打招呼

（2）双手递上产品目录

（3）索取名片

（4）把名片订在记录本上，认真记录客户信息

（5）介绍产品

2. 行为举止

在会展活动中，参展人员是公司的形象代表。衣着要整洁大方，形象端庄。接待顾客时要热情，言谈举止要富有感染力。要大力宣传自己的产品和企业。在参观者看来，你就代表着你的企业。你的言行举止和神情都会对参观者认识你的企业产生极大影响。留心观察每一个走过的

客户，看到有人朝展品看过5秒钟便去打招呼，并且尽量让他们走进你的展台，把第一个可以推荐的产品讲解给他听。注意不要有怠慢参观者的表现，哪怕几秒钟也不行，谁都不喜欢被怠慢。如果有人过来时你正忙，不妨先打招呼或让他加入你们的交谈。站立的位置不要拦路，也不要在展位前遮挡参观者视线的地方，要靠边站在过道边上。

3. 交换名片

交换名片遵循的原则是由尊到卑，如果搞不清楚关系，则由近及远。介绍时的顺序，遵循的原则是从卑到尊，从低职位到高职位。从辈分上讲，先幼后长。如果有女士的话，先男士后女士。自我介绍的时候，长话短说，废话不说，没话不要找话说，但介绍要完整。一般来说，常见的介绍顺序是把男士介绍给女士，并引导男士到女士面前作自我介绍。介绍的时候，一定把被介绍的女士的名字优先提到。把比较年轻的人介绍给年长者时，则要首先提到年长者的名字。在商务场所，会谈的时候都是先介绍职位高的，再介绍职位低的。一般不让长者或者高管们久等。这些都是基本常识，在商务场合，能体现介绍者的素养和知识层面。因此，在作介绍时一定要特别注意。

4. 接送客户

除非客户明确提出接机或送机要求，否则双方只要按照约定的时间和地点会见即可，工作结束以后客户会安排自己的其他行程，例如私人拜访、旅游等。

Useful Sentences

1. 首次见面（To Someone You Have Never Met Before）

(1) If I'm not mistaken, you must be Miss Anderson from Sydney.
如果没弄错的话，您应该是来自悉尼的安德森小姐吧？

(2) How do you do? I'm Tom Smith. I've been looking forward to meeting you.
您好，我叫汤姆·史密斯，我一直期盼与您会面。

(3) Excuse me, but aren't you Mr. Johnson from American Express?
不好意思，您不是来自美国运通的约翰逊先生吗？

(4) It is my pleasure to meet you, Mr. White. Welcome to China.
很荣幸能认识您，怀特先生，欢迎您到中国来。

(5) I am delighted to make your acquaintance.
很高兴和您认识。

2. 老友相逢（To a Friend You Haven't Seen for Some Time）

（1）It's so good to see you again, Mr. Simpson. How are you keeping?
很高兴再次遇见您，辛普森先生。境况如何？

（2）I'm so glad to meet you here in shanghai.
很高兴能在上海与您会面。

（3）Mr. Zhang, great to see you again!
张先生，很高兴再次见到您！

（4）I am happy to meet you, how is everything?
很高兴遇见您，一切如何啊？

（5）So nice to meet you here. Haven't seen you for ages!
真高兴能在这里遇见您。很久都没见到您了！

3. 介绍个人（Introducing an Individual）

（1）By the way, I don't think you've met my assistant, Jenny.
顺便说下，我觉得你们还没有见过我的助理珍妮吧。

（2）Mr. Brown, may I introduce you to Miss Wu, the assistant manager of our company?
布朗先生，我可以把您介绍给我公司经理助理吴小姐吗？

（3）Chen, I'd like you to meet Tom, a good friend of mine.
陈，我来给你介绍一下，这是我的好朋友汤姆。

（4）Our manager Mr. Deng asked me to say hello to you. He's sorry he can't come over to meet you personally.
我们的经理邓先生让我转达对你的问候，他很抱歉不能亲自来见你。

（5）I'd like you to meet Mr. Zhao, sales manager of our company.
我来给你介绍一下，这是我们公司的销售经理赵先生。

4. 介绍团体（Introducing a Group）

（1）Please allow me to introduce my colleagues. This is Bob Mondale, my partner. This is Charles Brown, my marketing manager. This is Allen Bell, my production manager. The last, is my right arm, Cindy Black, my secretary.
请允许我介绍下我的同事们。这位是鲍勃・蒙代尔，我的搭档。这位是查尔斯・布朗，营销部经理。这位是艾伦・贝尔，生产部经理。最后在我右边的是我的秘书辛迪・布莱克。

（2）Now, I'd like to introduce my people to you. This is Wang Dali, the counterpart of Mr. Brown. This is Dai Lian, our vice president of finance department. And this is Xiao Linlin, the head of my office.

现在我想把我方人员介绍给您认识。这位是王大力，与贵方布朗先生的职务相同。这位是戴连，我方财务部副主席。而这位是肖琳琳，我方办公室主任。

(3) This is one of the most important departments of our corporation — Business Department. Here is Mr. Wang, manager of the department and on his left is Ms. Liu, assistant manager of the same department.

这是我们公司的经营部，是公司最重要的部门之一。这位是经营部经理王先生，在他左边的是经营部副经理刘女士。

(4) May I have the honor to introduce our main members of the delegation to all of you present here? This is Mr. Liu, leader of our delegation, and here is Ms. Wu, secretary of our delegation.

请允许我很荣幸地为在座各位介绍我们代表团的主要成员。这位是我们代表团团长刘先生，而这位是代表团秘书吴女士。

(5) It gives me great pleasure to have a chance to be with the members of German Delegation, who have been invited to this country.

能有机会在这里与应邀到我国来进行访问的德国代表团成员们在一起，对我来说是莫大的愉快。

Chapter 4 产品介绍 (Introduction to Products)

Business Situation 1

Bruce Jackson and Bill Jones are visiting the booth, Denny Chen and Jack Wu are introducing the products to them.

布鲁斯·杰克逊和比尔·琼斯来到展位参观，丹尼·陈和杰克·吴向他们介绍产品。

Dialogue

B1 = Bruce Jackson　D = Denny Chen　J = Jack Wu　B2 = Bill Jones

D: Mr. Jackson, I'm greatly honored to have the opportunity to make the presentation to you. If you have questions, please feel free to interrupt at any time.

B1: OK.

D: Let's move along the booth. On display here, we have the right product range for today's market place. Look, this is our latest development. The model is with high performance. We put it on the market just two months ago.

B1: No wonder I have never seen it before. Can you give me some details about it?

D: With pleasure. As you can see, the Single Roller Shoes are made by PU upper and rubber sole with one durable PU wheel, it can be used for both ground skating and walking.

B1: Ah, it looks quite smart.

D: You said it. It is a good product suitable for sports, especially suitable for children's recreation and sports.

B1: This product seems so different.

D: Yes, we are on the cutting edge of design.

J: And yet, this particular model features its roller. Look, the roller can be retractable controlled by a button.

B1: It sounds quite creative.

D: Yes, it is so cool that it has become a great favorite with young people.

We have already had a large market share in the United States and the Europe.

B2: That's great. What's your model range?

J: We have size EU 29 to 44, MOQ 2,400 pairs per style including three colors and one size range. The styles and colors vary according to the clients' demand.

B1: Good, I think we have already seen some items we might like to order, although we would still like to study them a bit more.

D: We are willing to be at your service as always.

参考译文

陈经理：杰克逊先生，很荣幸能向您作产品介绍。如果您有什么问题，可以随时问我。

布鲁斯：好的。

陈经理：我们沿着展位来参观。陈列在这里的这些产品系列都是顺应市场需要的。这是我们最新开发的产品。这个型号产品的性价比很高，两个月前才投放到市场。

布鲁斯：难怪以前我没见过。能否请你更详细地介绍？

陈经理：好的。正如您所看到的，这种单轮溜冰鞋鞋面采用人造皮革，橡胶底上带有一个相当耐久的轮子，这种鞋可用来滑旱冰也可用来行走。

布鲁斯：啊，看上去挺不错的。

陈经理：是的。这是一种非常适合运动的产品，尤其适合孩子们休闲运动。

布鲁斯：挺与众不同的。

陈经理：是的，我们在设计方面很先进。

吴先生：这种产品的特别之处在于其滑轮。它的滑轮是可拉回的，由一个按钮来控制就行啦。

布鲁斯：挺有创意的。

陈经理：这种鞋挺酷的，所以极受年轻人的欢迎。它在美国和欧洲占有很大的市场份额。

比尔：很好。这种型号都有什么尺寸呢？

吴先生：尺寸从29码到44码不等。最小订货量2 400双，每款包三种颜色和全部尺码，款式和颜色均可按客户要求定做。

布鲁斯：好的。这些产品中有些将是我们会购买的，但是我们还需要进一步的了解。

陈经理：乐意之至。

Business Situation 2

Mr. Mark Schultz, marketing manager and Ms. Carolyn Cardinal, sales manager from Irwin Toy Inc. are visiting the booth of Chenghai Toy Trading Co., Ltd. Mr. Frank Li, sales manager and Miss. Anna Zhang, the chief seller are introducing their products.

Irwin 玩具公司的市场部经理马克·舒尔茨先生和销售部经理卡罗琳·卡迪纳尔女士来到澄海玩具贸易有限公司展位参观。澄海玩具贸易有限公司销售部经理李先生和业务主管张安娜小姐正在向他们介绍产品。

Dialogue

F = Frank Li	M = Mark Schultz
C = Carolyn Cardinal	A = Anna Zhang

F: Mr. Schultz, welcome to our booth.

M: Thank you. Would you please show us around? We would like to look over your selection first.

F: My pleasure. Mr. Schultz, Ms. Cardinal, this way, please. On display here, we have the right product range for today's market place.

M: Your products seem so different. I have never seen these ideas.

F: Thank you. As you know, we are on the cutting edge of design.

C: Mr. Li, could you tell us more about your line of toys?

F: With pleasure. Look, this Remote Control Dancing Car is our latest development. The car can move forward, backward and turn left or right. The selling point is its MP3 function and dancing function with flash light. What's more, it includes 4pcs of 1G Automatic Demonstration. We are sure this car would enjoy wide popularity among the kids.

M: It sounds quite creative.

C: How about the frequency?

F: The frequency is 27MHZ to 49MHZ.

C: What about the power?

F: 3. 6V battery. The vehicle comes with a 3. 6V rechargeable battery and a recharger. The controller requires 2 AA batteries which are not included.

C: How about the color and the painting of the vehicle?

A: Oh, the painting is the same as this sample. There are three colors: blue, yellow and green.

M: Good. One more thing, that's about the safety standard. We would like to know whether your products meet the CPSIA requirements?

F: You can be assured of that. All our products have passed the test under the CPSIA requirements. You see, the painting of this vehicle is in environmental protection paint.

M: Please provide us the Certificate of Conformity. It is quite necessary for us to decide the items of our order.

A: Here they are, Mr. Schultz.

M: Thanks.

(*Mark Schultz has a look at the Certificate.*)

M: I think some items here are of our interest. But we still need to study them a bit more and get back to you.

F: We are glad you stopped by our exhibit. We hope to hear from you soon.

参考译文

李经理：舒尔茨先生，欢迎参观我们的展位。

马克：谢谢。能否请您带我们看看？我们想先看看你们的展品。

李经理：好的。舒尔茨先生，卡迪纳尔小姐，这边请。陈列在这里的产品系列都是顺应市场需要的产品。

马克：你们的产品挺与众不同的。我从没见过这些创意。

李经理：多谢夸奖。众所周知，我们的设计很先进。

卡罗琳：李先生，能否请您详细介绍你们的玩具？

李经理：好的。这种遥控跳舞车是我们最新开发的产品。它能前进、后退、左转、右转。其卖点在于 MP3 功能和带闪灯的跳舞功能，而且还包含 4 个 1 G 的功能自动演示。相信这种跳舞车会深受孩子们的欢迎。

马克：听上去挺有创意的。

卡罗琳：频率是多少？

李经理：频率是 27 兆赫到 49 兆赫。

卡罗琳：电力是多少呢？

李经理：3.6 伏。随车配有一块 3.6 伏可充电电池和一个充电器。遥控器则需要 2 节 AA 电池，不过这不在配件里。

卡罗琳：车身颜色和图案怎么样？

张安娜：图案跟样品一样。有三种颜色：蓝、黄、绿。

马克：挺好的。还有一点就是关于安全标准。你们的产品是否达到了《消费品安全改进法案》的要求？

李经理：这点你大可放心。我们所有的产品均通过了《消费品安全改进法案》的检测。你看，车身上的油漆全部都采用了环保漆呢。

马克：那你们要提供相关合格证书。我们需要以此来决定订购的项目。

张安娜：舒尔茨先生，这是合格证书，请过目。
马克：谢谢。
（舒尔茨先生翻阅合格证书。）
马克：我们对有些产品挺感兴趣的，不过我们还要再研究后才能答复你们。
李经理：很高兴你们能参观我们的展位。希望能尽快得到你们的答复。

Business Links

1. 展台的类型

国际标准展台的尺寸是 10ft×10ft×8.3ft（国内为长 3 m×宽 3m×高 2.7m）。这种展台对一个小型企业或某一个单项产品的展出是很适宜的，而大型企业则可以考虑 3m×3m×4m，3m×3m×6m，3m×3m×8m，3m×3m×10m，或更大一些的。这要根据参展的实际情况和展出的内容多少来确定。总之，选择展台一定要大小适当。

展会组织者将展馆面积分割成两种形式进行出租。

其一是以标准摊位为基本单位出租。一般情况下，组织者在摊位中为参展商预先配置了一系列的基本设施，包括三面展板墙、地毯、公司中英文名称及展台号的楣板、两只射灯、一个电源插座、一张信息桌、两把折椅、一个废纸篓。不同的组织者会根据实际情况另行决定基本配置。一个展台的价格包含了基本设施的费用。参展商可按需租用面积更大的展台，或两个以上的展台。此类标准展台的特点是价格较低，便于参展商布置和展示产品，不需花费很多精力和时间即可完成布展。

另一种出租方式是以光地面积租订，通常规定在 $27m^2$ 或 $36m^2$ 以上起租。如参展商租用光地，则组织者仅需划定相应区域的面积给参展商即可，而无需另外提供基本设施。光地租订者需自行安排展台的设计、搭建以及展台设施的配备、电箱租用等。此类光地租用的特点是面积大，展示效果突出，对观众的吸引力大，适合于有经济实力的大公司和跨国企业的形象推广。

展览会中的展台主要有 4 种基本类型。由于展台的位置不同，展台开口也有差别。如果一个展台的左右侧都有展台，那么这个展台只有一面开口，称做“linear stand”。如果一个展台处于两条过道交叉口，这个展台就有两个开口，称做“corner stand”。如果一个展台三面都是过道，那么这个展台就称做“peninsular stand”或“head stand”。同理，四面都有过道的展台叫做“island stand”。4 种类型分别称为排式展台、环型展台、半岛型展台和岛型展台。所有租出的展台面积称为“net space”，而展会所使用的全部面积称为“gross space”。

2. 展台的布置

展台布置是在限定的时间内，将道具、展品、说明等放置在展台的最合适位置。展台布置对展示效果有直接的影响，主要分为展示的宣传内容与展示的物品内容。

（1）*展示的宣传内容*

展示的宣传内容要力求突出企业的名称（或团体的名称）、商标（徽标）、产品名称和要展出的主要内容名称。如果是企业，还要注意突出企业的领导人（企业无形资产的一部分）、企业的简介、主要的代表形象（如吉祥物、建筑物、标志等）。

（2）*展示的物品内容*

展示的物品内容是指一个企业或团体需要向外介绍或展示的新产品、新项目、新发明、新技术、新设备等。在展品的选择上，要选择能体现自身优势的展品。样品必须经过严格的挑选，一定不能存在质量问题。摆设展品时根据公司自己的摊位面积，把握好参展品的数量和质量，不宜过多，否则会给人一种拥挤感；当然也不宜过少，否则会给人空荡感。主打产品、新产品和热销产品应该摆放在醒目的位置。展品摆放时要具体设计好位置，做到高低起伏、错落有致、层次分明。

3. 资格认证、合格证书

根据2008年8月14日颁布的美国《消费品安全改进法案》，自2008年11月12日起，美国将执行新的消费品进口规定。自实施之日起，生产商和进口商必须提交书面证书，保证用于仓储或消费的进口产品符合美国消费品安全委员会的规章、禁令、规定或管理标准。

合格证书的要求包括：

（1）必须基于一个合理的检测程序

（2）必须由供应链上的两个或三个环节的经营者共同或单独出具（如：生产商、进口商和自有品牌商等）

（3）必须附在产品上或与产品一同装运

（4）必须提供给该产品的每个分销商或零售商

集装箱内的每个产品须配备一个独立证书。如发现产品无证书或证书错误，该批货物将可能不予通关或被销毁。合格证书必须包含生产商、进口商和保存检测结果记录人员的全部联系方式；必须列明该产品适用的具体标准；还必须标明生产地点和日期。除了这项规定外，《消费品安全促进法》还要求：自2008年年底起，所有儿童产品的生产商和进口商须提供由认可实验室出具的第三方检测证书。

4. 《消费品安全改进法案》

CPSIA 是 Consumer Product Safety Improvement Act 的缩写，即美国《消费品安全改进法案》。该法案除了对儿童产品中铅含量的要求更为严格外，还对玩具和儿童护理用品中的有害物质邻苯二甲酸盐的含量作出新的规定。此外，该法案还要求建立消费品安全公共数据库。《消费品安全改进法案》影响着美国所有生产、进口、分销玩具、服装和其他儿童产品及护理品的相关行业。所有制造商应该保证其产品符合该法案的所有规定。禁令、标准或者规则。现在，所有相关产品在进入美国市场以前，必须通过美国消费品安全委员会（CPSC）认可检测机构检测，否则将面临巨额罚款并导致出口中断。

Useful Sentences

1. 描述产品（Describing Products）

（1）— I have never seen this type of product before.
我从没见过这种产品。
— Yes. It is new on the market.
没错这是新产品。
— Is this available now in retail store?
零售店现在有卖的吗？
— It will be available starting next month.
下个月起开始有售。

（2）— What can you tell me about this product?
你能给我介绍一下这种产品吗？
— Sure. This one features its high quality and compact size.
当然可以。这种产品的特点在于其高质量和小体积。

（3）— Can you give me some information /details about this?
你能更详细地给我介绍一下这种产品吗？
— My pleasure. This is one of our newly developed products.
好的。这是我们新开发的一种产品。
— What is its material?
它是用什么材料做的？
— It is made of high-technology waterproof material. The distinction is its light weight.
它采用了高科技防水材料。其特点是非常轻。

（4）— Do any of your skates come with brakes?
你们的溜冰鞋带制动的装置吗？

— Yes, these skates are equipped with unique safety features.

是的，这些溜冰鞋都有特殊的安全装置。

— What's your model range?

都有什么型号呢？

— It ranges from 4 cubic feet to 5 cubic feet.

从4立方英尺到5立方英尺不等。

(5) — The toys look quite smart. Can you tell what's their features?

这些玩具挺有趣的。你能介绍一下它们的特别之处吗？

— Yes. They are specially designed for the children from 3 to 10.

好的。这些玩具是专门为3到10岁的孩子设计的。

— Are they safe?

它们安全吗？

— Yes. They have passed several inspections.

是的。我们的产品通过很多次检验。

2. 销售展示（Sales Demonstration）

(1) — Do you have the program with you?

你有这套软件吗？

— Yes, it is installed in this computer.

有，软件就安装在这台电脑里。

— Can I see how it works?

我能看一下它是怎样操作的吗？

— Sure, let me give you a quick demonstration.

行，我来给你作一个大概的演示。

(2) — Would you like to see a demonstration?

您要不要看看展示？

— Yes, but I have little time.

好，不过我时间不多。

— It won't take long. Look, ...

不会占用太多时间。看，……

— Good. The picture is really clear.

不错。图像挺清晰的。

(3) — Are people confused by all these buttons?

人们会不会被这些按钮弄糊涂了？

— It isn't complicated. Here, let me show you.

这并不复杂。我来展示给你看。

(4) — Could we see the specifications for the X200?

我们可以看一下X200型的详细规格吗？

（5）— Let me tell you about our product.
关于产品一事让我向你说明。

（6）— This is our most recently developed product.
这是我们最近开发的产品。

（7）— We'd like to recommend our new home health monitor.
我们想推荐我们新的家庭健康监测器。

3. 介绍产品（Introducing Products）

（1）We've already had a big demand for this product.
这种产品我们已有很大的需求量。

（2）This product is doing very well in foreign countries.
这种产品在国外很畅销。

（3）Our product is competitive in the international market.
我们的产品在国际市场上具有竞争力。

（4）Can you tell me about this model?
能请你介绍这一款产品吗？

（5）Yes. This particular model features much smaller occupancy of the space, and the capacity is very suitable to the needs of hotel rooms and college dormitories.
好的。这种型号所占空间较小，其容量特别适合酒店房间和大学宿舍用。

（6）Yes, our market analysis tells us our prime users will be between 40 and 60.
好的，我们的市场分析告诉我们，我们产品主要使用者的年龄将在40岁至60岁之间。

Chapter 5 商谈价格（On Prices）

Business Situation 1

Mr. Bruce Jackson is now having a talk with Mr. Denny Chen about the prices of the single roller shoes. Bruce would like to have 5% off, but Manager Chen insists 2% off only.

布鲁斯·杰克逊先生和陈经理正在商谈单轮滑冰鞋的价格。布鲁斯想要对方降价 5%，但陈经理只同意降 2%。

Dialogue

B1 = Bruce Jackson	D = Denny Chen	J = Jack Wu	B2 = Bill Jones

B1: Mr. Chen, we are quite interested in this single roller shoes, so can you give me your unit price on CIF Toronto?

D: Let me check the price brochure and figure out. Well, here it is. It only costs US$11.

B1: Is this the lowest price you can offer? I hope you can give us your best offer. If your price is competitive, I'll place an order with you right now.

D: It's very nice of you to say so. As we know, the costs of the materials for our commodities have risen a lot in recent years, but all our prices still keep reasonable. Moreover, this single roller shoes are in the latest design and of reliable quality.

B1: What you said sounds quite true. But you see, due to the financial crisis, our customers care so much about the price, and the sales volume in the supermarkets of our country have fallen rapidly. If you can cut down your price by 5%, I think it would do great help to push our sales.

D: Well, Mr. Jackson, I understand the sales situation in your country. But when we compare prices, we must take the quality of goods into consideration, right? I'm afraid the 5% reduction isn't going to be possible. It is as far as we could go. However, in order to promote our business relationship, we are prepared to reduce our price by 2% per unit, for a minimum order of over a 40 feet container.

B1: It's still too high. Can you drop another 2%?

D: I'm sorry, we really can't. This is really the best discount we can give.

B1: Hmm... I appreciate your sincerity in this transaction. OK, we accept this price.

D: I'm glad we've come to an agreement on price. Let's have a cup of coffee first, and we'll go on to the other terms and conditions later.

B1: OK.

J: Mr. Jackson, Mr. Jones, have a cup of coffee, please.

B1: Thank you.

B2: Thank you.

参考译文

布鲁斯:陈先生,我们对这款单轮滑冰鞋挺感兴趣的,请你给我们报多伦多成本、保险加运费的单价。

陈经理:让我查一查商品价目册算一下。哦,在这里。每双只需11美元。

布鲁斯:这是最低价了吗?希望你能给我们报最低价。如果你们的价格有竞争力,现在我就下订单。

陈经理:谢谢您这么说。您也知道,近年我们产品的材料费涨了许多,但我们的价格定位还是非常合理。再说了,这款鞋设计新颖,质量可靠。

布鲁斯:你说的也有道理。但你也知道,由于金融危机,我们的客户对价格非常在意,商场的销售额下滑得厉害。如果你能降价5%,这将有助于我们销售额的增长。

陈经理:嗯,杰克逊先生,我非常了解你们国家现在的销售情况。但比较价格时,肯定还要考虑质量因素。恐怕降价5%不太可能,我们实在做不到。不过为了促进我们的业务合作,我们准备给你们单价2%的优惠,最低订货量是一个40英尺的集装箱。

布鲁斯:价格还是太高了。能不能再降2%?

陈经理:对不起,我们做不到。这个价格已经是最大的折扣了。

布鲁斯:嗯……我很欣赏你们在这笔交易上的诚意。好,我们接受这个价格。

陈经理:很高兴我们能就价格达成一致意见。先喝杯咖啡,稍后我们再谈其条款和条件。

布鲁斯:好的。

杰克·吴:杰克逊先生,琼斯先生,请喝咖啡。

布鲁斯:谢谢。

比尔:谢谢。

Business Situation 2

Mr. Mark Schultz and Ms. Carolyn Cardinal are interested in the remote control dancing car produced by Chenghai Toy Trading Co., Ltd. Mr. Frank Li and Ms. Anna Zhang are negotiating on the price of the toy with them. They require to have a reduction of the price by 5%. But Mr. Frank Li and Ms. Anna Zhang only agree to 1% off.

马克·舒尔茨先生和卡罗琳·卡迪纳尔女士看中了澄海玩具贸易有限公司的玩具产品遥控跳舞车。李先生和张安娜正在与舒尔茨先生和卡迪纳尔女士商谈遥控跳舞车的价格。舒尔茨先生和卡迪纳尔女士要求享受5%的优惠，但李经理和张安娜只同意给1%的折扣。

Dialogue

L = Frank Li	M = Mark Schultz
C = Carolyn Cardinal	A = Anna Zhang

M: Good morning, Mr. Li.

F: Good morning, Mr. Schultz. Welcome to our booth. What can I do for you?

M: After studying your data, we are quite interested in your remote control dancing car 09003C, but we still need to learn more information about it. What's the price?

F: It's USD 19, FOB Shenzhen, or USD 22, CIF New York per piece.

M: Your price is more than we expected!

F: Could you give me an indication of a price that you consider workable?

M: I hope you can reduce your price by 5%.

A: Our quotation is well founded. Our products are of high quality and in the latest design. The cost of material has risen a great deal recently, but we still try to maintain the previous price. Moreover, we have spent high cost on the development of this style.

C: Compared with other suppliers, I find your price is on the high side.

F: Are you sure their products are the same with ours? Our remote control car is so popular that some other factories may imitate it.

C: Maybe it's the truth. But it's really difficult for us to open our market at your prices. You see, due to the financial crisis, many families cut lots of their daily expenses, and the toys' sales volume in the supermarkets in our country has fallen rapidly.

F: Well, for the sake of our long-term cooperation, we can make some concessions. I agree to USD 20 on CIF basis if you place an order no less than a 20 feet container.

M: I appreciate your cooperation. But I have to report to the head office for the final decision. We'll reply to you tomorrow.

参考译文

马克：早上好！李先生。

李经理：早上好！舒尔茨先生。欢迎来到我们的展位。我能为您做些什么？

马克：研究了你们的资料之后，我们对你们的09003C遥控跳舞车挺感兴趣的。不过我们想多了解一下该产品。它的价格是多少？

李经理：每架是深圳离岸价19美元或纽约成本、保险费加运费价22美元。

马克：您的报价比我们预期的要高。

李经理：能谈一下您认为合适的价格是多少吗？

马克：希望你们能降价5%。

张安娜：我们的报价是有根据的。我们的产品设计新颖，质量可靠。近几年材料价格涨了许多，可我们还是维持原有价格。而且我们在这种产品的开发上投放了大量资金。

卡罗琳：与其他供应商相比，你们的价格有些高。

李经理：您能肯定他们的产品跟我们的一样吗？我们的遥控跳舞车市场上很热销，有些厂家会可能会仿造。

卡罗琳：也许是那样的。但这个价格要打开市场真的很难。你也知道，由于金融危机，许多家庭都削减了日常的开支，我们商场的玩具销量迅速下降了许多。

李经理：为了我们长期的合作，我们可以作出一些让步。如果你们的订货量为一个20英尺的话，我们同意给你们纽约到岸价20美元的价格。

马克：谢谢你的合作。不过我还得向总部汇报才能作最后的决定。明天我给你答复。

Business Links

一、定价策略

1. 外贸谈判中如何定价主要有以下几点决定因素：

（1）因人因地定价——市场价格信息来源、销售价格控制等；

（2）客户关注点——合格率、产品性能、质量控制、产品研发、工厂环境等；

(3) 付款方式。

2. 两种常用的能吸引客户的报价方式：

(1) 高价留尾　西欧式报价。第一次报高一点的价格，有利于后来的讨价还价，这样的报价可以吸引中高档客户。老板报的价格永远比员工报的价格低，这是不会变的硬道理，因此在报价的时候一定要给自己留后路。

(2) 低价留尾　日本式报价。第一次价格就报的低一点，但规定一个比较高的起订量，或者交货期尽量延后，或者 100% 前T/T。这类报价主要是吸引对价格敏感的客户。无论采用何种方式，最重要的还是和客户进行沟通，在沟通中能更多地了解客户的心理，掌握客户的购买行为，这样在以后的合作中也就能报出一个更合适的价格，留住客户。

二、外汇风险防范

当美元汇率走软，人民币汇率走强的背景下，外贸公司在对外报价时面临两难局面。为防范汇率变化带来的风险，对外报价通常采用以下三种方法：

1. 美元报价。当交货期较近时，可按较低的美元汇率来计算。
2. 欧元或其他硬通货币报价。当交货期较远时，或外商不愿承担汇率风险时，可选用欧元或其他硬通货币报价。
3. 人民币报价。为了防止外汇变化给卖方带来的损失，我方可用人民币报价，在结算时用当时的汇率来结算外汇。电汇付款方式多采用人民币报价。

Useful Sentences

1. 询价与报盘（Inquiry and offer）

(1) — Would you give us an offer on FOB Shenzhen for your motor ZD 3812?

能给我们报一下 ZD 3812 型号电机的深圳离岸价价格吗？

— With pleasure. Please tell us the quantity you require so that we can work out the offers.

乐意之至。请告诉我们你们所需的数量，以便我们计算出价格。

— We would like to order 1 000 sets.

我们想预订 1 000 台。

— The unit price is FOB Shenzhen USD 46.

每台价格是每台 FOB 深圳 46 美元。

(2) — Could you offer us FOB Shanghai for your air fresher No. BG368?

能给我们报一下你们 BG368 型号的空气清新器的上海离岸价价格吗？

— Yes. Our offer is USD 106 per carton FOB Shanghai.

可以，价格是每台上海离岸价 106 美元。

(3) — I would like to make an inquiry about your sports wear.

我想咨询一下你们运动服的价格。

— OK. May I have the model number. and the quantity?

好的，能告诉我您要的型号和数量吗？

— I would like 500 pieces of No. GT 2130.

我想要订 500 件 GT 2130 型号的。

— Well, here it is. 500 pieces of sports wear No. GT 2130 at USD36 per piece, our loading port is Guangzhou.

嗯，找到了 500 件 GT 2130 型号的运动服，每件是 36 美元，装运港是广州。

(4) You had better supply us with your bottom price so that we could place an order.

你方最好报出底价，以便我方下订单。

If you could reduce the price by 2%, your goods will find a good market at our end.

如果你方降价 2%，你们的产品可在我方市场找到销路。

(5) Will you please tell us the specifications, quantity and packing you want, so that we can work out the offer as soon as possible?

能否告诉我们你们所需产品的规格、数量和包装要求，以便我方尽快计算报价。

2. 价格谈判（Price Negotiation）

(1) — Mr. Rudon, we are going to place 1 000 pieces each month for twelve months, so we'd like a 20% discount.

如东先生，我们将连续 12 个月每月订 1 000 件，所以希望你能降价 20%。

— Even with volume sales, our cost for this model won't go down much.

即使是大量订购，这个款式的价格也不可能降得这么低。

— Just what are you proposing?

那你的意见呢？

— We could take a cut on the price. But 20% would slash our profit margin. We suggest a compromise — 10% .

价格我们可以降一些。但降价 20% 我们会亏本。我们建议折中—10% 。

— That's a big change from 20% ! 10% is beyond my negotiating limit. Any other ideas?

这与 20% 差太远了！10% 远超过我的议价底线。有没有其他建议呢？

— I don't think I can change it right now. I have to consult my head office.

我想目前我也降不了价。我还得跟总部请示一下。

— Sure. I must talk to my office too. I hope we can find some common ground on this.

当然。我也得跟总部请示。希望我们双方都能就这点达成共识。

（2） — Miss Simon, your home health monitor are very good. But I'm afraid the price you're asking is too high for us. It's almost 25% higher than last year's.

西蒙小姐，你们的家用健康监测仪非常棒。但我认为你的报价太高了。几乎比去年的高了 25% 。

— That's because the price of raw materials has gone up.

这主要是因为原材料涨价了。

— It would be very difficult for us to push any sales if we buy it at this price.

但如果我们以此价格买入的话，销路会很难打开。

— I have cut the price the minimum. You know our monitor is a patent product, different from others, If it were not for your past large order, we could not have quoted it at such a low price.

我已经把价格降到最低了。您也知道我们的监测仪是专利产品，与其他家的不同。如果不是因为你们以前的订货量大，我们也不会报这么低的价格。

— Could you lower the price by 10% , which will lead to a large business between us?

你能否把价格降 10% ，这样我们之间的一笔大生意就能做成了。

— The price I'm offer is as low as I can go.

我报的价格已是最低的了。

— Then I am sorry to say I have to seek quotations from other suppliers.

那么，很遗憾，我只能去向别的供应商询价了。

— I'm sorry, Tom. But I hope you'll continue to approach us on other occasions.

汤姆，我很遗憾。不过，我还是希望我们以后有机会再次合作。

— OK.

好的。

(3) — We are interested in Article No. GX113 and GX 128, but we found that your prices are too high than those offered by other suppliers.

我们对你们的 GX113 和 GX 128 产品挺感兴趣的。但我们认为你们的价格比其他供应商的高很多。

— I'm sorry to hear that. But as you see, our commodities have always come up to the export standard. They are moderately priced.

我很遗憾。但您也知道我们的产品都是按照出口标准生产的，价位适中。

— I'm afraid I can't agree with you in this respect. It would be impossible for us to push any sales at such high prices. If you want to get the order, you'll have to lower the price.

这一点我不敢苟同。如此高的价格想要打开销路是根本不可能的。如果你们想要拿到订单，肯定要降下价格来。

— Well, in order to help you develop business in this line, we may consider making some concessions in your price.

好吧，为了帮助你们在行业内开拓市场，价格上我们可考虑作些让步。

(4) — Your price is too high for us to accept. It would be very difficult for us to push any sales at this price. If you can go a little lower, I'd be able to give you an order on the spot.

你方的价格太高，我们不能接受。按照这个价格我们很难推销产品。如果你们价格降一点，我现在就可以订货。

(5) — I'm sorry. It is our rock-bottom price. My offer was based on

reasonable profit, not on wild speculations. While we appreciate your cooperation, we regret to say that we can't reduce our price any further.

很抱歉。这是我们的底价了。我方的报价是以合理的利润为依据，不是漫天要价。虽然我们感谢贵方的合作，但是很抱歉，我们不能再降价。

Chapter 6 商谈付款方式 (On Payment Terms)

Business Situation 1

After having reached an agreement on price, Mr. Bruce Jackson and Mr. Denny Chen go on their talking about the payment terms. Mr. Bruce Jackson proposes to make a T/T payment, while Denny Chen insists on the payment by L/C.

布鲁斯·杰克逊先生与陈先生就价格问题达成一致意见，接着开始商谈付款方式。布鲁斯·杰克逊先生提议以电汇方式付款，而陈经理坚持以信用证方式付款。

Dialogue

D = Denny Chen　B = Bruce Jackson

D: Mr. Jackson, shall we go on with our business talk?

B: Sure, Mr. Chen, let's go ahead. There is another thing we have to discuss, the terms of payment.

D: As for the terms of payment, it is our usual practice for our new or regular customers to effect payment by L/C at sight.

B: I understand your position, for the payment by L/C is safe for the exporter. But you see, opening a L/C with a bank will involve us in a lot of expense and the tie-up of funds for a long time, and this would undoubtedly increase the cost of our import. In addition, this is not the first cooperation between us, so we request a payment on T/T.

D: I'm sorry that I can't be of help. Our company only allows us to do business by L/C at sight.

B: In that case, could we ask for a time L/C, such as 60 days after sight?

D: In view of our friendly cooperation we have had, we would consider your request. Please wait for a moment. I have to consult my boss.

B: Thank you.

(*Ten minutes after Denny made a phone call to his boss*)

D: Mr. Jackson, according to your request, we are prepared to make an exception to our policy of payment and accept a 30 days L/C. This is what we can do best.

B: 30 days? Anyway, it would do help to us. OK.

D: But we would like to make it clear that this accommodation is only for the view of opening up the market of this new product.

B: Thank you. You have been most helpful.

参考译文

陈经理：杰克逊先生，让我们继续好吗？

布鲁斯：好的，陈先生。我们继续。我们必须谈谈支付方式。

陈经理：关于支付方式，无论是新老客户，我们一贯的做法都是采用即期信用证付款。

布鲁斯：我能理解，用信用证支付对出口商有保障。但开立信用证使我们的开支太大了，而且还会使我们的资金周转不灵。这无疑会加大我们进口的成本再说了，这也不是我们的第一次交易，所以我想以电汇方式付款。

陈经理：这一点我爱莫能助。我们公司只允许用即期信用证付款。

布鲁斯：这样的话，能不能允许我们用60天远期信用证支付？

陈经理：介于我们之间良好的合作关系，我们可以考虑你们的请求。稍等一下，我得跟老板商量一下。

布鲁斯：谢谢。

（陈经理与老板通话10分钟后）

陈经理：杰克逊先生，根据你们的要求，我们将破例采用30天即期信用证的方式支付。这已经是我们所能做到的最好的了。

布鲁斯：30天吗？不管如何，这种付款方式还是对我们有帮助的。

陈经理：但我们要说明的是，正是为了开拓这种新产品的市场，我们才给你们这种优惠的。

布鲁斯：谢谢。你们的帮助真是太大了。

Business Situation 2

At the 107th American International Toy Fair in New York City's Jacob K. Javits Convention Center in New York City, Mr. Mark Schultz, marketing manager, and Ms. Carolyn Cardinal, sales manager of Irwin Toy Inc. went to the booth of Chenghai Toy Trading Co., Ltd. to inform Miss Linda Zhang that they agreed to place an order for a 20ft container at the price of $21.00 per piece CIF NewYork. Now they are talking about the terms of payment.

第107届美国玩具展在纽约的雅各布K. 贾维茨会议中心举行。来参加采购的美国Irwin玩具公司的市场部经理马克·舒尔茨先生和销售部经理卡罗琳·卡迪纳尔女士来到澄海玩具贸易有限公司的展台前，告知该公司的张琳达小姐，他们同意以每件21美元到达纽约的成本、保险费加运费的价格订购一个20英尺集装箱的货物。现在他们正在商谈付款方式。

Dialogue

M = Mark Schultz　C = Carolyn Cardinal　L = Linda Zhang

L: Good morning, Mr. Schultz. Good morning, Ms. Cardinal.

M: Good morning, Ms. Zhang. We have good news. Our head office agreed to order a 20ft container at the price of $21.00 per piece CIF NewYork.

L: That's great!

M: Shall we go on with business talk?

L: Sure. Let's go ahead.

M: There is another thing we have to talk about. That is terms of payment. We prefer to make payment by T/T.

L: However, it is our usual practice that customers are required to pay by irrevocable L/C at sight.

M: Payment by L/C is too complicated. Since we trust each other, why not do business in an easier way?

L: L/C is the safest method. It offers the bankers' guarantee.

M: To tell you the truth, payment by L/C is expensive. We have to pay a sum of deposit, which would increase the cost of our import.

L: Sorry, I can't help on the way of payment. Our company only allows us to do business by L/C.

C: In that case, could you accept a time L/C, say, 60 days after sight?

L: The best we can do is to accept 30 days L/C, with 20% of invoice value paid for order.

M: Thank you. You are most helpful. I hope you can set about production immediately after you get our L/C.

L: Don't worry about that.

参考译文

张琳达：早上好，马克·舒尔茨先生，卡罗琳·卡迪纳尔小姐。

马克：早上好，张女士，我们有个好消息要告诉你。我们公司同意以每件21美元到达纽约的成本、保险费加运费的价格订购一个20英尺集装箱的货物。

张琳达：太好了！

马克：我们继续谈吧。

张琳达：好的。继续吧。

马克：另一个问题就是关于支付方式。我们想用电汇方式付款。

张琳达：但我们一贯的做法都是要求客户采用即期不可撤销信用证付款。

马克：用信用证付款太复杂了。既然我们彼此信任，为什么不用更简易的方式做生意呢？

张琳达：信用证是最安全的方式。它提供银行担保。

马克：说实话吧，信用证的费用太贵了。我们得付一笔保证金，这会增加我们的进口费用。

张琳达：我想这一点我帮不了您。我们公司只允许用信用证付款。

卡罗琳：这样的话，你们能不能接受远期信用证，如60天？

张琳达：我们最多能接受30天远期信用证，但是要付发票金额的20%作为订金。

马克：谢谢。您真是帮大忙了。希望收到我们的信用证后你们能马上安排生产。

张琳达：这一点请您放心。

Business Links

1. 国际贸易中常见的支付方式

国际贸易中常见的支付方式有三种：汇付、托收和信用证。

（1）汇付（Remittance）

汇付是指买方通过银行或其他途径将货款主动寄给收款人，常用于预付货款、随订单付现和赊销业务，分为信汇（M/T: mail transfer）、电汇（T/T: telegraphic transfer）和票汇（D/D: demand draft）三种。目前，银行常用电汇和票汇方式。

（2）托收（Collection）

托收是指债权人出具汇票委托银行向债务人收取货款的一种结算方式，可分为付款交单（D/P: Document against Payment）和承兑交单（D/A: Document against Acceptance）两种。

付款交单分为即期和远期两种。即期交单（D/P at sight）指出口方开具即期汇票，由代收行向进口方提示，进口方见票后即须付款，货款付清时，进口方取得货运单据。远期交单（D/P after sight or after date）指出口方开具远期汇票，由代收行向进口方提示，经进口方承兑后，于汇票到期日或汇票到期日以前，进口方付款赎单。

承兑交单是买方对卖方开具的见票后天付款的跟单汇票，于提示时承兑，并应于汇票到期日付款，承兑后交单。承兑交单并不意味买方到期一定付款，这取决于买方的信誉。

（3）信用证（Letter of Credit）

信用证是银行有条件的付款承诺，保证在单证相符的情况下支付货款。信用证是国际贸易中最主要、最常用的支付方式。

2. 汇付、托收和信用证的区别

汇付和托收属于商业信用，信用证属于银行信用。汇付可以用于出口商了解的交易对象，但不宜用于对其信用不了解的交易对象。托收则对进口商较有利。信用证是目前国际贸易结算中被广泛应用的最为重要的支付方式。但开证人申请开证时，需向开证行支付一定比率的保证金或其他担保品，这在一定程度上增加了买方的资金负担，因此有时进口商会尽力说服出口商采用其他支付方式。

Useful Sentences

1. 客户询问付款方式（The Buyer's Inquiry about Terms of Payment）

（1）Shall we discuss the terms of payment?
我们来商谈付款方式好吗？

（2）What is your regular practice about terms of payment?
你们通常采用哪种付款方式？

（3）What are your terms of payment?
你们的付款方式是什么？

（4）How are we going to arrange payment?
我们如何安排付款？

（5）Could you tell me which kind of payment terms you'll choose?
你们会选择用哪一种付款方式？

2. 卖方回复询问付款方式（The Seller's Offer of Terms of Payment）

（1）We'd like you to pay us by L/C.
我们希望你们用信用证的方式付款。

（2）We always require L/C for our exports and we pay by L/C for our imports as well.
进出口我们都会用信用证。

（3）We insist on full payment.
我们坚持一次性付清货款。

（4）We have mainly adopted some usual international practices.
我们主要采用了一些国际惯例。

3. 客户建议付款方式（The Buyer's Suggestion about Terms of Payment）

(1) Now let's talk about the terms of payment. Would you accept D/P? I hope it will be acceptable to you.
现在我们来谈谈付款方式。你们接受付款交单吗？希望你们能接受。

(2) But I think it would be beneficial to both of us to adopt more flexible payment terms such as D/P term.
不过我认为采用像付款交单这样比较灵活的付款方式对我们双方都有利。

(3) As for regular orders in future, couldn't you agree to D/P?
那将来常规的订单能用付款交单吗？

(4) Payment by L/C is the safest method, but rather complicated. We hope you will accept T/T payment terms.
信用证支付是最安全的方式，但也相当复杂。希望你们能接受电汇。

(5) In view of this order of large quantity, we propose this payment by installments.
考虑到这笔订单数量巨大，我们提议分期付款。

4. 拒绝客人（Refusal to the Buyer）

(1) I'm sorry. We can't accept D/P or D/A. We insist on payment by L/C.
很抱歉，我们不能接受付款交单或承兑交单。我们要求信用证付款。

(2) I'm afraid we must insist on our usual payment terms.
恐怕我们还是得用一贯的支付方式。

(3) Payment by installments is not the usual practice in world trade.
分期付款并不是国际贸易的惯例。

(4) It is difficult for us to accept your suggestion.
所以我们很难接受你方建议。

(5) Sure. After several smooth transactions, we can try D/P terms.
当然。几次顺利地交易后我们可以试试用付款交单方式。

5. 让步与接受付款方式（Making Concession and Acceptance）

(1) Can we each make some concession?
我们双方能否各退一步？

(2) In order to conclude the business, we are prepared to ask for a 50

percent down payment first, the rest should be paid by T/T within one week on your receipt of our B/L copy.

为了能做成这笔生意，我们准备要求你方先付一半货款为定金，剩下的在你们收到我们的提单复印件后一周内电汇过来。

（3）— In what currency will payment made by?

我们用什么货币付款?

— We usually do business in U. S. dollars as world prices are often dollars based.

国际上的报价大都以美元结算，我们也如此。

（4）— When should we open the L/C?

信用证我们得什么时候开过来?

— Your L/C must reach us 30 days before the date of delivery so as to enable us to make all necessary arrangements.

你方的信用证在转运前 30 天开抵我处，以便我方及时作出各项安排。

（5）— Mr. Yao, we've got a cash flow problem for the time being. Would you allow us to postpone settlement of your account?

姚先生，最近我们的现金流比较紧张。你能否允许我方延期付款?

— Yes, we always adopt flexible ways of doing business. With a view of your good business reputation, we are prepared to allow you to pay by installments.

没问题，我们经常采用灵活的方式做生意。由于你方信用良好，我们打算允你方分期付款。

Chapter 7　商谈装运期 (On Shipment Date)

Business Situation 1

Mr. Bruce and Denny Chen are talking about the terms of shipment. Mr. Bruce Jackson requires a delivery before the first half month of June with his reasons.

布鲁斯先生和陈经理正在商谈有关装运的问题。布鲁斯先生要求货物于6月份上半月之前装运，并提出理由。

Dialogue

D = Denny Chen　B = Bruce Jackson　J = Jack Wu

B: Mr. Chen, we have set agreement on terms of payment; now let's come to the issue of shipment. Could you tell us how long it takes you to make delivery?

D: Generally, we deliver our goods within one month after receipt of the covering L/C. So your L/C should be opened 30 days before delivery so that we can make necessary arrangement.

B: Now it is May; I'm afraid your shipment 30 days after receipt of our L/C would be too late for our selling season. I want the goods to be delivered before the first half of June. You know, the coming summer holiday is the hot season for our sports shoes.

D: We do hope that the goods would arrive in time for your peak seasons. But you see, getting the goods ready, making out the documents and booking the shipping space, all these take time.

B: Mr. Chen, you certainly realize that time of delivery is a matter of great importance to us.

D: I understand. But our factories are heavily committed for this quarter, for many of our customers have placed orders for delivery in this quarter.

B: Could you possibly find some way to arrange the manufacture for an earlier delivery? A timely delivery means a lot to us.

D: OK. Jack, please get in touch with our factory and see what they say.

（*Several minutes after Jack called the factory manager*）

J: Mr. Jackson, we are glad to inform you that we can meet your requirements. The shipment can be effected within three weeks after receipt of your L/C.

B: Thank you very much. I'll have the L/C opened as soon as possible.

参考译文

布鲁斯：陈先生，我们已就付款方式达成一致意见，现在我们来谈谈装运的事情。你们要多长时间才能发货？

陈经理：通常我们收到信用证后一个月内就能发货。所以你们的信用证要在装运前30天开给我们，以便早作安排。

布鲁斯：现在已是5月份了，我怕你们收到信用证后30天才发货太晚了，会赶不上销售季节。我想这批货最好能在6月上半月发出，毕竟暑假是运动鞋销售的旺季。

陈经理：我们当然也希望货物能赶上你们的销售旺季。不过你也知道，备妥货物、制单证、预订舱位这些工作都是要花时间的。

布鲁斯：陈先生，你一定明白发货的时间对我们很重要。

陈经理：我能理解。可这一季我们工厂接的货很多，因为许多客户订的都是这一季的货。

布鲁斯：你能不能想想办法安排早点生产以便早出货？及时发货对我们很重要。

陈经理：好吧。杰克，你跟我们的工厂联系一下，看他们怎么说。

（杰克·吴跟工厂经理联系几分钟后）

杰克·吴：杰克逊先生，很高兴我们能满足你们的要求。我们将在收到你们的信用证之后三周内出货。

布鲁斯：太感谢了。我将尽快开立信用证。

Business Situation 2

Mr. Mark Schultz, marketing manager, Ms. Carolyn Cardinal, sales manager of Irwin Toy Inc. are talking with Mr. Frank Li, the sales manager and Ms. Anna Zhang, the chief seller of Chenghai Toy Trading Co., Ltd. about the terms of shipment.

Irwin 玩具公司的市场部经理马克·舒尔茨先生和销售部经理卡罗琳女士正在与澄海玩具贸易有限公司的销售经理法兰克·李和业务主管张安娜小姐商谈装运事宜。

Dialogue

M = Mark Schultz	C = Carolyn Cardinal	L = Frank Li	A = Anna Zhang

M: Is it possible to effect shipment by the end of September? You see, October is the season for this item.

L: We have stores for this item, so the goods can be dispatched in 10 days after we get your L/C.

A: Please issue L/C as soon as possible so as to ensure shipment will be made in stipulated time. I'll tell the head office to open L/C immediately after we sign the S/C.

L: By the way, please make sure the terms and conditions of L/C will be in strict in accordance with those stipulated in the S/C thus to avoid subsequent amendment.

C: That's undoubtedly.

L: It's a busy season. In order to ensure shipment be made promptly, we suggest transshipment be allowed.

M: I understand. But please make sure that partial shipment is prohibited.

L: Sure, don't worry about that. Furthermore, as to the consignment, we still wish 5% more or less be allowed.

M: No problem.

参考译文

马克：你们能不能在9月底安排装运？你看，10月份就是这种货物的销售旺季了。

李经理：我们这种产品有现货，收到你们信用证10天后就能发货。

张安娜：请尽早开立信用证以便货物能如期装运。合同一签下来，我就会告知总部立即开立信用证。

李经理：另外，请确保信用证条款要与合同条款一致，以避免后续的修改。

卡罗琳：当然会的。

李经理：现在是旺季，为使货物能及时装运，我们建议允许分批转运。

马克：好的。但不要分批装运。

李经理：好的，这点请放心。另外，请允许货物有5%的溢短装。

马克：好的。

Business Links

1. 国际贸易货物的运输方式

在国际贸易货物运输中，涉及的运输方式很多，一般有海洋运输、铁路运输、航空运输、集装箱运输、联合运输（即国际多式联运和大陆桥运输等）、河流运输、邮包运输、公路运输、管道运输等。其中海洋运输是最主要的运输方式。集装箱运输也是国际上普遍采用的一种重要运输方式。根据国际标准化组织的规定，集装箱规格有3个系列13种。在国际运输中常用的规格为20英尺（8 ft×8 ft×20 ft）（载货重量为17 500 kg，有效容积为25 CBM）和40英尺（8 ft×8 ft×40 ft）（载货重量为25 000 kg，有效容积为55 CBM）两种。目前国际上均以20英尺柜为标准箱，同时也是计算和衡量港口吞吐量和船舶大小的度量单位，通常以标箱TEU（twenty-foot equivalent unit）来表示，称为"相当于20英尺单位"。不同型号的集装箱一律折成TEU加以计算。

2. 装运期

装运期是交易过程中最重要的环节之一。能否适时收到货物，可能影响到收益，因此，买方在合同或信用证中关于装运时间的规定应当明确、灵活，尽量避免"immediate shipment（立即）"，"shipment ASAP（尽快）"之类的词语。有关装运期的规定常见的有："Shipment during/in May, 2009"（2009年5月发货），"Shipment on or before June 1, 2009"（在2009年6月1日或6月1日之前装运），"Shipment on or about June 15, 2009"（在2009年6月10日至6月20日之间装运），"Shipment not later than July 1，2009"　（不晚于2009年7月1日发货），"Shipment within 45 days after receipt of L/C"（收到信用证45天内发货）等。

《跟单信用证统一惯例》（简称《UCP600》）对有关时间规定的理解：

on or before（在……或在……之前），before不包含提及的日期。

on or about（在……或大概在……）被视为规定事件发生在指定日期的前后5个日历日之间，起讫日期计算在内。

Useful Sentences

1. 询问装运时间（Enquiry about the Shipping Time）

1）— Dick，what about the earliest delivery of the goods? As for shipment, the soon, the better.

迪克，货物最早什么时候装运？船运的话，越早越好。

— Yes，shipment is to be made in April，not allowing partial shipment.

货物4月份装运，不允许分批装运。

— Good.

好的。

2）— When can you effect shipment? I'm terribly worried about late shipment.
你们什么时候安排装运？我很怕装运迟了。
— We can effect shipment in December or early next year at the latest.
我们最迟安排在12月底或下年初装运。
— That's fine.
很好。

2. 要求尽早装运（Asking for an Early Shipment）

1）— Mr. Du, when will you deliver the products to us?
杜先生，你们什么时候能发货？
— The earliest delivery we can make is at the end of September.
最早在9月底。
— You know that time of delivery is very important to us. Could we expect an earlier shipment not later than the fist half of September?
你也知道发货时间对我们非常重要。你们能不能提早到9月上半月发货？
— As you know, our manufacturers are full committed and we have a lot of orders to fill. But we'll do our best to advance the time of delivery.
我们生产商的订单全满了，我们有许多货要发。不过我们会尽量快点。
— Thank you very much for your cooperation.
非常感谢你们的合作。

2）— Ted, will it possible for you to ship the goods before early October?
特德，你们能不能在10月初之前发货？
— Oh, our factory is heavily committed at the moment. If you desire earlier delivery, we can only make a partial shipment.
我们工厂目前的订单很多。如果你们想要提前发货的话，我们只能分批装运。
— The goods we ordered are seasonal goods, so we hope you can ship them all at one time.
我们订的货是季节性商品，所以希望你们能一次装运完毕。
— Well, we'll try our best to speed up the production in order to advance the time of delivery.
那我们就尽量加快生产速度，争取提前发货吧。

— Thank you very much.
非常感谢。

3. 提出转运要求（Asking for Transshipment）

1）— Mr. Simon, since direct steamers to your port are very few, I'm wondering whether transshipment can be allowed.
西蒙先生，由于到达你们那边港口的船只稀少，我希望你们能允许转运。

— Well, transshipment will prolong the delivery and cause the damage and additional expense, so we still hope the goods can be effected by direct shipment.
嗯，转运会延长船期，会有风险，而且增加费用，所以我们还是希望用直航。

— We will try our best to arrange direct shipment. But please understand that it is very difficult to book the space since it is hot season at present. If we can't get hold of a direct vessel, then we have to have the goods transshipped.
我们会尽量安排直航。但也请你们理解，目前是旺季，很难订到舱位。如果我们安排不了直航，那就只能转运了。

— It seems I have to agree to this proposal.
看来我只能同意这个方案了。

2）— Bob, I'm sorry to tell you that the liner space for Barcelona has been fully booked up, so direct streamer sailing is out of the question. Is there any chance for you to allow transshipment?
鲍勃，很抱歉到巴塞罗那港的舱位已满，直航是不可能了。你们能不能允许转运呢？

— Generally, we don't have our goods transshipped. You know, transshipment adds to the risks of damage and delays arrivals.
一般我们的货物都不会用转运方式的。你也知道，转运会有风险，还会延长船期。

— In that case, I'm afraid we can do little about it.
如果是这样的话，我恐怕会很难办。

— In order to promote our business relationship, we'd like to make an exception and agree to transshipment, and we propose to transship the goods via Hong Kong.
为了我们双方的贸易关系，我们会破例同意转运，但建议在香港转船。

— No problem.
好的。

Chapter 8 商谈包装（On Packing）

Business Situation 1

Bruce Jackson and Denny Chen are talking about the terms of packing. Bruce Jackson gives his suggestion for the packing.

布鲁斯·杰克逊和陈经理正在讨论包装的问题。布鲁斯·杰克逊提出了他对包装的建议。

Dialogue

D = Denny Chen B = Bruce Jackson

B: Mr. Chen, shall we get down to the matter of packing of the shoes?

D: Sure.

B: I wonder if you could give me some ideas about your packing.

D: The shoes are to be packed in exquisitely designed color boxes, each for one box, 80 pairs to one carton, 2,400 pairs per style including three colors and one size range, 8,400 pairs in a 40's container.

B: May I see the packing sample?

D: Yes. Here it is.

B: Good. They look quite beautiful and attractive. A well-designed package helps selling the goods.

D: That's just what we hope.

B: What about the outer packing?

D: We usually use standard export cartons.

B: I hope you make sure the cartons should be strong enough to stand long sea voyage.

D: Don't worry. Each carton is lined with waterproof paper, so that they can resist dampness or rain.

B: Very good. Besides, as for the labeling, we require that only Chinese and English be printed on the principal display panels on the label.

D: That can be easily done.

B: One more thing, each package should be marked with "KEEP DRY".

D: No problem.

参考译文

布鲁斯：陈先生，我们来谈谈鞋子的包装如何？

陈经理：好的。

布鲁斯：我希望你能谈谈你对包装的意见。

陈经理：我们将把鞋子用设计精美的彩色盒子包装，一盒一双，80 双一箱。每款 2 400 双，含三种颜色和全部尺码每个 40 英尺的集装箱装 8 400 双。

布鲁斯：能不能给我看看包装的样品？

陈经理：好的，给。

布鲁斯：不错，包装漂亮且挺吸引人的。设计精美的包装有助于产品的销售。

陈经理：这正是我们所希望的。

布鲁斯：外包装呢？

陈经理：我们通常采用标准出口纸箱。

布鲁斯：你们要确保纸箱必须很坚固，能承受长途海运。

陈经理：不用担心。每个纸箱均用防水纸做衬垫，这样货物就不会受潮或被雨淋了。

布鲁斯：很好。另外，关于标签，我们要求标签上的主要说明部分只印有中文和英文。

陈经理：这个好办。

布鲁斯：还有，每件包装上均需标明“防湿”。

陈经理：好的。

Business Situation 2

Mr. Mark Schultz and Ms. Carolyn Cardinal are asking about the terms of packing. Mr. Frank Li, the sales manager of Chenghai Toy Trading Co., Ltd. is explaining the packing of the goods.

马克·舒尔茨先生和卡洛琳·卡迪纳尔小姐正在询问有关包装的问题。澄海玩具贸易有限公司销售部经理李经理在向他们解释货物包装问题。

Dialogue

M = Mark Schultz　F = Frank Li　C = Carolyn Cardinal

M: Shall we get down to the matter of packing of the goods?

F: Sure.

M: I wonder if you could give me some ideas about your packing.

F: The toys are to be packed in carton, 18 pieces to one carton.

C: How about the inner packing? I wonder each piece be packed in an inner box.

F: Oh, since the inner box cost is not included in the unit price we offered, the goods just can be packed in poly bags.

M: But I think the lovely color boxes will help push the sales.

F: We agree with that. But if the goods are packed in inner box, undoubtedly it would add to our cost. If you insist on the inner packing, I'm afraid the extra cost has to be borne by you.

C: However, the sample you showed us was packed in the color box! We insist on the former price with the toys being packed in color boxes!

F: OK, to come to terms, we agree with the color box packing.

M: Thank you for your cooperation!

C: What about the outer packing?

F: We usually use standard export cartons.

M: I hope you make sure the cartons should be strong enough to stand long sea voyage.

F: Don't worry. Each carton is lined with waterproof paper, so that they can resist dampness or rain.

M: Very good. Besides, as for the marking, the main mark and side mark should be printed at our request. Carolyn will e-mail you our mark requirements.

F: No problem.

M: Thank you very much.

参考译文

马克：我们来谈谈货物包装的问题好吗？

李经理：好。

马克：我希望你能谈谈你对包装的意见。

李经理：这些玩具用纸箱包装，18 件一箱。

卡罗琳：内包装呢？我想知道每件玩具是否都有内包装。

李经理：哦，我们的报价并没有包括内包装的费用，内包装只能用塑料袋。

马克：但可爱的彩盒会有助于产品的销售。

李经理：这一点我们也同意。但每件玩具都用内盒包装无疑会增加我们的成本。如果你们一定要加内包装，费用应由你们承担。

卡罗琳：但你们给我们看的样品是用彩盒包装的，所以我们坚持还是原来的价格，而且彩盒包装。

李经理：好吧，为做成生意，我们同意加彩盒包装。

马克：谢谢你们的合作。

卡罗琳：那外包装呢？

李经理：我们通常采用标准出口纸箱。

马克：纸箱必须很坚固，能承受长途海运。

李经理：不用担心。每个纸箱均用防水纸做衬垫，这样货物就不会受潮或被雨淋了。

马克：很好。另外，关于唛头，我们要求正唛、侧唛必须按我们的要求来刷制。卡罗琳会把刷制要求电邮给你们。

李经理：好的。

马克：谢谢！

Business Links

1. 包装的分类

包装的分类方法有很多。通常，人们习惯把包装分为两大类，即运输包装和销售包装。专业分类有以下几种方法：

（1）以包装容器形状分类，可分为箱、桶、袋、包、筐、捆、坛、罐、缸、瓶等。

（2）以包装材料分类，可分为木制品、纸制品、金属制品、玻璃制品、陶瓷制品和塑料制品包装等。

（3）以包装货物种类分类，可分为食品、医药、轻工产品、针棉织品、家用电器、机电产品和果菜类包装等。

（4）以安全为目的分类，可分为一般货物包装和危险货物包装等。

2. 物品条码

物品条码（product code 或称 barcode）是一种产品代码，它是由一组粗细间隔不等的平行线及与之相对应的数字组成的标记。国际上通用的条码种类主要有以下两种：一种是美国统一代码委员会编制的 UPC 条码，另一种是由欧洲 12 国成立的欧洲物品编码协会（后改名为国际物品编码协会）编制的 EAN 条码。目前国际物品编码协会分配给我国的国别号为 690，691，692 和 693。凡有 690，691，692 和 693 开头的条形码的商品，即表示是中国的商品。

Useful Sentences

1. 商谈包装（Talking about Packing）

（1）— How are the shirts packed?
衬衣怎么包装?
— They're packed in cardboard boxes.
用纸箱包装。
— I'm afraid the cardboard boxes are not strong enough for ocean transportation.
我恐怕在海运中用纸箱不够结实。
— We can use hard fermented plastic padding to fix the goods inside the cartons and use metal straps to reinforce the outside.
我们会用硬泡沫塑料垫来固定箱内的货物，外面再用金属条加固。
— Fine.
好。

（2）— Mr. Clinton, let's come to the packing terms.
克林顿先生，我们来谈谈包装的问题吧。
— Our goods are often used as a small gift, so our buyers always pay great attention to packing. We wish the new packing will give our clients satisfaction.
我们的商品主要是用来做小礼物，所以我们的买家通常会很注意包装。我们希望新的包装能使客户满意。

（3）— I agree with you. Our packing would wrap each bag in a transparent bag first and then pack it in a box which is exquisitely designed. Here are the samples of packing available now. You may have a look.
我同意你的观点。货物会先用透明袋包起来，再用设计精美的盒子包起来。这是包装样品，你可以看看。
— Good. How about the outer packing?
很好。那外包装呢?
— We would pack them 120 boxes to one carton, and each is lined with waterproof paper to keep away from moisture.
120 盒一箱，每箱均内衬防水纸以防潮。
— All right.
好的。

（4）— The fragile goods should be wrapped in soft material and firmly packed in cardboard box.
易碎品要用软材料包起来，再稳固地放入纸箱内。

(5) — Packing must protect machines against dampness, moisture, rust and shock.
包装必须能防潮、防湿、防锈、防震，以保护机器。

2. 商谈标签（Talking about Marking and Labeling）

(1) — Mr. Brown, the next thing I'd like to bring up for discussion is labeling.
布朗先生，接下来我们要谈的是标签的问题。
— Please state your opinions about it.
请说说你的意见。
— Well, each package should be marked with "FRAGILE". No names of country or trade mark is to appear on the outside container.
是这样，每件包装上都要标明"易碎品"。外箱上不要出现国名和商标。
— OK, we will pass on your ideas to our manufacturers.
好的，我们会把你们的意见转告生产商的。
— Thank you.
谢谢。

(2) — Judy, it's time for us to discuss the labeling of the sports shoes.
朱迪，我们该谈谈运动鞋标签的事了。
— Well, for your reference, here is a label for sports shoes.
嗯，这是运动鞋的商标，你可以参考一下。

(3) — I don't think the present label works well. Is it possible for you to modify it?
我觉得现行的商标并不太好。能不能改改?
— What's your opinion about it?
你有什么建议呢?
— Only English can be used for label. The Chinese words must be deleted.
商标只用英文，中文删掉。
— Since your request calls for only a small change, we will act upon your idea.
你要求的改动不大，可以照办。
— Thank you very much.
太感谢了。

(4) Your must mark "HANDLE WITH CARE" on the face of the box.
箱面上必须标明"小心轻放"字样。

(5) Bar codes should be marked on the inner packing.
内包装上要有条形码。

Chapter 9 商谈保险（On Insurance）

Business Situation 1

The buyers and the sellers are discussing the insurance. Mr. Bruce Jackson, the marketing manager of Fashion Way Co., Ltd. asked the insurance about the CIF price terms and gave his suggestion.

买卖双方正在讨论保险条款。Fashion Way 公司的市场部经理布鲁斯·杰克逊先生询问了到岸价格条款的保险问题并提出他的建议。

Dialogue

B1 = Bruce Jackson	D = Denny Chen	L = Linda Zhang	B2 = Bill Jones

B1: Do you mind telling me what kind of insurance will be covered for this order of goods since it's based on CIF clause.

D: Of course not. As our usual practice, we'll have it covered under WPA.

B1: In my opinion, WPA is too narrow. I was wondering whether we can extend the coverage to All Risks and War Risk.

L: I think the premium rate will be a little higher.

B2: Yes, but the safety of the goods is more important. Do you think so?

L: Yes, absolutely.

D: In that case, we agree to change WPA to All Risks plus War Risk, but you have to bear the cost for the additional risk coverage, I mean the cost of War Risk.

B1: Deal.

L: The insurance coverage is All Risks and War Risk for 110% CIF invoice value. Any problem?

B1: May I know which insurance company you will choose?

D: We always work with PICC, the People's Insurance Company of China, which enjoys world reputation.

B1: Thank you.

D: Well, since all the details are settled, why don't we sign the contract now?

B1: Sorry, I think we should report to the head company for the final confirmation. Please get the contract ready. If everything goes well, I will come here and sign it tomorrow.

D: OK, we'll be waiting for the good news.

参考译文

布鲁斯：既然这批货是以到岸价条款成交的，您介意告诉我会投什么险吗？

陈经理：当然不介意。我们的惯例是投水渍险。

布鲁斯：我认为水渍险的范围太狭窄。把保险扩大到一切险和战争险如何？

张琳达：我想这样保险费会高些。

比尔：是。但是您不觉得货物安全更重要吗？

张琳达：这是肯定的。

陈经理：既然如此，我们同意改水渍险为一切险加战争险，但是您必须承担附加险的费用，也即是战争险的费用。

布鲁斯：成交。

张琳达：保险按照到岸价的发票金额的110%投一切险加战争险，还有问题吗？

布鲁斯：能告知你们将选择哪家保险公司吗？

陈经理：我们通常跟中国人民保险公司合作。这家公司享誉全球。

布鲁斯：谢谢。

陈经理：既然所有细节问题都解决了，我们为什么不现在就签合同呢？

布鲁斯：对不起，我觉得还是要跟总部最后确认一下。请先准备好合同。如果一切顺利，明天我就来这儿签合同。

陈经理：好，我们等您的好消息。

Business Situation 2

Mr. Mark Schultz and Ms. Carolyn Cardinal are having a discussion about the insurance terms which would be covered on the goods with Mr. Frank Li, sales manager of Chenghai Toy Trading Co., Ltd.

马克·舒尔茨先生和卡罗琳·卡迪纳尔女士正在跟澄海玩具贸易有限公司的销售经理李先生讨论货物投保何种险种的问题。

Dialogue

M = Mark Schultz F = Frank Li C = Carolyn Cardinal

M: Let's go on with our talk over the insurance.

F: OK. We always work with PICC, the People's Insurance Company of China.

M: Well, would you like to tell me what major categories of PICC underwrites?

F: PICC provides a broad range of coverage against all kinds of risks for sea transport, such as FPA, WPA, All Risks and Additional Risks.

C: Then what coverage will you take out for the goods?

F: Generally speaking, we insure the goods against All Risks.

C: Do you cover risks other than All Risks, such as War Risk?

F: Yes, if the buyers want to have the goods insured against those risks, we shall arrange for them, but if you want us to insure against any additional risks, the extra charge will be for your account.

M: OK. For this shipment, we request you to insure against All Risks and War Risk for 110% of the invoice value. Of course, the extra premium for the War Risk will be borne by us.

F: All right. We will do as you require.

C: How about the insurance claim? Could you give us some information about it?

F: Oh, suppose something happens, you begin by applying and obtaining in inspection from your claim settlement agent designated in your insurance policy, the claim settlement agent for this shipment would be the Seattle Department of PICC. Then, with all your documents like insurance policy, B/L, invoice, packing list and a list of your claim, you can present your formal claim in writing to PICC. As far as it is within the scope of coverage, PICC would be responsible for the claim.

C: Thank you.

参考译文

马克：我们继续谈保险吧。

李先生：好。我们一般跟中国人民保险公司合作。

马克：哦，您能告诉我中国人民保险公司的主要保险业务吗？

李先生：中保提供广泛的各种各样的海运保险，例如平安险、水渍险、一切险和附加险。

卡洛琳：那么你们打算怎样为货物投保？

李先生：一般我们货物是投一切险的。

卡洛琳：除了一切险，你们还投其他险种吗？例如战争险。

李先生：是的。如果买方想投那些险种，我们会替为安排。但是如果你们要我们投附加险，你们要承担额外费用。

马克：好吧。这批货我们要求你们按发票金额的110%投一切险和战争险。当然，我们会负担战争险的额外保险费。

李先生：好的。我们会按照您的要求去做。

卡洛琳：保险理赔如何？您能介绍一下吗？

李先生：噢，假设发生了什么事情，你们要先向保险条例里面指定的理赔机构提出勘查申请，这单货的理赔机构是中国人民保险公司的理赔部。然后你们向中国人民保险公司递交书面理赔书，同时提交所有单据，例如保险单、提单、发票、装箱单和索赔清单等。只要是在理赔范围里，中国人民保险公司会负责理赔的。

卡洛琳：谢谢。

Business Links

1. 海运货物保险合同中的保险条款

采用不同的贸易术语，办理投保的人就不同。凡采用FOB或CFR条件成交时，在买卖合同中，应明确由买方投保。凡以CIF条件成交的出口合同，均需按保险金额、险别和适用的条款向中国人民保险公司投保，并明确由卖方负责办理投保。

在CIF出口合同的保险条款中，必须明确下列内容：

1. 投保金额，或称保险金额；
2. 险别；
3. 以哪一个保险公司的保险条款为准。

2. 保险类别

我国的货物运输险别，按照能否单独投保，可分为基本险和附加险两类。

基本险可以单独投保，被保险人投保时，必须选择一种基本险投保。海洋货运保险的基本险包括平安险（F. P. A.）、水渍险（W. P. A. 或W. A.）和一切险（All Risks）。

附加险只能在投保某一种险的基础上才可加保。

3. 承保责任的起讫

根据保险条款规定，上述基本险承保责任的起讫，采用国际保险业通用的“仓至仓条款”（W/W Clause）。该条款规定，保险人的保险责任从被保险货物运离保险单所载明的起运地仓库或储存处所开始运输时生效，直到该货物到达保险单所载明的目的地的收货人的最后仓库或储存处所或被保险人用作分配、分派或非正常运输的其他储存处为止。如未抵达上述目的地，则在货物于最后卸载港全部卸离海轮后60天为止。在上述60天内如再需转运，则开始转运时保险责任终止。

Useful Sentences

1. 客人询问保险（Enquiry about Insurance）

（1）As for the insurance, I have quite a lot of things which I am still not clear about.
关于保险，我还有很多不清楚的地方。

（2）May I ask you a few questions about insurance?
我可否问你几个有关保险的问题吗？

（3）What do your insurance clauses cover?
你们的保险条款包括哪些？

（4）I wonder if the insurance company holds the responsibility for the loss.
我想知道保险公司是否对损失负责。

（5）What risks do you usually cover against?
你们通常会投保哪些险种？

2. 保险险种（Insurance Types）

（1）— Do you mind telling me what kind of insurance we've got for this order of goods?
能告诉我这单货物会投什么险种吗？
— We generally insure W. P. A. on CIF sales.
我们通常在成本、保险费加运费价基础上投水渍险。

（2）— We cover insurance on the 100 cartons of porcelain under F. P. A.
我们给这 100 箱陶瓷投了平安险。
— I was just wondering if the breakage of the goods is included in the F. P. A.?
我想知道平安险是否包括破碎险。

（3）— The goods are ready for shipment. We wish to cover insurance for the cargo.
货物已经准备装船了。我们想给这批货投保。
— We suggest this cargo be insured against partial loss.
我建议这批货物投部分损失险。

（4）— What are your terms of sale?
你们用什么贸易术语？
— The quotation is on CIF basis.
报价是到岸价。
— Is that CIF means the sellers are responsible for prepaying

shipping costs and arranging for the insurance policy.
到岸价是不是说卖方负责预付运费并安排保险?

— Yes, that is correct. We will afford the freight and cover insurance.
是的。我们会支付运输费用并办理保险。

(5) There are three basic covers, namely, Free From Particular Average, with Particular Average and ALL risks.
有三种基本险种，即平安险、水渍险和一切险。
ALL risk covers all losses occurring throughout the voyage caused by accidents at sea or land. In other words, it includes FPA, WPA, and general additional risks, with special additional risks.
一切险保险范围包括海洋或陆地运输过程中由于事故引起的一切风险。也就是说，包括平安险、水渍险、一般附加险和特殊附加险。

3. 保险费（Insurance Premium）

(1) This risk is coverable at a premium of...% .
这个险种的保险费是……% 。

(2) The additional premium is for the buyer's account.
增加的费用由买方负担。

(3) We can not comply with your request for insuring your order for 130% of its invoice value.
我们不能为你方的订货办理按发票金额 130% 的保险。

(4) This kind of additional risk is coverable at 2‰.
这种附加险的保险费是 2‰。

(5) The extra premium involved will be on your account.
额外的保险费有你方承担。

4. 承保范围（Insurance Coverage）

(1) The cover shall be limited to sixty days upon discharge of the insured goods from the seagoing vessel at the final port of discharge.
被保险货物在卸货港卸离海轮后，保险责任以 60 天为限。

(2) We adopt the warehouse to warehouse clause which is commonly used in international insurance.
我们采用国际保险中一贯用的“仓对仓”的责任条款。

(3) Which coverage do you usually provide?
你们通常提供哪种保险?

(4) We will insure against WPA for 110% of invoice value.
我们按发票金额 110% 投水渍险。

(5) Our goods are very valuable. I suppose they should be covered against All Risks.
我们的货物很贵重。所以我要保一切险。

5. 保险索赔 (Claim)

(1) The insurance company is responsible for the claim, as far as it is within the scope of coverage.
只要是保险范围内的，保险公司就会负责理赔。

(2) You should be liable for damage due to your own negligence.
你应该承担由于自己的疏忽所引起的损坏赔偿责任。

(3) Should any damage be incurred, you may, within 60 days after the arrival of the consignment, file a claim supported by a survey report, with the insurance company at your end.
一旦货物发生损毁，你可以在货物到达后的60天内，向投保的保险公司索赔同时提交一份调查报告。

(4) I'm an importer from Canada. I would file a claim about glass breakage.
我是来自加拿大的进口商，我要对这批玻璃破碎提出索赔。

(5) The insurance company is not responsible for the damage. You should file a claim against the seller.
保险公司对破损不负责任。贵公司应向卖方索赔。

Chapter 10 在商务中心 (At the Business Center)

Business Situation 1

Mr. Bruce Jackson negotiates with the sales manager of Shenzhen Ugo Sports Shoes Co., Ltd. about an order of the goods. He reports to the head company and sends a fax at the business center in the hotel.

布鲁斯·杰克逊先生与深圳 Ugo 运动鞋有限公司的销售经理商谈订单事宜之后,向总公司汇报,并在酒店的商务中心发传真。

Dialogue

S = Secretary B1 = Bruce Jackson B3 = Benson

(*In the hotel room*)

S: Good morning! Fashion Way Co., Ltd.

B1: Good morning! This is Bruce Jackson.

S: Hello, Mr. Jackson. How's your stay in China?

B1: Everything goes well. May I speak to Benson, please?

S: Hold the line, please.

B2: Good morning, Benson speaking.

B1: Good morning, Mr. Benson. This is Bruce Jackson.

B2: Hello, Bruce. Nice to hear your voice.

B1: Hello, Mr. Benson. I visited the fair today. It's fantastic!

B3: Good! Is there anything good for us?

B: I have a negotiation with the Shenzhen Ugo Sports Shoes Co., Ltd. Their sports shoes look nice with good quality.

B3: Did you take the catalogue?

B: Of course. I'm going to the business center to send you a fax about the details of the order we've come to today, together with specifications of the goods. If there are no problems, I suppose we can confirm the order tomorrow.

B3: Good. I'll give you a response as soon as possible.

B: I'm going to send the fax. Goodbye!

B3: Goodbye!

C = Clerk　B = Bruce Jackson

(*At the business center*)

C: Good evening, sir. Can I help you?

B: Good evening. I want to send a fax.

C: Where to, sir?

B: To Canada. Here is the fax number.

C: Please sit down and wait a moment, sir. I will send this fax at once.

B: OK, thank you.

C: Sorry, sir. The line is busy. I tried it a lot of times, but it's still busy. Is the fax number correct?

B: Let me see. Oh, it's my mistake. The right number is 001-416-3155. I'm sorry to bring you so much trouble.

C: It doesn't matter. All done, sir. Here you are.

B: How much do these pages cost?

C: Let me count. It's 18 yuan in all. How would you like to make the payment, sir?

B: I'd like to pay in cash.

C: Thank you.

参考译文

(*在酒店的房间*)

秘书：早上好！Fashion Way 公司。

布鲁斯：早上好！我是布鲁斯·杰克逊。

秘书：您好！杰克逊先生。您的中国之行如何？

布鲁斯：一切顺利。请问本森先生在吗？

秘书：别挂，请稍候。

本森：早上好！我是本森。

布鲁斯：早上好，本森先生。我是布鲁斯·杰克逊。

本森：你好，布鲁斯。很高兴听到你的声音。

布鲁斯：您好，本森先生。我今天去参加了展会。展会太棒了！

本森：好的！我们一切顺利吗？

布鲁斯：我与深圳 Ugo 运动鞋有限公司进行了谈判。他们的运动鞋看上去不错，质量也好。

本森：你拿了产品目录吗？

布鲁斯：当然拿了。我要去商务中心就今天讨论的订单的详细内容给您发个传真，其中包括产品的规格。如果没有问题，我想我们明天就可以把订单定下来了。

本森：好的。我会尽快给你回复。
布鲁斯：我去发传真了。再见！
本森：再见！
（在商务中心）
职员：先生，晚上好。能为您做些什么？
布鲁斯：晚上好。我想发一份传真。
职员：先生要发往哪里？
布鲁斯：加拿大。这是传真号。
职员：请坐，请稍候，先生，马上为您发送传真。
布鲁斯：好的，谢谢。
职员：对不起。线路忙。我试了好多次，一直占线。这个传真号码对吗？
布鲁斯：让我看看。哦，是我弄错了。应该是001-416-3155。很抱歉给您添麻烦了。
职员：没关系。好了，先生。给您。
布鲁斯：这些一共多少钱？
职员：让我数数。总计18元。您如何付款，先生？
布鲁斯：我想付现金。
职员：谢谢。

Business Situation 2

The assistant manager Ms. Dora Zhao sends a fax at the Business Center in Jacob K. Javits Convention Center, where she meets Lucy, a friend from Mexico, the marketing manager of an import and export company. They discuss their business at the fair.

公司经理助理赵女士在雅各布K. 贾维茨会议中心的商务中心发传真。在商务中心，她遇见了露西，墨西哥的一家进出口公司的市场部经理，她们谈论起各自在展会上的进展情况。

Dialogue

C = Clerk D = Dora Zhao

C: Good morning! Can I help you?
D: Good morning! Where can I make an IDD phone call and send a fax?
C: You may go to the Business Center. We have professional staff there, and they will help you.
D: That's great! Where is the Business Center?

C: It's on level 3, next to the Concierge Desk. When you get off the elevator, the Business Center is just on your right.

D: Thank you very much.

L = Lucy D = Dora Zhao

(*At the Business Center, Ms. Dora Zhao meets Lucy, a friend from Mexico, the marketing manager of an import and export company.*)

L: Hello, Dora! Nice to meet you!

D: Hi, Lucy! Nice to meet you!

L: How are the negotiations going on?

D: Our clients are quite satisfied with our products, but the negotiations are quite hard. They asked for a 5% discount.

L: Really? That's too much. But our company also met some problems this year.

D: Yeah, they said due to the financial crises, their sale decreases a lot. But we insisted on our products' good quality and original design, and then we finally agreed on a 2% discount.

L: Well done! How about the payment?

D: Our clients suggested by T/T, but we persisted that the payment should be made only by letter of credit. And they agreed.

L: Good. It's much safer. Many companies closed down this year, and sometimes we can't get the payment. Then you began to talk about the contract?

D: Yeah. We have come to terms in regard to shipment date, packing and insurance. And we have drafted the contract.

L: Congratulations!

D: Thank you. What about you?

L: Everything goes well. Although the clients are very choosy, we try to meet their demands.

D: Congratulations! Please visit our booth when you are free.

L: OK. If the economy recovers at the end of this year, we may need some products for Christmas. May I still have the preferential price?

D: Yes. Though we met difficulties this year, we have cooperated for 10 years. No problem. Welcome to our booth. This is our booth number.

L: Thank you. I'm going to phone my general manager. Goodbye!

D: Goodbye!

参考译文

职员：早上好！能为您做些什么？

赵女士：早上好！我在哪儿能打国际直拨长途电话并发传真？

职员：您可以去商务中心。那里有我们的专职员工，他们会帮助您的。

赵女士：太好了！商务中心在哪？

职员：在三楼，在接待员服务台隔壁。出了电梯，商务中心就在您的右手边。

赵女士：非常感谢。

（在商务中心，赵女士遇见了露西，一位来自墨西哥的朋友，她是一家进出口公司的市场部经理。）

露西：你好，多拉！很高兴见到你！

赵女士：你好，露西！很高兴见到你！

露西：谈判顺利吗？

赵女士：我们的客户对于我们的产品相当满意，但是谈判却很艰难。他们要百分之五的折扣。

露西：真的吗？太多了。但是我们公司今年也遇到一些问题。

赵女士：是的。他们说，由于金融危机，他们的销售下降了很多。但我们坚持认为我们的产品品质优良，而且是原创的设计，最后我们给了2%的折扣。

露西：做得好！如何付款呢？

赵女士：我们的客户建议用电汇，但我们坚持只接受信用证。他们也同意了。

露西：对，那要安全得多。今年很多公司倒闭，有时我们都收不回货款。你们开始谈合同了吗？

赵女士：是的。我们就出货的日期、包装和保险已经达成一致。我们已经草拟了合同。

露西：祝贺你！

赵女士：谢谢。你呢？

露西：一切顺利。尽管我们的客户很挑剔，但是我们努力地满足他们的需要。

赵女士：祝贺你！有空来我们摊位吧。

露西：好的，如果今年年底经济复苏，我们可能需要些圣诞节的产品。我还能享受优惠价吗？

赵女士：是的。今年虽然我们遇到了困难，可我们已经合作了10年了。没问题。欢迎你来我们摊位。这是我们的摊位号。

露西：谢谢。我去给我们总经理打电话。再见！

赵女士：再见！

Business Links

1. 商务中心介绍

商务中心是为商务旅行者提供“办公室之外的办公室”。商务中心对外的服务项目主要包括票务服务、商务秘书服务、会议商务服务、外币兑换服务等。票务服务包括为宾客提供代订国际、国内机票、车票等。文秘服务包括电传、传真、复印、打印、名片印刷、邮递服务等。会议商务服务包括会场内外布置策划等。

另外，有些饭店的商务中心还有秘书提供服务，专门负责给一些商务客人提供会议以及生活翻译服务，而且商务中心还对不住店的客人提供服务。

2. 商务中心的服务

(1) 服务项目与设备

商务中心设在前厅客人前往方便的地方。能够提供电传、传真、复印、打字、秘书等五种以上服务，配有现代化通信配套设备。

(2) 服务人员

要求服务人员能用两种以上外语和普通话提供服务，礼节礼貌和服务语言准确、规范，熟悉商务中心工作内容和程序。熟练掌握各种操作设备性能、作用和操作技术，能对设备进行简单保养和排除简单故障。

(3) 电传与传真服务

受理客人电传与传真，客人姓名、房号、发往的国家、地区及文稿内容，登记表格要填写清楚、准确，拨号、线路接通快速，操作技术熟练。

(4) 电脑打印服务

客人要打印文稿时，其文稿内容检查和客人的姓名、房号、打印格式、字体、时间要求等记录准确，电脑操作技术熟练，校对准确，打字每分钟不少于 100 字，错字要少于 2% 。

(5) 文件复印服务

客人要复印文件时，应对其原件内容检查清楚，客人姓名、房号、复印张数、纸的规格等登记好，复印操作技术熟练，复印效果良好。能够按客人要求装订，装订效果美观整齐。

(6) 通信服务

商务中心备有各商务机构通信名录，能为客人提供商务机构通信号码查询服务，收到海内外商务机构电码变动信息分类登记存放，适时通知有关商务客人。

（7）寄送快递服务

能够承担当地外贸系统寄送快递业务的公司下属酒店，商务中心与当地外贸系统签订业务合同，熟悉外贸部门寄送快件的业务范围和有关规定。

3. 酒店商务中心客房化

就在酒店经营者讨论商务中心运营时，各家电信企业提出了结合宽带接入的“酒店商务中心客房化”的解决方案。这个方案的核心是将商务中心的职能融入客房中，使酒店客房增加远程通信、收发传真、远程办公等功能，将酒店客房“写字楼化”。如网络传真就是通过某种技术，将传真收入互联网服务器上，客人可以随时上网，接收、发送传真，甚至能够完成普通传真机所无法完成的群发传真等功能。

Useful Sentences

1. 向公司报告（Report to the Company）

（1）This is Betty, phoning from England. We're at the conference.
我是贝蒂，现在在英格兰。我们正在会场。

（2）I want you to deal with it today, please, Betty! We spent a lot of money on the advertisement.
贝蒂，请你今天就处理好这个问题。我们在广告上花了一大笔钱。

（3）Well, I'll do my best, but I don't think we can change it.
好的，我尽力吧，但是我想恐怕无济于事了。

（4）How's the exhibition going? Is the stand busy?
展会进展如何？摊位来客多吗？

（5）They have agreed to the commission of 10%.
最后达成协议，他们同意 10% 的佣金。

2. 在商务中心（At the Business Center）

（1）发送传真（To Send a Fax）

1）I want to send a fax.
我想发一份传真。

2）I'll send this fax at once.
我要立即将这份传真发出。

3）Sorry, sir. The line is busy.
先生，对不起。线路忙。

4）I tried a lot of times, but it's still busy.
试了很多次，但是线路忙。

5）It's my mistake.
是我弄错了。

（2）复印的收费（The charges for copying）

1）Let me count, it's 15.5 yuan in all.
让我数一下，总计15.5元。

2）Could you tell me how you count this amount?
您能告诉我总数是如何计算的吗？

3）The regulation of charge in Business Center is on this board.
商务中心的收费标准在这块公告牌上。

4）The copy of each piece for size A4 is 1yuan.
每复印一张A4大小的页面收费1元。

5）To enlarge or lessen one piece of paper costs as much as two pieces of paper.
放大或缩小一张的费用是复印一页的两倍。

（3）使用因特网（To use the Internet）

1）May I use the Internet?
我可以上因特网吗？

2）Let me dial-up. Please sit down and you can use it already.
让我来拨号。请坐，现在您可以用了。

3）Can I type out my E-mail.
我可以打印我的电子邮件吗？

4）The Internet charge in 30 minutes is 5 yuan.
上网30分钟收费5元。

5）I'm sorry to bring you so much trouble.
对不起给您添麻烦了。

Chapter 11 签约（Signing a Contract）

Business Situation 1

Mr. Bruce Jackson visits the booth of Shenzhen Ugo Sports Shoes Co., Ltd. and prepares to sign the contract.

布鲁斯·杰克逊先生参观了深圳 Ugo 运动鞋有限公司的摊位并准备签订合同。

Dialogue

B = Bruce Jackson	D = Denny Chen	L = Linda Zhang

B: Good morning.

D: Good morning. Mr. Jackson, we have had the contract done. Please go over it and see if everything is in order.

B: Don't you think we should add the clauses about commodity inspection and certificate of origin?

L: Inspection Certificate of Quality will be issued by China Commodity Inspection Bureau.

B: OK. And please note that the Certificate of Origin should be forwarded to the bank together with other documents required.

L: No problem.

B: Yes, one more thing I would like to point out, that is, timely delivery. You know our customers are in urgent need of the goods. If you fail to deliver the goods at the time stipulated in the contract, we just can't stand the loss.

D: Well, we assure you that the shipment will be duly delivered, as long as your L/C reaches us at least one month before the time of shipment.

B: Of course. When I get back, I'll open an L/C as soon as possible.

D: Good! Please note that the stipulations in the relevant credit should strictly confirm to the terms stated in the contract in order to avoid subsequent amendment. Otherwise, shipment will possibly be delayed.

B: I see.

D: Any other questions?

B: No, nothing more. The contract contains basically all we have agreed upon.

D: I hope this will lead to further business between us. I was wondering whether you can stay here for one or two days after the fair? What about going to the White Cloud Mountain together? The scene is very beautiful.

B: It sounds good! I suppose we can have a day's holiday.

D: I'll arrange the trip.

B: Thank you very much!

D: My pleasure.

参考译文

布鲁斯：早上好。

陈经理：早上好，杰克逊先生。我们已经准备好合同了。请看看所有条款是否妥当。

布鲁斯：您不觉得我们必须增加商检和原产地证的条款吗？

张琳达：质量检验证书由中国商检局签发。

布鲁斯：好。请注意原产地证要和其他所需单据一起提交给银行。

张琳达：没问题。

布鲁斯：对了，还有一件事我要指出来，就是按时交货。您知道我们的顾客急着要这批货。如果你们没有按照合同规定的时间交货，我们是无法承担损失的。

陈经理：嗯。我们向您保证会按时装运的。只要我们最迟在装运期前一个月收到你们的信用证。

布鲁斯：当然了。我一回去就立即开信用证。

陈经理：好。请注意相关信用证条款必须与合同条款严格保持一致，以避免后续修改，从而延误装运。

布鲁斯：我知道。

陈经理：还有其他问题吗？

布鲁斯：没有其他问题了。合同基本上是符合我们的协定的。

陈经理：我希望这次交易能带来我们之间更多的合作。不知道你们能不能在交易会后在这儿待一两天。一起去白云山如何？那里的风景十分迷人。

布鲁斯：听起来很不错。我们能有一天假。

陈经理：我会安排旅程的。

布鲁斯：十分感谢！

陈经理：这是我们的荣幸。

Business Situation 2

Mr. Mark Schultz and Ms. Carolyn Cardinal checked all the terms listed in the contract and finally signed the contract with Ms. Dora Zhao and Frank Li.

马克·舒尔茨先生和卡罗琳·卡迪纳尔女士检查了合同中列出的所有条款，最后与赵女士和李经理签署了合同。

Dialogue

D = Dora Zhao　M = Mark　F = Frank Schultz Li　C = Carolyn Cardinal

D: The contract is ready for signature. Shall we sign the contract now?

M: Great! Let's have a look. Do you make it clear about the packing?

F: Sure. Every single toy will be packed in a color box. Don't worry about that.

C: Very good! And please make sure that the goods should be insured against All Risks and War Risk.

F: That's exactly what the terms of insurance write.

M: Very good! The contract contains all we have agreed upon during our negotiation. All the clauses have met with common understanding.

D: That's great.

F: Mr. Schultz, Ms. Carolyn, please sign your names here.

M: With pleasure.

C: My pleasure.

D: We hope this transaction will mark the beginning of long and stable business relations between us.

C: That's also our hope.

D: Welcome to China and visit our factory any time.

M: Thank you. We wish you a wonderful stay in America.

参考译文

赵女士：合同准备好了。我们现在就签合同吗？

马克：很好！让我看看。包装方面写清楚了吗？

李经理：当然写清楚了。每个玩具单独用一个彩盒装。不用担心。

卡罗琳：很好！请确认货物要投保一切险和战争险。

李经理：保险条款就是这么写的。

马克：很好！这份合同包含了我们在洽谈中所一致同意的。所有条款都达成一致。

赵女士：很好！

李经理：马克先生、卡洛琳女士，请在这儿签名。

马克：很乐意。
卡罗琳：很乐意。
赵女士：我们希望这次交易标志着我们长期稳定的贸易关系的开始。
卡罗琳：这也是我们的希望。
赵女士：欢迎随时来中国参观我们的工厂。
马克：谢谢。祝你们在美国有个愉快的旅程。

Business Links

一、商检证书

商检证书（Inspection Certificate）是各种进出口商品检验证书、鉴定证书和其他证明书的统称，是对外贸易有关各方履行契约义务、处理索赔争议和仲裁、诉讼举证，具有法律依据的有效证件，也是海关验放、征收关税和优惠减免关税的必要证明。

对外经济贸易关系人在向商检机构报验时，应按照商检机构的要求，真实、准确地填写申请单位并签名、盖章。商检证书是关系人申请商检机构检验的正式文件，也是商检机构进行检验的一种原始凭证。一般对于不同合同、不同发票、不同单证或装运单的商品应分别填写申请单。报验时除了提交申请单外，还应根据不同的情况分别提供各种单证。

二、原产地证明书

1. 什么是原产地证明书？

原产地证明书（Certificate of Origin）是出口商应进口商要求而提供的，由公证机构或政府或出口商出具的以证明货物原产地或制造地的一种证明文件。是商品进入国际贸易领域的“经济国籍”，是进口国对货物确定税率待遇，进行贸易统计，实行数量限制（如配额、许可证等）和控制从特定国家进口（如反倾销税、反补贴税）的主要依据之一。原产地证明书一般有三大类：①普惠制原产地证明书，②一般原产地证明书，③某些专业性原产地证明书。

2. 原产地证明书的类型

根据签发者不同，原产地证明书一般可分为以下三类：①商检机构出具的原产地证书，②商会出具的产地证书，③制造商或出口商出具的产地证书。在国际贸易中，应该提供哪种产地证明书，主要依据合同或信用证的要求。一般对于出口货物的实行普惠制的国家，都要求出具普惠制产地证明书。如果信用证并未明确规定产地证书的出具者，那么银行将接受任何一种产地证明书。

Useful Sentences

1. 签约（Signing a Contract）

(1) — Please go over it and see if everything is in order.
请过目，看看是否一切妥当。
— Don't you think we should add a sentence here like this?
您不觉得我们在这儿要加个句子吗？

(2) — Do you have any comment on this clause?
您对这个条款有何意见？
— I have no questions about the terms.
我对此没有意见。

(3) — My secretary drafted the contract yesterday. Please go over it.
我的秘书昨天拟好合同了。请过目。
— Let me check out all of the terms and conditions. Don't you think the packing should be improved.
让我核对一下所有条款。您不觉得包装应该改进吗？
— We'll have the contract amended. What about signing it in the afternoon?
我们会修改合同的。下午签合同如何？

(4) — Are there anything to be amended?
有什么要修改的吗？
— Delivery date. Our customer is in urgent need of the goods.
装运期要修改。我们的客户急着要这批货。
— We can try to ship the cargo in 15 days, but your L/C should reach us in a week.
我们可以尽量在15天内装运，但是您的信用证必须在一周内开到我司。
— I will have the L/C issued as soon as possible.
我会尽快开出信用证的。

(5) — Any other questions?
您还有什么问题？
— Please be sure to attach Quality Inspection.
请记得附上质量证书。
— The Quality Inspection will be issued by China Commodity Inspection Bureau.
质量证书将由中国商检局开出。
— No problem.
没问题。

2. 询问签单（Asking to Sign the Contract）

（1）When shall we sign the contract?
我们何时签合同？

（2）Mr. Brown, do you think it is time to sign the contract?
布朗先生，您认为我们该签合同了吗？

（3）Shall we go over the other terms and conditions of the contract to see if we agree on all the particulars?
我们是否对合同其他条款再看一下，看看是否对于所有细节都同意。

（4）Shall we sign the contract now?
我们现在就签合同吗？

（5）We have reached an agreement on all the clauses discussed so far. It is time to sign the contract.
到目前为止，我们对所有讨论的条款都达成了一致。我们可以签字了。

3. 产品质量证书条款（Clauses about Certificate of Quality）和原产地证书条款（Clauses about Certificate of Origin）

（1）The quality of the goods must be in conformity with Contract No. 87383.
货物质量须与87383号合同一致。

（2）Inspection Certificate shall be issued by government recognized agency.
检验证书由政府认可机构出具。
Certificate of Quantity/Weight must be issued by manufacturer.
质量/重量证明必须由生产商出具。

（3）Certificate of Chinese Origin issued or attested by C. C. P. I. T. states the name and address of manufacturer or producers and states that goods exported are wholly of domestic origin.
中国产地证由中国贸促会出具或证实，证明厂家或制造商名称和地址，并证明出口货物全部为国产。

（4）Generalized system of preferences certificate of origin form a showing Austria as importing country.
普惠制A式产地证显示奥地利为进口国。

（5）Certificate of Origin must be issued in English showing value of goods, number of the relative invoice.
产地证必须以英文出具，显示货值、相关发票号。

附　录

附录 1　美国海关出入境登记表

美国海关出入境登记表（I-94 FORM）

U. S. Department of Justice	美国司法部
OMR 1115-4077	OMR 1115-4077
Immigration and Naturalization Service	移民局
Welcome to the United State	欢迎来到美国
Admission Number 697385031 01	登记号码（＊举例说明）697385031 01
I-94 Arrival/Departure Record-Instructions	I-94 入境/离境记录说明
This form must be completed by all persons except U. S. citizens, returning resident aliens with immigrant visas, and Canadian Citizens visiting or in transit.	除了美国公民，美国海外侨民，永久居民和加拿大公民外，所有访问或过路的人士都必须填写此表
Type or print legibly with pen in ALL CAPITAL LETTERS. Use English. Do not write on the back of this form.	请用大写字母打字或用钢笔或用圆珠笔清楚填写。请用英文填写。不要在此表背面填写任何东西
This form is in two parts. Please complete both the Arrival Record（Item 1 through 13）and the Departure Record（Item 14 through 17）.	此表包括两部分，请填写入境记录（第 1 项至第 13 项）和离境记录（第 14 项至第 17 项）两部分
When all items are completed, present this form to the U. S. Immigration and Naturalization Service Inspector.	填写完毕后，请将此表交给美国移民局官员
Item 7 — If you are entering the United States by land, enter LAND in this space. If you are entering the United States by ship, enter SEA in this space.	第 7 项内容说明——如果你从陆地进入美国，请在空格内填写 LAND，如果你乘船进入美国，请在空格内填写 SEA
Form I-94（10-01-85）N	I-94 表（10-01-85）N
Admission Number 697385031 01	登记号码 697385031 01
Immigration and Naturalization Service	移民局
I-94 Arrival Record	I-94 入境记录
1. Family Name	1. 姓
2. First（Given）Name	2. 名
3. Birth Date（Day/Mon. /Yr. ）	3. 生日（日/月/年）
4. Country of Citizenship	4. 哪个国家公民

5. Sex (Male or Female)	5. 性别（男填 MALE 或女填 FEMALE）
6. Passport Number	6. 护照号码
7. Airline & Flight Number	7. 航空公司和航班号
8. Country Where You Live	8. 你在哪个国家生活
9. City Where You Boarded	9. 你在那个城市降落
10. City Where Visa Was Issued	10. 在哪个城市得到签证
11. Date Issued (Day/Mon. /Yr.)	11. 得到签证的日期（日/月/年）
12. Address While in the United State (Number and Street)	12. 在美国的住址（门牌号及街名）
13. City and State	13. 在美国的住址（市名及州名）
Departure Number 697385031 01	离境号码 697385031 01
Immigration and Naturalization Service	移民局
I-94 Departure Record	I-94 离境记录
14. Family Name	14. 姓
15. First (Given) Name	15. 名
16. Birth Date (Day/Mon. /Yr.)	16. 生日（日/月/年）
17. Country of Citizenship	17. 哪个国家公民

附录2　美国海关申报表

美国海关申报表

WELCOME TO THE UNITED STATES	欢迎来到美国
DEPARTMENT OF THE TREASURY	财政部
UNITED STATES CUSTOMS SERVICE	美国海关署
CUSTOM DECLARATION	海关申报
Each arriving traveler or head of family must provide the following information (only ONE written declaration per family is required):	每个入关的旅游者或一家之主必须提供如下资料（一个家庭只须申报一份）:
1. Name:	1. 姓名:
Last　First　Middle	姓　名　中间名
2. Number of family members traveling with you:	2. 与你同行的家庭成员人数:
3. Date of Birth:	3. 出生日期:
4. Airline/Flight:	4. 航空公司/航班号:
5. Month　Day　Year	5. 月　日　年
6. U. S. Address:	6. 在美居住地址:
7. I am a U. S. Citizen　YES　NO	7. 你是一个美国公民吗　是　否
If No, Country:	如果不是，你是哪个国家的公民:
8. I reside permanently in the U. S. YES　NO	8. 你是在美国永久居留吗 是　否
If No, Expected Length of Stay:	如果不是，预期停留多久:
9. The purpose of my trip is or was BUSINESS　PLEASURE	9. 此次旅程的目的是 商务　旅游
10. I am/we are bringing fruits, plants, meats, food, soil, birds, snails, other live animals, farm products, or I/we have been on a farm or ranch outside the U. S. YES　NO	10. 你携带水果，植物，肉类，食品，土壤，鸟类，蜗牛，其他动物和农产品，或你一直居住在美国以外的农村或牧场吗 是　否
11. I am/we are carrying currency or monetary instruments over $10,000 U. S. or the foreign equivalent. YES　NO	11. 你携带现金或珍贵物品，其价值超过10 000 美元或相当于10 000 美元的外币吗 是　否

12. The total value of all goods I/we purchased or acquired abroad and am/are bringing to the U. S. is (see instructions under Merchandise on reverse side; visitors should report value of gifts only): U. S. Dollars	12. 你境外购买或获得并带入美国所有物品总价值(参看背面商品栏目;访问者只须申报礼品价值):__________ 美元
SIGN ON REVERSE SIDE AFTER YOU READ WARNING. (Do not write below this line.)	在你阅读警告之后请在背面签字(不要在此线下面签字)
INSPECTOR's NAME: (STAMP AREA)	检察员姓名:(盖章区域)
BADGE NO. :	徽章号码:

附录3　各类会展邀请函样板

▶Sample 1

Notice of Overseas Exhibitors Recruitment

华交会境外参展商网上参展申请须知

1. Schedule

1.1 Preparation and arrangement　　February 26th to 28th, 2010

1.2 Exhibition open for business　　March 1st to 5th, 2010

9:30AM - 6:00PM (Stay Open at Noon)

(9:00AM entrance open to the exhibitors)

1.3 Exhibition hall evacuation　　4:00PM, March 5th, 2010

1. 日程安排

1.1 布展：　2010年2月26日—2月28日

1.2 展览洽谈：2010年3月1日—5日

9:30—18:00（中午不闭馆）

（每天上午9:00参展工作人员进馆）

1.3 撤展：　2010年3月5日16:00以后

2. Venue

Shanghai New International Expo Centre

(2345, Long Yang Rd., Pudong District, Shanghai)

2. 展馆

上海新国际博览中心（上海浦东新区龙阳路2345号）

3. Registration Qualification for Overseas Trade Delegation

3.1 Applicants shall be the companies legally registered by eligible law in any country or region (including Hong Kong, Taiwan and Macau regions of China). Copy of the Company

Business License issued by the government or other valid certificates shall be submitted.

3.2 Applicants shall be the companies legally registered over one year.

3.3 All the exhibitors shall be employees of the companies.

3.4 In case the Applicants entrusts its branches, official agents or manufacture plants to participate the fair, the Applicant shall apply to the Organizer and submit: (1) The Business Licenses of both the Applicants and its branches, official agents or manufacture plants; (2) The contact method (including Telephone No. and E-mail Address) of the Applicants, and one of the exhibitors should come from the Applicants.

3.5 The application from foreign invested companies in mainland of China which has no overseas head office is not accepted.

3. 参展准入条件

3.1 境外企业需拥有政府颁发的正规营业执照，且注册地为境外国家或地区（包括中国港澳台地区）。

3.2 企业自注册日期起一年后方可报名。

3.3 境外企业直接报名参展，参展人员均须为境外企业员工。

3.4 境外企业的如通过境内分公司、办事处或境内工厂报名参展，需提供境外总公司以及境内分公司、办事处或境内工厂的正规营业执照，且需提供境外总公司联系人的有效联系方式（电话和邮箱），并由境外总公司委派至少一名员工作为参展人员。

3.5 如境内外资公司在境外没有总公司，则不接受其参展请求。

4. Registration Deadline: Nov. 15th, 2009

4. 报名截止日：2009 年 11 月 15 日

5. Booth Rate

5.1 Standard Booth (3m × 3m): 22,000 RMB for each.

5.2 Facilities for Standard Booth: a table, a lockable cup board, 4 chairs, 2 spotlights (100W), an outlet (220V), and a Chinese-English signboard for each booth.

5.3 Raw Space Rate: 20,000 RMB for 9sqm (18sqm at least, the total space should be integers multiples of 9sqm)

5. 境外企业展位价格及配置

5.1 国际标准展位（3m × 3m）：22 000 元人民币/个。

5.2 标准展位配置：洽谈桌 1 个、锁柜 1 个、椅子 4 把、短臂射灯 2 个（100W）、220V 电源插座 1 个、中英文楣板 1 块。

5.3 光地价格：20 000 元人民币/9 平方米（18 平方米起租，总面积应为 9 的整数倍）。

6. On-site Service

6.1 Provide preferential price for reserving hotels.

6.2 Set up drink-provided spot and provide food and beverage service.

6.3 Provide medical emergency service.

6.4 Set up taxi station, provide shuttle bus (from Metro Station Long Yang

Rd. to Exhibition Hall), the bus especially for rainy days.
6.5 Invite the bureau and organization of Customs, Industry and Commerce, Entry-Exit Inspection & Quarantine, Intellectual Property Rights, the Bank of China, Insurance, Civil Aviation, Post, Delivery, etc. to provide service on-site.
6.6 Provide fax, domestic and international long distance phone, copy and etc. service and public telephone set-up in the hall.
6.7 Set up grocery and provide service including booth decoration stuff, film, drink, business-card quick-print, etc.
6.8 Provide and organize the logistic service of equipment, staff and exhibition-stuff rental.
6.9 Provide information service for exhibitors.
6.10 Provide interpreter service, and business assistant, law consultancy, public Internet room, etc.

6. 现场服务

6.1 提供酒店预订优惠价格。
6.2 设饮水供应点，室内外餐饮点。
6.3 设医疗急救室。
6.4 设出租车站，区间班车（地铁龙阳路站至展馆），免费疏散车（雨天）。
6.5 邀请海关、工商、进出口检验检疫、知识产权、中国银行、保险、民航、邮寄、快递等单位，在展馆设点提供现场服务。
6.6 在商务中心设传真、国际国内长途电话、复印等服务，馆内设市内公用电话。
6.7 设小卖部，提供布展用品、胶卷、饮料、快印名片等服务。
6.8 组织搬运设备和人员提供展品搬运服务和展具租赁服务。
6.9 为参展客商提供咨询服务。
6.10 提供外语翻译、商务助理、法律顾问、公共网络室等。

7. Contact Method

Permanent Office of East China Fair (International Trade Promotion Co., Ltd.)
Add:
Tel:
Contacts:
Fax:
E-mail:

7. 联系方式
华交会常设联络办公室（世博集团 上海外经贸商务展览有限公司华交会项目部）
地址：
电话：
传真：
电邮：

▶Sample 2

Invitation Letter

2nd China International Conference
on Digital City Construction Technology
第二届中国国际数字城市建设技术研讨会
2nd China International Expo on Digital City Construction
Technology & Equipment
第二届中国国际数字城市建设技术与设备博览会

Suzhou International Expo Center
Jul. 10th to 12th, 2008
中国 · 苏州 · 国际博览中心 2008 年 6 月 10 — 12 日

Held by: 主办单位：
Leading Office of Information Affairs of Ministry of Construction
建设部信息化工作领导小组办公室
High-tech. Department of Ministry of Science 科技部高新司
Science & Technology Department of Ministry of Construction 建设部科技司
Suzhou Municipal Government 苏州市人民政府
State Bureau Of Surveying And Mapping 国家测绘局
China E-business Association 中国电子商务协会
China Geographical Information System Association 中国地理信息系统协会
Digital China Institute of Peking University 北京大学数字中国研究院
Venue：Suzhou International Expo Center 地点：苏州国际展览中心
Address: Exhibition Plaza of Modern Road, Suzhou Industrial Park
苏州工业园现代路会展广场
Post code: 215021 邮编：215021
Tel: 电话 Fax: 传真 E-mail: 邮箱 Website: 网址 Contact：联系人

第二届中国国际数字城市建设技术与设备博览会

1. Conference Theme 大会主题

- Digital city & Harmonious society
  建设数字城市，建立和谐社会
- Digital city & Sustainable development of city
  数字城市与城市可持续发展

2. Conference Objective 大会宗旨

Dedicated to the integration and discussion between the nation, government and the construction field, IT field, financial field and news field. Under the macro guidance of the government, encourage innovation and discuss tactics in the perspective of policy & regulation, operation system, scientific & technical tackling and development of the industry. Meanwhile, with the direct view of the exhibition, summarize and demonstrate the e-city works during 11th 5-year plan, exhibit domestic and foreign e-city construction achievement, and the latest trend for technical innovation. Introduce related digital technology, equipment and product, promote extensive cooperation on e-city between domestic and foreign cities, government and enterprises, and realize the multi-span development of e-city.

致力于国家及城市，政府与建设界、科技界、IT 界、金融界、教育界等人士的互动研讨。在宏观决策指导、政策法规配套、建设运作机制、科技创新攻关、行业应用实践、产业发展思路等方面，激发创新精神、商议对策。同时借助展览的直观可视性，总结和展示“十一·五”城市信息化工作，展示中外数字城市建设现状与成果，技术创新最新动态，推介相关数字技术、设备及产品，促进中外城市之间、政府与企业之间在“数字城市”领域的广泛合作，培育“数字城市”产业链，实现“数字城市”的跨越式发展战略。

3. Conference Format 大会形式

The conference will take rich contents, high-leveled background, foreseeing theme and integration style, and obtain high attention from all fields of the society and the media.

大会将以丰富的内容、高层次的背景、具有前瞻性的主题和互动的风格，赢得社会各界和传媒的高度关注。

Suzhou, as the center of global e-information industry and manufacturing, will welcome domestic and foreign industrial and commercial magnates with its unique charm.

作为全球电子信息产品制造业中心，苏州将以独特的魅力迎来中外工商企业巨头。

4. Time and Venue of the Conference 大会时间、地点

Venue: Suzhou International Expo Center, China

地点：苏州国际博览中心

Time: Jun. 10th, 2006 (Saturday) to Jun. 12th, 2008 (Monday)

时间：2008年6月10日（星期六）至6月12日（星期一）

5. Organization of the Conference 大会组织

(1) Holding Organizations 举办单位

Leading Office of Information Affairs of Ministry of Construction

建设部信息化工作领导小组办公室

High-tech Department of Ministry of Science

科技部高新技术发展与产业化司

Science & Technology Department of Ministry of Construction 建设部科技司

Suzhou Municipal Government 苏州市人民政府

China E-business Association 中国电子商务协会

(2) Supporting Organizations 支持单位

China Computer User Association 中国计算机用户协会

(3) Undertaking Organizations 承办单位

China Construction Branch of E-business Association 中国电子商务协会建设分会

Suzhou International Expo Center 苏州国际博览中心

(4) Supporting Media 支持媒体

Journals and Magazines:

Science & Technology Daily, China Construction Newspaper, China Computer Newspaper, China Electron Newspaper, Yangzi Evening, Construction Science & Technology, Internet Weekly, Safety World etc.

期刊和杂志：《科技日报》、《中国建筑报》、《中国计算机报》、《中国电子报》、《扬子晚报》、《建设科技》、《互联网周刊》、《安全世界》等。

6. Theme of Conference 会议内容

(1) Seminar 研讨会

Introducing and discussing the informationalization of policy, standard, technology, equipment and experience of domestic and foreign digital city construction, demonstrate the applicable achievement of digit, website, telecom, related technology and equipment in domestic and foreign informationalization practice. Strengthen & push the research and development of information technology in construction industry, promote the application, cooperation and communication.

介绍与讨论国内外数字城市建设信息化的政策、标准、技术、设备及经验。展示国内外信息化领域的数字、网络、通信以及相关的技术与设备的应用成果，加强和推进建设领域信息技术的研究开发、推广应用与合作交流。

- National Macro-policy Forum 国家宏观政策论坛
- Mayor Forum and Scientist Forum 市长论坛和科学家论坛
- Informationalization Forum of Construction Enterprises 建设企业信息化论坛
- E-government Forum 电子政府论坛
- E-business forum 电子商务论坛
- City Construction Informationalization Forum 城市建设信息化论坛
- Key Technology Forum for Digital City 数字化城市建设关键技术论坛
- Digital Community Forum 数字社区论坛
- Internet Forum 因特网论坛

(2) Achievement Exhibition of Digital City 数字城市成就展

- Exhibition Areas for E-government, E-business Products, Infrastructure Toll Management System
  中国国际电子政务、电子商务技术产品与基础设施收费管理系统展览会
- Exhibition Areas for City Space Information Technology
  中国国际城市空间信息技术及产品展览会
- Exhibition Areas for Telecom and Websites Technology
  中国国际通信及网络技术设备展览会
- Exhibition Areas for Intelligent Community Technology
  社区智能化产品展览会

(3) Round Table Conference for Academicians, Mayors and Entrepreneurs 院士、市长、企业家圆桌会议

(4) Conference and other Affiliated Activities 大会其他配套活动

- Publication of Achievement Collection of China City Informationalization Construction 出版《中国城市信息化建设成果汇编》。
- Publication of the Conference Proceedings and Paper Collection
  出版大会会刊与论文集

7. Fees for Participation 参展费用

(1) Exhibition Fee and Exhibition Attending Procedure 参展费用及参展程序

1) Toll Standard: 参展收费标准

Booth Types and Specification 展位类型及规格

Standard Booth (3m × 3m) = 9 m^2 标准展位 (3m × 3m) = 9 m^2

Price 价格

Domestic: RMB 国内：人民币　International: USD　国外：美元

Equipment of the standard booth: equipments for every 9 square meters of the standard booth include: 3-sided white exhibition board, door head of participating company, both English and Chinese, full-covered carpet of the exhibition booth, 2 chairs, 1 table for consultation, 1 socket (220V/5A), 2 intensified lamps (or daylight lamp)

Floor space (minimal 36 square meters)

Domestic: RMB 720 yuan/m^2　　International: US 280 dollars/m^2

标准展位配置：每 9m^2 标准展位设施包括：三面白色展板、参展公司的中英文门楣、展台满铺地毯、2 把椅子、1 张咨询桌、1 个电源插座 (220V/5A) 和 2 只射灯（或日光灯）。

室内光地 (36 m^2 起租)

国内：人民币 720 元/m^2

国外：280 美元/m^2

2) Specially Recommended Advertisement 特别推荐广告

A. Information Bag RMB 7,000 (per 1,000) 资料袋 7 000 元（每 1 000 个）

B. Gate Ticket RMB 5,000 (per 10,000) 门票 5 000 元（每 10 000 张）

C. keepsake RMB 5,000 (per 100) 纪念品 5 000 元（每 100 份）

Releasing date for site advertisement of the exhibition: 3 day-exhibition, including on-site advertisements and plugs of the conference.

展览馆现场广告发布时间：展期 3 天内，包括现场广告和大会宣传品。

3) Exhibition Attending Procedure 参展程序

① The participants fill in the application form of the exhibition, stamped with the common seal, post or fax to the commission.

参展商请详细填写《参展申请表》并加盖公章，邮寄或传真至组委会。

② Remit related payment of all exhibition fees to the appointed account in 10 days after application.

企业报名后 10 天内将各项参展费用汇至大会指定账号。

③ The committee will obey the principle "pre-application, payment and arrange" and is entitled to remove or cancel the unpaid booth. 大会按"先报名、先付款、先安排"的原则，对未按规定付款的展位有权移动或取消。

④ Other related issues: such as the delivery of the articles to be exhibited and deposit etc. please read *Exhibition Brochure*, which shall be handed out one month in advance.
其他相关事宜，如展品发运、存放等，请参见《参展手册》，《参展手册》于大会前一个月统一发放。

（2）Forum Cost 论坛费用
1）Presentation Fee for the Forum 论坛发言费用
20 minutes will be given to each presentation maker that attends the forum, and the fee is 10,000 yuan. The presentation will be collected into the paper collection, and 2 free paper collections will be presented. Cooperation cocktail party and discussion conference fund will be designed, which is 30,000 yuan for each practice, with one quota for presentation designed for the forum.
参加论坛演讲的每位演讲者时间为20分钟，费用10 000元。演讲内容收入论文集，并免费获得论文集2本。另设合作酒会及合作洽谈会的赞助，费用为每项30 000元，并获得1个论坛发言名额。

2）Registration Fee for the Forum 论坛参会费用
Registration Fee for Domestic Representatives: 国内代表参会费用
Remit before Jan. 31st, 2008, the registration fee is 1,200 yuan/person.
2008年1月31日前汇款，注册费1 200元/人。
Remit before Mar. 31st, 2008, the registration fee is 1,600 yuan/person.
2008年3月31日前汇款，注册费1 600元/人。
Remit after May. 31st, 2008, the registration fee is 2,200 yuan/person
2008年5月31日之后汇款，注册费2 200元/人。
Registration Fee for Foreign representatives: 外国代表参会费用
Remit before Mar. 31st, 2008, the registration fee is US 400 dollars/person. 2008年3月31日前汇款，注册费400美元/人。
Remit after Mar. 31st, 2008, the registration fee is US 500 dollars/person.
2008年3月31日后汇款，注册费500美元/人。
(The registration fee includes conference, conference meal and information fee, accommodation will be arranged by the commission with the cost born by the attendees.)
注册费包括：会议费用，会议就餐费用，信息咨询费用，住宿由大会统一安排，费用自理。

8. 2nd China International Conference on Digital City Construction Technology Feedback of Exhibition Application

第二届中国国际数字城市建设技术研讨会展位申请回执

Name of Company: 单位名称		
Address: 地址		Post Code: 邮编
Contact 联系人		Position: 职务
Company Website: 公司网站		E-mail: 邮箱
Phone: 电话	Fax:	Mobile: 手机

You know the Expo. by: Fax Post Website Industrial communication Media Others
得知本展会途径：□传直 □邮寄品 □网站 □业内人士 □媒体 □其他

The contents to be exhibited: 参展内容

We would rent: 展位租赁

1. ______ standard booth (3m×3m), with the number ______, counting to RMB ______ yuan, specially decorated booth (minimal 36 square meters), with the number ______, counting to RMB ______
______标准展位（3m×3m），展位数 ______，合计人民币金额 ______ 元，特别装修展位面积（最低36平方米）______ 展位数 ______ 合计人民币金额 ______

2. On-site advertisement: 现场广告 ____________

3. Special advertisement: 特别广告 information bag 资料袋 ticket 门票 exhibition/visit passport 参展/参观通行证

4. ____________ forums 论坛

Above fees add up to (minuscule): ______ yuan, 以上费用合计（小写）______ yuan in print（大写）(Above fees shall be remitted to the appointed account no later than May 15th, 2008. 以上费用须在2008年5月15日前汇到指定的银行账户)。

We have carefully read through the items of the information made by the organization committee, and agree to rent above booth or make advertisement items. The faxed or posted copy of the application/agreement for the exhibition to the committee made by our company will come to be valid after it is made, and we agree to obey payment requirement and related regulations issued by the committee.
我们已经认真阅读了组委会提供的各项信息，同意租赁以上展位或申请广告项目。我公司通过传真或邮寄发给组委会的参展申请或签署的协定，一经作出即有效。我们同意遵守组委会做出的付款要求和相关条款。

Signature of the person in charge: 负责人签字　Date: 日期　(Seal 盖章)

Account Name: 账户名称	Account No.：账号

Address: 地址 Post Code: 邮编 Phone: 电话 Fax: 传真 Website: 网址
Contact: 联系人

▶Sample 3

2007 中国国际食品工业经贸洽谈会采购商邀请函

Invitation to Purchasers

2007 China International Foodstuffs Trade Fair

展会名称：2007 中国国际食品工业经贸洽谈会

展会时间：2007 年 11 月 9 日至 11 月 11 日

展会地点：中国广东省中山市黄圃国际会展中心

Name: 2007 China International Foodstuffs Trade Fair

Duration: November 9 – November 11, 2007

Venue: Huangpu International Exhibition & Conference Center, Zhongshan City, Guangdong Province, China

理想平台

Ideal Platform

由中国食品工业协会、广东省中山市人民政府、欧中联合商会、广东省食品行业协会与香港中小企业总会联合主办的中国国际食品工业经贸洽谈会迄今已成功举办了两届，在促进中外食品行业间的经贸交流、投资与合作等诸多方面作出了重大贡献，并成为了中国华南地区的食品盛会之一。

China International Foodstuffs Trade Fair is jointly held by China Food Industry Association, Zhongshan Municipal People's Government, Europe-China Commercial Union, Guangdong Food Industry Association and Hong Kong Small and Medium Enterprises General Association. It has been successfully held twice. The fair has made great contributions to promoting foreign economy and trade exchanges as well as investment and cooperation, it is becoming one of the grand events for the food industry in South China.

作为中国腊味名镇，中山市黄圃镇地处中国经济最活跃地区——珠三角腹地，拥有国内第一个中国食品工业示范基地，现有各类食品工业企业 300 多家。当地具有良好的食品产业发展优势与诱人的投资环境，已经吸引法国、荷兰、英国、巴哈马等多个国家的企业来当地发展投资，其巨大的商贸发展潜力为一年一度的“食洽会”提供了强有力的保障。

Huangpu Town, China's Famous Township for Preserved Meat and Foodstuff, is located in the hinterland of the Pearl River Delta, which is China's most dynamic economic region. Huangpu Town boasts of China's first domestic food industry demonstration base, in which more than 300 food industry enterprises has been set up. Huangpu's booming food industry and advantageous investment environment has attracted foreign investment from

France, the Netherlands, the United Kingdom, Bahamas, etc. Huangpu's enormous potential for commerce and trade has provided considerable momentum for the Foodstuffs Trade Fair.

2007 中国国际食品工业经贸洽谈会为期三天，将举办丰富的对接洽谈活动，其中包括“欧洲食品荟萃”、东盟食品展示会、中国大型连锁超市采购专场活动以及中国地理标志产品推广日活动，协助您获取可观的经贸成效，并建立新的商业网络。

Held during the three days of the 2007 China International Foodstuffs Trade Fair will be various business talks, including European Food Combo, ASEAN Food Exhibition, procurement activities of China's big supermarket chains and Day of Promoting China Geographic Indication Products, which will assist you to obtain considerable benefits and establish a new commercial network.

成绩斐然

Fruitful Achievements

2006 中国国际食品工业经贸洽谈会吸引了全球 30 多个国家和地区以及中国 20 多个省市的 400 多家企业前来参展，其中来自国外的食品企业有 130 多家，占总参展企业的 30% 以上，包括欧洲三大酒庄之一的西班牙桃乐丝、法国美夏以及法国航空食品公司在内的知名展商；包括泰国正大集团、日本贸易振兴机构、沃尔玛集团等在内的近千个采购团队前来贸易洽谈，观展人次达到 30 多万，落实投资贸易合作项目 100 多个，成交额达 7 亿多美元。

2006 China International Foodstuffs Trade Fair attracted more than 400 enterprises from over 30 countries and regions worldwide and over 20 provinces and cities in China. More than 130 exhibitors, accounting for over 30% , were foreign food enterprises, such as world-famous Bodegas Torres of Spain, one of the three biggest wineries in Europe, France Summergate and France Air Food Company. The fair appealed to nearly one thousand group purchasers, including Chia Tai Group from Thailand, Japan External Trade Organization, Wal-Mart Group etc., and over 300 thousand visitors. More than 100 business projects were set up in contract. The turnover was over US $ 700 million.

拓新领域

Exploring New Opportunities

大会将安排多项交流活动，为买家提供良机，在轻松氛围下与国际同行畅叙交流。业内人士亦可参加企业论坛及专题研讨会和其他精彩的专题活动等，获得有关市场、产品、服务的最新资讯，有助于开拓市场的新领域。

The Fair will arrange a number of interactive activities for buyers to exchange ideas and information with global counterparts in a relaxed atmosphere. Industrial insiders can also participate in enterprise forums and symposia as well as other exciting features, so as to obtain latest information concerning the market, products and services, which helps to explore new opportunities in the market.

采购便捷

Convenient Purchase

为充分满足买家需求，2007 年食洽会继续将展品进行专题展示，并在去年的“法国食品专题活动区”基础上，增设主题展区三个，分别是“欧洲食品荟萃专题展区”、“东盟食品专题展区”、“中国地理标志产品专题展区”，充分创造更多的采购商机。

In order to fully satisfy the buyers' needs, 2007 China International Foodstuffs Trade Fair will not only include French Food Special Fair, but also add new exhibit areas, such as European Food Combo Area, ASEAN Food Special Area and China Geographic Indication Products Promotion Area, in which more business opportunities are created.

同期精彩

Other Activities

展会期间，企业论坛及专题研讨会、国际食品贸易港推介会、美食节暨啤酒节、中国优势产业县市推介会也将热烈盛开，届时您将发现更多商业机会。同时，主办方还将举办烟花综艺晚会、黄圃工业成果专线游及民俗文化体验游等系列独具特色的文化艺术活动。

During the fair, Enterprise Forums & Seminars, International Food Trade Harbor Promotion, Food Festival & Beer Festival, Seminar for Chinese Cities with Advantageous Industries will be held, in which you will find more business opportunities. Meanwhile, a variety of unique cultural and arts activities such as fireworks gala, Huangpu industry tour, folk culture experience tour will be the features of the fair.

买家评语

Buyers' Comments

这是一个很有效的洽谈平台，特别是上届的法国食品专题日活动，通过现场对接与法国红酒企业的接触与洽谈，我们顺利地达到了参会的预期目标。2007“食洽会”值得期待。

中山市食品进出口有限公司

冯先生

This is a very effective platform for business negotiations. Especially in last year's French Food Special Fair, through contacts and negotiations with French red wine enterprises, we have got what we expect from the fair. We are looking forward to the 2007 session.

Mr. Feng, Zhongshan Food Import & Export Company Limited

"食洽会"越来越趋于国际化，活动内容也越来越丰富。作为采购商，我们已经连续参加了两届，每次都能采购到我们满意的产品。面对"食洽会"中将来出现的更多合作商机，我们一定会给予更多的关注。

香港食品委员会食品贸易商

刘先生

The fair becomes more and more international with greater variety of activities. As a purchaser, we have consecutively participated in two sessions and have bought back the satisfying products every time. We would pay more attention to cooperation opportunities arising from the fair.

Mr. Liu, Food Trader from Hong Kong Food Council

"食洽会"的影响逐年扩大，服务也更趋专业完善，参展的项目方资质更加优秀，这些都为我们寻找满意的投资项目提供极为有利的条件。

法国美夏（SUMMERGATE）国际贸易有限公司

销售总监 Mr. Francois Nakkachdji

The fair is showing greater impacts year by year and provides more professional and better service, and exhibitors bring better projects to the fair, all of which provide highly advantageous conditions for us to find new investment projects.

Mr. Francois Nakkachdji, Sales Supervisor

SUMMERGATE International Trading Co., Ltd.

来会必看

Must Read

展会日期及开放时间

11月9日	10：00—17：30
11月10—11日	09：00—17：30

Fair Date and Opening Hours

November 9	10:00 - 17:30
November 10 - 11	9:00 - 17:30

展馆地点

中山市黄圃镇国际会展中心

Venue

Zhongshan Huangpu International Exhibition & Conference Center

买家登记地点

中山市黄圃镇国际会展中心主会馆入口处

Registration Location for Buyers

Main Entrance of Zhongshan Huangpu International Exhibition & Conference Center

买家登记时间

11 月 9 日　　09:00 — 17:00

11 月 10 — 11 日　　08:30 — 16:30

Registration Time for Buyers

November 9　　09:00 - 17:00

November 10 - 11　　08:30 - 16:30

入场费

免费入场，只供 18 岁以上的业内人士用名片换领采购商证，凭证进入参观。

Admission Fee

Admission is free of charge with the buyer's badge, which is only offered to industry insiders aged over 18 with business cards.

参会方式

请填妥“参会登记表”、“交通补助回条”，传真、邮寄或者 E-mail 至“食洽会”广州办事处或组委会秘书处。

(广州) 电话：86-20-38372372, 38372117 传真：86-20-38372460

地址：广州市珠江新城华穗路 263 号双城国际东塔 1306 房

邮编：510623　邮箱：diancai _1996@126. com

(中山) 电话：86-760-3300111, 3300222, 3970333

传真：86-760-3978838

地址：中国广东中山市黄圃镇中国食品工业示范基地国际会展中心

邮编：528429　邮箱：hpicec@126. com

或登录“中国国际食品工业经贸洽谈会”网站 www. chinafood-hp. gov. cn (现用) www. foodonline. gov. cn (8 月起用) 进行在线报名。

Ways of Participation

Please fill in the Application Form for Buyers/Visitors and the Application Form for Traffic Allowance, and send it to Guangzhou Office of the fair or the Secretariat of the fair through fax, mail or E-mail.

(Guangzhou) Tel: 86-20-38372372, 38372117　Fax: 86-20-38372460

Add: Room 1306, Shuangcheng International East Tower, 263 Huasui Road, Zhujiang Xincheng, Guangzhou
Post Code: 510263 E-mail: diancai _1996@126. com
(Zhongshan) Tel: 86-760-3300111, 3300222, 3970333
Fax: 86-760-3978838
Add: China Food Industry Demonstration Base International Exhibition & Conference Center, Huangpu Town, Zhongshan City, Guangdong Province, China
Post Code: 528429 E-mail: hpicec@126. com
Or log on to the website of China International Foodstuffs Trade Fair *www. chinafood-hp. gov. cn* (currently in use) *www. foodonline. gov. cn* (to be in use from August) to sign up online.

主办单位
中国食品工业协会
中山市人民政府
欧中联合商会
广东省食品行业协会
香港中小企业总会
Sponsors
China National Food Industry Association
Zhongshan Municipal People's Government
Europe-China Commercial Union
Guangdong Food Industry Association
Hong Kong Small and Medium Enterprises General Association

承办单位
中山市经济贸易局
中山市黄圃镇人民政府
中山市黄圃镇工业开发有限公司会展中心
Organizers
Zhongshan Economic and Trade Bureau
Huangpu Township People's Government, Zhongshan
Huangpu International Exhibition & Conference Center of Huangpu Industrial Developing Co., Ltd.

协办单位
广州市食品行业协会

中山市文化局
中山市工商联合会

Co-organizers

Guangzhou Food Industry Association
Zhongshan Bureau of Culture
Zhongshan Federation of Industry & Commerce

策划单位

广州点彩策略

Planning Agent:

Guangzhou Diancai Strategy Agency

展品种类

- 食品工业产品：腊味、干果、糕点、糖果、饼干、巧克力、咖啡、可可、罐头、蜂蜜制品、果蔬制品、蜜饯、奶粉、酱菜、肉制品、食用菌、熟食及腌制食品、冰淇淋、乳制品、奶制品、蛋制品、豆制品、固体冲剂、粮油食品、糖制食品、速冻食品、酒类产品、饮料、精制茶叶、方便食品、休闲食品、儿童食品、旅游食品、烘烤食品、营养保健食品、有机食品、绿色食品及水产品加工食品
- 食品添加剂与食品配料：调味品、植物油、香精香料、着色剂、防腐剂、乳化剂、抗氧化剂、品质改良剂、营养强化剂及各种配料
- 各地名特优产品
- 酒店、餐饮连锁加盟及美食
- 食品加工机械及包装设备
- 食品科研项目展示

Exhibition Scope

- Foodstuff products: preserved meat and foodstuff, dry fruit, cakes, candies, biscuits, chocolate, coffee, coco, canned food, honey produce, fruit and vegetable produce, confection, milk powder, pickles, meat produce, edible fungus, cooked food and cured food, ice cream, dairy produce, egg produce, bean produce, dissolved granule, grain and edible oil, sugar-made food, frozen food, alcoholic products, beverages, refined tea, instant food, snacks, children's food, food for traveling, baked and roasted food, health food, organic food, green food, processed aquatic food and local specialties.
- Food additive and seasoning: dressing, plant oil, spicery, colorant, preservative, emulsifier, antioxidant, quality-improving agent, nutrition-enhancing agent, etc.
- Local famous brand and high-quality products
- Franchise hotels and restaurants and delicacies

- Food processing machinery and packaging equipment
- Exhibition of food scientific research items

服务周到

食洽会组织完善，面向专业买家提供十分周全的专业服务及设施，其中包括：

- 免费电邮中心：设有舒适的电邮中心，供专业买家进行远程联络，彰显现代便捷的商务服务。
- 交通补助计划：专门针对提出申请的业内买家，提供份额有限的价值为200元人民币的交通补贴。
- 穿梭巴士：特设免费巴士服务，接载参观买家往来国际会展中心与中山、黄圃各主要酒店和客流点。
- 买家贵宾室：贵宾买家可在舒适宁静的贵宾室使用电脑上网，以及免费享用食品。
- 特惠酒店：买家可以根据各自的需要，选择周边的合适酒店入住。

Considerate Service

Considerate and professional service are offered to buyers, including:

- Free and Comfortable E-mail Service Center: Access to long distance connection.
- Traffic Allowance Program: Limited Traffic Allowance worth of RMB 200 available to industrial buyers subject to previous application.
- Free Shuttle Bus: To and from International Convention & Exhibition Center, major hotels, shopping centers and tourist attractions in Zhongshan and Huangpu.
- VIP Room for Buyers: Computer and internet access as well as free drink and snacks are available in VIP Room for VIP buyers.
- Preferential Hotels: Buyers may find satisfying hotels near the fair venue.

特惠酒店名录

名　称	电　话	地　址	星　级	车　程
中山市香格里拉大酒店	8386888	东区起湾北道16号	5星	30分钟
中山国际酒店	8633388	西区中山一路142号	5星	30分钟
三角真善美酒店	5403999	三角镇金三大道	4星	15分钟
汇东酒店	3303388	黄圃南三新圃路段	3星	5分钟
宜必思酒店	3970000	黄圃兴圃路黄圃地税局南	商务酒店	8分钟

Preferential Hotel List

Name	Tel	Add	Star Level	Traveling Time by car
Zhongshan Shangri-La Hotel	8386888	#16 Qiwan Rd. North, East District	Five stars	30 min
Zhongshan International Hotel	8633388	#142 Zhongshan No. 1 Rd., West District	Five stars	30 min
Sanjiao Mascot Hotel	5403999	Jinsan Avenue, Sanjiao Town	Four stars	15 min
Huidong Hotel	3303388	South Sanxinpu Rd., Huangpu	Three stars	5 min
Hotel Ibis	3970000	Xingpu Rd., Huangpu (south to Huangpu Local Taxation Bureau)	Business Hotel	8 min

免费穿梭巴士服务详情

路 线	上落客点	开出时间
南三线	南三公路路口	上午8时至下午4时
新圃线	汇东酒店	上午8时至下午4时
兴圃线	宜必思酒店	上午8时至下午4时

附：巴士服务为每30分钟一班。

Free Shuttle Bus Service

Line	Stops	Business Hours
Nansan Line	Intersection of Nansan Rd.	8:00AM - 4:00PM
Xinpu Line	Huidong Hotel	8:00AM - 4:00PM
Xingpu Line	Hotel Ibis	8:00AM - 4:00PM

Note: Every 30 min. a turn.

参展商其他自选服务

在会间进行定向推介会；在食洽会会刊、食洽会网站刊登广告；在会展中心展馆内外发布广告；协助聘用翻译人员及临时工作人员；协助安排企业间的交流；食洽会指定物流服务（包括展品运输）及清关；食洽会指定承建商提供展台设计、搭建及租借额外工具；食洽会指定旅游代理提供租住酒店、申请签证及代订机票、车票等服务；如有其他特别需求，请联络主办单位！

Other Optional Service for the Exhibitors

In-session promotional seminar; advertisement on the Fair Journal and the fair website; advertisement within and outside the exhibition center; hire translators and temporary staff; assistance to inter-enterprise communication; designated logistics service (including transportation of the exhibits) and customs clearance; booth designing, building by the designated contractor; extra equipment leasing; hotel booking, visa application, air and train tickets booking by the designated tour agency.

Should you need any more information or service, please feel free to contact us.

“食洽会”向登记采购商、投资商及其他专业买家提供以下优待服务:

Special Service for Registered Buyers, Investors and Other Professional Purchasers:

在指定地点集合，免费安排巴士前往会场；派发免费入场证及展会会刊（价格为人民币 30 元）；免费赠送专题研讨会门票（名额有限，赠完为止）；免费使用买家休息室，享用饮料及食品；免费商贸配对服务；中山当地酒店及美食折扣优惠。

Free shuttle bus between the fair venue and designated places; free admission badge and free copy of *Fair Journal* (at RMB 30); Free seminar tickets (first come, first serve); free access to the Buyers' Lounge with beverage and snack; free business matching service; discounts for local restaurants and hotels.

附录 4　参展商向展会组织方预订展位

第十七届北京国际广播电影电视设备展览会

Beijing International Radio, TV & Film Equipment Exhibition 2008

November 5 - 8,2008 — China International Exhibition Center, Beijing, China

SPACE RESERVATION FORM 展位预订表				Deadline: June1,2008	
Company 公司:					
Person in Charge 负责人:		Title 职务:			
Address 地址:					
Zip/Postal Code 邮编:		E-mail 电邮:			
Tel 电话:		Fax 传真:		Mobile 手机:	
Contact Person 联系人:		Title 职务:			
Address 地址:					
Zip/Postal Code 邮编:		E-mail 电邮:			
Tel 电话:		Fax 传真:		Mobile 手机:	

We would like to reserve the followings: 我们希望预定如下场地:

Raw Space: (minimum 36m²) 空场地 (36 平方米以上)

RMB 2,750 / m² × Total Area ________ m² = RMB ________ □ Upper Floor Area of Double-decker RMB 1,375/m² × Total Area ________ m² = RMB ________

(1) Standard Booth: (minimum 9m²) 标准空地 (9 平方米或以上)

(2) RMB 3,150 / m² × Total Area ________ m² = RMB ________

(3) □ Outdoor Raw Space: 室外空场地

RMB 1,250 m² × Total Area ________ m² = RMB ________

Total Amount: RMB ________

Remarks: □ Same location as BIRTV2007 与 BIRTV2007 的展位相同

□ Request new location 要求新位置

Products For Exhibit 展品内容:	
□ Video/Audio Production 音视频制作与播出设备	□ Computer Production & Network 计算机及网络产品

□ Digital TV and New Media 数字电视和新媒体	□ Monitoring Equipment & Accessories 测试设备和仪器工具
□ Transmission System 广播电视传输和发射系统	□ Film Production 电影制作和放映设备

Company Chop (seal) & Signature   Please print full name   Date

Please Complete this form and return to the organizer.

附录5　展会承办商向展馆预订展位

场地预订申请表

Reservation Form

日期（年/月/日）：

Date（Y/M/D）：

<table>
<tr><td rowspan="2">展览会名称
Show Name</td><td>中文 Chinese</td><td colspan="2"></td></tr>
<tr><td>英文 English</td><td colspan="2"></td></tr>
<tr><td colspan="2">主办单位 Sponsor</td><td colspan="2"></td></tr>
<tr><td colspan="2">承办单位 Organizer</td><td colspan="2"></td></tr>
<tr><td rowspan="3">展览时间 Open Date</td><td>布展 Move In</td><td colspan="2"></td></tr>
<tr><td>开展 Exhibition</td><td colspan="2"></td></tr>
<tr><td>撤展 Move Out</td><td colspan="2"></td></tr>
<tr><td colspan="2">展览面积 Exhibition Space</td><td colspan="2"></td></tr>
<tr><td colspan="2">展出内容 Exhibition Content</td><td colspan="2"></td></tr>
<tr><td colspan="2">申请公司名称 Name of Company</td><td colspan="2"></td></tr>
<tr><td colspan="2">联系人 Contact Person</td><td colspan="2"></td></tr>
<tr><td colspan="2">联系电话 Telephone</td><td colspan="2"></td></tr>
<tr><td colspan="2">电子邮箱 E-mail</td><td colspan="2"></td></tr>
<tr><td colspan="3">备注 Remarks:（1）展馆方在收到此申请表之后，将在5个工作日内做出同意或者不同意安排的书面确认函。
We should send you the confirmation relating to your reservation within five working days after we have received your reservation form.
（2）申请方在收到本展馆安排档期确认函后，需在5个工作日内以书面形式回函确认，并落实合同签署事宜；逾期如未收到申请方回复本场馆将不予保留该档期。
Please give us your reply in written form within five days after your having received our confirmation and arrange the signing the contract. We shall reserve the right to cancel this reservation confirmation, once we don't receive any responds from you before the above deadline.</td><td>申请人签名
Signature of Applicant
单位公章
Seal</td></tr>
</table>

附录 6　世界博览会概况

1851 年万国工业博览会（Great Exhibition of the Works of Industry of All Nations）成为全世界第一场世界博览会，在英国首都伦敦的海德公园（Hyde Park，London）举行，展期是 1851 年 5 月 1 日至 10 月 11 日，主要内容是世界文化与工业科技，其定名中的“Great”在英文里有伟大的、很棒的、壮观的意思，借此博览会英国在当时展现了工业革命后，英国技冠群雄、傲视全球的辉煌成果。

1867 年巴黎世博会已经具备了现代世博会的雏形。

二战后，世界人民在满目疮痍的废墟上重建家园，并在恢复生产，复苏经济的基础上，于 1958 年在比利时首都布鲁塞尔（Brussels）举行战后第一个世界博览会（Brussels World's Fair 1958），主题为科学、文明和人性（A World View — A New Humanism）。为了体现科学这个主题思想，布鲁塞尔世博会建造了一座原子能结构的球型展馆，代表着人类进入了科技进步的新世纪的象征，它独特新颖的造型，虽然时隔快半个世纪之久，但仍然历历在目。博览会的辉煌和丰富，几乎使以往的所有世博会都黯然失色。

1962 年美国西雅图举办了一次规模不大的专业性的博览会“太空时代的人类”。博览会展出全新的先进科技，自动售货机和单钢轨铁路，使其获得了巨大的成功。

历届世博会标志

1964 年为了纪念纽约建城 300 周年，纽约又一次举办了世界博览会（1964 New York World's Fair），虽然主题的格调高雅“通过理解走向和平”。然而这次世博会浓重的商业气氛，使观众驻足不前，失去了纪念活动的意义。1970 年在日本大阪首次举办了世界博览会，日本人称之为“万国博览会”，体现人类的进步与和谐，向观众展示了继东京奥运会之后，日本在各方面的发展和成就。得益于这次博览会，日本在以后 10 年的经济发展中，一直保持强劲的势头。

1985 年日本再次举办世界博览会，会址是在新城筑波市，一座距东京 50 多公里的全新科学文化城。博览会的主题是居住与环境人类的家居科技。时隔一年，加拿大为纪念温哥华建城100周年，举办了一次以“交通运输”为主题的博览会。

1988年是英国人在澳洲建立居住点200周年，为铭记这一日子，澳大利亚在东部黄金海岸城市布里斯班举办了世界博览会（Brisbane: Expo '88）。这次博览会的主题是“科技时代的休闲生活”。体现了人类在当今科学技术极其发达的时代中休闲和娱乐。各国都围绕这个主题，以体育、文娱、旅游、休闲、烹调、园艺等各种内容来体现人类生活的丰富多彩。

1990年日本大阪举办了A1类专业性的国际花与绿博览会，主题是人类与自然。展出以世界园艺为内容，作为庆祝大阪“新的开端”100周年的纪念活动。这次展览会共有82个国家参加，55个国际组织与日本各省市和大企业都单独设了展馆或展台。首次在亚洲实现了大型国际园艺博览会，取得了巨大的成功。

历届世博会标志

1992年，是哥伦布发现美洲500周年，为此，西班牙政府在塞维利亚（Seville）举办了世博会，把博览会的主题命名为“发现的时代”。世博会占地面积478万平方米，有100多个国家参加，观众达6 000多万人次。中国馆展出四大发明及长征系列火箭等，被评为“五星级展馆”。

1993年，韩国大田（Daejeon）博览会，这是世界上第一次由发展中国家举办的世界博览会（认可类）。主题为新的起飞之路。中国馆展示了航天科技、三峡工程等，共接待观众350万人次，为各展馆之最，被评为五大最佳展馆之一。

1998年，葡萄牙里斯本（Lisbon）世界博览会。1998年是联合国批准的国际海洋年，博览会的主题为海洋——未来的财富。

2000年，德国汉诺威世博会，主题是人类、自然、科技。参展国家和组织共计172个，为往届世博会参展国家、地区和组织最多的一届。

2005年，日本爱知世博会，主题是自然的睿智，是最近的一次注册类世博会，中国馆接待观众570万人次，为接待观众最多的展馆。

2008年，西班牙萨拉戈萨（Zaragoza）世博会，水塔是2008年萨拉戈萨世博会的标志性建筑，也是萨拉戈萨城市最高的建筑。水塔是世博园中三大主题展馆之一，展览“水，生命之源”（“Water and the Sustainable Development”）为主题的场所，为此也称“水塔馆”。

◆ **世界博览会一览表（List of world expositions）**

时间	举办国/城市	名称
1851 年	英国/伦敦 London	万国工业博览会
1855 年	法国/巴黎 Paris	巴黎世界博览会
1862 年	英国/伦敦 London	伦敦世界博览会
1867 年	法国/巴黎 Paris	第 2 届巴黎世界博览会
1873 年	奥地利/维也纳 Vienna	维也纳世界博览会
1876 年	美国/费城 Philadelphia	费城美国独立百年博览会
1878 年	法国/巴黎 Paris	第 3 届巴黎世界博览会
1883 年	荷兰/阿姆斯特丹	阿姆斯特丹国际博览会
1889 年	法国/巴黎 Paris	世界博览会
1879 年	澳大利亚/悉尼 Sydney	悉尼博览会
1881 年	意大利/米兰 Milan	米兰博览会
1884 年	美国/新奥尔良 New Orleans	新奥尔良博览会
1888 年	西班牙/巴萨罗纳 Barcelona	巴萨罗纳世界博览会
1893 年	美国/芝加哥 Chicago	芝加哥哥伦布纪念博览会
1900 年	法国/巴黎 Saint Louis	第 5 届巴黎世界博览会
1904 年	美国/圣路易斯 Saint Louis	圣路易斯百周年纪念博览会
1908 年	英国/伦敦 London	伦敦世界博览会
1910 年	比利时/布鲁塞尔 Brussels	比利时世界博览会
1915 年	美国/旧金山 San Francisco	旧金山巴拿马太平洋博览会
1925 年	法国/巴黎 Paris	巴黎国际装饰美术博览会
1933 年	美国/芝加哥 Chicago	芝加哥世界博览会
1935 年	比利时/布鲁塞尔 Brusselse	布鲁塞尔世界博览会
1937 年	法国/巴黎 Paris	巴黎艺术世界博览会
1939 年	美国/纽约 New York	纽约世界博览会
1958 年	比利时/布鲁塞尔 Brussels	布鲁塞尔世界博览会
1962 年	美国/西雅图 Seattle	西雅图 21 世纪博览会

（续）

时间	举办国/城市	名称
1964 年	美国/纽约 New York	纽约世界博览会
1967 年	蒙行利尔/蒙特利尔 Montreal	蒙特利尔世界博览会
1970 年	日本/大阪 Osaka	大阪世界博览会
1974 年	美国/斯波坎 Spokane	斯波坎世界博览会
1982 年	美国/诺克斯维尔 Knoxville	诺克斯维尔世界博览会
1984 年	美国/新奥尔良 New Orleans	新奥尔良世界博览会
1985 年	日本/筑波 Tsukuba	筑波世界博览会
1986 年	加拿大/温哥华 Vancouver	温哥华世界博览会
1988 年	澳大利亚/布里斯班 Brisbane	布里斯班世界博览会
1992 年	西班牙/塞维利亚 Seville	塞维利亚世界博览会
1993 年	韩国/大田 Daejeon	大田世界博览会
1998 年	葡萄牙/里斯本 Lisbon	里斯本世界博览会
1999 年	中国/昆明 Kunming	昆明世界园艺博览会
2000 年	德国/汉诺威 Hanover	汉诺威世界博览会
2005 年	日本/爱知 Aichi	爱知世界博览会
2008 年	西班牙/萨拉戈萨 Zaragoza	萨拉戈萨世界博览会
2010 年	中国/上海 Shanghai	上海世界博览会
2015 年	意大利/米兰 Milan	米兰世界博览会

附录 7 重要国际展览行业组织

国际城市、体育及多用途场馆协会 Internationaler Verband der Stadt-, Sport- und Mehrzweckhallen

国际船展组织者协会 International Federation of Boat Show Organizers

国际会议和参观者协会 International Association of Convention and Visitors Bureau

国际商会 International Chamber of Commerce

国际展览服务联合会 International Federation of Exhibition Service

国际展览管理协会 International Association for Exposition Management

国际展览会和展览会协会 International Association of Fairs and Expositions

国际展览会联盟 Union of International Fairs

国际展览局 Bureau of International Expositions

国际展览运输联合会 International Exhibition Logistics Associates

国际展览者协会 International Exhibitors Association

国际展览业协会 The Global Association of the Exhibition Industry

欧洲旅游贸易博览会协会 European Tourism Trade Fairs Association

欧洲农业社团和展览组织者咨询委员会 European Agricultural Society and Show Organizers Consultive Committee

欧洲主要展览中心联合会 European Major Exhibition Centres Association

附录8　广交会参展商服务指南主要内容

Main Contents of the SERVICE GUIDELINES OF EXHIBITORS of the 106th Canton Fair

前言　Preface

欢迎参加第106届中国进出口商品交易会（简称广交会）。

自2007年4月第101届广交会起，设立了进口展区，诚邀海外企业参展。第106届广交会进口展区设于琶洲展馆B区9.3和10.3展厅，展出时间为10月15日—19日，展览面积约1.5万平方米。按照类别设机械设备、小型车辆及配件、电子信息及家电、五金工具、建材及厨卫设备、原材料、日用消费品、装饰品及礼品、食品及农产品9个产品区。

广交会迄今已有逾50年的发展历史，到会客商已达20万人次，已经成为非常成熟的贸易盛会，为参展商提供了展示公司实力，提升品牌形象，交流最新信息的重要平台。参加广交会，与国际采购商直接接触，寻找合作机遇，进入中国潜力巨大的市场，一定让你的事业获得巨大成功！

参加广交会你将获得无限的商机！

Welcome to the 106th session of China Import and Export Fair (the Canton Fair for short).

Since its 101st session in April, 2007, the Canton Fair has set up an International Pavilion inviting overseas enterprises to participate. The International Pavilion of the 106th session of the Canton Fair will be held in Hall 9.3 and 10.3 of Area B of Pazhou Complex from Oct. 15 to 19 with an exhibition area of 15,000 square meters. Exhibits will be shown according to classification in 9 sub-sections, including (1) Machinery and Equipment; (2) Small Vehicles and Spare Parts; (3) Electronics, IT Products, and Household Electrical Appliances; (4) Hardware and Tools; (5) Building Materials, Kitchen and Sanitary Equipment; (6) Raw Materials; (7) Consumer Goods; (8) Decorations and Gifts; (9) Foodstuffs and Agricultural Products.

With over 50 years' development, the Canton Fair, has already grown to be a mature trade fair which has loyal buyers reaching 200,000. It provides the exhibitors with a platform for showing company strength, upgrading brand image, and exchanging latest information. Direct contact with international buyers and opportunities for cooperation, and the entry into the huge potential Chinese market will assure you of a great success!

Welcome to the Canton Fair with boundless opportunities!

Part I 展会简介 A Brief Introduction to the Exhibition

第一章 展会简介

一、展览名称 Official Fair Name

第 106 届中国进出口商品交易会（以下简称广交会）

The 106th Session of China Import and Export Fair (hereinafter referred to as the Canton Fair)

二、主办单位 Hosts

中华人民共和国商务部 广东省人民政府

Ministry of Commerce of the People's Republic of China

People's Government of Guangdong Province

三、承办单位 Organizer

中国对外贸易中心 China Foreign Trade Centre

四、展览地点 Venue

广州市海珠区琶洲中国进出口商品交易会展馆

China Import and Export Fair Complex, Haizhu District, Guangzhou

五、进口展区位置 Location of the International Pavilion

广交会展馆 B 区 9,10 号馆三层展厅（简称 9.3,10.3）

Third floors of Hall 9 and Hall 10 (abbreviated as Hall 9.3 and Hall 10.3)

六、展览时间 Exhibition Time

2009 年 10 月 15—19 日　每天 9:30—18:00

October 15 - 19, 2009　9:30 - 18:00

七、筹、撤展时间 Stand Construction and Dismantling Schedule

筹展：特装展位搭建：2009 年 10 月 10—12 日　每天 8:30—17:30

特装及标准展位展品进馆布置：2009 年 10 月 13 日　8:30—24:00

2009 年 10 月 14 日　8:30—12:00

展馆于 2009 年 10 月 14 日中午 12:00 封闭，参展商应在此时限前布展完毕。

撤展：2009 年 10 月 19 日 18:00 至 20 日 11:00，10 月 19 日晚展馆通宵开放

Stand Construction: Custom-built Stand Setting-up: October 10 - 12, 2009　8:30 - 17:30

Move-in Exhibits of Standard and Custom-built Stand:

October 13, 2009　8:30－24:00

October 14, 2009　8:30－12:00

Exhibitors should have their stand construction accomplished by 12:00 at noon on October 14, 2009 when the complex will be closed.

Stand Dismantling: 18:00, October 19－11:00, October 20,2009

The complex will be open for 24 hours October 19, 2009.

八、主场承建商 Recommended Contractor

中国对外贸易中心（集团）客户服务中心展览工程部

参展商对展位进行特装搭建，必须选择具备广交会特装布展资质的承建商。

Exhibition Construction Department of Customer Service Center, Canton Fair Foreign Trade Centre (Group)

Exhibitors of Custom-built stands shall choose contractors with qualification certification issued by the Canton Fair.

九、大会推荐进口展品承运商 The Shippers Recommended by the Canton Fair

海程邦达国际货运代理有限公司广州有限公司

广州中远物流有限公司

保昌国际货运有限公司广州分公司

泛联国际货运代理（上海）有限公司广州分公司

AirSea Transport Inc. (Guangzhou)

Cosco-logistics (Guangzhou)

Baltrans International Cargo Ltd., Guangzhou branch

Trans-link International Forwarding (Shanghai) Ltd. Guangzhou branch

十、交通 Transport

（一）地铁 By Metro

中国进出口商品交易会展馆位于中国广州市海珠区阅江中路 382 号。参展商可通过以下途径前往展馆：

Import and Export Fair Complex, is located at No. 382 Yuejiangzhong Road, Haizhu District, Guangzhou, China. Exhibitors can get to the Complex through following means:

地铁 2 号线（三元里站—万胜围站）：于新港东站下车前往广交会展馆 A 区，或琶洲站下车前往广交会展馆 B 区；

地铁 1 号线（广州东站—西朗站）：于公园前站下车，换乘 2 号线；

地铁 3 号线（天河客运站—番禺广场站）：于客村站下车，换乘 2 号线；

地铁 4 号线（万胜围站—金洲站）：于万胜围站下车，换乘 2 号线。

Metro Line 2 (Sanyuanli Station - Wanshengwei Station): Get off at Xingangdong Station to Area A of China Import and Export Fair Complex or at Pazhou Station to Area B of China Import and Export Fair Complex.

Metro Line 1 (Guangzhou East Railway Station - Xilang Station): Take Metro Line 1 and get off at Gongyuanqian Station. Then transfer to Line 2, directions are same as above.

Metro Line 3 (Guangzhou Tianhe Bus Station - Panyu Square Station): Take Metro Line 3 and get off at Kecun Station. Then transfer to Line 2 for the Complex.

Metro Line 4 (Wanshengwei Station - Jinzhou Station): Take Metro Line 4 and get off at Wanshengwei Station. Then transfer to Line 2 for the Complex.

（二）出租车 By Taxi

广州出租车起步价（含 2.3 公里）人民币 7 元，每公里租价人民币 2.60 元，另加收人民币 1 元的燃油附加费。出租车计费器安置在车前靠门处。

The fixed taxi start fee in Guangzhou is RMB 7 yuan for the first 2.3 kilometers, plus one-yuan fuel surcharge. After 2.3 km the rate of RMB 2.60 yuan per kilometer is added. The taximeter is located in a visible position at the front of the car near the door.

（三）酒店穿梭巴士 By Hotel Shuttle Bus

酒店穿梭巴士信息请咨询酒店。

Hotel Shuttle Bus Information is available in the hotels.

十一、气候 Climate

广州属南亚热带典型的季风海洋气候，10 月份温度为摄氏 18℃ ~ 34℃，属于少雨季节。

Guangzhou is of typical subtropical monsoon marine climate in South Asia. October in Guangzhou is in rainy season with the average temperature between 18℃ and 34℃. Have an umbrella and raincoat handy just in case.

十二、货币 Currency

中国境内使用人民币。外币可以在酒店和各银行网点兑换成人民币。中国银行和有银联标识的柜员机可办理外币信用卡提现业务。

RMB is the circulating currency in China. Foreign currencies can be exchanged for RMB in hotels and bank outlets. Bank of China and the ATMs with the sign of "China Union Pay" provide cash withdrawal via credit cards.

十三、时区 Time Zone

广州较格林尼治标准时时间早 8 小时（+8 小时 GMT）。

Guangzhou time is 8 hours earlier than Greenwich Mean Time (+8 hours GMT).

十四、电力 Power Supply

中国境内电压为 380/220 伏特 50 赫兹。

The voltage standard in China is 380/220V 50Hz.

第二章　广交会进口展区参展流程

一、申请展位 Stand Application

登录广交会官方网站 www. cantonfair. org. cn 查阅国内/海外招展代理联系方式或直接通过“参展易捷通”（英文版）在线申请展位。

Find contact telephone. of domestic/overseas agents at *www. cantonfair. org. cn* or apply directly via online Easy Exhibitor system.

二、获取展位 Get Stand

与招展代理确认取得广交会展位，并向其领取展位号，展位图和《参展商服务指南》。

Confirm with agents about getting stand and get stand number, Stand Layout and Service Guide.

登录广交会官方网站“参展易捷通”栏目（http://exhibitor. cantonfair. org. cn/en），在线登记详细展品资料。详见展品网上登记章节。

Visit the Canton Fair's website is at *http://exhibitor. cantonfair. org. cn/ en* to register/update information of exhibitors and exhibits, find details in Exhibitor/Exhibit Online Registration.

三、办理入馆证件（筹展证、参展商证、撤展证）

Handle Badges (Badge for Stand Construction, Exhibitor Badge, and Badge for Stand Dismantling).

进口展区参展商的相关证件需通过招展代理办理。具体流程参见证件服务章节。

Badges for exhibitors will be handled by agents. Find details in Certificate Service.

四、展位搭建 Stand Construction

详见标准展位布展服务及约定章节。

Find details, in Standard Stand Construction Service Provisions.

五、展位布置及展品摆放 Stand Arrangement and Exhibit Setting

六、参展 Exhibition

现场洽谈 on-site negotiation

进口成交统计 import turnover statistics

知识产权维护 IP protection

七、撤展 Stand Dismantling

（一）具体撤展时间安排详见撤展安排及约定章节

Find details in "Chapter 6 Stand Dismantling"

（二）展样品回运服务

Return Transportation of Exhibits and Samples

（三）办理撤展证，样品放行条

Handle badges for stand dismantling and Release Note for Exhibits and Samples

Part II　服务指南和服务规定 Service Guide and Stipulation

第一章　证件服务

设立证件服务中心，为参展相关人员提供证件办理服务

The Registration Service Centre shall issue exhibitors badges and passes of various kinds

一、办证地点 Application and Collection Places

地铁 2 号线琶洲站 A 出入口人行道（办理参展商证、筹展证、撤展证、车证、换证）

Sidewalk of Exit A to Pazhou Station of Metro Line 2 for Exhibitor Badge, Stand Construction Badge, Stand Dismantling Badge, Vehicle Pass application and badge replacement

二、证件种类及办证标准 Types of Certificate and Issuing Criteria

（一）参展商证——供参展商进馆使用（参展商证在筹、撤展期间可以使用)，请填写表格 A1。

Exhibitor Badge — applicable to exhibitors for the entry into the Exhibition Halls (Exhibitor Badge is also valid during the periods of stand construction and dismantling). In case the badge is needed, please fill in

Form A1.

办证标准：Issuing Criteria

每 9m² 标准展位可办理：

Every standard stand（9 ㎡）can apply for:

参展商证 3 张（免费）。可多届使用（每届需注册），请妥善保管。

Three Exhibitor Badges (free) can be used for multi-sessions (have to be registered every session), please safekeep it properly.

（二）筹展证——筹展期间供协助参展商进行布展的人员使用，参展商需要可填写表格 A2。

Stand Construction Badge — applicable to persons assisting exhibitors in stand construction. In case the badge is needed, please fill in Form A2.

办证标准：Issuing Criteria

每 9 ㎡标准展位可办理筹展证 2 张。

One standard stand（9 ㎡）can apply for two Stand Construction Badges.

（三）撤展证——撤展期间供协助参展商撤展的人员使用，参展商需要可填写表格 A3。

Stand Dismantling Badge — applicable to persons assisting exhibitors in stand dismantling. In case the badge is needed, please fill in Form A3.

办证标准：Issuing Criteria

每 9 ㎡标准展位可办理撤展证 1 张（需收费：人民币 10 元/张）。

One Stand Dismantling Badge shall be allocated for every 9 ㎡ of standard stand (RMB 10 /one).

（四）停车证——供参展商车辆进馆使用，如有需要，请填写表格 A4。

Parking Permit — applicable to exhibitors' vehicles for the entry into the exhibition halls. In case the Parking Permit is needed, please fill in Form A4.

车证、车位指标安排标准：

Arranging Criteria:

每个招展代理单位均只安排一个地下停车场车证（每证每天收费人民币 15 元）。

One Parking Permit in underground parking lot of China Import and Export Fair Complex is arranged for one Agent. (RMB 15 yuan per day per permit).

每 40 名参展商可办理 1 个大客车证，每 3 个大客车证安排 1 个停车位（每个车位每天收费人民币 45 元）。

One Coach Parking Permit is arranged for every 40 exhibitors, and 1 parking space is arranged for every 3 coaches (RMB 45 yuan per day per parking space).

(五) 筹展车证、撤展车证——供参展商筹、撤展期间运送展样品进出广州市区及展馆的车辆使用，如有需要，请填写表格 A5，A6。筹、撤展车辆在装、卸货物后必须马上驶离展馆，不得在展馆范围内任何地方停放。

Stand Construction Vehicle Pass and Stand Dismantling Vehicle Pass — applicable to exhibitors' vehicles during the periods of Stand Construction and Dismantling when the vehicles carrying exhibits move in and out the city of Guangzhou and the Fair Complex. Should exhibitors require the Passes, please fill in Forms A5 and A6. During the periods of Stand Construction and Dismantling, vehicles shall leave the complex after loading or unloading exhibits. No parking anywhere within the complex is allowed.

三、办理时间 Application Time（内容略）

四、办理方法 Application and Collection Methods

(一) 申办参展商证（含换证和补办）由中介代理机构指定专职办证人员通过广交会（进口展）网络管理与服务系统 http://import.cantonfair.gov.cn 进入办证系统，提交办证申请，申办筹展证、撤展证和车证由专职办证人员到证件服务中心指定的办证地点统一现场办理。由专职办证人员负责从证件服务中心领取证件并发放到参展人员手中，原则上不受理参展企业和个人的独自申请。

The application for Exhibitor Badge (including re-placement and re-application) shall be submitted to Website Management and Service System (International Pavilion) at *http://import.cantonfair.gov.cn* by nominated full-time personnel of agency organization. The application and collection of Stand Construction Badge, Stand Dismantling Badge, and Vehicle Passes shall be submitted on-site in a unified manner to nominated place of Registration service Centre by full-time certificate personnel.

专职办证人员需凭招展代理机构证明到 C 区一楼办证中心参展商证组办理《专职办证员证》，然后凭大会证件和《专职办证员证》办理其他证件业务。

All the badges shall be collected by full-time personnel from the Registration Service Centre, and distribute them to the exhibitors. In principle, the individual application of the exhibitor or his staff shall not be accepted.

(二) 参展企业需交齐参展费用后才能领取与参展有关的各类证件。请各中介代理机构在收到“参展通知”和参展企业递交的办证资料后方可通过广交会（进口展）网络管理与服务系统 http://import. cantonfair. gov. cn 进入办证系统提交办证申请，先到先办。如因未能及时提交办证申请而延误办证，不能及时进馆参展的，责任自负。

Only after the payment of all the exhibition fees has been made shall the exhibitor be granted related badges. After receiving Notice of Stand Confirmation and materials submitted by exhibitors, agents can apply for badges via Website Management and Service System (International Pavilion of the Canton Fair) at *http://import. cantonfair. gov. cn.* Application will be accepted based on arrival priority. Responsibilities will be born by agency organization and exhibitor in case of any failure to enter the complex which is caused by late submit of applications.

（三）因非人为原因未能按要求提前通过办证系统提交办证资料的参展企业，经证件服务中心现场管理负责人审查同意后，由中介代理机构专职办证人员在现场通过网络提交资料，或由证件服务中心协助其提交资料后办证。

In case exhibitors fail to submit application materials through Registration System due to force majeure, upon approval of the person in charge from the Registration Centre, full time personnel from the agency can submit application materials on the spot submit materials with thc assistance from the Registration Centre.

（四）办证资料的总体要求：

Requirements of Materials for Application

1. 护照（或身份证）的复印件必须能清楚地辨认出人像和字迹。

The picture and letters on the copy of the passport (or ID card) shall be clearly recognizable.

2. 凡提供通过扫描录入的证件专用彩色照片（尺寸为 40MM × 50MM），必须是用相片纸洗印出来的光面照片，不得使用由普通打印纸打印出来的相片。彩色照片必须五官清晰，头部占相片的 2/3。直 接提交数码照片的，必须采用 jpg 格式，文件大小在 100k 以内。为提升证件打印相片的清晰度，首次办证者，要求提交白底或蓝底相片。凡照片不符合要求的，将不予受理。

A color photo (40mm × 50mm) shall be submitted. The photo shall be developed on glossy photo paper, while the photo printed on ordinary printing-paper is not acceptable. The picture shall be clearly recognizable and the head shall cover two thirds of the whole photo. The digital picture submitted directly shall be in the jpg format and less than 100k. The photos failing in meeting the requirements shall be rejected.

3. 办理车证需提供介绍信、行驶证（正、副证）复印件、驾驶证复印件。

For the vehicle passes, a letter of recommendation, a copy of vehicle registration certificate (the original and the copy), a copy of the driver's license shall be submitted.

（五）参展企业向中介代理机构提供办证资料时，必须在申请表上的护照或身份证复印件加盖骑缝章给以确认才予受理。

When an exhibitor submits its registration materials to the agency, the copy of passport or ID card on the Application Form is accepted with a seal on the perforation of the exhibitor or agency.

第二章　展览现场服务

本章所介绍的项目服务点位置，详见附件 3 "广交会展馆 B 区功能区域示意图"。

Please refer to the Appendix 3: "Functional Layout of China Import and Export Fair Complex Area B" for the locations of service spots described herein.

一、展览服务受理 On-site Service

（一）广交会设立进口展区参展商服务中心，下设服务咨询、现场服务、标摊搭建、运输等项目组，为参展商提供方便快捷的与展位相关的项目申报服务。

The Service Center for Exhibitors of the International Pavilion is set up at site of Canton Fair to provide exhibitors with convenient service of application for items associated with exhibition stands. The Centre has several project teams such as Service Consultation, On-site Service, Standard Stand Setting-up, and Transportation.

（二）审图组服务内容：特装审图、标准展位改装申报

服务地点：广交会展馆 A 区西侧来宾报到处（两层玻璃房）

Drawing Verification Team

Service covered: Custom-built Verification, Application for Modification of Standard Stand

Location of service: Buyer Registration Office (two-floor building covered with glass), west side of Area B, China Import and Export Fair Complex

现场服务约定 Stipulations of Service

1. 部分服务项目可能会因库存不足、资源不足或超过安全警戒线而无法提供。

Parts of the service may not be provided due to insufficient stocks, the lack of resources or demand overtops the warning limit.

2. 可提供的服务项目，保证在参展商交清费用后 2 小时内完成服务（10 月 13 和 14 日现场繁忙时段除外）。

The service available shall be fulfilled within two hours after full payment has been made by the exhibitor (except for the peak hours on Oct. 13 and Oct. 14).

3. 10 月 13 日和 14 日现场繁忙时段，服务完成时间相对较长，请参展商耐心等候，并请参展商尽量选择在非繁忙时段申报服务。

During the busy hours on October 13 and October 14, it may take longer time to fulfill the required services. The exhibitors are therefore advised to wait patiently and try to avoid applying at peak hours.

4. 如参展商对现场服务有任何不满意，请拨打服务与投诉电话。

Exhibitors dissatisfied with the on-site service could lodge a complaint by dialing the service and complaint numbers.

5. 除特别注明受理截止时间的服务项目外，以上服务受理截止时间均为 2009 年 10 月 19 日。

Deadline for applying for the aforesaid service will be Oct. 19, 2009, except for those whose application deadlines have been specified.

二、展品运输、仓储、搬运服务

Exhibit Transportation, Storage and Portage

广交会推荐海程邦达国际货运代理有限公司广州有限公司、广州中远物流有限公司、保昌国际货运有限公司广州分公司、泛联国际货运代理（上海）有限公司广州分公司为本届广交会进口展区展品承运商，负责向进口展区参展商提供境内外的展品国际货运代理、仓储、进出口通关、出入境检验检疫及广交会展馆进口展区现场搬运等服务。参展商可登陆广交会网站 www. cantonfair. org. cn 查询展品运输服务指南，或直接向四家展品承运商索取详细的资料。

The Canton Fair will recommend Air Sea Transport Inc. (Guangzhou), Cosco-logistics (Guangzhou), Baltrans International Cargo Ltd. Guangzhou branch and Trans-link International Forwarding (Shanghai) Ltd., Guangzhou branch to be the transporter to take charge of exhibit transportation, storage, customs clearance, inspection and quarantine, and portage of the exhibits of the International Pavilion, China Import and Export Fair Complex. The exhibitor can ask for detailed Transportation Service Guide from the four transporters directly or visit *www. cantonfair. org. cn*.

三、电子商务服务 E-commerce Service

电子商务中心设在珠江散步道，提供宽带上网、收发传真、文件打印等电子商务服务。

E-commerce Centre is located at Pearl River Promenade, providing with broadband Internet access, fax and document printing.

四、知识产权与贸易纠纷投诉服务
Complaints for IPRs and Trade Disputes

广交会在展馆内设立知识产权与贸易纠纷投诉接待站。

A Reception Station of Complaints and Settlements for IPRs and Trade Disputes has been set up by the Canton Fair in the exhibition venue.

五、财物遗失申报及失物认领服务
Property Loss Registration and Claim of Lost Articles

服务部门：大会保卫办展馆保卫科

Service Department: Security Section of the Security Office of Canton Fair:

六、外汇兑换服务 Foreign Exchange Service

广交会在展馆内安排中国银行和中国建设银行提供外汇兑换等银行服务。

Bank of China and China Construction Bank will offer foreign exchange service in the exhibition halls.

七、餐饮服务 Catering Service

展馆内设有中餐、西餐、清真食品及麦当劳快餐等服务点。详见附件 3：广交会展馆 B 区功能区域示意图。

There are catering service spots inside the exhibition halls to serve food of various kinds such as Chinese food, Western-style food, Muslin food and fast food like McDonalds. Please refer to Appendix 3: the Functional Layout of the China Import and Export Fair Complex Area B for details.

八、商旅及票务服务 Business Travel and Ticket Service

广州交易会国际旅行社有限公司可为参展商提供商务旅行及飞机票、直通车票的订票服务。

The Canton Fair International Travel Agency Co., Ltd. shall be able to arrange business travels and offer tickets booking service for exhibitors.

九、翻译人员雇请服务 Translator & Interpreter Service

广交会为参展商提供翻译人员雇请服务，主要语种有英语、西班牙语、意大利语、俄语、日语、法语、阿拉伯语等，如参展商需要其他语种翻译人员，广交会将尽力安排。

Canton Fair provides exhibitors with the service of hiring translators and interpreters with different languages mainly including English, Spanish, Italian, Russian, Japanese, French, Arabic, etc. In case that translators and interpreters of other languages are required, the Canton Fair will make arrangements for the exhibitors with efforts.

收费标准：Charge Criteria

- 英语翻译：每人每天人民币 400～500 元，每天工作 9 小时（包括午餐时间 1 小时）。
- 日语、法语、俄语、西班牙语、意大利语、阿拉伯语翻译：每人每天人民币 500～700 元，每天工作 9 小时（包括午餐时间 1 小时）。
- English interpreter: RMB 400 - 500 yuan each person per day of 9 hours (including 1 hour for lunch).
- Japanese, French, Russian, Spanish, Italian or Arabic interpreter: RMB 500 - 700 yuan each person per day of 9 hours (including 1 hour for lunch).

十、医疗服务 Medical Treatment

服务地点：珠江散步道综合服务区 9 号馆南侧

服务时间：10 月 10—19 日

服务电话：0086-20-89124120

Service Spot: South of Hall 9, Comprehensive Service Area, Pearl River Promenade

Service Time: October 10 - 19

Service Tel: 0086-20-89124120

第三章　特装布展施工管理约定

（供租用光地的参展商及其委托的特装布展施工单位使用）

(For raw-space-exhibitors and their entrusted contractors of custom-built stands)

一、特装展位 Custom-built Stands

参展商租用广交会光地（18 ㎡起租），委托通过广交会特装布展资质认证的布展施工单位进行的木结构装修布展或使用其他与广交会标准展位装搭材料不同的制式材料进行复杂装修布展的展位。

Refer to the stands, on rental raw space (minimum 18 ㎡), that exhibitor entrusts the contractor with qualification certification of the Canton Fair to set up and decorate either in the wooden structure or with materials which are different from those used in the standard stands.

二、特装布展施工单位 Contractor of Custom-built Stands

参展商须委托通过广交会资质认证的特装布展施工单位负责展位的设计搭建，凡未获广交会特装布展施工资质认证的单位，一律不得在广交会承接工程或进行特装布展施工。广交会审图组不接受未通过资质认证的特装布展施工单位报图。Exhibitor shall entrust the contractors with qualification certification of the Canton Fair to design and set up the stands. Contractor without qualification certification of the Canton Fair shall be prohibited to undertake such project or construction works. The design and drawings submitted by such contractor without qualification certification will be rejected by the Drawings Verification Team of the Canton Fair.

三、特别提醒 Reminder

参展商与施工单位之间的任何约定或安排纯属双方之间的合约，如发生任何意外、事故或纠纷，双方应循法律途径解决，广交会不承担任何责任。

Any Agreements between the exhibitor and his entrusted contractor shall be deemed to be contracts of the two parties only. Any incidents, accidents or disputes hence arising shall be subject to the legal procedures by the two parties involved, and the Canton Fair shall assume no responsibilities for such consequences.

第四章　标准展位布展服务及约定

(For Standar-booth-exhibitors)(供标准展位的参展商使用)

广交会指定中国对外贸易中心（集团）客户服务中心展览工程部（以下简称工程部）为标准展位搭建单位，负责所有标准展位搭建、展位配电、展具配置等工作。

Recommended Contractor — Exhibition Construction Department, Customer Service Center, of China Foreign Trade Centre (Group) (hereinafter referred to as Construction Department) is in charge of setting up all standard stands, distributing electricity, and configuring stand equipment.

一、标准展位 Standard Stand

基本配置 Basic equipment

包括：三面围板、一块楣板、地毯、射灯 4 支、日光灯 1 支、洽谈桌 1 张、椅 4 张、矿泉水一箱（一箱 24 瓶，三千尺配水质量监督电话：0086-20-XXXXXXXX）、电话机一部。

Including: Three-side walls, one fascia board, one carpet, four spotlights, one F/L light, one aluminum table, four chairs, and one box of mineral water (24 bottles in one case, Quality Supervisory Telephone of SQC mineral water: 0086-20-XXXXXXXX), and one telephone.

展位尺寸:2 970mm × 2 970mm，围板高度为 2 500mm，楣板最低点距地面距离为 2 200mm。

Stand dimension: 2,970mm × 2,970mm, height of walls: 2,500mm, distance between the nadir point of fascia board and floor: 2,200mm

搭建规范

1. 展位内配置的射灯、日光管均按以上图例所标注的位置搭装。

2. 转角位展位只搭两面展板，面向通道的两面不搭展板。

Setting-up Specifications:

The spotlight and the F/L light shall be installed at the positions indicated in the above picture.

For stands located at corners, panels will only be set up at two sides of the stands with other two sides facing the aisle open.

注意事项：

参展商不得擅自更改展位围板、楣板及主体框架，如需增加展具，或拆除标准展位之间的隔板、额外申请增加用电设备，需提前与审图组联系。

Reminders:

No variations of wall, fascia board and main framework will be allowed unless the approval of the Canton Fair is obtained. In case that the increase of stand equipment, the dismantling of partition panels between adjacent stands and separate application for increasing electric equipment is needed, please contact the Drawing Verification Team in advance.

二、标准展位改装约定及申报指引

Stipulations and Submission Guide on Modification of Standard Stand

（一）标准展位改装约定 Stipulations on Modification of Standard Stand

受理改装范围：Acceptable Modifications

1. 拆除或增加同一参展商两个或两个以上相连接展位之间的展板 (Dismantling or installing partition panels between adjacent stands of 2 or greater than 2 of the same exhibitor);

2. 在装搭可行的情况下，增加展柜、展架等展具；

Increasing stand equipment such as show case and shelf stand provided that the installation is feasible;

3. 在不超用电负荷及安装可行的前提下，增加照明灯具及插座；

Increasing lightings and sockets provided that the power consumption will not exceed the designed capacity and the installation is feasible;

4. 在有库存可用的前提下，增加桌、椅等家具。

Increasing quantity of furniture under the condition that the storage is available.

不受理改装范围 Scope of Unacceptable Modifications

1. 拆除楣板（Dismantling fascia board）；

2. 拆除背面及外侧展板（Dismantling panels at the back and exterior sides of the stand）；

3. 同一标准展位间隔为两个半个展位（Separating one standard stand into two stands）。

约定 Stipulations

1. 9月30日前申请改装涉及的展具、灯具、家具数量不超过标准展位基本配置数量的，免收费用。如多于基本配置数量的，增加的数量应另交纳费用。

For the submission of stand modification prior to September 30, in case that the involved stand equipment, lights and furniture are not exceeding the basic configurations of the standard stand in quantity, the service will be free of charge. In case of an excess, the exceeding amount shall be separately charged.

2. 9月30日后申请的改装，无论是增加还是减少基本配置数量，均应交纳改装费用。

For any submission later than September 30, no matter to increase or decrease the basic configurations, modification fee shall be charged.

3. 提前申报与现场申报实行不同收费标准。9月30日前（包含该日）的申报均视为提前申报，9月30日后的申报均视为现场申报。

Different charge criteria will be placed on the advance and on-site application respectively. Application prior to September 30 (including September 30) shall be treated as an advance one while an application after September 30 shall be regarded as an on-site submission.

4. 拆除展板如影响到照明灯具安装位置的，除参展商申报时有特殊要求外，均就近移位。

In case that dismantling the panels would affect the installation location of lights, those lights will be shifted toward the nearest places unless the exhibitor has particular requirements in his application.

5. 拆除的展板两侧如已安装有展具的，除参展商申报时要求拆除展板后恢复展具安装外，均不予恢复安装。

In case that there has been stand equipment installed on either side of the show shelf dismantled, the equipment will not be re-installed after the dismantling of the show shelf unless the exhibitor requires to do so during the application.

6. 申请增加插座的，统一安装在展位左侧靠近展厅通道处或右侧靠近展厅通道处。

The additional power sockets applied will be installed at the left side or the right side of the stand near to the aisle.

7. 标准展位围板高度为2 500mm，布展限高2 430mm。

Walls of standard stands are 2,500mm, while the stand height shall be below 2,430mm.

8. 进口展区标准展位标配的射灯、日光灯及租用的插座的统一供电时间为10月13日9:30；标准展位标配的桌椅统一开始配送的时间为10月13日13:00。

Power will be supplied starting at 9:30, Oct. 13 for the spotlights, F/L lights and rented power outlets installed at all standard stands in the International Pavilion. Tables and chairs for standard stands will be delivered starting at 13:00, Oct. 13.

（二）标准展位改装提前申报指引 Advance Application Guide for Modification of Standard Stand

申报内容 Contents of Application

1. 标准展位改装申请表，请填写表格B2。

Application Form for Modification of Standard Stand. Please fill in Form B2.

2. 标准展位改装方案平面图及文字说明，请填写表格B2-1。

Modification Plan and Descriptions for Standard Stand. Please fill in Form B2-1.

3. 如涉及需要额外增加展具配置的，请填写表格B2-2。

As for additional stand equipment, please fill in Form B2-2.

4. 如涉及需要租用配电箱的，请填写表格B2-3。

As for concerning the rental of distribution box, please fill in Form B2-3.

三、标准展位使用约定 Stipulations of Use of Standard Stand

1. 在任何情况下，参展商不得擅自拆装、改动展位配置的楣板、展板、展具及照明灯具。如有需要改装的，应向广交会提前申报或到广交会进口展区参展商服务中心申报，经广交会同意，并缴清费用后，由广交会安排人员负责实施。

Under no circumstances shall the exhibitor dismantle or modify the configured fascia board, show shelves, stand equipment and lighting lamps without authorization. In case any modification is needed, the exhibitor shall apply for it to the Canton Fair in advance or submit the application at the Service Section in International Pavilion. Upon approval by the Canton Fair and full payment made by the exhibitor, certain personnel will be assigned by the Canton Fair to execute the modification work.

2. 广交会在标摊展位内安装有标配电箱的，不允许对该配电箱安装位置进行移动，参展商在布置时应注意避开。

In case that any distribution box is installed inside the stand, the Canton Fair will not alter its position, and exhibitors are also not allowed to remove it. Exhibitors, during the course of stand decoration, are reminded to avoid it.

3. 参展商租用展馆的电箱由展馆方电工负责安装到展位，电箱开关下桩即展商自带设备与展馆电箱之间的接电工作由参展商自行负责，并由展馆方电工监管。展馆不提供电箱开关下桩即展商自带设备与展馆电箱之间的接电服务。

The electrician from the Canton Fair organizer is responsible for installing the distribution box rented by exhibitors at the proper stand. Any power connection beyond the switch of the distribution, including connection between the box and exhibitors' own equipment, should be done by exhibitors themselves, under the supervision of the organizing host's electrician. The Fair does not provide such power connection service beyond the switch.

4. 标准展位增租的射灯和日光灯不能装于展位的外侧。

Spotlights and F/L lamps additionally rented at the standard stand shall not be installed on the exterior side of the stand.

5. 标准展位配置的楣板、展具及照明灯具等，是中国对外贸易中心（集团）的财产。参展商不得将上述展材带出展厅，不得损坏所有展位的配置，不得锯裁展位的展板、铝材或在铝材、展板、展具上油漆、钻孔、打钉等。

The configured fascia board, stand equipment and lighting lamps in standard stands are properties of China Foreign Trade Centre (Group). Exhibitors shall not take any of the properties out of the exhibition hall. Exhibitors shall by no means damage any configurations of the stand, cut the show shelves and aluminum products, or paint, drill and nail on the show shelves, the aluminum products, stand equipment and the like.

6. 参展商不得在展板上进行任何粘贴，如确有需要，应向广交会进口展区参展商服务中心提出申请，经同意并按广交会认为不损坏展板的方式粘贴。

No sticking on the show shelves will be permitted. In case that the sticking is needed, exhibitors shall apply to the Service Center for Exhibitors of the International Pavilion for approval and thereafter operate without damaging the show shelves.

7. 标准展位不允许安装参展商自带的照明灯具，也不允许参展商携带相同或类似搭装材料进场安装。

No lighting lamps brought by exhibitors will be permitted to install in the standard stand; no identical or similar setting-up materials will be permitted to be brought to the exhibition for installation.

第五章 展品运输服务及约定

根据中国海关、出入境检验检疫机关有关规定，本届广交会进口展区所有进口展品的进出口通关、出入境检验检疫申报，按广交会属地管理办法，应在广州口岸办理展品相关的进口申报手续。从非展出地口岸进口的展品，应当在中国进境地口岸办理相关的转关手续。按照海关的要求，进口展区现场实施封闭式管理，筹撤展及展览举办期间，展馆范围内的展品搬运服务必须由广交会推荐的进口展区展品承运商承接。

According to related provisions of China Customs, Entry and Exit, Inspection and Quarantine Bureaus, import declaration procedures such as custom clearance and application for entry and exit, quarantine and inspection shall be conducted in Guangzhou Port in conformity with Managing Regulations on Dependent Territory. Related transfer procedures for exhibits imported from ports other than Guangzhou shall be conducted in the port of entry. Upon the request of China Customs, the site of International Pavilion will follow closed-end management. During the stand construction and dismantling period and throughout the exhibition, the exhibit move in & out service within the range of fair complex will be carried out only by the recommended transporters for International Pavilion of the Canton Fair.

参展商将进口展品运输出入境可通过三种途径，但无论采用何种途径都应在广交会进口展区筹展期前，通过各自申报参展的招展代理向广交会进口展区招展主管部门提交《第106届广交会进口展区参展展品清单》（见附表C4），以作进口展区参展品信息报备、统计、进出展馆查验放行之用。三种运输途径如下：

Exhibitors' inbound and outbound of exhibits may be conducted via three approaches as below. No matter which approach is adopted, before the stand construction period, the exhibitor shall submit the "Exhibit List for the International Pavilion of the 106th Session of the Canton Fair" (See attachment C4) through its own agent to the managing department of exhibitor recruitment for the International Pavilion of the Canton Fair. The lists will he used to collect and record exhibit information, as well as pass inspection at the exhibit move in & out. Three approaches are:

1. 参展商委托广交会推荐的进口展区展品承运商，采用"门对门"一站式服务，由广交会推荐的相关展品承运商提供境外上门收货、境外运输、检疫、报关入境、国内运输、仓储、展品搬运上展位、展后展品不同处置方式应办理的相关手续、清关核销、展品复运出境到参展商所在地等。

The exhibitor will entrust the Recommended Transporter of International Pavilion of the Canton Fair to provide "Gate to Gate" one-stop service which will include overseas collection of exhibits, overseas transportation, customs clearance, quarantine and inspection, local transportation, storage, exhibits portage on exhibition stands, related procedures for different methods of disposing exhibits subsequent to exhibition, customs cancellation subsequent to verification, re-transportation of the exhibits out of the territory to the exhibitors' locality.

2. 参展商可在当地自行选择货运公司，将展品运输到广州口岸后，再由广交会推荐的相关展品承运商接关（须提前办理相关委托手续），提供进出口通关及出入境检验检疫、国内运输、仓储、展品搬运上展位、展后展品不同处置方式应办理的相关手续、清关核销、展品复运出境前境内运输等服务。

Exhibitor may entrust his own transporters locally to deliver the exhibits to Guangzhou Port where these exhibits will be transferred to the recommended transporter who will offer service such as customs clearance, quarantine and inspection, local transportation, storage, exhibits portage on exhibition stands, related procedures for different methods of disposing exhibits subsequent to exhibition, customs cancellation subsequent to verification, re-transportation of the exhibits out of the territory to the exhibitors' locality. Please note that relevant entrust procedure is required in advance.

3. 参展商可自行安排全程货运，则广交会推荐的相关展品承运商可为参展商提供代办展品出入境手续服务（须提前办理相关委托手续），一种是由展品承运商负责代为参展商办理展品出入境报关、清关手续及展会期间的仓储、海关监管、展品搬运服务；另一种是参展商按一般贸易进口货物的方式自行申报进口，缴纳相应税金后，则展品承运商只负责代办展会期间参展商的展品仓储、搬运服务。其中：

In case that the exhibitor arranges transportation for the entire process, the recommended transporter may conduct outbound and inbound procedures for the exhibits on behalf of the exhibitor. One approach will be that the Recommended Transporter carries out outbound and inbound procedures and customs clearance of the exhibits on behalf of the exhibitor and provide service such as storage, customs supervision and portage of the exhibits during the course of the exhibition; the other approach will be that the exhibitor imports the exhibits as common goods and carries out relevant customs procedures and pays in relevant duties while the Recommended Transporter will only provide services such as exhibits storage and portage during the course of the exhibition. Please note that relevant entrust procedure is required in advance.

以快递方式安排展品入境的，快递的收货人必须是广交会推荐的4家展品承运商之一，并注明是第106届广交会进口参展展品。

For exhibits imported by express delivery, the nominated receiver must be one of the four transporters recommended by the Canton Fair. Please specify as the exhibit of International Pavilion of the 106th Session of the Canton Fair.

以随身携带方式安排展品入境的，请务必注意中国海关的相关规定，对于超过中国海关规定的自用物品范围之外的展品，必须按进口展品常规的报关手续予以申报入境（完税入境或委托广交会推荐的四家展品承运商之一代理报关入境）。

For exhibits imported as personal belongings, exhibitors shall pay attention to relevant regulations of China Customs. For exhibits that fall out of the categories of personal belongings stipulated by China Customs, one should carry out the import of exhibits with normal customs procedures and pay in relevant duties, or entrust one of the four transporters recommended by the Canton Fair to carry out the customs procedures.

参展商可使用国际展品ATA单证册办理展品的进出口通关手续，广交会推荐的相关展品承运商可提供协助服务。

Exhibitors shall carry out import and export customs procedures with

ATA Certificate for International Exhibits, and the recommended transporter could offer assistance.

参展商非选择广交会推荐进口展区展品承运商安排运输服务的（含随身携带展品），则在展品抵达广交会展馆现场后，凭参展前向招展代理提交的《第106届广交会进口展区参展展品清单》（见附表C4）复印件，到广交会推荐的进口展区相关展品承运商现场服务点，办理相关参展展品的进馆登记与放行手续。

In case that the exhibitor entrusts other transporters than the recommended four to carry out the transport of exhibits, or import exhibits as personal belongings, exhibitor should, upon the arrival of the exhibits at China Import and Export Fair Complex, carry out relevant registration and release procedures at the service spot of the recommended transporter for the International Pavilion of the Canton Fair, against the "Exhibit List for the International Pavilion of the 106th Session of the Canton Fair" formerly submitted to the agent.

广交会推荐进口展区展品承运商根据参展商所选择的服务类别收取相应的费用，基本费率参照相关收费标准执行，政府机构因监管需要另外产生的费用按实际发生的金额由参展商缴纳，并缴纳相应的手续费。如需特别的服务，所需费用由参展商向展品承运商自行交纳。

The exhibitor will be required to pay the recommended transporter for the International Pavilion of the Canton Fair relevant fees in accordance with the chosen service scope. Basic rate will be determined as per relevant criteria specified Extra administrative fees charged by the government sectors will be paid by the exhibitor as per real situation including relevant procedure fees. Fees for special services shall be paid by the exhibitor to the Recommended Transporter.

参展商注意事项 Reminders

1. 参展商无论选择哪一种方式将展品运入中国境内，都应该提前与广交会推荐的进口展区相关展品承运商取得联络，并特别注意展品到达及报关文件的报送截止期（以进口展区展品承运商通知为准）。

No matter what approach to be chosen for exhibits transportation to China, the exhibitor will be required to contact in advance with relevant Recommended Transporter for the International Pavilion of the Canton Fair with more attention to the deadline of arrival of exhibits and submission of customs application documents (subject to the notice given by the Recommended Transporter).

参展商需提供的展览文件（所需文件要求以进口展区展品承运商通

知为准）

Exhibition Documents (subject to the notice of recommended transporter)

（1）暂准进口展品报关清单 List of Temporary Import Exhibits

此清单是中国海关确定的清关报表，各参展商均须无例外地填写清楚并交进口展区展品承运商。

This list will be a compulsive customs clearance form stipulated by China Customs and shall be filled in by all exhibitors and be submitted to the recommended transporter.

（2）致进口展区展品承运商的付运确认书［详见表格 C2］

Exhibit Delivery Confirmation to Recommended Transporter [refer to from C2]

为了让进口展区展品承运商清楚每一位参展商对展品运输的要求从而作出适当的安排，请参展商填妥此指示书并在截止期前送回进口展区展品承运商。

All exhibitors will be requested to fill in this Delivery Confirmation and return the same to the transporter prior to the deadline to enable the transporter to thoroughly understand the transportation requirements of every exhibitor so as to make appropriate arrangements.

（3）送中国海关审查的说明书、纪念品、赠品、消耗品及现场播放的录像带、光盘、幻灯片等样本各两份预先寄往进口展区展品承运商

As for brochures, souvenirs, gifts, consumables and video tapes, CDs, slides to be demonstrated in the exhibition and to be submitted to the customs for inspection, the exhibitor shall furnish two samples of each to the recommended transporter beforehand.

（4）正本海运提单、空运主单副本及各类货运文件

Original Bill of Lading, Copy of Master Air Way Bill, and various shippers' papers.

（5）原产地正本木质烟熏消毒证书或非木质包装证书

Original Certificate of Origin, Certificate of Fumigation and Disinfection or Non-wood Packing Certificate.

（6）机械设备及高新科技产品需要提供产品说明书

Product specification of machinery and equipment and high-tech products shall be submitted.

（7）国际展品 ATA 单证册（参展商使用该单证册进口展品的。）

ATA Certificate for International Exhibits (The exhibitor use this certificate for importing exhibits.)

请参展商携带暂准进口展品清单、付运确认书的副本、产品原产地证明书，按一般贸易办理进口手续的报关单、完税证明等到展览现场作参考用。

The exhibitor will be required to bring the List of Temporary Import Exhibits, copy of Delivery Confirmation to Transporter, Certificate of Origin, Customs Declaration as General Import and Certificate for Taxation to the exhibition hall for reference.

2. 参展商须在规定期限内向进口展区展品承运商提出申请，提供所需文件及展品，参展商应如实申报，单货相符。若由于单货不符、申报不全、延误申报而造成不能顺利通关、不能按时送货，参展商应承担因自身失误引起的责任。

The exhibitor must apply to the recommended transporter within the time specified and provide the required documents and exhibits. The exhibits applied will be consistent with relevant documents. Otherwise, the exhibitor will be responsible for any deferment in customs clearance and delivery caused by inconsistency of goods and documents, incomplete application and delay in application.

3. 展览免税品审批：参展商提供清单，由进口展区展品承运商在展览会备案时或开幕前向海关提出展览消耗品免税的书面申请。

Approval of Duty-free Exhibits: The transporter will apply in written to the customs for duty-free consumables with a list furnished by the exhibitor in the registration time of Canton Fair or prior to the opening of the Canton Fair.

第六章　撤展安排及约定

广交会进口展区总体撤展时间安排为 10 月 19 日 18:00 至 10 月 20 日 11:00，19 日晚展馆通宵开放。由于撤展时间紧，请各参展商及施工单位务必抓紧时间撤展，确保不影响广交会第二期的布展工作。

The entire stand dismantling of the International Pavilion of Canton Fair will be from 18:00, October 19 to 11:00, October 20, 2009. The hall will be opened overnight on the October 19, 2009. In respect of the tight time schedule for dismantling, all exhibitors and contractors are required to carry out timely dismantling without influencing construction works for the next phase of exhibition.

广交会对进口展区的撤展工作作如下安排及约定，请各参展商务必

配合并遵守:

Following arrangements and stipulations of dismantling works determined by the Canton Fair should be abided by all exhibitors:

注意事项:

1. 为了更好地服务参展商，加快撤展进度，届时广交会会对进口展区撤展工作安排作进一步细化，并向参展商、进口展区展品承运商及特装布展施工单位另发进口展区撤展工作通知。

In order to provide better services to the exhibitors and expedite the stand dismantling process, Canton Fair will put forth more detailed arrangements for the dismantling works of the International Pavilion and a Notice on Dismantling Works of the International Pavilion will be separately issued to the exhibitors, recommended transporter and contractors of the customs-built stands.

2. 任何迟于10月20日23:00后的延迟撤展行为将会给广交会造成损失，广交会保留向参展商或其委托的特装布展施工单位追讨赔偿的权利。

Any dismantling works later than 23:00, Oct. 20, 2009 will cause losses to the Canton Fair, who shall therefore reserve the right to claim from the exhibitor or his contractors for such losses.

3. 特装展位已清场或预装（含现场租用）的电箱已回收的，特装施工单位应立即联系大会相关服务工作人员办理现场确认登记手续。未按时办理及手续不齐备的，视同违反约定，其中未及时清场的特装展位，按照每标准展位面积扣除1 000元人民币的标准作为代为清场费用；未交还电箱的，按照每个电箱1 000元的标准作为赔偿费用。

Contractors of custom-built stands shall contact the Canton Fair's staff immediately to handle the on-site confirmation and registration procedures after dismantling the stands and returning the pre-installed or rented distribution box. Those who cannot finish procedures in time or finish procedures incompletely shall be regarded as violations. The Fair shall be entitled to deduct RMB 1,000 per standard stand for not dismantling in time, and fine RMB 1,000 per distribution box for those who do not return the distribution box. The on-site signature confirmation and registration procedures are as follows:

现场签名确认手续办理程序如下:

On-site signature to confirm the completion of stand dismantling.

（1）特装展位清场完毕的现场签名确认手续。特装施工单位应于10月20日11:00前将特装材 料清理出馆并立即联系现场展厅管理员查看，由展厅管理员在《特装施工管理收费确认单》（黄色顾客联）上签名确认。办理时间：10 月 19 日 22:00—20 日 11:00，服务电话：89120500、89120503。

The contractors shall contact immediately the on-site management staff to check the stand after the contractors remove the decorative materials prior to 20:00, October 20. The staff of on-site management shall sign to confirm on the "Payment Note of Construction Management of Custom-built Stand" (yellow customer copy). Service Time: 22:00, October 19 - 20:00, October 20. Service Tel: 89130651, 89131206 .

(2) 电箱回收的现场签名确认手续。10 月 19 日撤展当晚，特装施工单位应派员留守展位待大会配电施工人员回收电箱时，要求该工作人员在《特装预装电箱确认单》或《特装租用设备确认单》（黄色顾客联）上粘贴特殊标记，并凭此特殊标记联系展厅值班电工在已缴款的《特装预装电箱确认单》或《特装租用设备确认单》上签名确认。

办理时间：10 月 19 日 18:00—20 日 11:00。

On-site sign to confirm return of the distribution box. On the evening of Oct. 19 when power distribution staff collects the distribution box of the stand, a person nominated by the contractor shall stay behind in the stand and require the power distribution staff to paste special label on the "Confirmation Slip for Preinstalled Distribution Box in Custom-built Stand" or "Leased Equipment Note of Custom-built Stand" (yellow customer copy). The electrician of exhibition hall on duty shall sign to confirm on the "Confirmation Slip for Preinstalled Distribution Box in Custom-built Stand" or "Leased Equipment Note of Custom-built Stand" against that special label.

Service Time: Oct. 19, 19:00 - Oct. 20, 20:00

上述手续缺一不可，请各特装施工单位务必按时办理。前述手续办理及时并齐备的，外贸中心财务处将根据大会相关规定，于本届广交会闭幕后清退特装施工单位的保证金。

Neither procedure is dispensable. The contractors shall handle them on time. According to relevant Regulations on the Canton Fair, after the closure of the Canton Fair, Finance Department of China Foreign Trade Centre shall return the deposit to the contractors who finish procedures completely and in time.

现场申报改装展位及租用电箱的，由参展施工单位持《押金单》参照前述特装展位程序及时间办理相关签名确认手续，并于 10 月 19 日 18:00—20 日 11:00 至进口展区参展商服务中心直接办理押金清退。

For those stands declaring decoration and leasing distribution box on site, the contractors shall bring the "Deposit Note" and handle relevant signed confirmation procedures according to the above mentioned procedures and during the above mentioned period, they shall take their deposit back at the Service Center for Exhibitors of the International Pavilion from 19:00 -24:00, Oct. 19 and from 9:00 - 20:00, Oct. 20.

第七章　展品网上登记

为了更有效地宣传参展商的公司与展品，方便与会采购商更准确、便利、快捷地查找到展商信息，广交会官方网站继续为参展商提供展品网上登记服务。请参展商登录广交会网站“参展易捷通（英文版）”（http://exhibitor.cantonfair.org.cn/en）登记展品详细资料。

In order to better promote your company and exhibits, facilitate buyers' search for information of target exhibitor and exhibits in a more accurate, fast and convenient way, the Canton Fair official website continues to provide free online exhibitor registration for exhibitors. Please visit the Easy Exhibitor (English Version) on our website for online registration of exhibits with detailed information at *http://exhibitor.cantonfair.org.cn/en*.

登记时间：2009 年 9 月 1 日至 9 月 27 日

Registration Time: from September 1st to 27th, 2009

登记方法：Procedure

1. 获取“参展易捷通”的账号和密码。在确认已分配了进口展区摊位后，请参展商登录已登记的电子邮箱，查收附有“参展易捷通”账号密码的邮件。

Acquire the account and password. Sequent to the stand confirmation of International Pavilion, exhibitor should check e-mail address which is registered in stand application form, for e-mail attached with the account and password for Easy Exhibitor.

2. 凭账号密码登录广交会网站“参展易捷通（英文版）”（http://exhibitor.cantonfair.org.cn/en），登记或更新展品详细资料，自行选择产品类别并上传展品图片。

Log on Easy Exhibitor (English Version) on *http://exhibitor.cantonfair.org.cn/en* with the account and password. Register or update the detailed information of exhibits by selecting product category and uploading exhibit pictures.

3. 登记或更新参展商的详细资料（包括联系方式等重要信息）。

Register or update the detailed information of exhibitors, such as the contact means.

4. 注意：无法通过电子邮箱获取账号密码的参展商，请与所属的招展代理联系，获取“参展易捷通”的账号及登录密码。

Note: In case that the exhibitor fails to acquire the account and password through e-mail, please contact the agent of exhibitor recruitment for acquiring.

Part III 规则与条例 Provisions and Regulations

第一章 安全与防火条例

为确保广交会安全有序，防止各类安全事故及违法活动，依据《中华人民共和国消防法》、中国海关监管条例及有关社会治安管理法律法规，结合广交会的安全需要，广交会特制定以下安全与防火条例，参展商应严格遵守。共同维护好广交会的秩序，确保广交会安全。

To ensure the order and safety of the China Import and Export Fair (hereinafter referred as the Canton Fair or the Fair) and avoid various safety accidents and illegal events, the following safety and fire-prevention provisions have been formulated by the Canton Fair in accordance with Fire-prevention laws of P. r. China, Chinese Customs Supervision Regulations and relevant laws and regulations on social security administration as well as safety requirements of the Canton Fair, which shall be strictly abided by all exhibitors.

1. 参展商应加强和提高其参展人员的安全防范与防火意识，积极配合广交会安全和消防部门，共同维护好广交会的秩序，确保广交会安全。

The exhibitor shall reinforce and enhance the safety and fire-prevention awareness of his participants and proactively cooperate with the fire-prevention and security sectors of the Canton Fair to maintain its good order and safety.

2. 参展商应通知及约束其参展人员严格遵守中华人民共和国法律法规，在参加广交会期间不参与任何违法活动，特别是不得在展馆内从事任何违法活动。

The exhibitor shall notify and restrict his participants to strictly comply with the Laws and Regulations of the People's Republic of the China without conducting any illegal activities during the course of the Canton Fair especially in the exhibition hall.

3. 参展商人员应凭有效进馆证件进入展馆，并在展馆逗留期间内始终将有效进馆证件挂于胸前，随时配合和接受广交会保卫人员的检查。

参展商证件只限使用人本人使用，不得将证件转借他人或变卖、涂改。

The exhibitor shall only be allowed to enter the exhibition hall with a valid badge wearing in front during his stay in the exhibition hall for the inspection of the security guards of the Canton Fair at any moment. Such badge shall only be used by the owner and not be allowed to be transferred to any other people or sold out or revised.

4. 除广交会特许的免检人员外，其他参展商人员均应自觉服从和接受门卫保卫人员的安全检查。

Except for those who have been specially exempted by the Canton Fair, all other exhibitors shall accept the safety inspection conducted by the guards of the Canton Fair.

5. 参展商应重视防盗工作，妥善保管好个人随身财物（如手提电脑）和展品。

The exhibitor shall pay special attention to guarding against theft and safekeeping his personal properties (e. g. laptops) and exhibits.

6. 带剧毒展品、易燃易爆展品和带放射性展品，参展商不得携带展品实物进入展馆，只能使用图片、仿制代用品或模型展出。此类展品包括烟花、鞭炮、汽油、酒精、天拿水、氢气及广交会消防保卫部门认为可能威胁展馆安全的其他物品。

No poisonous, inflammable and explosive and radiation exhibits shall be directly displayed in the exhibition hall. Those exhibits shall only be displayed through pictures, copy substitute or models. Goods falling into this category include fireworks, cracks, gasoline, spirits, thinner, hydrogen and other items may be treated by the security sector as threatening to the safety of the exhibition hall.

7. 除指定吸烟区外，展馆室内的展厅、休息区、就餐区、咖啡厅、卫生间、会议室等任何区域禁止吸烟。Except for specified places, smoking shall be forbidden in the exhibition areas such as exhibition halls, lounges, dinning areas, cafe, toilets, meeting rooms and so forth.

8. 无论任何时候任何情况，消防通道均应保持畅通无阻。

The fire-prevention aisles shall be accessible under any circumstances.

9. 展品的布置或摆放应注意做到牢固与安全，参展商如需展品的演示或其他演示活动，事先应向广交会提出书面申请，经批准同意后方可安排，演示时也应注意安全与维护展馆内秩序，确保不存在任何潜在的安全隐患或对参观者、第三方构成任何潜在危险或骚扰。

Collocation and arrangement of the exhibits shall be stable and safe.

Exhibitors shall submit written applications to the Fair in advance for demonstration of the exhibits or other items. And these demonstrations shall not be arranged before being approved. During demonstration, exhibitors shall be in considerations of safety and good orders within the exhibition hall without any potential dangerous outcomes or disturbance to the visitors and any third parties.

10. 所有展品属海关监管物品，展品因毁坏、丢失或被窃而不能复运出境的，参展商应及时向中国海关报告，对于毁坏的展品，海关根据毁坏程度估价征税；对于丢失或被窃的展品按照进口同类产品照章征税。

All exhibits shall be under the control of the China customs. The exhibitor shall give timely report to the China customs concerning any inability of the exhibitor to return any exhibits to original countries/regions because of damages, losses or pilferages. As for the damaged exhibits, the customs shall levy a tariff on basis of the extent of such damages. A tariff shall accordingly be levied on lost or pilfered exhibits in accordance with relevant regulations.

11. 展位搭装应办理申报手续及进场手续，并参照本指南第二部分第三章《特装布展施工管理约定》的相关约定进行搭装施工，该约定是本条例的组成部分之一。

Stand shall be set up on basis of completion of relevant application and entry procedures. Setup works shall then be executed in accordance with relevant regulations stipulated in Chapter 3, Part II herein, i. e. Stipulations of Construction Management for Custom-built Stand, since this regulation shall be an integral part of the regulations.

12. 展览期间，参展商及其委托的特装布展施工单位应安排已申报备案的值班电工留守值班，随时消除可能出现的安全隐患。

During the course of exhibition, the exhibitor as well as his entrusted contractor shall arrange electricians who are recorded on files of the Canton Fair to be on duty so as to eliminate any kind of hidden safety trouble at any moment.

13. 参展商应特别注意用电安全，严禁使用不合格或有故障电器，避免在操作中的使用不当。

The exhibitor shall pay special attention to safety in electricity usage and shall not utilize any unqualified or malfunction electric devices or violate rules during operations.

14. 搭建两层展位特殊安全条例

Special Safety Regulations for Two-Storey Structures

（1）展位第二层不允许使用任何电热器具。

No electronic heating devices shall be allowed on the second storey of the stand.

（2）展位第二层不允许安排任何演示活动及开展中华人民共和国公安部门和消防部门认为不安全的其他活动。No demonstration and other activities which may be unsafe in accordance with the Regulations on the security and fire-prevention sectors of P. R. China shall be allowed on the second storey of the stand.

（3）展位第二层每平方米范围内洽谈人员不应超过 0.5 人，所摆放的展品及洽谈人员的总重量和单位面积重量均不超过通过审核的设计总活载值和单位面积活载值。

Negotiation persons on the second storey of the stand shall not be greater than 0.5 person per square meter. Similarly, the total weights of the negotiation persons and exhibits and average weight on unit area shall not be greater than the total designed loading capacity of this storey.

（4）广交会安排保卫人员定时进行巡查，参展商应积极配合，并随时确保展位第二层不摆放超重展品或人员不过于密集等。The Canton Fair shall arrange guards to go on inspection tours timely. The exhibitor shall proactively cooperate with these guards and ensure only acceptable exhibits weight and person numbers are allowed on the second storey of the stand.

15. 施工或筹展完毕后，所有施工工具、施工余料、包装材料及辅料等均应于展馆封馆前清理出展馆外，不应存放于展位内或展位背面（侧面）的空间内。如需临时存放的，请联系进口展区展品承运商。参展商由中国境外携带入境的施工工具、施工余料、包装材料及辅料视同进口展品管理，需按中国海关的指示办理相关手续。

All constructional tools, surplus constructional and packing materials and accessories shall be cleared out of the exhibition hall prior to closure and subsequent to completion of construction works. The aforesaid items shall not be stored in the stand or any spaces behind (or beside) the stand. The exhibitor shall contact the recommended transporter in case of any temporary storage of such items. Constructional tools, surplus constructional and packing materials and accessories brought from overseas by exhibitors shall be managed equal to import exhibits, and shall go through related procedures under the instructions of the China Customs.

16. 展览期间，参展商应积极配合现场保卫人员做好清场工作。

The exhibitor shall proactively cooperate with the guards at site to carry out clearance work during the course of exhibition.

(1) 清理展位内杂物、熄灭火种和消除可能存在的其他安全隐患。

Clear all rubbish in the stand, extinguish kindling and other possible safety troubles.

(2) 切断展位电源。

Switch off the electricity supply in the stands.

(3) 存放好贵重物品(展品),给配备锁具的展柜上锁。

Safekeeping valuables (exhibits) and lock up the exhibition cabinets.

第二章　卫生保障规则

1. 参展商负责人应负责其参展人员的卫生保障工作,密切掌握其参展人员的身体健康状况,及时向广交会卫生保障办公室提供与卫生防疫有关的个人信息。

The exhibitor in charge shall guarantee the sanitation situations of his exhibitors through mastery of health conditions of all participants and provide the Sanitation Protection Office of the Canton Fair with timely personal information with regard to sanitation and epidemic prevention.

2. 参展人员要及时搞好工作、居住环境和个人卫生;前往人群密集的公共场所要采取防护措施;注意饮食卫生,不随便在外就餐;注意室内自然通风;注意天气变化,防寒保暖、劳逸结合、保重身体、不要带病工作。

Exhibitors shall carry out timely personal and living environment sanitary works. Protection measures shall be undertaken while approaching to any public areas with dense population. Casually dinning out shall be forbidden and all exhibitors shall care about food sanitation. Living rooms must be opened to fresh air. All exhibitors must pay attention to climate changes so as to balance live and work well and not to work with illness.

3. 参展人员在入住宾馆出现发热、咳嗽、头疼、呕吐、腹泻或其他身体不适症状时,要立即报告参展商负责人,及时到就近医院检查、治疗,不要带病坚持工作,更不要进入馆内。如在展馆内出现上述症状时,要立即报告广交会卫生保障办公室值班室,安排送往指定医院检查、治疗。

The exhibitor should report to the person in charge in case of fever, cough, headache, vomit, diarrhea or other uncomfortable symptoms when registering in the hotels. He should then conduct a medical examination and treatment immediately in the nearest hospital. The exhibitor shall not be allowed to work with illness and enter the hotel under such circumstances. If such cases are found in the exhibition hall, the exhibitor should give immediate notice to the sanitary duty office of the Canton Fair. And the Fair shall arrange a medial examination and treatment for the patient in the appointed hospital.

4. 参展人员应自觉遵守以下约定：不随便议论、打听、传播有关信息，自觉维护广交会正常秩序。

All exhibitors shall consciously comply with following regulations: not to discuss, inquire about or diffuse any relevant information of such cases and consciously maintain regular order of the Canton Fair.

5. 广交会通过《个人卫生防病知识》、《卫生保障工作简报》、《广交会通讯》等，向参展人员介绍宣传个人卫生防病知识，公布有关卫生保障信息。参展人员应及时了解、掌握卫生动态和防病知识，增强防病意识。

The Canton Fair will introduce to the exhibitor knowledge of personal sanitation and release sanitary guarantee information through brochures of "Knowledge of Personal Sanitation", "Work Briefing on Sanitation Guarantee" and "Messages of the Canton Fair". The exhibitor should enhance his awareness of sanitation and grasp timely information and knowledge of personal sanitation.

6. 为了保障参展商的身体健康，广交会安排符合卫生安全要求的供餐单位现场提供餐饮服务，建议参展商不要从展馆外其他供餐单位购买中餐、西餐等食品并携带进入展馆内，违者后果自负。

To ensure personal health of the exhibitors, the Canton Fair shall arrange restaurants to provide healthy meals for the exhibitor in the exhibition hall. The exhibitor shall therefore be suggested not to order Chinese or Western foods from other sources or bring the same into the hall. the Canton Fair shall not be responsible for any consequences arising there from.

7. 广交会在展馆内设立医务室，为参展商提供临时应急医疗服务。请参阅本指南第二部分第二章《展览现场服务》。

Clinics shall be set up in the hall by the Canton Fair to provide exhibitors with timely first aid service. Please refer to Chapter 2 "On-site Service" of Part II herein for details.

第三章　展位使用条例

1. 广交会展位只允许已与广交会签订《参展合同》的参展商使用，未经广交会书面同意，参展商不得转让展位或与第三方共同使用全部或部分展位。除非已事先征得广交会书面同意，否则，符合以下条件之一者，将被认定为违约使用展位：

The stands in the exhibition hall shall be exclusively utilized by the exhibitor who has signed the "Participation Agreement" with the Canton Fair. The exhibitor shall be forbidden to transfer or share any stand or parts of the stand with a third party without prior written consent of the Canton Fair. Any of following cases shall be treated as violation of the use of stand regulations herein unless advance permission has been issued from the Canton Fair to the exhibitor:

（1）在展位内派发非备案参展商人员名片、产品目录或宣传资料；

Distribution of business cards, product catalogs or promotional materials of non-recorded exhibitor in the stand;

（2）参展商遮挡展位楣板或另自行制作非备案参展商名称的展位楣板；

The exhibitor makes the fascia board of stand shelter or fascia board with titles of any non-recorded exhibitors.

（3）以非备案参展商的名称进行签约活动的；

Entering into any kinds of agreement in the name of a non-recorded exhibitor.

（4）违反《参展条款》中展位使用的规定；

Violating regulations for stand use stipulated in "Participation Provisions".

（5）广交会有其他充分的证据。

The Canton Fair has other adequate evidences for such misconducts.

2. 参展商因签证理由不能派人参展，必须在征得广交会书面同意的情况下，才可委托第三方参展或使用展位，而该第三方必须持参展商委托书并与广交会签署有关文件以确认其接受《参展合同》及本服务指南规定的所有条款。

In case of absence at the Fair due to visa issues, the exhibitor shall then delegate a third party to participate in the exhibition or use the rented stands with a written consent from the Canton Fair. The aforesaid third party shall hold the Power of Attorney from the exhibitor to sign related exhibition documents with the Canton Fair to confirm that the Participation Agreement and all service provisions hereof have been accepted by such third party.

第四章　展品管理条例

1. 中国海关将进口展品列入暂准进出境货物，展品应当接受海关监管，按规定办理海关手续。属中国海关监管的进口展品包括下列货物、物品：

The China customs shall treat all import exhibits as temporary import and export goods. The exhibitor shall therefore accept the supervision of the Chinese Customs and carry out specified customs procedures. Exhibits under the supervision of China Customs include:

(1) 本届广交会进口展区展示的货物；

Goods and articles displayed or demonstrated in the International Pavilion of this session of the Fair.

(2) 为示范展出的机器或器具所需用的进口物品；

Imported goods and articles required for demonstrating machines and apparatus.

(3) 境外参展商设置临时展台而进口的建筑材料及装饰材料；

Imported constructional and decoration materials used by the overseas exhibitor to set up temporary stand.

(4) 供展品作示范宣传而进口的电影片、幻灯片、录像带、录音带、说明书、广告、光盘、显示器材等；

Imported films, slides, video tapes, tapes, specifications, advertisements, discs, and display equipment used by the exhibitor for demonstration and publicity.

(5) 其他用于展示的进口物品。

Other imported goods and articles displayed or demonstrated in the exhibition hall.

2. 广州海关是本届广交会进口展区展品的主管海关。广交会举办期间，广州海关对进口展区展品实行口岸转关、展出地申报查验的集中监管方式。原则上，各参展商应在广州海关办理展品进口申报手续；非从广州海关进口的展品，应当在进境地海关办理转关手续。

Guangzhou Customs is the local customs of exhibits in the International Pavilion of the Canton Fair. During the Canton Fair, Guangzhou Customs shall adopt concentrating supervision of port transfer, declaration and inspection of exhibiting place. In principle, exhibitors shall conduct the import declaration procedures in Guangzhou Customs. Transfer procedures of exhibits imported from ports other than Guangzhou port shall be conducted in entry customs.

3. 本届广交会进口展区展品将享受免领进口许可证、免交进口关税和其他税费等特别待遇。中国海关要求进口展区展品承运商及海外参展商对每一件进口展品负责，对其进行担保。敬请各海外参展商严格遵守中国海关的有关规定，包括但不限于以下规定：

Exhibits of the International Pavilion of this session of the Canton Fair fall into the scope of the custody of China Customs, and shall enjoy such special treatments as exempt from getting import permit, exempt from pay for import tariff and other taxes. Transporter and overseas exhibitors of the International Pavilion are required by the China Customs to be responsible for every article of imported exhibits and guarantee them. Exhibits imported under customs bonds shall strictly comply with relevant Chinese customs regulations, include but not limit to the following:

4. 展出或者使用的宣传品和技术数据，包括电影片、幻灯片、录音带、录像带、唱片、光盘、照片、地图、说明书、广告等，展出单位应当事先送交广州海关，审查同意后，始得使用。在未经海关审查同意前，参展商不能发放或使用这些物品。对中华人民共和国政治、经济、文化、道德有害的以及侵犯知识产权的印刷品和音像制品，不得展出或使用，并由海关根据情况予以没收、退运出境或责令参展商更改后使用。

All promotional materials and technical data to be used or demonstrated including films, slides, tapes, video tapes, CD-ROMs, pictures, maps, descriptions and advertisements should be submitted to Guangzhou Customs by the exhibitor for prior approval. Without permission from the customs, the aforesaid items shall not be used or distributed. All printing materials and audio-visual products harmful to the politics, economy, culture and morality of the People's Republic of China and infringing any IPRs shall not be used or demonstrated. Otherwise, they shall be confiscated, returned by the customs as per real situation or be forcibly modified prior to any kind of utilization.

5. 根据中国出入境检验检疫法律法规，暂准进出境的货物免予检验。但是，法律、行政法规另有规定的除外（如动物、水果类展品需经检疫合格后才可入境）。检验不收任何费用，检疫则按检疫的种类与要求收取一定费用，相关的收费按国家颁布的标准执行。参展商持国际展品 ATA 单证册办理进口货物出入境的，在检验检疫方面未有豁免或优待的政策。

In accordance with laws and regulations on entry-exit, inspection and quarantine of China, temporary import and export goods shall be exempted from inspection unless otherwise specified by laws and other administrative regulations (Entry of exhibits such as animals and fruits shall be approved after the quarantine). Inspection is conducted free of charge, and quarantine is charged according to the categories and requirements. Related charges are paid in accordance with national standards. Exhibitors who conduct the entry and exit procedures with ATA certificate shall enjoy the exemption or special treatment in terms of inspection and quarantine.

6. 境外动植物、食品类的展品在入境前必须得到中国出入境检验检疫机构确认、批准才可进口，参展商必须在进口前 20 天把有关展品或样本或展品清单提供给展品承运商以提交中国有关部门审批。广州出入境检验检疫局是本届广交会进口展区展品检验检疫直接管辖机构。

Overseas animal, vegetation and foodstuff exhibits shall be validated/approved by China's entry-exit. inspection and quarantine authorities prior to entry to China. The exhibitor shall be required to furnish to the recommended transporter with exhibits/samples/list of exhibits for approval from related authorities 20 days prior to import of such goods. Guangzhou Entry-Exit, Inspection and Quarantine Bureau is responsible for the inspection and quarantine of exhibits of the International Pavilion of the 106th session of the Canton Fair.

按国家相关法规规定属于禁止出入境、禁止随身携带或通过邮寄出入境的物品，有关需办理动植物检疫审批的进出境展品目录及具备的条件，办理相关手续需提供的有关文件及资料等，可登录广交会网站 www. cantonfair. org. cn 在《展览品运输服务指南》中查询，或直接向广交会推荐的进口展区展品承运商索取详细的资料。

For exhibits, according to related laws and regulations, which are forbidden to enter or exit, be carried, or posted, exhibitlist and conditions for inspection and approval for animal and vegetation, documents and materials for related procedures, please refer to Service Guide of Exhibit Transportation at *www. cantonfair. org. cn* or ask for detailed materials from the recommended transporters of the International Pavilion of the Canton Fair.

7. 展览现场发现参展的农产品类展品存在明显不符合中国出入境检验检疫有关规定而带有安全隐患的，参展商必须立即进行彻底消杀，并按规定送到广州市政环卫行政部门指定的填埋场深埋或焚毁，由此产生的费用由参展商自行负责。

In case farm products are found not in conformity with related regulations on entry-exit, Inspection and quarantine and with safety hazard, the exhibitors shall destroy these products immediately and bury or burn them in the landfill nominated by Bureau of City Appearance, Environment, and Sanitation of Guangzhou Municipality. The expense occurred therefrom shall be borne by the exhibitors.

8. 参展商只允许在展位内展出《参展合同》约定或经广交会书面同意备案的参展展品，并携带或向广交会提交以下文件备查：

Only exhibits stipulated in the Participation Agreement or with written consent by the Canton Fair shall be exhibited by the exhibitor in the stand. The exhibitor shall bring along and submit the following documents in advance to inspection:

（1）前述《展品运输服务及约定》中“参展商注意事项”所列各类文件，以及《第 106 届广交会进口展区参展展品清单》。

Documents listed by the Exhibitor Notices of the Services and Stipulations of Exhibit Transportation, as well as the Exhibit List for the International Pavilion of the 106th Session of the Canton Fair.

（2）凡是涉及商标、专利、版权等知识产权及质量认证的参展展品，应携带《商标、专利、版权、质量认证情况备案清单》（请填写表格 D1）及附上商标、专利、版权、质量认证的合法权利证书复印件。

All exhibits involving IPRs such as trademark, patent and copyright and quality attestation should be attached with “List of Files for Trademark, Patent, Copyright & Quality Attestation” (please fill in Schedule D1) and copies of legal certificates of such trademark, patent and copyright and quality attestation.

（3）非参展商直接生产的展品，应与供货商签订允许其参展的协议书。

For exhibits not produced directly by the exhibitor, agreement should be reached and signed with the suppliers on the exhibits' participation in the Fair.

（4）自行选择非广交会推荐的进口展区展品承运商安排展品运输的，请提供与货运公司的付运确认书（复印件）供广交会进口展区组织机构核查并登记备案。

In case that exhibitor entrusts other transporters than the recommended ones to carry out the transportation of exhibits, exhibitor should provide the copies of letter of confirmation on transportation from the trusted transporter to the organizing committee of the International Pavilion for the purpose of inspection and registration.

9. 根据中国海关的要求，中国台湾地区企业参展需办理备案手续。

中国台湾地区参展商经确认准许参展后，请预先向招展代理索取并填报《台湾同胞赴祖国大陆参展备案表》，由招展代理提交给广交会招展主管部门以便向中国海关申请办理台湾地区企业参展备案手续。若未办理该备案手续，广交会推荐的进口展区展品承运商将无法承接台湾地区参展商的“一站式”展品运输服务委托。

According to the regulations of China Customs, exhibitors from Taiwan region of China shall be filed for record. Subsequent to the confirmation of participation, Taiwan exhibitors shall receive from the agent of exhibitor recruitment and fill in the Registration Form of Participation by Taiwan Exhibitors at Mainland Exhibition, with which the agent will carry out the relevant registration procedures at China Customs. Without the above registration procedures, the recommended transporter will fail to fulfill the one-stop exhibit transportation service entrusted by the Taiwan exhibitors.

10. 符合下述条件之一的展品，均视为违约展品，均按违约处理。

Exhibits fall into one of the following categories shall be treated as breach exhibits and shall be disposed as breach products.

（1）超出《参展合同》约定或经广交会书面同意备案的参展展品范围的展品。

Exhibits not included in the exhibit scope specified in the Participation Agreement or exhibit scope approved by written consent of the Canton Fair.

（2）涉及商标、专利、版权等知识产权及质量认证的展品，无法提供合法权利证书。

Exhibits involving IPRs such as trademarks, patent, copyright and quality attestation without relevant legal certificates.

（3）非参展商直接生产的展品，无法提供供货商允许其参展的协议书。

Exhibits not directly produced by the exhibitor without signed Participation Agreement with the manufacturer.

（4）按中国法律法规应实施检验检疫的展品而未经检验检疫的。

Exhibits, which shall go through the procedures of inspection and quarantine according to Chinese laws and regulations, are not inspected or quarantined.

（5）未经中国海关、出入境检验检疫机构同意，在展会期间提供试销、试吃的展品。

Exhibits, without the consent of China Customs and entry-exit, inspection and quarantine authorities, are sold or eaten on a trial basis during the Fair.

(6) 其他不能说明合法来源的展品。

Other exhibits without legal origins.

11. 所有参展展品不得在展馆内销售。

No exhibits shall be sold in the hall.

12. 参展商不得在展馆内以任何形式陈列、展示、宣传任何其他展览会的资料及为该展览会进行任何形式的宣传活动，除非已事先征得广交会书面同意。

The exhibitor per se shall not be allowed to display, demonstrate and publicize any materials of the exhibition in any format in the hall or carry out any kind of publicity for the exhibition in any forms without prior written consent of the Canton Fair.

第五章 参展行为规则

1. 参展企业自备的企业介绍、产品目录或宣传单张等，内容仅限于介绍本企业和本届参展的产品，仅限于在本企业展位内派发。参展商的一切参展行为，包括展出、演示、派发礼品，只能在《参展合同》约定的展位范围内进行，不得对周边参展商造成骚扰或影响广交会的参展秩序，并严格遵守《安全与防火条例》。

Content coverage of any company introduction, products directory or brochure leaf brought by exhibitors is restricted on the exhibitor's own company introduction or products exhibit in the current fair, and any distribution of these material outside exhibitor's own stand is prohibited. All activities of the exhibitor including exhibition, demonstration, distribution of product catalogs and promotional materials or gifts shall have to be carried out only within the stand area stipulated in the Participation Agreement without disturbing the neighboring exhibitors or exhibition order of the Canton Fair. The exhibitor shall strictly abide by the Safety and Fire-prevention Regulations.

2. 参展商应教育和约束其参展人员及雇请人员，保持良好的参展行为。

The exhibitor shall instruct and restrict his participants to behave themselves in the exhibition.

(1) 不偷窃其他参展展位的展品。

No pilferage of exhibits of other exhibitors.

(2) 未经其他展位使用人许可，不偷拍或偷录其他参展展位的展品。

No photographing or recording of exhibits on other stands shall be allowed without others' permission.

（3）如非经展位使用人邀请，不擅自进入其他参展展位。

No entry into any other stands without invitations from their users.

（4）不在展馆内滋扰参观者（采购商）或其他参展人员。

No disturbance to the visitors (buyers) or other exhibitors.

（5）服从和配合广交会现场保卫人员的管理，不无理取闹。

Obey to and cooperate with the guards of the Canton Fair without being deliberately provocative.

（6）不损伤、损坏展馆任何活动或固定的设施，包括但不限于：

No damage to any fixed or movable installations in the hall include but not limit to:

① 不损伤、损坏标准展位内配置的展具、展板、铝材、灯具、桌椅，请参阅本指南第二部分第四章《标准展位布展服务及约定》的相关约定。

No damage to any exhibit accessories, boards, aluminum materials, lighting, tables and chairs in the standard stand. Details shall be referred to Chapter 4, "Services and Stipulations of Standard Stand Decoration", of Part II.

② 不在展馆天花、地面、柱子或墙壁上打钉、钻孔或粘贴。

No nailing, trilling or sticking shall be allowed on the ceiling, floors, pillars or walls in the hall.

（7）在展馆内拾获的任何物品应及时送交广交会保卫办公室展馆保卫科登记处理，不应据为己有或擅自处理。

Any lost articles found in the hall shall not be pocketed and shall be handed over to the security sector of the Canton Fair.

第六章　涉嫌侵犯知识产权的投诉及处理办法

1. 为加强中国进出口商品交易会（以下简称广交会）期间知识产权保护，维护正常交易秩序，保护参展企业和知识产权权利人的合法权益，根据国家有关法律和行政法规制定本办法。

The regulations herein are formulated in accordance with related laws and regulations to protect IPRs, maintain good trading order, and to protect the legal rights and interests of the exhibitors as well as the owners of such IPR rights during the period of the China Import and Export Fair (hereinafter referred to as the Canton Fair).

2. 本办法仅适用于在广交会期间对有关知识产权的保护。

The regulations are only applicable to the protection of IPRs during the period of the Canton Fair.

3. 参展企业应与广交会相关部门签订承诺书。其样式见表格 D2。

The enterprises shall sign Letter of Undertaking with related department of the Canton Fair.（See Form D2）

4. 大会业务办设立的知识产权和贸易纠纷投诉接待站（以下简称投诉站）是广交会唯一接受知识产权相关内容投诉的机构。广交会邀请当地政府有关知识产权行政执法部门驻会参加投诉站的工作。

Reception Station of Complaints and Settlements for IPRs and Trade Disputes（hereinafter referred to as Complaint Reception Station）established by the Business Office of the Canton Fair is the only station receiving the complaints concerning IPRs infringement. The Canton Fair invites relevant government administrative department of IPRs to work with the Complaint Reception Station.

5. 投诉站仅受理当届广交会举办期间发生在展馆内的涉嫌侵犯知识产权（以下简称为“涉嫌侵权”）的投诉。

The Complaint Reception Station shall merely accept and hear complaints concerning with being suspected of infringement on IPRs（hereinafter referred to as infringement）arising in the exhibition hall during period of the session of the exhibition.

6. 广交会举办期间发生在展馆内的知识产权纠纷，应按本办法规定的投诉程序处理。对不通过投诉站，擅自与涉嫌侵权方进行交涉而影响展馆秩序的人员，按违反大会展馆秩序管理规定处理。

All disputes concerning IPRs during the Canton Fair shall be handled in accordance with complaint procedures stipulated herein. Those who tend to avoid the Complaint Station and negotiate with the infringing party directly thus cause a disorder in the exhibition shall be treated as disobeying the Exhibition Order Managing Regulations.

7. 广交会参展企业的展品、展品包装、宣传品及展位的其他展示部位拥有自主知识产权的，应当带上相关的权属证明文件前来参展，以备必要时接受大会的检查。

In case that the exhibitor's exhibits, packaging of exhibits, promotional materials and any part of his stand has independent IPRs, the exhibitor shall bring the certificate documents of ownership for inspection of the Fair.

8. 参展企业如违反与大会签订的相关协议，在其展品、展品包装、宣传品及展位的其他展示部位上出现侵犯他人知识产权行为而导起纠纷的，应当赔偿当事人由此而导致的一切费用与损失。

In case that the exhibitor violates relevant agreements signed with the Canton Fair, he shall be obliged to compensate for all expenses and losses in case of disputes arising from his exhibits, packaging of exhibits, promotional materials and any part of his stand infringing IPRs of others.

9. 投诉人如按照本办法向广交会提出投诉，并要求广交会对被投诉人按本办法处理，应当同意支付广交会各相关单位因处理该投诉而引致的费用，并赔偿被投诉人可能因此造成的损失。

In case that the appellant lodges a complaint to the Complaint Reception Station and requests the station to deal with the defendant as per regulation herein defined, the appellant shall accordingly agree to pay to the station all expenses brought about, and compensate to the defendant for all losses arising therefrom.

10. 持有参加当届广交会有效证件的与会人员，在展馆内发现展位上陈列摆放的展品、宣传品及任何展示部位涉嫌侵权，可到投诉站投诉。投诉、处理流程见附件 9、附件 10、附件 11。

Exhibitor with a valid badge of the Fair can lodge a complaint to the Complaint Station in case that any infringements have been detected in the exhibits, promotional materials in the stand or in any displaying parts of the stand. Please refer to Appendix 9, 10, 11 for the complaint procedure.

11. 投诉人投诉，应当首先向投诉站工作人员出示权属证明。对上届投诉站已经处理过的专利、版权投诉，而本届再次发现的同一侵权个案，投诉人还应出示在上届广交会闭幕后通过法律途径跟踪处理的法律文件。如投诉人不能出示相关文件的，不予受理。投诉站不受理同一投诉人就同一知识产权向同一被投诉人提出的重复投诉。

The appellant shall be required to show to the staff in the Complaint Station the ownership certificate. Appellant shall be further required to demonstrate relevant follow up legal documents in case such patent and copyright infringing shall be a repetition of previous session of Canton Fair and had been settled by this Complaint Station in previous session of Canton Fair. The case will not be accepted unless relevant documents from the appellant have been furnished. A repeated complaint upon the same defendant for the same infringing on IPR will not be accepted by this Complaint Station.

12. 上述有关文件经投诉站工作人员审验有效后，投诉人应按要求填写《提请投诉书》。《提请投诉书》样式见表格 D3。

The appellant shall be required to fill out the "Letter of Complaint" upon verification of the above documents by the staff of the Complaint Station. Please refer to Form D3 for details.

13. 投诉站收到《提请投诉书》后，即安排投诉站工作人员处理投诉。被投诉方应以在广交会正式备案的参展企业代表协助投诉站处理投诉事宜。

The Complaint Station shall nominate staff to deal with the case upon reception of the "Letter of Complaint". The defendant shall cooperate with the Complaint Station to deal with the case on behalf of the person in charge of the stand recorded.

14. 投诉站处理涉嫌侵犯专利或版权的个案，适用举证责任倒置原则。被投诉方在被告知其展出的展品及宣传品或其他展示部位涉嫌侵权后，应当立即出示权利证书或其他证据以证明其拥有被投诉内容的合法权属，作出不侵权的举证，并协助投诉站工作人员对涉嫌侵权物品进行查验。

Principle of Invert the Burden of Proof shall be employed to handle cases of infringement of patent and copyright. In the event that he shall be accused of being suspected of infringing in his exhibits, promotional materials or any parts of his exhibits, the defendant should immediately prove his non-infringement by demonstrating relevant certificate of rights or other evidences to prove he is in possession of legal rights and interests for the items alleged. The defendant shall accordingly be required to examine the alleged items with the staff of the Complaint Station.

15. 如被投诉方不能当场对被投诉涉嫌侵权的物品作出"不侵权"有效举证的，投诉站工作人员对涉嫌侵权的物品作暂扣处理。同时被投诉方应立即签署《承诺书》，承诺自被投诉起，如不能提供有效举证的，不再经营或展出该涉嫌侵权物品。《承诺书》一式两份，分别由被投诉方和投诉站保存。其样式见表格 D4。

In case that the defendant shall be unable to effectively prove his non-infringement immediately, the accused items shall be temporarily detained by the Complaint Station. The defendant shall meanwhile sign on the Letter of Undertaking to commit that he shall not operate or exhibit the accused items in case of his inability of furnishing effective evidences subsequent to such accuse. The Letter of Undertaking shall be made in duplicate and the defendant and the Complaint Station shall hold one copy respectively. Please refer to Form D4 for details.

16. 如被投诉方对投诉站的处理结果有异议，可在一个工作日内（以广交会会场作息时间表为准）到投诉站提出不侵权的补充举证。举证有效的，投诉站立即发回暂扣物品，并允许其继续展出；举证无效或不作补充举证的，广交会对暂扣物品予以没收，终止该物品展出。

In case that he disagrees with the settlements of the Complaint Station, the defendant shall furnish supplement evidences of non-infringement to the Complaint Station within a workday (base on the schedule of Canton Fair). The temporarily detained items should be immediately returned to the exhibitor provided that the proof shall be effective. Otherwise, those items shall be confiscated by the Complaint Station and forbidden in the exhibition.

17. 为维护广交会的交易秩序，在投诉站按照本办法作出处理且被投诉方接受此处理后至当届广交会结束前，投诉人不得在展馆内对被投诉方采取进一步的法律行动。

The appellant commits not to take any legal measures against the defendant in the exhibition hall prior to closing of this fair and subsequent to the Complaint Station has settled the case in accordance with the regulations herein defined and the outcomes have been accepted by the defendant.

18. 当届广交会结束后，投诉站将当届受到广交会处理的涉嫌侵权的参展企业名单在广交会网站上予以公布。

All settled infringing exhibitors at the Fair shall be filed on the website of the Canton Fair by the Complaint Station subsequent to closing of this fair.

19. 发生在展位上的涉嫌侵权行为，由在广交会正式备案分配使用该展位的参展企业承担侵权责任并接受大会的处理。

Responsibility for all infringement happened in the stand shall be borne by the exhibitor who has entered into the Participation Agreement with Canton Fair and been registered by Canton Fair. The exhibitor shall accordingly accept the settlements finalized by Canton Fair.

20. 涉及商标侵权的投诉，由投诉站会同驻会商标管理行政执法部门按《商标法》规定的程序进行处理。对侵权行为属实的参展企业，认定为“构成侵权”并根据《商标法》的有关条款进行处罚。

Any complaint involving infringement of trademark shall be resolved according to the Trademark Law by the Complaint Station cooperating with relevant government trademark administrative departments. The exhibitor proved to be infringed shall be treated as infringement and be punished in accordance with the Trademark Law of P. R. China.

21. 涉及专利、版权的投诉，由投诉站按本办法规定的程序进行处理，对不能作出“不侵权”有效举证的参展企业，认定为“涉嫌侵权”，终止涉嫌侵权展品展出，并按本办法的规定进行处罚。

Any complaint involving patent and copyright infringement will be settled by the Complaint Station as per procedures stipulated herein. Exhibitor who is unable to prove himself as “non-infringement” shall be regarded as being “suspected of infringement” and the infringing exhibits will be forbidden in the exhibition and be disposed as per regulations herein defined.

22. 如被投诉的参展企业业务员（参展商）对投诉站的查处工作拒绝合作，在劝说无效的情况下，可以收缴当事人的参展证件，并可以对该企业进行大会通报警告或取消下一届参展资格。

In case that the exhibitor's staff refuse to cooperate with the Complaint Centre regarding any kind of investigation and inspection, the Complaint Station and the security office of the Canton Fair shall be authorized to confiscate the badge of such person and stop such person from entering the hall afterwards subsequent to an invalid persuasion of the staff of the station.

23. 投诉站对涉嫌侵权展品作出初步处理后，如发现涉嫌侵权的参展企业在同一展位再次展出同样的涉嫌侵权展品，大会可以立即没收该展位全体业务人员的参展商证，取消其当届广交会的参展资格，并在《广交会通讯》对该参展企业进行通报批评。

Should the exhibitor be found out to exhibit the same infringing exhibit in the same stand subsequent to an initial settlement has been performed by the Complaint Station, the Complaint Station and the security office of the Canton Fair shall be authorized to confiscate the badges of all participants in such stand, stop them from entering the hall afterwards and circulate a notice of criticism of the exhibitor on Newsletter of the Canton Fair.

24. 对一届发生涉嫌侵权行为的参展企业，大会将予以书面警告；对连续两届或累计三届发生专利、版权涉嫌侵权行为；或累计两届发生商标涉嫌侵权行为；或故意假冒、冒充他人专利或注册商标行为的，取消该企业六届广交会参展资格，并进行大会通报。

Those exhibitors who are suspected of infringement for one session shall be given written warning by the Canton Fair; those exhibitors who are suspected of infringement of patent and copyright for consecutive two sessions or accumulative three sessions; those exhibitors who are suspected of infringement of trademark for consecutive two sessions; those exhibitors who purposely counterfeit and fake other's patent and registered trademark shall be refused to participate in six sessions of the Canton Fair and be criticized in the circulating notice.

25. 对一方经司法或行政已生效判决或裁定为侵权而又将该侵权展品摆上广交会展位的，或曾被取消多届广交会参展资格，恢复参展后又再一次涉嫌侵权的，将永久取消该企业的广交会参展资格并进行大会通报。

Those exhibitors who get effective judgments of infringing IPR through administrative or judicatory approaches show the alleged exhibits in the stand, and those exhibitors who have been refused to participate in several sessions of the Canton Fair and are suspected of infringing IPR after they resume the participation of the Canton Fair, shall be disqualified the participation of the Canton Fair permanently and be criticized in the circulating notice.

26. 对在同届广交会期间，涉及 10 家企业以上同时侵犯 1 个权属号的（即大面积侵权），或 1 个企业涉嫌侵权 3 个以上权属号的，予以大会通报警告，并可以取消下一届广交会参展资格。

In case that during the same session of the Canton Fair, over ten exhibitors infringing one ownership number (extensive infringement) or one exhibitor is suspected of infringing over three ownership No. shall be disqualified the participation for the next session of the Canton Fair and be criticized in the circulating notice.

第七章　违约处理条例

任何法人、自然人或其他组织申请参加广交会，即为接受本《参展商服务指南》约束的意思表示，参展商与广交会签订《参展合同》参加广交会，即表示接受本《参展商服务指南》的约束。违反本指南的任何规则、条例或约定，即构成违约，应按本章约定接受违约处理。

Legal person, natural person or other organizations applying for participating in the Canton Fair shall accept the Exhibitors' Guide and be bound by it. Exhibitors participating in the Canton Fair through entering into the Participation Agreement with the Canton Fair shall accept the Exhibitors' Guide and be bound by it. Violation of any regulation, regulations or stipulation of the Exhibitors' Guide shall be regarded as a breach. The default party shall accept related breaching punishment in accordance with stipulations herein defined.

1. 违反展位使用条例

广交会对所有违反展位使用条例的参展商将采取以下处理措施：

The In Violation of Regulations for Use of Stand

The Canton Fair shall deal with those exhibitors who violate the regulations herein defined through measures as follows:

（1）没收违约展位所有参展人员证件，并拒绝其参展人员进入展馆。

Confiscate the badges of all exhibitors of the breaching stand and stop those exhibitors from entering the exhibition.

（2）封闭违约展位，并将该展位的参展商备案，以后不受理其参展申请。

Close down the breaching stand and have it recorded so as to refuse its application in the future.

2. 违反展品管理条例

In Violation of Regulations for Exhibits Management

（1）涉嫌侵犯知识产权的展品，按照本部分第六章《涉嫌侵犯知识产权的投诉及处理办法》处理。

Suspected infringing exhibits shall be dealt with pursuant to Complaint and Settlement Provisions of Being Infringing IPR of Chapter 6 herein.

（2）超出《参展合同》约定或经广交会同意备案展品范围的展品而参展商拒不自行清出展馆的，广交会将移走违约展品，并对由此而造成的任何损失不承担任何责任。

Exhibits excluded in scope defined in the Participation Agreement or in the records agreed by Canton Fair shall be removed from the exhibition hall by the The Canton Fair in case that the exhibitor refuses to clear the same from the exhibition hall. The Canton Fair shall not bear any responsibilities for any losses arising therefrom.

（3）违法或参展商不能说明或证明其合法来源的展品，广交会将予以收缴，并对由此而造成的任何损失不承担任何责任。

The Canton Fair shall confiscate all illegal exhibits or exhibits which the exhibitor is unable to illustrate or proof their legal origins without bearing any responsibilities for any losses arising therefrom.

（4）因参展商违反中华人民共和国海关规定擅自处置进口展品或展出违法展品而造成广交会遭受中华人民共和国海关或其他政府执法部门处罚的，广交会保留向参展商追索损失的权利。

In case that a punishment imposed by the Chinese customs or other governmental legal departments upon the Canton Fair is caused by the exhibitor's violation of the Regulations on the Chinese customs in disposing per se import exhibits or exhibiting any kind of illegal exhibit, the Canton Fair shall retain the power to claim from the exhibitor for any losses arising therefrom.

（5）未经广交会书面同意，参展商擅自在展馆内以任何形式陈列、展示、宣传任何其他展览会的资料及为该展览会进行任何形式的宣传活动，广交会有权没收其宣传资料并对参展商进行劝告。劝告不听而继续进行此类违约活动的，广交会将没收违约展位所有参展人员证件，并拒绝其参展人员进入展馆。

In case that the exhibitor shall demonstrate, display and publicize any other materials of the Canton Fair in any forms and publicize the Canton Fair in the exhibition hall in any forms without written consent of the Canton Fair, the Canton Fair shall be authorized to confiscate these promotional materials and expostulate the exhibitor. The Canton Fair shall confiscate the badges of all participants of such stands, in which the exhibitors ignore the expostulations and continue the aforesaid breaching activities. These participants shall furthermore be refused to enter the exhibition hall.

3. 违反参展行为规则 In Violation of Code of Conduct for Participation in the Fair

（1）在《参展合同》约定的展位之外的展厅通道及其他展馆内任何公共区域派发宣传小册子、宣传光盘、产品目录等资料及礼品或摆放的，广交会将对以上宣传资料、礼品或展品进行收缴并对参展商进行劝告，劝告不听而继续进行此类违约活动的，广交会将收缴违约展位所有参展人员的参展证件，并拒绝其参展人员进入展馆。非参展人员分发以上资料的，广交会将没收派发资料及分发人员证件，并将该分发人员清理出馆。

Exhibitor who distributes promotional booklets, CDs, product catalog and displays gifts in areas other than what specified in the Participation Agreement such as aisles and any public areas in the exhibition hall shall be expostulated by the Canton Fair and the aforesaid materials shall be confiscated. The Canton Fair shall confiscate the badges of all participants of such stands, in which the exhibitors ignore the expostulations of the Fair and continue the aforesaid breaching activities. These participants shall furthermore be refused to enter the exhibition hall. Non-exhibitors who perform so shall be confiscated of their badges and materials and hence be driven out of the hall.

（2）未经其他展位使用人同意，偷拍或偷录其他展位的参展展品或展位设计的，广交会将没收胶卷或摄录设备内存条。

Any spy filming or recording of exhibits on other stand or its designs without permission from the owner of the stand concerned, Canton Fair shall be entitled to confiscate such films or memory sticks of the recording devices.

（3）未经其他展位使用人同意，偷拿其他展位的参展展品的，广交会将收缴进馆证件，并拒绝其再次进入展馆；对偷拿贵重展品的，视为偷窃处理，广交会将收缴该人员进馆证件，并移送公安部门处理。

Badges of those who take exhibits from other stand without permission from the owner of the stand concerned shall be retained by the Canton Fair who shall be authorized to refuse such person to enter the exhibition hall again; Person who pilfers precious exhibits shall be treated as a theft and his badges shall be confiscated by the Canton Fair and the person shall be transferred to public security sectors for settlement.

（4）不服从和配合广交会现场保卫人员的检查和管理而无理取闹者，广交会将没收该人员进馆证件，并拒绝其再次进入展馆。

Those who refuse to obey and cooperate with the guards of the exhibition and create any troubles shall be confiscated of their badges and be refused to enter the exhibition hall again.

（5）展位内演示（包括演示使用的音响设备音量超过 70 分贝）对周边参展商造成骚扰或影响广交会的秩序，广交会将进行劝告，劝告不听者，广交会将采取切断该展位供电电源处理并有权采取进一步处理措施，如没收该展位所有参展人员证件并拒绝其再次进入展馆。

In case that demonstration in the stand (including noise of the acoustics used shall be greater than 70 decibels) causes a disturbance to the neighboring exhibitors or orders of the exhibition, the Canton Fair shall be entitled to expostulate such exhibitors. Exhibitor refuses to accept such expostulations shall be punished by a electricity cut to the stand by the Canton Fair, and the Canton Fair has full power to handle such misconducts through measures, such as confiscating badges of all exhibitors and refuse them to enter the exhibition hall in future.

（6）在展馆天花板、地面、柱子或墙壁上打钉、钻孔、粘贴或损伤损坏展馆天花板、地沟、柱子、墙面上的消防设施、监控设施、配电设施、照明设施、通信设施等设施、卫生间设施、可移动消防设施以及展馆内其他任何活动或固定设施，广交会将采取以下处理措施：

Following measures shall be undertaken by the Canton Fair to handle misconducts such as nailing, drilling, sticking on ceilings, floors, pillars or walls of the exhibition hall, or damage and destruction to the fire-prevention installations, monitoring systems, electricity distribution structures, communication facilities on the ceilings, ditches, pillars and walls of the exhibition hall, or toilet establishments, mobile fireproofing equipments and other portable or fixed installations in the exhibition hall:

① 责令责任人所属的参展商或施工单位负责恢复原状。

The responsible exhibitor or contractor shall be forcibly required to renew the damaged settings to the original status.

② 不能修复原状的，责任人所属的参展商或施工单位应负责按广交会修复估价进行赔偿。

Or the responsible exhibitor or contractor shall compensate to Canton Fair as per assessment of such renewal in case the renewal has not been accomplished.

4. 违反特装展位申报与搭装约定

In Violation of Stipulations of Application & Setting-up for Customs-Built Stand

（1）特装展位搭装设计图纸未申报或已申报但没有通过审核的，广交会不允许特装布展施工单位进场施工。

In case the design drawings of the custom-built stand have not been submitted for approval or have not been verified and approved, the Canton Fair shall not allow the related contractor to execute construction works in the hall.

（2）特装展位搭装设计图纸逾期申报的，广交会有权不予受理并不允许特装布展施工单位进场施工。

In case the design drawings of the custom-built stand shall not be submitted for approval within the time limits, the Canton Fair shall be entitled to refuse such drawings and stop related contractor from executing construction works in the hall.

（3）特装布展施工单位未办理施工证等进场手续而擅自进场施工的，广交会将责令其退出展馆，并依程序补办进场手续。

Contractor of custom-built stand without Construction License shall be forcibly requested by the Canton Fair to withdraw from the exhibition hall and the contractor shall afterwards be required to accomplish all move-in procedures in accordance with stipulated processes.

（4）特装展位不按约定进行施工的，广交会将给予警告并责令施工单位停工整改，拒不整改或整改后仍未通过验收的，广交会将不予接电，已接电的将采取切断展位电源处理。对拒不整改者，广交会还将取消其施工证，并取消该施工单位下届广交会的施工资质，同时参照与施工单位的约定，扣除部分或全部施工安全保证金作为违约金，一切后果由施工单位自负。这类违约行为包括但不限于：

In case the custom-built stand shall not be constructed in accordance with the stipulations, the Canton Fair shall hence warm the related contractor and forcibly order such contractor to terminate all construction works for modification. No electricity shall be connected to such stand in case of a refusal for modification or completed modification not be accepted by the Canton Fair. Connected electricity under such circumstances shall therefore be cut off. Construction License of those who refuse to carry out such modifications shall be cancelled by the Canton Fair and whose construction qualifications for next the Canton Fair shall accordingly be terminated. Furthermore, parts or the entire constructional safety deposits of the contractor shall be deducted as a penalty for such misconduct following the stipulations agreed upon between the contractor and the Canton Fair. All consequences arising therefrom shall be borne by the contractor. Such breaches shall include but not limit to the following:

① 不按已经广交会审核通过的设计图纸进行施工，包括超高、违约封顶等。

Execution of works not comply with design drawings verified by the Canton Fair including over height and putting a roof on the stand.

② 不按约定使用不燃或难燃搭装材料或使用非不燃或难燃搭装材料，不按广交会要求采取适当及足够的安全防火措施。

Not utilize fire-resisting construction materials as stipulations or not take adequate measures for fire-prevention as per requirements of the Canton Fair even stipulated materials have been employed.

③ 不按约定使用合格的电气材料和设备设施。

Not utilize qualified electric materials and equipment as stipulations.

④ 不按约定进行电气设备设施的安装操作及施工操作。

Electric equipment is not installed and operated as stipulations.

⑤ 阻挡消防设施或阻挡配电通讯设施而没有预留足够的安全距离。

Obstruction to fire-prevention installations or electricity distribution and communication establishment however not adequate safe distance has been reserved.

⑥ 改变展位内或展位附近任何固定设施，利用展馆天花、地面、柱子或墙壁上任何设施，进行固定、悬挂或装饰。

Modification of any fixed installations inside or nearby the stand; any fixation, suspension or decoration on/to the ceiling, floors, pillars or walls of the exhibition hall.

⑦ 展位背面或侧面裸露部分未采用双饰面美化处理及外饰面含装饰广告内容。

Exposed components of the back side or flanks of the stand have not been beautified through double decoration covers and advertisements have not been decorated from outside.

⑧ 施工时未将施工证悬挂在展位内明显位置，超出施工证范围施工。

Construction License is not hanging in a prominent location in the stand during construction; construction works exceed the scope covered in the license.

5. 违反标准展位使用约定

In Violation of Regulations on Use of Standard Stand

（1）未经广交会同意，参展商擅自拆装改动标准展位及展位内配置展板、铝材、展具、灯具、配电线路的，广交会将暂扣违约展位参展人员参展证件，并采取以下处理措施：

In case that the exhibitor per se dismantles or alters the standard stand and the fascia, aluminum materials, exhibition accessories, lightings and distribution circuits without permission of the Canton Fair, the Canton Fair shall be authorized to temporarily detain the badges of all exhibitors in the breaching stand and afterwards settle the case through following measures:

① 要求参展商恢复原状，并承担恢复原状的所有费用。

The exhibitor will be required to renew the stand to the original state and bear all expenses incurred therein.

② 如恢复原状不可行的，广交会将按每展位人民币 600 元收取违约赔偿金，如造成展板、铝材、展具、灯具、配电线路损坏的，参展商还应承担额外的损坏赔偿责任。

The exhibitor shall compensate to the Canton Fair RMB 600 yuan for per stand as penalty if aforesaid renewal becomes the impossible. The exhibitor shall furthermore pay to the Canton Fair extra penalties in case of damages to the fascia, aluminum materials, exhibition accessories, lightings and distribution circuits.

（2）未经广交会同意擅自更改展位楣板文字或对楣板进行任何形式的覆盖，广交会将要求参展商恢复原状，并交纳广交会协助恢复原状所需费用及人民币 100 元作为违约赔偿金。

In case that he shall modify any wordings of the fascia or cover up the fascia by any means, the exhibitor shall be required to have it renewed to the original state by the Canton Fair. The exhibitor shall accordingly pay to the Canton Fair all expenses arising therefrom and an amount of RMB 100 yuan as a default penalty.

（3）未经广交会同意和办理登记手续，擅自携带与广交会标准展位搭装材料相同或类似的展材、展具等搭装材料进入展馆的，广交会将予以收缴，由此而引起的损失由参展商自负。

All identical installation materials for standard stand or similar exhibition materials and accessories to the Canton Fair brought into the hall by the exhibitor without permission of or registration with the Canton Fair shall be confiscated and all losses therefrom arising shall be borne by the exhibitor.

（4）锯裁展位配置展板、铝材或在展板、展材上油漆、打钉、钻洞或造成展板、铝材遗失的，广交会将按每块受损或遗失展板人民币 300 元，每根受损或遗失铝材人民币 500 元收取损坏或遗失赔偿金。

Any cuttings on the allocated exhibition panel and aluminum materials, or painting, nailing and trilling on the penal or exhibition materials, or losses of exhibition penal and aluminum materials happened, the Canton Fair shall charge from the exhibitor RMB 300 yuan for each lost or damaged penal, and RMB 500 yuan for each damaged or lost aluminum material as penalty.

（5）在展板上进行任何粘贴的，广交会将收取每展位人民币 500 元的清场押金，押金在参展商 清理干净后退还，如不能清理干净的，广交会将没收押金作为展位清洁及维护费用。

The Canton Fair shall collect RMB 500 yuan as a clearance deposit in case of any sticking on the exhibition panel. Such deposit will be only reimbursed to the exhibitor provided that clearance of the sticking has been accomplished or otherwise it shall be confiscated by the Canton Fair.

（6）未办理申报手续擅自在展位内增加安装照明灯具或乱拉乱接电源的，广交会将给予切断该展位电源处理，参展商应赔偿因此可能给广交会带来的一切损失。

In case of the exhibitor's installation of extra lighting or casual connection to electricity supply without application to and approved by the Canton Fair, the Canton Fair shall switch off the electricity supply to the stand and the exhibitor shall accordingly compensate to the Canton Fair for all losses may arise therefrom.

（7）损坏展位内配置的灯具、配电线路、配电箱或造成这些设备遗失的，广交会将按灯具每盏 人民币 100 元、配电线路每米人民币 100 元、配电箱每个人民币 500 元标准收取损坏或遗失赔偿金。

The Canton Fair shall charge penalties for the damaged items in the stand in the following criteria: RMB 100 yuan for per light, RMB 100 yuan for per meter of distributor wire, and RMB 500 yuan for per electricity distributor.

6. 违反《安全与防火条例》及其他约定

In violation of "Regulations on Safety and Fireproofing and other Regulations"

（1）在展位内或展位背面（侧面）空间内存放包装箱（包装材料）、施工工具等物料的，广交会将强行清理，由此而产生的费用由违约展位的参展商或施工单位承担。

All articles such as packaging cases (packaging materials), constructional tools storing inside or beside the stand shall be forcibly cleared by the Canton Fair and all expenses arising therefrom shall be borne by the breaching exhibitor or the constructional contractor.

（2）在展馆内非吸烟区吸烟的，广交会将采取以下处理措施：

Following measures will be undertaken by the Canton Fair to deal with smokers who smoke in the non-smoking areas in the hall:

① 参展人员：暂扣参展证件，在参展人员提交保证此后不再违反的书面承诺后退还证件，但违反此约定两次以上的参展人员，参展证件不予退还。

Exhibitor: The exhibition badge will be temporarily detained and the same will be returned only subsequent to the exhibitor's submission of a written commitment of non-repetition of such violation in future. The badge will not be returned to those who repeat such violations for more than twice.

② 非参展人员：没收进馆证件，清理出馆。

Non-exhibitor: The badge will be confiscated and the person will be driven out of the hall.

（3）所有两层展位的第二层展位是广交会的重点检查对象，如参展商有以下违约行为，广交会将提 出警告，参展商应立即整改。拒不整改或不服从管理的，广交会将强行封闭展位的第二层，并对第二层摆放的物品进行强行清理。如因参展商拒不整改而造成展位坍塌等安全事故的，一切后果由参展商及施工单位自负。广交会将追究参展商和施工单位的安全责任，扣除施工单位全额施工安全保证金，并保留向参展商及施工单位追偿因此而可能造成的一切损失。

The second storey of two-storey structures shall be mainly inspected. The exhibitor will be warned in case of following defaults, and he shall immediately correct such misconducts. If no correction is carried out or the exhibitor refuses to obey such regulations, the Canton Fair shall be entitled to close down this storey and forcibly clear up all items in this area. In case of stand collapse due to exhibitor's refusal to carry out the required corrections, the exhibitor and his constructor shall then be responsible for all consequences arising therefrom. The Canton Fair will accordingly investigate the safety responsibilities of the exhibitor and the constructor and deduct all safety security of the constructor. Furthermore, the Canton Fair shall be entitled to claim from the exhibitor and contractor for all losses that may arise therefrom.

① 在展位第二层使用电热器具。

Utilization of electronic heaters on the second storey.

② 在展位第二层安排演示活动及中华人民共和国公安部门和消防部门认为不安全的其他活动。

Demonstration and other activities on the second storey which may be treated as unsafe in accordance with the Chinese Security and Fire-prevention Department.

③ 擅自摆放超重展品或聚集人员超过设计标准。

Weight of exhibits or numbers of people excess the designed criteria.

(4) 撤展时不按约定时间将展品或特装材料清出展馆，或特装材料虽清出展馆但乱堆放于展馆室外光地或广交会展馆周边道路的，广交会不退还清场押金，并保留向相关单位进一步追偿由此而给广交会造成的一切损失。

In case the exhibitor shall be unable to remove his exhibits or special constructional materials from the hall or have them stored on spaces outside the hall or on roads surrounding the China Import and Export Fair Complex subsequent to stand dismantling, the Canton Fair shall not return the clearance deposit to the exhibitor and shall further retain the power to claim from the competent authorities for all losses arising therefrom.

(5) 10 月 14 日 12: 00 后仍未布置展品的空展位，广交会有权收回展位，并由该展位参展商承担一切损失。

The Canton Fair shall be entitled to draw back all stands which have no exhibits in display after 12: 00 on Oct. 14, 2009, and the exhibitor of the stands shall be responsible for any losses arising therefrom.

第八章 广交会展馆宽带服务管理规定（部分内容省略）

为加强展馆宽带网络安全管理工作，保证展馆网络系统的正常运行和网络用户的使用权益，营造安全、稳定、高效的网络使用环境，根据《中华人民共和国计算机信息网络国际互联网管理暂行规定》和有关计算机网络法律法规，结合广交会展馆的实际情况，特制定本规定。

In order to strengthen safety management of broad band, ensure network's normal operation and using rights of network users, and create safe, stable and efficient environment for using network, the regulations are stipulated according to "Interim Provisions on Computer Information and Internet Management of PRC" and relevant laws and regulations.

参展方、承建商和其他需通过展馆方提供宽带服务的单位及人员适用本规定。

The regulations are applicable to exhibitor, contractor, and other parties who need the broad band service provided by the Canton Fair exhibition hall.

一、展馆宽带概况 Broadband Internet Access on the Fair Premises

展馆方提供的宽带服务是指有线宽带及无线宽带服务，所提供的标准服务包括 HTTP，QQ，MSN，E-mail 服务。对标准服务以外的互联网服务，如使用证券软件、VPN 等需使用特殊协议端口的业务件进行联网，需另外交费申请开放权限端口服务（BT、迅雷、游戏等网络端口除外）。注：展馆提供的无线宽带服务不提供权限端口开放服务。

The Canton Fair provides both cable and wireless broadband Internet access in its exhibition halls. Exhibitors, contractors, and other parties concerned may choose either one according to their need. Cable access users have to apply for the service from *http://www.cantonfair.org.cn* beforehand. Multiple access users can apply for multiple cable connections or broadband network.

Wireless access users may rent wireless adapter if needed. Both wired and wireless Internet access in the exhibition halls only provide HTTP, QQ, MSN and E-mail service. Wired access users can apply for internet service like network ports for stock information and some special software.

二、展馆宽带网络使用和管理

Proper Use and Management of Broadband Internet Network

（一）用户不得私自使用交换机、集线器和其他网络交换设备利用展馆方提供的宽带服务接入多台电脑上网。

If users use wireless AP, wireless router or other wireless network facilities to connect or disturb the network signals of the exhibition, interfering other users' normal operation, the Canton Fair is entitled to disqualify the users from broadband service and confiscate the users' facilities.

（二）用户不得私自使用无线路由器、无线 AP 进行自行组网，同时不得使用任何其他可能干扰展馆无线网络信号的设备连接或干扰展馆网络。

If users use router, network hub or other switch facilities to connect the network, the Canton Fair is entitled to disqualify the users from broadband service and confiscate the user's facilities.

（三）严禁用户安装盗号木马软件、病毒工具和其他恶意电脑程序对展馆网络进行非法攻击或侵入，干扰其他用户的正常使用。

If users install password-stealing Trojan, virus tools or other vicious computer software to attack the network illegally or disturb other users, the organizer is entitled to pursue the user's liability according to the seriousness of the case.

（四）严禁用户使用迅雷、网际快车、BT、电驴等多线程或 P2P 下载软件下载电影、视频以及其他占用网络带宽较大的应用软件。

If users' virus attacked computer affects the normal operation of the exhibition's network because the user does not install anti-virus software, or affects other network for downloading through BT or other download software, the organizer is entitled to disqualify the user from broadband service and not to reimburse fees and deposit for broadband access.

（五）附件 Appendixes（略）

（六）相关表格　　Relevant Forms（略）

（七）技术数据　　Technical Data（略）

附录9 海外参展注意事项

面对WTO和更加激烈的国际市场，“走出去”的发展战略已经成为行业内企业尤其是大型企业的共识。作为国际商贸活动的重要形式，在海外商品博览会上展销产品无疑是出口推销卓有成效的方式，同时也是走向国际化的最佳途径。

一、海外参展的优点

与参加国内相关展会相比，企业海外参展有着不同的优势：1. 扩大商务接触面，开阔视野，启发思路；2. 货比三家，寻求最佳的供货厂商与合作对象；3. 增强营销力度，直接面对客户，寻求代理合作和商贸机会；4. 可以直接订货；5. 可以宣传企业。

二、海外展会的选择

由于地理、文化、习俗及各国政府规定的不同，出国展销与国内展销有很大的差异。很多参展单位在海外进行的展览，往往历经坎坷，花费巨大，却收效甚微。究其原因，当然有产品、市场、包装、价格、广告和销售网络等多方面的问题，但是，展览能不能达到预期的目标，却大多出于展览本身的组织实施问题。例如，事先对展览会的市场调查不周导致选择失当、展览品配置不对或是运输中对展品造成重大损坏等，而这一切又大都是因为参展方对海外展览实务基本知识和经验的缺乏。

（一）参展前必问的“为什么”

企业在计划参加某个展会前18~24个月就要开始做计划和调查，并需要提出以下一些问题：该次展览能满足我们市场拓展的需要吗？展会日期是否合适？同期有别的展会举办吗？展会地点是否便利？有多少与会者是来自目标市场的？有多少与会者是来自我们主要的服务地区的？主办单位怎样推广展会？等。

（二）选择前的准备工作

1. 分析展会资料，了解展会的性质；
2. 了解宣传方式与进展情况；
3. 了解展位预订情况；
4. 了解展会场地情况；
5. 探寻同行看法；
6. 分析研究结果：在对展会做了分析之后就要作出决定，即是否参展？展位的大小？是参观考察作市场调查还是搜集有关资讯？

总之，就是从营销计划入手，将展会销售纳入企业的总体营销策略。通过与展会的组织者、先期参展的单位和有关的贸易机构取得联系，了解观展客商的人数及其职业经营范围，从而确定某一展会是否是本公司产品最理想的推广和竞争场所，并让全球参展人员对公司既定的展会营销目标做到胸有成竹。

三、海外参展流程

企业一旦决定想要参加海外展会，就要拟定出一套详细的参展计划，一般需要提前一年开始进行各项准备。

（一）了解相关知识

1. 海外参展的方式及费用

海外展览的方式一般包括租用摊位、租用整个场馆还是部分场馆、自设场馆等。企业海外参展，所需费用中外汇支付占最大比例。究竟租用多少摊位合适，租用多大展馆为宜，采用哪种方式进行展出最佳等都要慎重考虑，要根据实际需要和“低投入、高产出”的效益原则，对展会的费用项目进行全面的了解、比较并作深入探讨，跟主办方进行巧妙的洽谈，争取较多的服务和相对低廉的价格。

2. 海外参展展品的运输和保险

国内企业想要将展品安全、准时、经济地运到参展国的展馆，一般需要全权委托外运公司进行（他们通常与展会所在国的运输代理公司合作）。按照外运公司的要求，如展会组织者应提供展品的有关资料，如展会地址、日期，收件人以及展品的箱号、尺码、毛重、净重及总的体积和重量等。

对于展品的保险，我国企业一般是在国内投保，所投项目一般是火险、水险、盗窃险等。但对于展品来说，丢失后即使能获得赔偿，但也失去了市场时机，其看不见的损失是难以估量的。所以，防患于未然更重要。防火处理和装置、防盗措施、安全守卫与检查制度，都应完善和健全，并贯穿于开箱至装箱的整个展会活动过程。

（二）海外参展详细计划表

列出计划之前也有几个“为什么”要问清楚：该展览的覆盖地区有多大？参展的外国同行业公司有哪些？自己的产品若销往展会举办国需缴纳什么样的税？自己产品的 FDB 价和 CIF 价分别是多少？如果收到订单，履约有无困难，能否迅速组织到需要的货源，在运输、出口等方面是否需要预先作安排等。

1. 12 个月前

（1）从展会的规模、时间、地点、专业程度、目标市场等各方面综合专家意见，选定全年参展计划；

（2）与展会主办单位或代理公司进行联系取得初步资料；

（3）选定场地（一般而言，首次参加国际大展较难取得最佳位置）；

(4) 了解付款形式，考虑汇率波动，决定财务计划；

2. 9个月前

(1) 设计展览结构；

(2) 取得资料管理公司的设计批准；

(3) 选择并准备参展产品；

(4) 与国外潜在客户及目前顾客联络；

(5) 制作展览宣传册。

3. 6个月前

(1) 以广告或邮件等方式进行推广活动；

(2) 确定旅行计划；

(3) 支付展览场地及其他服务所需预先付款；

(4) 复查公司的参展说明书、传单、新闻稿并准备必要的翻译；

(5) 安排展览期间翻译员；

(6) 向服务承包商及展会主办方订购广告促销。

4. 3个月前

(1) 继续追踪产品推广活动；

(2) 最后确定参展样品，并准备大量代表企业产品品质及特色的样品，贴上公司标签，赠送索取样品的客商；

(3) 将展位结构设计作最后的决定；

(4) 计划访客回应处理程序；

(5) 训练参展员工；

(6) 安排展会期间的约谈；

(7) 安排展览现场或场外的招待会；

(8) 购买外汇。

5. 4天前

将运货文件、展览说明书及传单等额外影印本放好带齐至目的地。

6. 3天前

(1) 抵达，视察展厅及场地；

(2) 咨询运输商，确定所有运送物品的抵达；

(3) 指示运输承包商将物品运输至会场；

(4) 联络所有现场服务承包商，确定一切准备就绪；

(5) 与展览组织代表联络，告知通信方法；

(6) 访问当地顾客。

7. 2天前

(1) 确定所有物品运送完成；

(2) 查看所订设备及其他用品的使用和功能；

(3) 布置展位；

(4) 将所有活动节目做最后的决定。

8. 1天前

（1）将摊位架构、设备及用品做最后的检查；

（2）将促销用品发送到直接分配中心；

（3）与公司参展员工、翻译员等进行展览前的最后简单报告。

9. 展览期间

（1）尽早到会场；

（2）展会第一天即将新闻稿送到会场的记者通讯厅；

（3）实地观察后尽早预约下一年的场地；

（4）详细记录每一个到访客户的情况及要求，不要凭事后记忆；

（5）对于没有把握的产品需求，不要当场允诺，及时上报并作出合理答复，一旦承诺，必须按质按量如期完成；

（6）每日与员工进行沟通；

（7）每天将潜在商机信息及顾客资料送回公司，以便及时回复与处理。

10. 展览结束

（1）监督摊位拆除；

（2）处理商机；

（3）寄出感谢卡。

（三）海外展会上如何与外国人交流

在展会上我们能碰到各式各样的买家。在偶然的交流中如果能发挥得好一些，就能增加获得订单的几率，要想在一次难得参加的海外展会上达到利益最大化，跟外国人的交流就显得尤为重要，那么怎样才能更好地与外国人交谈呢？以下几点希望对大家有所帮助。

1. 欧洲人、美国人是非常喜欢互动交谈的，同他们交谈时不要太拘谨，在与之对话的时候，适当的时候要称呼对方。假如你在对话中经常称呼对方，对方也会称呼你，这样可以让客户容易对你有印象，对后续跟踪客户是十分有益的。外国客户名字，如果不会读可以直接问客户，这样是不失礼的，切忌自以为是，弄巧成拙。

2. 母语是英语的人说话可能会很快，很少停顿。如果听不懂可以让对方稍微放慢语速，这是不失礼的。千万不要不懂装懂，随意接客户的话。一旦语不达意，客户就会觉得和你沟通很困难，就离开了。

3. 有外国人在展台前坐下来的话，就要和他们多交谈，在你完全了解对方的情况下，再介绍你自己。和欧洲人、美国人谈话的时候，你可以让客户简单地说一下此行的目的，希望得到一些什么样的信息等，这样你可以有针对性地跟客户进行进一步的沟通和交流。

4. 假如有幸碰到头衔是 Director（主管）或者 Vice President（副总）等职务的买家，要多说一些有战略性的东西，因为他们很可能是来找

Strategic Partners（战略合作伙伴）的，因此更要小心谨慎，如果有可能的话，也可以对他们直接提出参观的邀请。

5. 其实很多大公司的买手最关心的不是价格、质量，而是可靠性。差不多的商品，买手从不同的供应商处购买，价格有点小差距，国外的很多大公司都是可以接受的。但是，买手找的供应商出问题的话那麻烦就大了。所以，我们要站在客户的角度考虑问题，要让买手觉得在所有的供应商里面你是最可靠的，包括质量、价格、长期供货能力等。

附录 10　美国签证常见英语解析

Admission Number（准许入境编号）：表 I-94 上所用编号（在 F-1 或 M-1 非移民签证的情况下，则是 I-20 ID 印件上所用编号），供移民归化局（INS）查询此人时备用。也称“身份编号”（Identification Number）。

Alien Registration Number（外侨登记号码）：简称“A”号码（“A” Number）。本来是美国政府给予移民的身份编号（Identification Number），在某些情况下，由美国移民归化局斟酌决定。这种登记号码也可能给予非移民学生和交流学者。不过，多数持有 F-1，J-1 和 M-1 签证留学美国的学生没有“A”号码。

“Arrival/Departure record”（Form I-94）（表 I-94，入境-出境记录）：移民归化局文件，在美国入境地点签发，作为外国国民合法进入美国的证明。表上明确注明证件持有者许可在逗留的期限，或是确定一个固定的“截止日期”（expiration date），或是注上“D/S”字样。“D/S”意为“身份有效期”（duration of status），允许证件持有者在美国逗留到达成业经批准的目的为止。

“Certificate of Compliance”（守法证书）：付税情况审查记录文件，签发给离境外国国民，以证明当事人业已付清全部所得税。在一般情况下，F-1，J-1 和 M-1 非移民签证的持有者需要守法证书。守法证书也称“离境签证”（Exit Visa）或“离境许可证”（Sailing Permit）。

“Certificate of Eligibility”（身份合格证书）：即表 I-20 A-B、表 I-20 M-N 或表 IAP-66。表 I-20A-B 和表 I-20 M-N 由同意录取该外国学生为正规全日制学生来美学习的得到承认的美国高等院校、职业学校或其他非学术性院校签发。表 IAP-66（交流学者身份合格证）则由组织该项交流活动的单位或同意其进入该校的美国高等院校签发。表 I-20 和表 IAP-66 均非签证，它们只是申请签证的先决条件，仅仅说明持有者具有申请非移民学生签证的资格。

Change of Status（改变身份）：即变换所持非移民签证的种类。改变身份一定要得到移民归化局的批准。

Dependent（家属）：需依靠另一人支持者。从移民归化局处理有关事项的角度说，“家属”仅指本人的配偶和十八岁以下的未婚子女。

Deportation（驱逐出境）：指从一个国家将另一国被认定为非法入境或其居住有碍公共利益的公民强行赶走。

Duration of Status（身份有效期）：简称“D/S”。移民归化局在表 I-94（参阅“入境—出境记录”（Arrival/Departure Record）栏目）上的用词，意为该外国留学生或交流学者在美国逗留的期限为完成一个（或若干个）业已批准项目的需用时间另加 30 天。

Employment（就业）：一个人参加拿薪水的工作通称就业。为了保障美国公民的就业，外国留学生、交流学者及其配偶的就业要受有关条例的限制。

Exchange Visitor（交流学者）：持有 J-1 签证，根据某个“交流学者”项目来美从事文化、教育方面活动的外国公民。

Exit Visa（离境签证）：参阅“Certificate of Compliance”（守法证书）栏目。

Extension of Stay（延长居留期）：签证持有者在美国逗留时间超过表 I-94 入境—出境记录所注明的截止日期须经移民归化局批准。

F-1 签证：美国非移民签证的一种，专门签发给由一座得到承认的美国高等院校同意录取来美进行学术性正规学习的正式学生。

F-2 签证：美国非移民签证的一种，专门签发给 F-1 签证持有者的家属（指配偶和 18 岁以下的未婚子女）。

Foreign Student Office（外国留学生办公室）：设在各大学的校园内办事处，负责为外国学生和交流学者提供帮助和咨询服务。有些地方称为“国际服务办公室”（Office of International Services）、“国际教育事宜办公室”（Office of International Education）、“国际交流项目办公室”（Office of International Programs）等。参阅 Form I-20 A-B（表 I-20 A-B）：“Certificate of Eligibility”（身份合格证书）栏目。

Form I-20 ID Copy（表 I-20 ID 印件）：签发给持有 F-1 和 M-1 非移民签证者，他们或是在入境地点领取，或是在美国境内获得这种身份时领取，用以记录与 F-1 或 M-1 学生非移民身份有关的一切事项。对持 F-1 非移民签证的学生，表 I-20 ID 印件可纳入表 I-20 A-B，成为它的一个部分。对持 M-1 非移民签证的学生，表 I-20 ID 印件则可纳入表 I-20 M-N，成为它的一个部分。

Form I-20 M-N（表 I-20 M-N）：即“Certificate of Eligibility”（身份合格证书）。

Form I-94（表 I-94）：即“Arrival/Departure Record”（入境-出境记录）。

Form I-538（表 I-538）：持有 F-1 或 M-1 非移民签证者，要求延长在美国逗留期限、申请部分时间就业、从事实习或转换学校时，需要填写的申请表。

Form IAP-66（表 IAP-66）：由授权组织交流学者在美国活动的学校、单位、代理机构或基金会签发给安排在美国从事某项特定教育或文化项目的学生的表格。必须先得到这一表格才能申请进入美国所需的 J-1“交流学者”非移民签证。

Full-time Student（全部时间用于学习的正规学生）：正规入学、念满学校规定的全部课程的学生。一般情况下，大学本科生至少要念满 12 个学分课时（credit hours）或学分（units），研究生至少要念满 9 个学分课时或学分。持有 F-1，J-1 和 M-1 非移民签证的学生必须在学年的每个学期（不包括暑期）遵守这一规定。

Home-Residence Requirement（学成归国的规定）：某些持有 J-1 签证的交流学者，在美国完成其“交流学者”项目后，必须回祖国至少 2 年，然后才有资格以移民身份或者“H”或“L”类非移民身份（“H” or “L” non-immigrant classifications）再来美国。

Identification Number（身份编号）：参阅“Admission Number”（准允入境编号）栏目。

Immigrant（移民）：到不是本人祖国的另一国家长期定居的人。

Immigration and Naturalization Service（移民归化局）：缩写为 INS，美国司法部所属的一个政府机构，主管移民事宜，并执行有关法律。

INS：美国移民归化局是 U. S. Immigration and Naturalization Service 的缩写。

J-1 签证：美国非移民签证的一种，专门签发给交流学者，即为某个教育或文化目的来美国从事指定交流项目的人。

J-2 签证：美国非移民签证的一种，专门签发给 J-1 签证持有者的家属（指配偶和 18 岁以下的未婚子女）。

Notarization（公证）：由一名执行公务的官员（在美国称为 notary public（公证人））出具的证明，证明某个文件、声明、报告书或签名的真实可靠性。

Naturalization（归化）：加入另一国家（非本人祖国）的国籍。

Part-time Employment（部分时间就业）：每周工作时间达 20 小时的有偿就业。持 M-1 签证的外国学生不得从事兼职工作。在某种情况下，可以允许学习时间超过一年并取得优良成绩的持 F-1 签证的外国学生兼职工作，也可允许持 J-1 签证的交流学者从事部分时间就业。

Part-time Student（只有部分时间用于学习的非正规学生）：正规注册入学，但所修课程少于正规学生应修的全部课程的学生（参阅 Full-time Student“正规学生”栏目）。不允许外国留学生仅用部分时间学习，他们必须在学年的所有学期（暑期除外）念满学校规定的课时。

Passport（护照）：一种正式文件，用以证明持有该文件者的身份和国籍，由一个国家的政府有关机构（诸如：外交部）发给本国的公民。有效（而非过期）的护照允许持有该文件者出境和重新进入本人所在国籍的国家。在另一个国家签发签证的情况下，护照持有者可以在这一国家境内旅行。注意：在美国的外国留学生和交流学者所持的护照必须有至少 6 个月的有效期。

Permanent Resident（长期定居者）：得到许可在美国无限期居留的外国国民，也即移民（immigrant）。

Practical Training（实习）：一个学生在其专业领域内从事的获得批准的全职工作（full-time employment），可以是在一个教育项目执行期间，也可以是在该项目完成之后。具有 F-1 非移民身份的外国学生最多可以从事 12 个月的实习；J-1"交流学者"最多可以从事 18 个月的实习，称为"学业培训"（academic training）。具有 M-1 非移民身份的外国学生，只有在他们的教育项目完成之后才能申请实习。每个学生在校正规学习 4 个月后可从事 1 个月的实习。持有 F-1，J-1 和 M-1 签证的学生都必须具备大学或交流项目主管机构的推荐书。F-1 学生自愿从事实习（optional practical training）和 M-1 学生完成学业之后的实习（post-completion practical training）都必须得到移民归化局的批准。

Responsible Officer（负责人）：按照美国新闻署（U. S. Information Agency）的规定，负责主管一个具体的"交流学者"项目的人员，称之为 Responsible Officer（负责人）。负责人应在诸如同意就业、延长签证期、改变 J-1 签证类别、转换学校之类事宜上协助 J-1 签证持有者。

Sailing Permit（离境通行证）：即 Certificate of Compliance（守法证书）。

Transfer（转科或转学）：包括改换学业项目、学习赞助人和学习单位。学生要求开始一项全新的学业项目必须事先得到移民归化局的批准。仅仅转换学习单位而不改变学业项目则不需要申请同意。但无论出于何种考虑，任何转科或转学都应事先征得有关学习单位外国学生咨询顾问的同意，并须领取一份新的"身份合格证书"（Certificate of Eligibility）。

U. S. Immigration and Naturalization Service 是美国移民归化局。

Visa（签证）：一项签署，由护照持有者意愿进入的国家的一个特定授权机构盖印在护照上面。签证表示该护照业已经过审查，入境的各项条件均已具备，护照持有者已得到许可通行。得到签证并不等于一定能批准入境，真正的批准要在入境地得到。

附录 11　美国商务签证常见问题

一、何为美国商务签证?

外国公民到美国从事商务、参加会议、赴展等都必须申请 B-1 签证。B-1 签证为商务签证类别。此类签证分为三个月、半年、一年、三年有效、五年有效、十年有效。入境次数分为一次入境和多次入境。一般在中国领区，核发的商务签证最长的有效期为最长一年多次入境。美国商务签证的核发的原则是：申请人不能违反美国签证法案 214（b）条款，即“ 移民倾向条款”，申请人必须要向签证官证明：

1. 赴美的目的是商务考察，生意谈判和参展，而非其他目的；
2. 在美国只做短暂的停留，在签证到期前会按时离美返回中国；
3. 在中国有强烈的纽带，即拥有强烈的返回中国的原因，例如稳定的工作，社会地位，富有的财产，和睦的家庭等；
4. 完整真实地提供在美国邀请文件，旅行及生活的证明材料。

二、B-1/B-2 签证的概况：

B-1 签证颁发给从事短期商务活动的申请人。商务活动包括签订合同，参加展览或会议，或与客户洽谈业务。该签证为三个月一次有效。申请 B-2 签证的事由相当广泛，美国驻外使领馆也没有明确的限制。一般来讲，凡到美国观光旅游、商务、娱乐、探亲访友、就医、参加会议、赴展、处理个人事物等都可以申请 B-1/B-2 签证。B-1/B-2 签证可分为三个月有效期，一年有效、三年有效、五年有效、十年有效和永久性有效。入境次数也分为一次和多次入境有效。不同国家和地区的美国使领馆或同一使领馆的不同领事，对签证的有效期或入境次数都有极大的酌处权。

三、B-1 签证所提交的材料：

B-1 签证签发给从事短期商务活动的申请人。商务活动包括签订合同，参加展览或会议，短期培训 或与客户洽谈业务。该签证持有者不得在美国停留期间就业。B-1 签证申请人应出示其拟在美从事商务活动的相关文件，包括：

1. 美国邀请方的邀请函原件（需详细说明访美目的、在美停留时间以及由谁提供所有费用）
2. DS-156 申请表
3. 有效护照（有效期必须是 6 个月以内）

- 与美方合作伙伴签订的合同、其他协议或来往信件等证明与美国邀请方的合作关系，如赴美检测、购买机器、软件或其他设备，请提供该设备的相关信息，如产品宣传手册或产品目录等

4. 证明在中国的公司真实性的文件，如公司的营业执照、信用证明

以及所从事的商务活动的证明文件

• 申请人还需提供文件证明中国对其具有非常牢固的约束力，如：存折（不要银行存款证明）、在职证明、财产证明、结婚证、家庭合影，最好也能提供往返机票等

5. 如申请人曾经访美，请提供相关证明文件

6. 2—4 张半身免冠照片

7. 个人简历（请注明是否在美国有亲属，是否曾在美国有商业活动或进行学术访问）

8. 不可退还的使馆签证申请费 810 元人民币

四、B-2 签证所提交的材料：

B-2 签证签发给赴美国旅游的申请人，包括观光、治病、探亲访友以及参加会议。该签证持有者不得在美国停留期间就业。申请人需要出示：

1. 美方亲友的身份证明，如：护照和签证复印件、绿卡复印件

2. 美国的亲属或朋友的邀请信，或证明参加了旅游团或会议的信件

3. 证明申请人经济能力或在美国亲友的经济能力的文件

4. 如果申请人有任何既往病史，申请人应该出示在赴美期间的旅游或健康保险

5. 证明申请人个人情况的文件，如结婚证书、在职证明、银行存款证明、工资单、等

五、申请 B-1 或 B-2 签证的关键因素：

要获得赴美国的商务或旅游签证，申请人必须证明其短期进入美国的目的仅为旅游或短期商务活动，有合理的旅游目的，有足够经济能力支付申请人旅游和在美国期间所需费用；在国外有不可放弃的居住权；有短期暂停留后必须回国的不可分割的社会，经济和其他关系。根据 1952 年《移民与国籍法》修正案条款中第 214（b）段，如果申请人不能向领事官员提交上述材料以消除对其假定的移民倾向，领事官员将不会为其签发签证。

B-1 或 B-2 签证的签发由美国海外领事机构自行决定，美国境内的移民局不予过问。同 B-1 签证一样，由领事当场决定，因此又带有浓厚的主观性。一般来讲，签证领事考虑的主要因素是申请人赴美的必要性和申请人是否有移民倾向。经济能力在理论上是个重要考虑因素，但在签证实例中往往并非最重要，而且自己会准时返国。

六、何为移民倾向？

所谓移民倾向，是指任何一个申请美国非移民签证的外国人，都要被美国签证官视为有移民美国的潜在可能性，签证官有绝对权力拒绝申请人的签证。除非该申请人能在面试中反驳签证官，让签证官确信自己

不可能在进人美国后留美不归，才可以使签证官发放签证。

事实上，移民倾向这个问题对于商务签证的申请人，并不完全针对他们滞留或者移民的可能性，而是要求申请人必须证明去美国的真实目的和自身在中国的优越情况，从而打消签证官的疑虑，并颁发赴美签证。商务签证的申请人要充分准备书面材料和面谈问题问答，才能令签证官对赴美商务目的信服，避免怀疑有移民倾向的问题。

绝大多数没有经验的申请人应面签前，在专家的指导下进行有针对性、有逻辑性的充分准备，才能顺利获得签证。

七、B-1 或 B-2 签证申请被拒绝怎么办?

B-1 或 B-2 签证申请如果受到拒签是不可以申述的。领事拒绝 B-1 或 B-2 签证申请，要么是申请的事由不充分，要么就是申请人没有返国的打算，或两者皆反思有。不过由于 B-1 或 B-2 签证是一种随时都可申请的签证，因此申请者应反思被拒的原因，待有了充分的理由或能提交新的材料时，再行申请。有人在申请被拒后更换护照，再重新申请，虽然美国在全世界的使领馆对拒签的护照盖上印记，但在实践中，更换护照和使用原护照再次申请，获得签证或签证被拒两种情况都有。所以如第一次签证被拒，再次申请签证时，应重点考虑提供充分的事由或有返国打算的证明材料。

附录 12　商务旅行与会展相关词汇

公示语

1. Business Hours 营业时间
2. Office Hours 办公时间
3. entrance 入口
4. exit 出口
5. push 推
6. pull 拉
7. shut 此路不通
8. on 开
9. off 关
10. open 营业
11. pause 暂停
12. stop 关闭
13. closed 下班
14. menu 菜单
15. fragile 易碎
16. This Side Up 此面向上
17. introductions 说明
18. One Street 单行道
19. Keep Right/Left 靠左/右
20. Buses Only 公交专用
21. Wet Paint 油漆未干
22. danger 危险
23. Lost and Found 失物招领处
24. Give Way 快车先行
25. Safety First 安全第一
26. Filling Station 加油站
27. No Smoking 禁止吸烟
28. No Photos 请勿拍照
29. No Visitors 游人止步
30. No Entry 禁止入内
31. No Admittance 闲人免进
32. No Honking 禁止鸣喇叭
33. Parting 停车处
34. Toll Free 免费通行
35. F. F. 快进
36. REW. 倒带
37. EMS (邮政)特快专递
38. Insert Here 由此处插入
39. Open Here 由此处开启
40. Split Here 由此处撕开
41. Mechanical Help 车辆修理
42. “AA” Film 成人电影
43. Do Not Pass 禁止超车
44. No U-turn 禁止掉头
45. U-turn OK 可以 U 形转弯
46. No Cycling in the School 校内禁止骑车
47. SOS 紧急求救信号
48. Hands Wanted 招聘
49. Staff Only 员工专用
50. No Litter 请勿乱扔杂物
51. Hands Off 请勿用手摸
52. Keep Silence 保持安静
53. On Sale 减价出售
54. No Bills 不准张贴
55. Not for Sale 恕不出售
56. pub 酒店
57. cafe 咖啡馆，小餐馆
58. bar 酒吧
59. laundry 洗衣店
60. travel agency 旅行社

世界旅游胜地

Asia 亚洲

the Himalayas 喜马拉雅山

the Great Wall，China 中国长城

the Forbidden City, Beijing, China	中国北京故宫
Mount Fuji, Japan	日本富士山
the Taj Mahal, India	印度泰姬陵
Angkor Wat, Cambodia	柬埔寨吴哥窟
Bali, Indonesia	印度尼西亚巴厘岛
Borobudur, Indonesia	印度尼西亚婆罗浮屠
Sentosa, Singapore	新加坡圣淘沙
Crocodile Farm, Thailand	泰国鳄鱼湖
Pattaya Beach, Thailand	泰国芭堤雅海滩
Babylon, Iraq	伊拉克巴比伦遗迹
the Mosque of St. Sophia, Turkey	土耳其圣索非亚教堂
Africa	**非洲**
the Suez Canal, Egypt	埃及苏伊士运河
the Aswan High Dam, Egypt	埃及阿斯旺水坝
Nairobi National Park, Kenya	肯尼亚内罗毕国家公园
the Cape of Good Hope, South Africa	南非好望角
the Sahara Desert	撒哈拉沙漠
The Egyptian Pyramids	埃及金字塔
The Nile, Egypt	埃及尼罗河
Oceania	**大洋洲**
the Great Barrier Reef	大堡礁
Sydney Opera House, Australia	悉尼歌剧院
Ayers Rock	艾尔斯巨石
Mount Cook	库克山
Easter Island	复活节岛
Europe	**欧洲**
Notre Dame de Paris, France	法国巴黎圣母院
the Eiffel Tower, France	法国埃菲尔铁塔
Arch of Triumph, France	法国凯旋门
the Elysee Palace, France	法国爱丽舍宫
the Louvre Museum, France	法国卢浮宫
Kolner Dom, Koln, Germany	德国科隆大教堂
the Leaning Tower of Pisa, Italy	意大利比萨斜塔
the Colosseum, Rome, Italy	意大利古罗马圆形剧场
Venice, Italy	意大利威尼斯
the Parthenon, Greece	希腊巴台农神庙
Red Square, Moscow, Russia	俄罗斯莫斯科红场
Big Ben, London, England	英国伦敦大本钟
Buckingham Palace, England	英国白金汉宫

Hyde Park, England	英国海德公园
Tower Bridge, London	伦敦塔桥
Westminster Abbey, England	威斯敏斯特大教堂
Monte Carlo, Monaco	摩洛哥蒙特卡罗
the Mediterranean	地中海
America	**美洲**
Niagara Falls, New York State, USA	美国尼亚加拉大瀑布
Bermuda	百慕大
Honolulu, Hawaii, USA	美国夏威夷火奴鲁鲁
Panama Canal	巴拿马大运河
Yellowstone National Park, USA	美国黄石国家公园
the Statue of Liberty, New York City, USA	美国纽约自由女神像
Times Square, New York City, USA	美国纽约时代广场
the White House, Washington DC., USA	美国华盛顿白宫
Central Park, New York City, USA	美国纽约中央公园
Yosemite National Park, USA	美国尤塞米提国家公园
Grand Canyon, Arizona, USA	美国亚利桑那州大峡谷
Hollywood, California, USA	美国加利佛尼亚好莱坞
Disneyland, California, USA	美国加利佛尼亚迪士尼乐园
Las Vegas, Nevada, USA	美国内华达拉斯维加斯
Miami, Florida, USA	美国佛罗里达迈阿密
Metropolitan Museum of Art, New York City, USA	纽约大都会艺术博物馆
Acapulco, Mexico	墨西哥阿卡普尔科
Cuzco, Mexico	墨西哥库斯科

主要职称及部门名称

职称

Chairman	董事长
President/Managing Director	总裁
Vice-president	副总裁
Senior Managing Director	资深常务董事
Managing Director	常务董事
Director	董事
General Manager, × ×Department	某部部长（总经理）
Manager, × ×Section	某科科长（经理）
Assistant Manager, × ×Section	某科副科长（副经理）
Manager of Branch office	某分公司经理

主要部门名称

Head Office	总公司
Branch Office	分公司
Business Office	营业所
General Affair Department	总务部
Accounting Department	会计部
Finance Department	财务部
International Department	国际部
Domestic Sales Department	国内业务部
Overseas Sales Department	国外业务部
Purchasing Department	采购部
Export and Import Department	进出口部
Technical Department	技术部
Development Department	开发部
Production Department	制造部
Product Section	商品科
Stock Control Section	库存管理部
Quality Control Section	品质管理科
General Merchandise Section	资料科
Customer Section	顾客服务科

会议词汇

通用词汇	**General Terms**
reach common ground	达成共识
on behalf of all the committee members	代表全体委员
take preventative measures	防患于未然
chat freely	随意聊聊
shoulder the responsibility	担起责任
high-level and all-directional dialogue	高层次、全方位的对话
stack up (against with)	相比；比得上
call out the media hounds	唤起舆论的注意
exchange views	交换意见
get the show started	揭开序幕；开始
get together	聚集一堂
lay sth. out	口头详细说明
cliché	陈词滥调
shoot in the dark	盲目尝试
jump the gun	冒失行动

turn things around	扭转乾坤
go bankrupt; go belly up	破产；倒闭
pull the wool over sb's eyes	欺骗
be all in for	全力投入
damage control	伤害控制
jack up	使上涨；提高
suffer a heavy loss	损失惨重
make a special mention of	特别提到
take sb. to court	向法院控诉
clear up misunderstandings	消除误解
live in peace with oneself	心安理得
bite the bullet	咬紧牙关硬撑
in an unofficial capacity	以非官方身份
in one's own name	以个人名义
in a private capacity	以私人身份
advance with times	与时俱进
miscellaneous	杂项；其他事项
verbatim record	逐字记录
make a brief report/account of	做简要报告/介绍
会议类型	**Types of Meetings**
ministerial meeting	部长级会议
video conference	电视会议
ad hoc meeting	非例行会议
senior officials meeting (SOM)	高官会
public price hearings	价格听证会
forum	论坛
annual	年会
fair	洽谈会
celebration	庆典
plenary meeting	全体会议
summit (meeting)	首脑会议
conference setup	会议机构
editing group	编辑组
auditing committee	财务审核委员会
finance committee	财务委员会
preparatory committee	筹备委员会
the secretariat of the meeting	大会秘书处
organization committee	大会组委会
committee of heads of delegation	代表团团长委员会
committee of enquiry	调查委员会

committee on legal questions	法律问题委员会
advisory committee	顾问委员会
observer team	观察员小组
committee on contribution	会费委员会
mixed committee	混合委员会
plan coordination committee	计划协调委员会
technical cooperation committee	技术合作委员会
hospitality committee	接待委员会
state Council Office for Rectifying Malpractices	国务院纠风办
resolution committee	决议委员会
joint working party	联合工作组
joint liaison group	联合联络小组
joint committee	联合委员会
liaison committee	联络委员会
interim working party	临时工作组
interim committee	临时委员会
ladies committee	女宾委员会
drafting committee	起草委员会
drafting group	起草组
personnel committee	人事委员会
discussion group	讨论组
special autonomous working party	特别自治工作组
nomination committee	提名委员会
good offices committee	斡旋委员会
sub-committee	小组委员会
coordination committee	协调委员会
committee of consultation	协商委员会
electoral committee	选举委员会
standing orders committee	议事规则委员会
budget control committee	预算控制委员会
steering committee	指导委员会
panel of arbitration	仲裁组
committee of experts	专家委员会
special committee	专门委员会
consultative committee	咨询委员会
credentials committee	资格审查委员会
general committee	总务委员会
organizing committee	组织委员会

会议成员	Meeting Personnel
permanent delegate	常驻代表
head of a delegation	代表团团长
member as of right	法定代表
alternate；deputy	副代表
co-opted member	互选会员
member status	会籍
officers of the conference	会议职员
senior members	年长会员
interim chairman	临时主席
chairman on duty；rotating presidency	轮值主席
honorary president	名誉主席
former chairman	前任主席
by-elect members	递补委员
plenipotentiary	全权代表
full-fledged member	全权会员
chief delegate	首席代表
retiring chairman	卸任主席
representatives present at the meeting	与会代表
life-member	终身会员
the host country	主办国
keynote speaker；keynoter	主要发言人
会议文件	**Documents**
white paper；white book	白皮书
aide-memoire；memorandum	备忘录
supplement	补编
supplementary report	补充报告
addendum	增编
preliminary report	初步报告
keynote speech	主题发言
act	法案
code	法典；准则
bill	法规
laws and decrees；decree；order；statutes	法令
additional protocol	附加议定书
appended document	附属文件
survey	概览
progress report	工作进展报告
working document	工作文件
bulletin	公告

official letters	公函
convention	公约
regulations	规则；规定
repertory	汇编
minutes	会议纪要
report on the activity	活动报告
confidential document	机密文件
quarterly report	季报
summary record	简要记录
recommendations	建议书
resolution	决议
blue book	蓝皮书
provisional report	临时报告
temporary document	临时文件
covenant	盟约
internal regulations	内部规定
annual report	年报
yearbook	年鉴
information report	情况报告
full powers	全权证书
optional protocol	任意议定书
statement	声明
administrative program	施政纲领
time table	时间表
factual report	事实报告
credential	授权证书
private document	私人文件
rules	条例
treaty; pact	条约
circular	通报；通函
notification	通知；通告
contributions	文稿；论文
reference number of document	文件编号
classification of document	文件类别
questionnaire	调查表；问卷
charter	宪章

program	项目；大纲
agreement	协定
press release	新闻稿
manifesto；declaration	宣言
mandate	训令
study program	研究大纲
agenda	议程
draft agenda	议程草案
items on the agenda	议程项目
rules of procedure	议事规定
monthly report	月报
abstract	摘要
constitution	组织法；组织条例
statutes	章程
official document	正式文件
interim report	中期报告
award	仲裁书
expert report	专家报告
会议程序	**Meeting Procedure**
requisite majority	必要多数
draw lots	抽签
the theme of the conference	大会主题
rectify	订正
address… on the topic of	对……就……为题发言
challenge a result of votes	对表决结果质疑
challenge the ruling	对裁决表示异议
deliver a speech	发表讲话
required majority	法定多数
negative vote	反对票
ballot papers null and void	废票
veto	否决权
alternation	更改
program of work	工作日程
blow the whistle	公开揭发；指控
approved by acclamation	鼓掌通过
election at expiration of office terms	换届选举

simple majority	简单多数
approved agenda	经批准的议程
absolute majority	绝对多数
corrigendum	勘误
provisional agenda	临时议程
equality of vote	票数相等
other business	其他事项
abstention	弃权票
cancel a vote	取消所投的票
approved unanimously	全体通过
confirm a vote	认定表决有效
two-thirds majority	三分之二多数
take the floor	上台发言
qualified majority	特定多数
defer/postpone a vote	推迟/延期表决
map sth. out	详细说明
address oneself to	向……发表讲话
exercise the power of veto	行使否决权
amendment	修订
revise	修正
declare the vote closed	宣布表决结束
declare a vote to be final	宣布为最后表决
pack it in	宣告结束
overwhelming majority	压倒多数
modify	修改
ask for a ruling	要求裁决
unanimous approval	一致通过
address the meeting	在会上发言
provisional regulations	暂行规定
affirmative vote	赞成票
direct election	直接选举
interrupt a vote	中断表决
the central subject under discussion	中心议题
a bank order	银行汇票
a bank transfer	银行汇款
a bill	账单，货物验收单

会展及课文词汇

a complaint	抱怨
acceptable	可接受的
accommodation	调整，和解
account	会计
accountant	会计师
account book	账簿，会计账簿
accrual accounting	全责发生制记账法
a customer	顾客
a counter offer	还价
additional	另外的，附加的
additional risks	附加险
admission	入场办法
administrative overhead	行政管理费
advertising	广告
advisory committee	顾问委员会，咨询委员
a firm condition of the order	订单的拒绝通知书
an inconvenience	不便
an insurance company	保险公司
an order of acknowledgement	接受订单确认书
an order form	订单表格
airport	机场
all Risks	一切险
all - inclusive	总括
a bill of exchange	汇票
a cash against documents basis	凭单付现
a cash basis	现金支付
a cash on delivery basis	交货付现
a check	支票
a partial payment	部分付款
a payment	付款
a postal check	邮政支票
a postal order	邮政汇票
advance (payment)	预付（款项）
allow credit facilities	同意信用交易

allow monthly account tern	同意月结
amount	总数，数值
an account	账单
an account opened on the book	信用交易账户
an advice of payment	支付通知
an extension of payment	延长支付期限
aluminum	【化】铝
an inquiry	询盘
an agency	代理商
an offer	报价
amend	修改
amendment	修改，修改通知书
amendment to L/C/amendment of L/C	信用证修改书
American International Toy Fair	美国纽约国际玩具博览会
a parcel	小包
arrange delivery	安排交货
a responsible person	经办人
a retailer	零售商
a payment on T/T	以电汇方式付款
aperitif	开胃酒
appetizer	开胃菜
apply for	申请
appendixes	附件
Application Form for Overseas Exhibitor badge	参展商证申请表
Application Form for Stand Construction badge	筹展申请表
Application Form for Stand Dismantling badge	撤展申请表
approved	已被承认的；赞许的；有效的；安全的，试验证明的
Arrangements and Stipulations of Stand dismantling	撤展服务与约定
approach sb. for sth.	就某事与某人联系
a quotation	报价单
assets	资产
assistance	协助
at-home party	家庭宴会
a time L/C, 60 days after sight	60天远期信用证

attendee's Card	参展商证
a wholesaler	批发商
available	可用到的，可利用的
avenue	林荫道，大街
avoid legal action	避免法律行动
avoid subsequent amendment	避免后续的修改
be held in strict	极机密文件
business hours	营业时间
bulk sale	整批销售
bookkeeping	簿记
budget	预算
budget revenues	预算收入
budgeting	编制预算
banquet	酒宴
birthday party	生日宴会
board of directors	董事会
box supper	慈善聚会
budget committee	预算委员会
balance	余额
balance sheet	资产平衡表
balance of payments	（国际）收支
balance of trade	贸易差额，国际贸易平衡
baked	烤的
bank Reference	交易银行的信用照会状
banking services	银行业务
barrel	琵琶桶
be enclosing	随信寄上
bill	汇票（美作 check）
bill of exchange	汇票
booth catering	摊位饮食服务
business Center	商务中心
be a part of sth.	参加（某项活动）
be familiar with	熟悉
be featured with	有……的面貌特征
be for one's account	记在某人的账上，费用由某人承担
be fully committed	接满订货
be heavily committed	接的订货很多（注意用被动语态）
be in conformity with	与……一致
be on the cutting edge of	在……方面很先进

be prepared to…	准备做……事
be satisfied with	对……感到满意
be over committed	接受订货过多
black market	黑市
block	街区
book the shipping space	预订舱位
booth	市场内的摊棚；（商展等的）摊位
Booth No.	摊位号
breakage	破损
breakout session	小组讨论
Broadway	百老汇
broccoli	花椰菜
budget	预算
buffet party	立食宴会
business cards	名片
Business Center	商务中心
business hours	营业时间
busy season	旺季
buyer	买主，买方
by way of	途经，经过
cash on delivery	交货付现，货到付款
cash payment	现金支付，付现
clear the balance	付清余额
clear the bill	付清账单
compensation	赔偿，补偿
credit inquiry	信用照会
confidence/be treated in strict confidence	处理
cover insurance on	为……投保
cash sale	现货
client/customer	客户，顾客
commerce/trade/trading	贸易
commercial channel	商业渠道
commercial transaction	买卖，交易
competition	竞争
competitive	有竞争力的
competitor	竞争者
concessionaire/licensed dealer	受让人，特权获得者
consumer	消费者，用户
customs	海关

customs duty	关税
consumption	消费
cash accounting	现金记账法
cash balance	现金余额，现款结存
cash on hand	留存现金，库存现金
cashbook	现金出纳簿
credit balance	贷方余额
consultative committee assembly	大会
christmas party	圣诞晚会
cocktail party	鸡尾酒会
commemorative party	纪念宴会
committee of experts	专家委员会
committee/commission	委员会
concurrent session	分组会议
conference	会议
congress	代表大会
convention	会议
corporate meeting	公司会
cancel an order	取消订单
Canton	广州（旧称）
carpet	【建】磨耗层
carton	纸板箱
carrier	承运商
case	箱
cash price	现货价格，现金价格
catalog	目录
certificate of Conformity	资格认证、合格证书
CFR（Cost and Freight）	含运费价格
CIF（Cost Insurance Freight）	含运费、保险费在内的价格
charge the additional fee	收取额外费用
Chicago	芝加哥
China Import and Export Fair	中国进出口商品交易会（广交会）
classic	经典的
Code of Conduct for Participation at the Fair	参展行为规则
chief	主要的
circle-line	环线
cleaning	清洁

commodity tax/ VAT (value added tax)	商品税/增值税
Co. , Ltd.	有限公司
cost price	成本价
cost of transport	运费
cost of freight	空运费
cost of delivery	发送费用
come to terms	达成协议
come to the details	就细节问题达成一致
comes with	配套（指某种产品原本附带有某种配件）
commit	接了订货
common sense	常识
common understanding	共识
Complaint and Settlement Procedure	投诉处理
confirm	确认
confirm the order	确认订单
confirmation of order	确认订单通知书
continental	欧洲大陆的
contractor	【商】立约人，承包人
convenient	方便的
conveniently	方便地
Convention Center	会议中心
Corner Booth	角落摊位
count	数
CPSIA Requirement = Consumer Product Safety Improvement Act	美国《消费者产品安全改进法案》
crossing	交叉口，十字路口
cuisine	烹调风格，烹饪
currency	通货，货币
customs clearance	进出口通关
cutting edge	先进的
daily expenses	日常开支
deduct the amount	扣除该金额
difference	差额
down payment	预付定金
deferred payment	延期付款
draw a bank order	开具银行汇票
Dun Report	信用照会报告书
dealer	经销商

dumping profit margin	倾销差价，倾销幅度
demand	需求
debit	借方
debit balance	借方余额，借方差额
deficit	亏空
double-entry bookkeeping	复式簿记
dance party/ball/fandango	舞会
dinner party	晚餐会
drafting committee	起草委员会
deal	成交
decline an order	婉拒订单
decrease	减少
delicate	精致的
delivery	交货，送货
delivery within ~ day(s)	~日内发送
department stores	百货商店
deposit	押金
description	型号
discount	折扣
distinctive	与众不同的
direct flight	直达飞机
dispatch	发运
decoration	装修
denomination	（度量衡等的）单位，面额
departure	启程，出发
deposit	保证金
dessert	甜点
detail	细节
double room	双人间
downtown	市中心
drum	铁皮圆桶
durable	耐久的，持久的
executive council/executive board	执行委员会
estimation/estimate/valuation	估价
export/exportation	出口
exporter	出口商
establish an open account with	与……信用交易
e-banking	网上银行
economy (class)	经济舱

effect	安排，进行，办理
effect insurance	办理保险
effect payment	办理付款
effect shipment	办理装运
electrical	电的，电气
elevator	电梯，自动扶梯
e-mail	电邮
End-cup Booth	三面开口摊位
entrust	委托
entrust procedure	委托手续
equipment rental	设备租用
exact	确切的
exchange	兑换，把……兑换成……
exchange rate	兑换率
executive (class)	商务舱
exhibition	展览，展览会；陈列品
exhibitor	展出者，显示者
Exhibition Categories	展出内容
Exhibition Dates and Hours	展览日期及时间
Exhibitor/Exhibit Online Registration	展品网上登记
exporter	出口商
export packing	出口包装
express	专门的，快的
exquisitely	精美的
ex warehouse	仓库交货价
ex works	工厂交货价
full amount	全额
facsimile number	传真号码
foreign trade/external trade	对外贸易，外贸
free-trade area	自由贸易区
financial year/trading year	财政年度
fixed expenses	固定费用
fancy ball	化装舞会
fancy fair	义卖场
farewell party	惜别会
final sitting	闭幕会
fishing party	钓鱼会
formal sitting	隆重开会
fund-raisers	捐款会

faulty goods	不良品
foresight/forecast	预测
Fair Information Services	展会资讯服务
factory price/manufacturer's price	出厂价
FAS（Free Along Ship）	船边交货价
fixed price	固定价格
FOB（Free On Board）	装运港船上装货价
FOR（Free On Rail）	火车上交货价
function	功能
fascia	（店门上的）招牌
feature	特征；特别之处在于，以……为特色
fill in the form	填写表格
financial crisis	金融危机
first class	头等舱
figure out	计算
five-star hotel	五星级酒店
flow	流
for the sake of	为了……
for the view of doing sth.	为了……；希望……；考虑到……
frequency	频率
front desk	前台
garden party	游园会
general committee/general officers/general bureau	总务委员会
general meeting, general assembly	会员大会
governing body	主管团体
guarantee	保证
General Additional Risks	一般附加险
get back to sb.	与某人联系
get in touch with sb.	与某人联系
get stand	获取展位
get the goods ready	备妥货物
ginger	姜
global Travel Agency	环球旅行社
goods which are not existing in the catalog	目录上未刊载的商品
gross price	含各种费用的价格
Ground Zero	“9·11”遗址
guaranteed price	保证价格

gunny bag	麻袋
hire-purchase	分期付款购买
home market	国内市场
hectares	公顷
height limit	限高
Hongqiao Airport	虹桥机场
Honolulu	火奴鲁鲁（即“檀香山”，美国夏威夷州的首府）
host	主办单位
hotel reservation service	订房服务
inspect the damage	调查损失
import/importation	进口
importer	进口商
internal trade/interior trade	国内贸易
international trade	国际贸易
item	项目，细目
income and expenditure/receipts and expenditure/output and input	支出和收入
incentive meeting	激励性会议
ID card	身份证
IDD telephone	国际直拨长途电话
imitate	仿造
in accordance with	与……一致
inbound	入境的
include in the price	包含在价格中
insurance / premium	保险费
inner packing	内包装
inquire	询问，打听
in regard to	关于
in stock	有现货
insurance	保险
interchange station	换乘站
International Exhibition Center	国际会展中心
introduce	介绍
in urgent need of	急着要
invitation	邀请
invitation card	请帖
involve	使陷入……（某种情况）之中
involve sb. in expense	使某人破费

irrevocable L/C at sight	不可撤销即期信用证
island booth	岛型摊位
Jacob K. Javits Convention Center	雅各布 K. 贾维茨会议中心
journal	日记簿
keg	小圆桶
keep the price	维持价格
liabilities	债务，负债
line items	科目
luncheon party	午餐会
large-scale	大规模的
layover	中途停留
L/C at sight	即期信用证（或 sight L/C）
usance L/C; time L/C; term L/C	远期信用证
line of toys	玩具系列
open a L/C; establish a L/C; issue a L/C	开立信用证
less insurance	保险费除外
letter of credit	信用证
letter of invitation	邀请函
linear Booth	道边摊位
literature	商品价目册
Location of the International Pavilion	进口展馆位置
Location Map of Exhibition Venue	展馆位置图
look forward to sth.	期待……的到来
Low/dead/dull/slack season	淡季
lunar calendar	农历
monthly payment	月度付款
manufacturer	制造商，制造厂
merchant	商人（英）批发商（美）零售商
middleman	中间商，经纪人
marketing	销售学，销售业务，
monopoly	垄断
meeting in camera	秘密会议
magnetic card	磁卡
mail…under separate cover	另函寄送
main course	主菜
main mark	正唛
maintain the previous price	维持原来的价格
make an exception to… / make sb. an exception/do sth. exceptionally	在……上破例也可说

make amendment	做出修改
make delivery	交货
make some concession	做些让步
make out the documents	缮制单证
market	市场
market price	市场价
maximum price /ceiling price	最高价
minimum price	最低价
market share	市场份额，市场占有率
mean	对……有意义，对……有价值
meet your requirements	满足你方要求
mean a lot to us/ mean much to us/be very important to us	对我们很重要
menu	菜单
mineral water	矿泉水
MOQ = minimum order quality	最低订货量
5% more or less is allowed	允许5%溢短
modernity	现代性
move-in	入驻
New Year's Banquet	新年会议
negotiation	商议谈判
net price	净价，实价
neutral packing	中性包装
noticeable	显而易见的，明显的
one third of the payment	支付1/3款
overdue account	过期未偿付的金额
outside business hours	营业时间外
offer	报盘，发价
open market	公开市场
outlet	销路
opening sitting	开幕会
official builder	大会指定承建商
offer a substitute	建议替代品
official carrier	官方承运商
official contractor	展览会指定装修代理公司
official forwarder	展会运输代理公司
official publication	展会指定刊物
official website	展会指定信息网
on a lump-sum basis	一次（整笔）总付办法

on-site service	现场服务
one size range	全部尺码
one-way	单程
open-end ticket	未经确定的不定期机票
open the market	开拓市场
order	订单；订购，订货
order form	订单
organizer	承办单位
outbound	出境的
outer packing	外包装
out of stock	缺货
overtime drayage rates	加班运输费
overseas co-organizer	海外协办单位
oversea passports	境外护照
pay in ~ installment	分～次付清
payment due	支付期限
payment in arrears /outstanding payment	拖欠款项
payment in kind	以实物付款
payment in specie	以其真正形式付款
pro forma invoice	估价单，估价发票
promissory note	本票，期票
purchase	购买，进货
plan	计划
planning	计划编制
program	计划，方案
pace of activity	活动间隔
packing	包装
paper notes	纸币
partial shipment	分批装运
participate	参与，参加
Participation Application Form	参展申请表
Participation Procedures of the International Pavilion	进口展区参展流程
passport	护照
payment (term)	付款方式
payment terms/terms of payment	支付方式，支付条件
Pazhou Complex, Guang Zhou	广州琶洲展览馆
personal photo	个人照片

peninsula booth	半岛型摊位
photocopying printing	影印
piece price /unit price	单位价格，单价
PICC = People's Insurance Company of China	中国人民保险公司
place an order with sb. for sth.	向某人订购某物
place an order	下订单
place a substantial order	下达订单
place a trial order	实验性订单
place regular order	定期下单
plain steamed crabs	清蒸螃蟹
porch	门廊，大门内停车处，入口处
portage	搬运
preferable	受欢迎的，招人喜爱的
preferential rates	优惠价格
preferential price	优惠价
premium rate	保险费率
prestigious	有声望的，有威信的
price control	物价管制
price fall	价格下降
price fixing	限价，限定价格
price free on board	装船港往船上装货价
price freeze	价格冻结
price index	物价指数
price per unit	单价
prime cost/first cost/first price/initial cost	最初成本
procedure	手续
procedures for the registration	参展程序
product	产品
Provisions and Regulations	展会规则
Provisions of Sanitation Protection	卫生保障规则
Pudong Airport, Shanghai	上海浦东机场
PU upper	人造 PU 革
quarantine and inspection	检验检疫
quantity	数量
quota	配额，限额
quote the best quantitative discount rate	报出口价格
quote the most competitive price	报数量折扣价

quote	报价
receipt	收据
records / books	账簿
refund/repayment	归还，调换证券
remuneration	报酬，补偿
refer	进行信用照会
reference	照会状、照会
repair charge	修理费用
reshuffle of the company staff	人事变动
registered office /head office	总公司，总店
registered trademarks	注册商标
retail trade	零售业
retailer	零售商
return on investment	投资收益
raw space	光地展位
receptionist	接待员，前台工作人员
reduce the price	减价
reduce your price by 5%	降价 5%
registration	登记
Registration Service	登记服务
Regulations on Exhibit Management	展品管理
Regulations on Safety and Fire-prevention	安全与防火
Regulations on Use of Stand	展位使用
relevant forms	相关表格
relevant rental	相关的地租［租金］总额；出租的财产租册
representative	代表
reserve	预订，保留
reservation	预订
retail price	零售价
rise in price	价格上涨
retractable	可拉回的，可缩回的
rockery	假山，假山庭园
roller Shoes	滑轮鞋/溜冰鞋
room rates	客房费用
round / return	往返，返程
rubber sole	橡胶底
statement of accounts	账目表，账单
sale	销售

stocks	存货，库存量
salmon	鲑鱼
sale price	卖价，销售价格
scope of coverage	保险责任范围
sculpture park	碑林
seal	图章
Secretarial & Translation Service	秘书与翻译服务
send by sea freight	海运送货
send by air freight	空运送货
send by registered	航空挂号送货
schedule of delivery	发货日程细节
service charge	服务费
services and Stipulations of Exhibit transportation	展品运输服务及约定
Service Guide and Stipulations	服务指南与服务约定
Services and Stipulations of Standard Stand Construction	标准展位布展服务及约定
selling packing	销售包装
selling season/hot season/peak season/high season/busy season	销售季节，旺季
settle an account	付清
shipment	出货
shipment date	装运日
shipping instruction	出货指示单
shopping center	购物中心
show hours	展出时间
shuttle	梭子，往返移动之物；班车
shuttle bus	往返汽车
side mark	侧唛
sign up the contract	签合同
single-entry bookkeeping	单式簿记
sign	签名
size range	尺码范围
small packing	小包装
sobriety	庄重
sorghum	高粱
soya sauce	酱油
Special Additional Risks	特殊附加险
spot light	射灯

spotlight	聚光灯，反光灯，照明灯；荧光源，车（头）灯
stable	稳定的
stand	承受；经受；忍受
stand	展位
Stand Arrangement and Exhibit Setting	展位布置及展品摆放
stand application	申请展位
stand construction	展位搭建
station	台，所，站，车站
the Statue of Liberty	自由女神像
stipulated in the contract	合同中所规定的
Stipulations of Construction Management for Custom-built Stand	特装布展施工管理约定
storage	仓储
store	库存
stock	存货，储存；置备，进行存储
Out of stock	缺货，无现货
From stock / ex stock	从仓库交货
strong	（味道）重的，偏咸的，（酒）烈的
subway	地铁
subway station	地铁站
sum	总数，全额
Succeed to the position	接任者
take … into consideration /take into consideration of…	考虑
take no responsibility	不负任何责任
target customer	目标顾客
taxi	出租汽车
terms of payment	支付条件
terms of trade	贸易条件
T-bone steak	T 骨牛排
telecommunications	电讯，远程通信
terms of payment	付款条件
texture	质地
the admission fee to the scenic spots	景点门票
Javits Tool Kit	贾维茨工具包（贾维茨会议中心服务手册）
the Metropolitan Museum of Art	大都会博物馆
the selling point	卖点

arrange/make/effect shipment	安排装运事宜
the tie up of funds	资金难以动用
the oversea buyer's card	海外采购商证
the…day(s) promissory note	……天的期限
the summer vacation	暑假
thoughtful	体贴人的，考虑周到的
tie up	捆绑，阻碍
timely delivery	准时出货
time of delivery	交货时间
timetable	时间表
Time for Stand Dismantling	撤展时间
Time and Venue for Exhibitor Registration	参展商登记时间、地点
total price	总额
Trademark Infringement Claims	商标侵权处理
transaction	交易
tradesman	零售商
transport packing	运输包装
transportation fare	交通费
transshipment	转运
T/T = Telegraphic Transfer	电汇（汇付方式中的一种）
toll-free	免费
Trade Show and Events Marketing Committee	美国玩具工业协会贸易展览与活动策划委员会
transfer	换车
turnover/volume of business	营业额，销售额
underwrite	负责保险
underwriter	承保人
unfair competition	不合理竞争
unified	统一的，统一标准的，一元化的
unique	独特
unwind	放松
usual practice	一贯做法，常规做法
variable expenses	可变费用
vary	变化，改变
venue	展览场地
view	景色，风景
visa card	维萨信用卡
voucher	凭单，收据

wake-up call/ morning call	催醒电话
War Risk	战争险
waterfall	瀑布
Wireless & Broadband Internet	无线宽带网络
wholesale	批发
wholesaler	批发商
wholesale price	批发价
WPA	水渍险
wooden box	木箱
workable	可行的，合适的
zero-based budgeting	零预算编制法

参考文献

[1] Harold E Meyer. 全美英文信函百科［M］. 薛京玉译. 北京：中国轻工业出版社，1999.

[2] Lan Wood. Cambridge Business English 3［M］. 北京：经济科学出版社，2001.

[3] Malcolm Goodale. The Language of Meetings［M］. Thomson Heinle, 2006.

[4] Mark McCraken. Business Skills in English［M］. Delta Publishing Company, 2003.

[5] 程丛喜. 导游英语［M］. 武汉：武汉大学出版社，2005.

[6] 崔进. 新编旅游英语［M］. 武汉：武汉大学出版社，2007.

[7] 丁衡祁，李欣，白静. 会展英语［M］. 北京：对外经济贸易大学出版社，2008.

[8] 杜清萍. 商务英语［M］. 北京：中国计量出版社，2009.

[9] 理查兹·沙特雷. 商务旅游英语［M］. 北京：北京大学出版社，1999.

[10] 梅德明. 通用口译教程［M］. 北京：北京大学出版社，2007.

[11] 裘果芬. 国际商务英语洽谈［M］. 上海：上海交通大学出版社，2000.

[12] 沈银珍，孙静，丁萍萍，等. 会展英语［M］. 北京：中国物资出版社，2003.

[13] 王义静，李秀英. 英语听说 2000［M］. 大连：大连理工大学出版社，2002.

[14] 王伟，刘武年. 出国英语口语［M］. 西安：西北工业大学音像电子出版社，2007.

[15] 吴建华，肖璇. 现代会展英语实务教程［M］. 广州：广东世界图书出版社，2009.

[16] 吴庆雯. 商务会议英语 1000 句［M］. 北京：机械工业出版社，2009.

[17] 徐小贞，赵敏懿，刘建珠. 商务现场口译［M］. 北京：外语教学与研究出版社，2006.

[18] 张翠萍. 商贸英语口语一本通［M］. 北京：对外经济贸易大学出版社，2004.

[19] 张文. 英汉汉英高级口译教程［M］. 北京：旅游教育出版社，2004.

[20] 张占军，张宝敏，张宏杰. English for Conference and Exhibition［M］. 北京：中国商务出版社，2005.

[21] 贺雪娟. 商务英语［M］. 北京：外语教学与研究出版社，2007.

[22] 陈文钊，张文克，刘云飞. 商务英语会话与函电［M］. 北京：中国财政经济出版社，1997.

[23] 胡润生. 商务英语会话手册［M］. 西安：出界图书出版公司，2000.

[24] 周保国. 商务交际英语听说教程 [M]. 武汉: 武汉大学出版社, 2007.
[25] 彭青龙, 蓝星, 葛建光. 会展英语 [M]. 上海: 上海交通大学出版社, 2009.
[26] 钟乐平, 韩江红. 出国留学英语 [M]. 北京: 机械工业出版社, 2006.